The World War I Diary of José de la Luz Sáenz

D1736084

Number Thirteen:

C. A. Brannen Series

J. Luz Saenz

■

The WORLD WAR I DIARY *of*
JOSÉ DE LA LUZ SÁENZ

Edited and with an Introduction by

EMILIO ZAMORA

Translated by

Emilio Zamora with Ben Maya

■

TEXAS A&M UNIVERSITY PRESS

COLLEGE STATION

Manufactured in the United States of America
The paper used in this book meets the minimum requirements
of the American National Standard for Permanence
of Paper for Printed Library Materials, Z39.48-1984.
Binding materials have been chosen for durability.

Frontispiece: José de la Luz Sáenz, US Army photograph, 1918
The editor gratefully acknowledges Alberto Jiménez, who photographed the oil
painting that appears on the cover of the book.

Library of Congress Cataloging-in-Publication Data

Saenz, José de la Luz, 1888–1953, author.
[México-americanos en la Gran Guerra. English]

The World War I diary of José de la Luz Saenz / edited and with an introduction
by Emilio Zamora ; translated by Emilio Zamora with Ben Maya. — First edition.
pages cm. — (C. A. Brannen series ; number thirteen)

Translation of: Los méxico-americanos en la Gran Guerra: y su contingente en pró de la democracia, la humanidad y la justicia, first published in original Spanish in San Antonio by Artes Graficas, 1933.
Includes bibliographical references and index.

ISBN 978-1-62349-113-0 (cloth : alk. paper) —
ISBN 978-1-62349-114-7 (pbk. : alk. paper) —
ISBN 978-1-62349-151-2 (e-book)
1. United States. Army. Infantry Division, 90th—Biography. 2. World War, 1914–1918—
Regimental histories—United States. 3. Saenz, José de la Luz, 1888–1953. 4. Mexican
Americans—Texas—Biography. 5. Civil rights workers—Texas—Biography. 6. World War,
1914–1918—Personal narratives, Mexican American. 7. World War, 1914–1918—
Participation, Mexican American. I. Zamora, Emilio, translator, editor. II. Maya,
Ben, –2012, translator. III. Title. IV. Series: C. A. Brannen series ; no. 13.
D570.390th .S2413 2014
940.4'12730922—dc23
2013035951

To my dear and long-suffering wife and my loving children, with the sole intent of maintaining the memory of the heroic sacrifice that our American soldiers of Mexican origin made in the past world war, all the while preserving democratic principles and proclaiming JUSTICE for our suffering humanity!

—J. Luz Sáenz

I am grateful to the Sáenz family for the trust they placed in me. I also thank my wife Angela, and our daughters Clara and Luz for their love and support and welcome Clara's husband Felix Gonzales and their beautiful boy Felix Jr., "Feliciano," to the family.

—Emilio Zamora

Contents

Illustrations

"For Democracy, Humanity, and Justice"

Introduction

José de la Luz Sáenz,[1] the author of the only extant war diary published by a World War I doughboy of Mexican origin, was born on May 17, 1888, in Realitos, Texas.[2] His widowed paternal grandmother, Marcelina, moved her family from the Mexican border town of Ciudad Mier, Tamaulipas, to San Diego, Texas, in the 1860s to work for a Mexican family with ranch properties that extended into Texas.[3] The arrival of a family on its way from San Antonio to Mexico led to the expansion of the Sáenz household when the newcomers' daughter, Cristina Hernández, stayed in Realitos to marry Rosalío, one of Marcelina's sons. Their union produced six children, including José de la Luz Sáenz. His first name, José de la Luz, suggests an abiding Christian faith as it denotes the biblical José and the heavenly message that he received and obeyed. This association with the divine may explain why Mexican parents give both boys and girls the name "Luz," a term Sáenz family members affectionately used with him. His adult friends and colleagues preferred his surname. I defer to this more formal salutation.[4]

The young Sáenz-Hernández family led a difficult life that depended on Rosalío's meager earnings as an itinerant railroad worker and migratory farm laborer. Cristina's passing, on June 28, 1896, brought even greater hardship, as Rosalío now had to depend on the help of relatives and his oldest daughter, Marcelina, to care for their home and raise the children. Sáenz, who was eight years old when his mother died, recalled spending time with other relatively unsupervised boys, seeking youthful adventures in the ubiquitous chaparral brush. Rosalío's concern with the welfare of his children may have contributed to his decision in 1900 to marry a woman named Petra Ramos. According to Sáenz, Petra raised them with the same deep love that they had been accustomed to receiving from Cristina. Soon after their marriage, Rosalío and Petra made another important decision: they moved the family to the nearby town of Alice so the children could attend school. This move had a profoundly positive effect on Sáenz's social and intellectual development.

Six years later, at eighteen years of age, Sáenz graduated from the town's public high school with an exemplary academic record. He also completed studies in two independently operated community schools, each taught by local intellectuals named Pablo Pérez and Eulalio Velázquez. The latter was the editor of *El Cosmopolíta*, a well-known newspaper in South Texas.[5] The lower incidence of school segregation in the predominantly Mexican region of South Texas where the Sáenz's family lived explains his fortuitous opportunity to obtain a public education. Although he was able to enter a public school, this did not shield him from racial discrimination, as we shall later see. Private learning institutions were also present in some communities to supplement the official curriculum because the public schools either misrepresented or entirely excluded Mexican history and culture, even in places like South Texas. The Pérez and Velázquez schools appear to have offered a third alternative. They provided instruction in Spanish and taught Mexican history and culture by choice, and not as merely a response to school segregation and exclusion. Sáenz's broad educational experience accounts for his intellectual confidence and curiosity in adulthood, and for the noticeable skill with which he expressed encyclopedic knowledge in his diary.[6]

The schools he attended prepared Sáenz in nonacademic ways as well. He remembered fights with Anglo youth and confrontations with teachers in the public school—experiences that encouraged him to develop self-pride and a righteous sense of responsibility to defend his community. Some teachers in the public school stood out as caring and effective instructors, however. They helped Sáenz develop the confidence to stand up to discrimination and other subtler forms of racist behavior. He reserved his highest praise for his Mexican teachers, especially Velázquez, who modeled civic participation and opened his apparently vast personal library (which included among its many subjects books on Mexican history and culture) to Sáenz and other students.[7]

If the public school provided Sáenz with a mostly instrumentalist and practical form of education and the Mexican schools a more culturally affirming type of learning through a curriculum that emphasized an exalted form of Mexico's history and culture, the lessons he received from the Mexican community and at home gave special meaning to both. His difficult experiences as a young migrant worker, traveling with his father to the cotton fields of South and Central Texas, and exposure to stories of violence toward Mexicans in the region where he grew up had already implanted in Sáenz an awareness of the racially charged environment that victimized Mexicans and found daily expression in his public school. Also, Sáenz acknowledged a home-based Mexican education that included the use of Spanish as well as a family history of epic proportions. His mother, Cristina Hernández, was descended from the Canary Island settlers of San Antonio. His father's family traced its lineage from members of the Aztec communities that escaped the violence of the Spanish conquest in 1519 and made their way from the central valley of Mexico to the present-day Mexico-Texas border in the late nineteenth century.[8] Although the Mexican schools Sáenz attended may not have explicitly incorporated such home-based knowledge of high drama and decline, they reinforced it. Velázquez, for instance, shared with students his deep admiration for Benito Juárez, the Zapotec Indian who served as president of Mexico between 1858 and 1864. He also no doubt underscored Juárez's important role in unifying the nation during the French intervention in Mexico in the early 1860s. Juárez led the resistance as an inspiring head of state on the run and resumed the presidency after the defeat of the French. Velázquez also encouraged a small group of graduating students, including Sáenz, to organize a public commemoration of Juárez. Sáenz later recalled that organizing the event and serving as its principal orator gave prideful expression to his deeply held Mexican and indigenous identity.

When a group of parents from El Palo del Oso, a nearby community of railroad workers, read about the Juárez program and Sáenz's leading role in it, they immediately offered him a teaching job in a private Mexican school they named La Escuela Laica Vicente Lozano. Still young but clearly mature for his age, Sáenz accepted the offer to teach children during the day and adults in the evening.[9] He stayed in El Palo del Oso for about three years and continued teaching throughout South and Central Texas for well over forty years. By the time of his death in 1953, he had taught all grades in thirty public schools and served as a principal in elementary schools and high schools in the Texas communities of La Joya, Benavides, Oilton, and McAllen. According to one of his grown children, Sáenz often moved because he always protested the segregation of Mexican children, thus angering local school officials.[10]

By the 1910s, Sáenz had found his way to the area south and southeast of San Antonio. There he worked mostly in public, but separate, Mexican elementary schools and established himself as a respected educator and frequent critic of segregation and discrimination against Mexican youth in the schools. While living in Moore, he joined the Mexican Protective Association, a federation of mutual aid societies in Central Texas, and involved himself in organizing Mexican patriotic celebrations and school-related activities. He married María Petra Esparza from San Agustín, a small Mexican-origin community founded and settled by the Esparza family. San Agustín is located near Pleasanton, about fifty miles south of San Antonio, where Sáenz taught in a separate Mexican elementary school. María Petra, who was born in August 1898, was a descendant of José María (Gregorio) Esparza, who died defending the mission known as the Alamo during the famous battle that took place there in 1836.[11] Sáenz and María Petra raised nine children (Adán, María de la Luz, Evangelina Lucía, Eduardo Francisco, Enrique León, Eva Olivia, Cristina Antonia, Beatriz, and José de la Luz). Between the 1910s and the 1950s, the family lived in Moore, New Braunfels, Pleasanton, Poteet, Alice, Premont, Peñitas, La Joya, and McAllen.[12] Sáenz was teaching Mexican children in San Agustín in 1917, when the US government began calling on all able-bodied men between nineteen and forty years old to register for the military draft. Although he could have secured an exemption from military service due to his position as the head of a household with children, Sáenz registered and joined the army in February 1918. His diary provides a detailed account of the next sixteen months of his life, from enlistment through discharge.

Sáenz resumed his political work in the community when he returned from the war in 1919. One of his most popular initiatives involved a campaign to build a statue in San Antonio to commemorate the contributions of Mexican soldiers in World War I.[13] His efforts included giving lectures sponsored by Mexican organizations throughout South and Central Texas, writing letters to potential supporters, and submitting articles for publication in newspapers like the San Antonio daily, *La Prensa*. Sáenz also continued to speak out against the discrimination and segregation that plagued Texas schools, and he called on Mexicans to engage racial problems by increasing their participation at the polls and in other aspects of the civic life of the community.[14]

In the late 1920s, Sáenz began a long association with the League of United Latin American Citizens (LULAC). The organization became known for advancing what historians have come to call an ethnic, or Mexican Americanist, political identity and for promoting a strategy for securing constitutional rights through claims of citizenship. He joined with such civil rights political stalwarts as Alonso Perales, an attorney from San Antonio, and José Tomás Canales, a former school official and state representative from Brownsville, in a campaign to form the first statewide civil rights organization. Their initial attempt failed when most of the Mexico-born delegates representing mutual aid societies bolted the 1927 meeting. They accused Perales of seeking to establish an organization exclusively for US-born Mexicans. Sáenz, Perales, Canales, and other civil rights activists from South Texas regrouped and established LULAC in 1929. The organization focused on US citizens of Mexican origin, although the leadership often claimed to be speaking for the entire population of Mexicans living in the United States.[15]

In addition to his extensive postwar efforts to find funding for the statue to

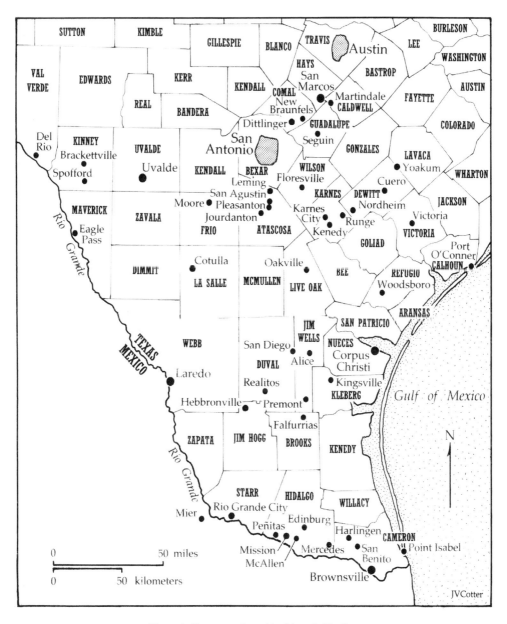

Places in Texas mentioned by Sáenz in his diary

commemorate his fellow soldiers' patriotism and bravery during World War I, Sáenz was involved in securing financial support for the historic *Salvatierra v. Del Rio* antisegregation case of 1933.[16] Possibly because of his frustration in raising enough funds for the statue, he turned the money he had collected over to the legal fight. Although the *Salvatierra* verdict did not outlaw discrimination against Mexican children when pedagogical reasons were used to justify their segregation, it favored the plaintiffs by acknowledging the segregation of Mexican children. Sáenz's financial contribution was a lesser-known detail in the historic legal fight, yet it serves as a symbolic tribute to the military service and battlefield sacrifice of Mexican soldiers in World War I.

Sáenz was known for his numerous political essays, published in both English- and Spanish-language newspapers, in which he sharply condemned discrimination and inequality.[17] He also worked on behalf of Mexican candidates for public office, especially in South Texas, where Mexican American voters represented a significant portion of the electorate. He did much of this work as a member of various local and statewide organizations with a civil rights focus. During his more than forty years of activism and public service, Sáenz worked especially closely with LULAC and parent-student organizations, as well as with the American GI Forum, the Veterans of Foreign Wars, the American Legion, the American Council of Spanish Speaking Persons, La Sociedad Mutualista of Sacred Heart Church (McAllen), and the Texas Good Relations Association.[18] He took special pride in his work with LULAC, including his role in its organizing campaigns, its founding convention in Corpus Christi, and its eventual status as the leading Mexican American civil rights organization in the country.

When Sáenz's life ended in 1953, Alonso Perales, perhaps the best-known Mexican civil rights figure in Texas, described him as "one of our most distinguished and honest leaders in the United States of America."[19] Santos de la Paz of Corpus Christi, the editor of the weekly paper *La Verdad* and a popular civil rights leader in the Gulf Coast area, added that Sáenz was a man of "true civic courage."[20] The editors of *La Prensa* offered this extraordinary praise:

> *Profesor* Sáenz always distinguished himself with his love and interest for the people of Mexican origin in this country. He always defended them when it was necessary and few people were speaking out. Consequently, his passing is without a doubt an irreparable loss for our people in the United States, especially in the state of Texas.[21]

THE DIARY

Sáenz's diary, a handsome, cloth-covered, 298-page book titled *Los méxi-co-americanos en la Gran Guerra y su contingente en pro de la democracia, la humanidad, y la justicia* details his thoughts, observations, and interactions with fellow military men as a newly recruited private in the 360th Infantry Regiment of the 90th Division of the US Army, over a sixteen-month period beginning in 1918. The book was published in 1933 by the San Antonio–based Artes Gráficas, one of the most successful publishers of literary and historical works in the Americas.[22] Friends, most of whom were fellow veterans and civil rights activists from South and Central Texas, made the publication possible with subscriptions, or advanced payments, for part of the $4 cost of the diary. Sáenz salutes these benefactors, noting at the end of the diary that "they deserve to be called collaborators because this publication would not have been possible without their help."

The diary draws on wartime notes Sáenz had entered into small, bound travel guides, blank-page booklets, the backs of postcards, loose sheets of paper, letters to his loved ones, and articles that he submitted to *La Prensa*. He sent most of these notes home during the war, asking friends and relatives to keep the materials, as well as copies of his articles, so that he could later review and prepare everything for publication as a diary. Few copies of the published volume have survived, largely because the publisher released only one thousand imprints, and most public libraries in the United States apparently overlooked its historical value and failed to purchase copies.[23]

Although Sáenz made his first entries on February 23 and 24, 1918, when he bid his family farewell, he declares the diary's official start as February 25, the date he enlisted for military duty at New Braunfels, Texas. The diary omits only five days from its chronological entries between February 1918 and June 1919. In addition to introductory and concluding remarks that Sáenz wrote after the war, as he prepared the book for publication, the book includes photographs of fellow soldiers, battle scenes, towns, and US and European national leaders. The last chronological entry, recorded on June 21, 1919, announces his release from the military and mentions a visit with family in Alice. As Sáenz explains in his introduction to the volume, he intends the diary to be a record of military service and battlefield sacrifice that justifies claiming equal rights at home. It is a call to action based on the nation's foundational principles of justice and democracy—principals the war had reinforced.

In between its first and last entries, the diary chronicles Sáenz's movement through approximately three months of training at San Antonio's Camp Travis, followed by a trip by rail to New York City, where he and his fellow soldiers boarded the steamship *Olympic* to cross the Atlantic. They arrived at Southampton, England, during the latter part of June. After crossing the English Channel, they passed by Paris and ended their journey in southeastern France, where they underwent additional training in preparation for battle in the northeastern part of the country. Sáenz and his buddies began seeing action in August and participated in two major battles at war's end, the Saint-Mihiel offensive of September 12–15, 1918, and the Meuse-Argonne offensive of September 26–November 1, 1918. Once the fighting ended, in anticipation of the armistice signed on November 11, the 90th Division entered Luxembourg and Germany. After approximately four months in occupied territory, they swung back into France and headed for Saint-Nazaire. There, on May 28, 1919, they embarked on the steamship *Mongolia* to return to the United States. The ship reached Boston on June 7. After a six-day trip by rail, the soldiers arrived in San Antonio, where they were subsequently discharged.

During training at Camp Travis, Sáenz was assigned to headquarters as a clerical worker. This position provided a vantage point he uses effectively in the diary to anticipate and then narrate large-scale events, such as training plans and assignments, troop movements in Europe, coordinated activities with allied troops, the scale of fighting at the different fronts, and news of world events. His dedicated service, as well as his rapid learning of French, earned him intelligence and messenger assignments. In addition, he was responsible for teaching English to a class of fellow Mexican soldiers from Texas. His position at headquarters and his knowledge of Spanish, English, and French also made Sáenz a popular figure among the soldiers. They often asked him for help in writing letters to their loved ones, and they questioned him about the contents of the telegrams and other news arriving daily at headquarters from around the world.

Sáenz's high-level assignments at headquarters were not without drawbacks, however. He reports witnessing unfair practices that colored his view of the military and reminded him of the discrimination Mexicans faced at home. One of his earliest such experiences occurred when his superiors at Camp Travis refused to grant the petition of an old and blind Mexican man who asked that one of his two sons be allowed to remain at home to care for him. Sáenz also reveals a keen sense of self-worth as he notes his growing irritation with superiors who fail to acknowledge his skills and dedication by promoting him to a rank commensurate with the demanding and skilled

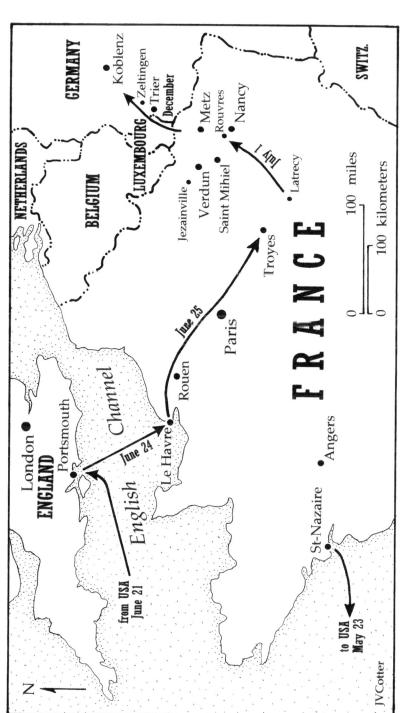

Routes taken by Sáenz at the war front

work he is regularly assigned to do. This lack of recognition and appreciation becomes especially unbearable when his application for admission to an officer training school is denied—twice—and without explanation. He remained a private throughout his military service.

Sáenz, who lived among the soldiers, provides accounts of their difficult day-to-day experiences, including forced marches, bloody battles, remarkable acts of heroism, terrifying deaths, hand-to-hand fighting, scouting missions conducted in the dead of night, constant back-and-forth shelling, and the sad, boring, and terrifying life in the trenches. He also describes the close relationships men developed amid the widespread carnage and devastation, the life and culture of local peasant communities, and the soldiers' difficulties with haughty and unfair superiors. He describes the different kinds of Mexicans serving alongside him—the poor recruits from Texas farms, ranches, towns, and cities whose arduous working-class lives prepared them for the physical demands in the military, the illiterate and the well-schooled, the self-confident and uncertain recruits, the long-term foreign-born residents, the Americanized, and the large number of Spanish or bilingual speakers. Sáenz also discusses his numerous conversations with the Mexican soldiers, during which he usually is exhorting them to act honorably, fight bravely, and commit to the social cause back home.

Sáenz seems to have spoken to the Mexican soldiers with notable confidence, probably because of the deference they showed him. He was older and better-educated and possessed impressive reading and writing skills, as well as being a reliable conduit for news and information they valued greatly. Sáenz also assumed a leadership position that his fellow soldiers obviously accepted. This is especially evident in the response to his call for a gathering on March 2, 1919, during an extended encampment in Zeltingen, Germany. Fifty-one Mexican soldiers from the 360th Infantry Regiment showed up. As he visited with individuals and groups, Sáenz delivered the message that had prompted him to call for the meeting: Mexicans had faced discrimination at home and survived the fighting in Europe, but they now had the opportunity to use their improved standing as patriots to prepare for the cause for respect, dignity, and equal rights at home.

The gathering at Zeltingen led Sáenz to believe that his fellow Mexican soldiers would lead a popular social movement when they returned home. They did not. Instead, the returning veterans mostly involved themselves in the joy of coming home and in the time-consuming tasks required of them as they resumed their family responsibilities. The concluding section of Sáenz's book reveals the magnitude of his disappointment. He offers a moving lamentation over the violent response by government troops in 1932 to the

"Bonus Army" of over forty thousand destitute veterans and their families who camped in the nation's capital to draw attention to their demand for payment of certificates issued to them by Congress in 1923.[24] He surmises that the continuing discrimination against Mexicans in Texas and the reappearance of war clouds over Europe demonstrate that Americans, Texans, and Europeans do not appreciate the lessons of the war, including the service and sacrifice of Mexican soldiers. He also regrets the lack of support in the Mexican community for a statue to honor the Mexican soldiers in the war.

His harshest critiques appear in the epilogue. In some cases, the leadership in the Mexican community had failed to understand the historic opportunity the soldiers' battlefield sacrifices offered. Sáenz aims his most vehement criticisms, however, at government officials who showed their insensitivity by denying veterans their promised bonus, and at society as a whole, for forgetting the soldiers' wartime contributions. No doubt, his concluding thoughts are also colored by the Interior Department's decision to reject his proposal that land and other resources be allotted to establish a Texas farming colony of Mexican American veterans. Still, showing his characteristic refusal to be completely daunted by disappointment or poor treatment, Sáenz closes with a reworking of an exhortation that appears throughout the diary: "We need more sacrifices and these offerings require more broad-minded men prepared to fight for the common good of our *raza.*"[25]

Sáenz's prescription for sacrifices and broad-mindedness was not limited to his call for action on behalf of Mexicans in the United States. He also made note of the abject conditions of peasant life in France and Germany, prejudice and discrimination against African Americans and Native Americans, and the calamity of war that was threatening humanity in Europe. Sáenz, however, was not above the prejudice and narrow-mindedness that he condemned. He spoke disparagingly of Romani (Gypsies) and other poor people from Europe who had taken to begging and haggling over the price of goods they were selling to the soldiers. Sáenz also characterized Jewish merchants and peddlers in negative terms when he suggested that they were especially given to scheming ways. He also expressed discomfort when he saw women accompanying African-origin soldiers in Paris. Sáenz's disparaging observations, however, were very limited, and they did not undermine his overall arguments and perspective related to military life, wartime experiences, and the cause for Mexican rights. They in fact stand in sharp contrast to his overall critique of prejudice and discrimination. Moreover, he was likely unaware of his own prejudices since he did not have a lived, personal experience with the people he disparaged. His critical views of Anglos in Texas, on the other hand, were based on lived experiences as a member of an aggrieved community, and this imbued him with a substantive critique of Anglo prejudice and discrimination in racial terms.

Fourteen years elapsed between Sáenz's final diary entry and the book's publication. His family responsibilities, along with his work commitments and political activities may account for much of this delay.[26] Still, the length of time he spent preparing the diary for publication is sufficiently long to raise questions regarding the extent to which Sáenz revised the text of his original entries. It is not unreasonable to wonder whether an understandable concern for amending or modifying the narrative for the sake of clarity and consistency might have resulted in major alterations that would undermine the integrity of the diary as a firsthand account of experiences and events.

To address that concern, I compared Sáenz's twenty-five postcard notes and twenty letters included among his personal papers with their corresponding entries in the published volume. The results of that comparison suggest a high degree of validity in the diary as the personal chronicle that it purports to be.[27] Although he did occasionally revise the content of his original materials, Sáenz recognized his responsibility to maintain the integrity of the diary as a reliably close rendering of events and a consistently trustworthy document. This is especially evident in the verbatim appearance in the diary of the three articles he wrote for *La Prensa* while at the front.[28] Sáenz made substantial revisions in only one document, a letter from a young pen pal named Robert E. Hoey, the original copy of which is in his archival collection. The letter appears in two places in the diary as revised copies of the original. This represents an inconsistency in an otherwise dependable narrative.[29] Sáenz emphasizes his belief in the validity of the diary in his concluding remarks. He claims that he has met his responsibility of commemorative vigilance, that he has created a record of the extraordinary service and sacrifice achieved by the Mexican soldier, and that this witnessed account stands as a source of inspiration and a basis for recuperative justice.

READING SÁENZ

The veterans and their family members, including relatives of soldiers who did not return from the war, must have seen the diary as a valuable record and an evocative guide to their own and others' experiences as young men in distant lands more than a dozen years earlier. Sáenz takes care to identify many of his fellow soldiers and to describe their warfront experiences, including the circumstances surrounding the death of some of his comrades. His frequent use of "we," whether referring to Mexican soldiers or to the entire army of men, also underscores the war as a collective American experience that Mexican readers could claim in their own identification with the nation and their quest for equality. Sáenz's references to the names and hometowns of the soldiers, as well as to the familiar Spanish-named bridges, streams, roads, and towns in Texas and his use of colloquial, archaic, and indigenous terms popular in Texas and Mexico would have encouraged Mexicans to read their community and their history into the narrative and to embrace Sáenz's bold and even defiant method of inscribing their world onto the larger narrative of the war. Finally, his frequent references to sayings, literary works, and historical events from Mexico and Texas also reinforce a sense of community that earns recognition if not respect. Sáenz's vast cultural repertoire, especially his command of history and literature, no doubt exceeded some readers' comprehension, but these readers also may have accepted and even expected this from a learned and assertive person like Sáenz.

Moreover, Sáenz projects a sense of self-respect and righteousness his readers would have been likely to recognize and admire as an idealized cultural type—a larger-than-life man who always stood up to any Anglo who would dare question his integrity or deny him his rights. This image takes form as Sáenz records his confrontations with prejudiced Anglos in Texas and unfair officers in the military, as well as when he repeatedly refers to extraordinarily brave and principled figures in Mexico's history. Sáenz also casts the racial tensions and conflicts prevalent in Texas in terms that favor Mexicans. A case in point is the story of a father and two sons—described by Sáenz as the Velázquez men—who refused military service because they had never been made to feel they were a part of the nation, but as draftees, they were now expected to fight on the country's behalf. The ensuing shootout with local authorities results in the death of the father and one son, but their indifference and even opposition to the draft is understandable under the racialized circumstances Sáenz describes. In acknowledging an underlying resentment that often ran deep, Sáenz validates an alienated identity and justifies a common thread that binds the Mexican community together. It also lays the necessary groundwork for Sáenz to propose military service and sacrifice as the basis for a new form of unity and social incorporation that capitalizes on the nation's reenergized principles of justice and democracy.

Some readers, of course, must have disagreed with Sáenz as they read the diary. The Mexicanists who reacted against Sáenz and his fellow Mexican Americanists in 1927, when the first efforts to launch LULAC were proposed at the Harlingen convention, for instance, may have interpreted the diary as an attempt to shore up citizenship claims with demonstrations of loyalty in the form of military service and battlefield sacrifice. Perales and Sáenz encouraged this view when they visited the offices of *La Prensa* on the eve of the publication of the diary. Perales reportedly praised the book for its treatment of Mexican American military service and sacrifice by men he considered loyal citizens: "Mexican Americans know how to meet their duties as citizens, including the supreme obligation to offer their lives in fulfillment of those responsibilities."[30]

The newspaper's readers would have been familiar with Perales's advocacy of civil rights and recognized that his claim of entitlement was premised on constitutional guarantees to the US-born and the naturalized. They could also see that Sáenz was now binding the theoretical contract with a pen dipped in blood shed on European soil. Although readers of the diary would soon discover that Sáenz had not given US citizenship such importance, his silence when Perales made his pronouncement could have been misinterpreted as full acquiescence.

Allowing Perales to read US citizenship into the diary conformed to LULAC's constitutional strategy and Sáenz's commitment to it, but his book does not offer an outright endorsement of the strategy. Sáenz does, however, often attribute US nativity and citizenship to the soldiers by using the term *Mexican American* and by referring to some of the soldiers as having been born or raised in Texas. Sáenz also provides grist for the citizenship mill by criticizing Mexican-origin slackers. Such individuals prompt prejudiced Anglos to suspect all Mexicans of being disloyal to the United States. He also uses the term *México Americanos* in the diary's title and encourages his readers to embrace a cause for equal rights that logically would lead to both political and cultural incorporation.

Sáenz's moral and practical arguments on using warfront contributions to gain the incorporation of Mexicans into US society on an equal basis, however, stand on their own. He may have encouraged the readers of *La Prensa* to interpret the previously noted visit to the newspaper as allowing Perales to impose LULAC's purpose on his writing, but he makes it clear throughout the diary that it is primarily intended as a record of the military service and sacrifice of all the Mexican recruits. His concern is that the same anti-Mexican attitude that has historically denied the Mexican community its rights in Texas will overlook the meaning behind the Mexican community's response to the nation's call to military service. Creating a written, published record, therefore, serves this higher purpose. The service and sacrifice that Sáenz recounts achieves greater importance as he repeatedly reminds his readers that US- and Mexico-born Mexicans who took part in the war did so despite the discriminatory treatment they had received in Texas.

Despite Sáenz's efforts at describing the Mexican community as mostly unified in its response to the call to arms, he makes nativity and citizenship

distinctions that conform to the views that many US-born civil rights leaders would later inscribe into LULAC. This no doubt reinforced social difference and inequality among Mexicans, as well as between Mexican immigrants
and the larger nativist-minded population. Sáenz's other possibly unintended
masculinist approach to the telling of the Mexican war experience also shored
up a gendered hierarchy, one that privileged Mexican men as the sole repre-
sentatives of a Mexican military heritage who sacrificed everything for the
Mexican community and the nation. Mexican men clearly made extraordinary contributions that could become currency to secure equal rights. Sáenz,
however, pays little attention to women who made sacrifices of their own,
including his wife, who assumed greater and largely unrecognized family and
community responsibilities when the men went to war and resumed their
unequal roles as the men returned from Europe armed with self-aggrandizing
claims of heroism and sacrifice. Sáenz obviously assumed that wartime heroism and sacrifice was restricted to the men on the battlefield and that men
would lead the cause for equal rights and that they would focus on the US-
born and immigrants aspiring to be Americans, ideas that predominated in
patriarchal and nativist regimes within and outside the Mexican community.
These appear as the most obvious inconsistencies in an otherwise self-aware,
inspiring, and even unpretentious account of wartime experiences.

Drawing a contrast between the dejected state of a socially submerged
group at home and this same group's distinguished record of military service
abroad grants Mexicans a morally superior position that Sáenz uses to build
his argument for equal rights. He uses a second technique when he juxtaposes
the loyal Mexican-origin recruits with the undetermined number of both US-
and Mexico-born Mexicans who avoided the draft by escaping to Mexico.
Sáenz also advances the essentialist notion that Mexico's history of wars and
revolutions against colonial powers, foreign intruders, and conservative ideas,
equips its people with a singular appreciation for the values of justice and
democracy. The convergence of such possibilities with the historic opportunity to capitalize on the Allied spirit of democratic values now requires that
Mexican-origin soldiers serve honorably and bravely to leverage change at
home. Sáenz concludes that this type of service is precisely what the recruits
had rendered.

Sáenz builds an even more elaborate edifice on the bedrock of military
service and sacrifice. He suggests throughout the diary that Mexicans had
earned a special place in the national project of forging a new nation on the
restored principles of justice and democracy. He adds that the segregationists at home, some of whom are of German origin, are like their counterparts in Europe, men who violated these same civilizing values and caused

great harm to entire nations, including their own. A fight against such evil forces at home requires that Mexicans ready themselves by promoting a truly patriotic social movement—namely, one that opposes discrimination and segregation.

Sáenz most often defines patriotism as a devotion to the principles of justice and democracy rather than an admiration for the flag or a jingoistic allegiance to the nation. In his view, high moral principles provide the basis both analogizing the cause for equal rights at home with the war against Germany, and for inverting the relationship between segregationists and advocates for expanded rights. Predicating a just cause for equal rights on military service and sacrifice reinforces a nation-building principle of just rewards for the nation's soldiers and their communities.

Other writers whose works appeared in Spanish-language newspapers shared Sáenz's observations on Mexicans in the military and applauded their individual sacrifices as expressions of their loyalty. Some of these writers included soldiers whose letters and articles appeared in the Spanish-language press as well as family members who recounted their own wartime sacrifice and admiration for the soldiers. However, today, *Mexican Americans in the Great War* is the only available work by a Mexican from the United States that provides a firsthand account of the war and the bravery of the Mexican soldiers as a basis for political action on behalf of their communities. Sáenz also stands apart from other writers in that excerpts from his highly elaborated narrative appeared in Spanish-language newspapers during and after the war.

Sáenz's prescription for action, which emphasized military service and battlefield sacrifice, began to be advocated in newspaper articles and in speeches by other leaders. This trend became especially pronounced beginning on the eve of the US entry into World War II, as members of the so-called Mexican American generation of upwardly mobile, US-born Mexican leaders began to embrace the cause of the war as an expression of national loyalty and an opportunity to once again include wartime contributions in the civil rights agenda.[31]

Current readers of Sáenz's diary can read his wartime account with an eye on its contributions to various histories. For instance, Sáenz's explicit statements about military service and battlefield sacrifice as points of leverage in the cause for equal rights underscore the importance of the diary to the Mexican community, its history and the histories of other marginalized groups in US history. His own ability to recognize the importance of the war to minority rights and to offer sophisticated understandings on the political meaning and uses of military service and battlefield sacrifice also represents a valuable contribution to intellectual history and the troubled history of racial and class relations in Texas history. Sáenz's account also stands as a thoughtful portrayal of military life and warfront experience that the common soldier endures. The war diary, in other words, expresses the spirit of foxhole solidarity, even as it calls for a good measure of empathy to be extended to the always brave Mexican soldiers, their community in the United States, and the "suffering humanity" in war-torn Europe that Sáenz laments.

A PERSONAL NOTE FROM THE TRANSLATOR

When I first read the diary in 1979, I was deeply impressed by its historical significance and promptly incorporated it into my university classes on Mexican American and Texas history. At the same time, though, I was amazed that no one else appeared to be engaging the diary as a record of singular importance for the study of Mexican, intellectual, Texas, and military history. I assumed that most scholars had overlooked the book because they were not proficient in Spanish. I then thought I might translate it. The diary deserved a distribution much wider than could be achieved by the few Spanish-language copies available in some US university libraries. My initial research on Sáenz led me to interview his sons and daughters. When I discovered that their father's rich collection of personal papers had been saved (distributed among the siblings), I suggested they reassemble the collection and donate it to the Mexican American Library Program within the Nettie Lee Benson Latin American Collection, located at the University of Texas at Austin. Family members did this in 1989. My subsequent research in the Sáenz Papers, along with findings presented in a 1989 scholarly article by Carole E. Christian on Mexican soldiers from Texas, spurred me to edit and translate the diary.

I made a commitment to the project around 1996, when Mary Lenn Dixon, an editor at Texas A&M University Press, reviewed my proposal to translate Sáenz's diary and offered an advance contract. Also, Fran Vick, a fellow Texas historian, editor, and generous benefactor, provided me with the necessary financial support to obtain the translating assistance of the late Ben Maya, a certified court interpreter and translator from Austin. I had translated about one-fifth of the diary in order to get a sense of the scope of the work that lay ahead. Ben conducted a first translation of the entire book while I edited its contents. I began revising the translated material as it became available from Ben. After I had completed at least five detailed revisions of the translated and edited version of Sáenz's book, I wrote several drafts of the introduction, revising in response to suggestions from readers. Polishing the remainder of the manuscript also took time.[32]

I began to publish my research findings in 2002, with an essay in which I described Sáenz as a key intellectual who provided valuable philosophical justifications for the Mexican cause in Texas. I also devoted a section of my recent book to Sáenz's important role in guiding this social movement in its transition from a Mexicanist, or inclusive political orientation, to a more narrow, Mexican Americanist identity and outlook. A forthcoming essay uses the concept of autobiographical consciousness to explain Sáenz's political philosophy and views.[33]

Despite my early confidence-building research and writing about Sáenz, I did not fully grasp the magnitude of the work the diary project would involve. The book's sheer length and small font size, the arduous task of identifying rare sources, and the difficulties of translating a variety of forms of communication, as well as accurately rendering the meaning of colloquial, archaic, and indigenous terms and sayings, posed serious challenges. Tracking down basic information about the numerous places, people, and events mentioned in the diary required research and the addition of explanatory notes. Finally, as I discovered, translating the meanings embedded in esoteric words and complex idioms no longer in use requires developing explanations that go far beyond a literal rendition of a text.

I am aware of the pivotal role I play as a translator and editor, orchestrating an exchange between subjectivities across a cultural divide that separates the historical moment when Sáenz put pen to paper and my own very different time and place. Inevitably, my surroundings and sensibilities influenced how I have interpreted the meanings he gave his words. To put this a little differently, translating Sáenz's diary places me in the position of a mediator with a special determining role in interpreting observations, thoughts, and opinions. I believe my professional training in history, Spanish, and literature; my record of research and writing in Mexican American and Texas history; and my cultural citizenship in the Mexican community of Texas combine to make me especially sensitive to the language and meanings in the diary. It is my hope that these attributes have resulted in a form of coauthorship that reveals and celebrates the creative work of Sáenz while also acknowledging my own interventions and embedded interpretations.

My effort to bring Sáenz's work to a broad audience is tied directly to my personal and professional interests. I am a socially engaged scholar who conducts research in Mexican history to explain the persistence of class and racial inequalities and to draw attention to the organized initiatives to ameliorate and change conditions that contribute to this problem. I have translated the diary because I recognize Sáenz's masterful critique of these inequalities, his bold reconfiguration of the Mexican cause, and his sensitive treatment of

Mexican people and their veterans. I also admire his expansive and far-reaching statements about a shared Mexican history and culture and his ability to speak prophetically about a Mexican cause that continues to draw on the United States' foundational principles to justify itself.

The candid historian that I am requires that I admit an uncertainty about Sáenz. I am not able to fully understand the source of his extraordinary insight and bold judgment. I appreciate his keen intellect and ability to assemble and then present an array of ideas as coherent, effective arguments—and often to do so in indifferent or even hostile settings. Similarly, I am not surprised by his mastery of the Spanish language and Mexican history and culture. Here and elsewhere, I have credited his good schooling and mentoring in Alice, along with his studious nature and determined personality, to explain his analytical skills and self-assuredness. I have also suggested that loving parents and a hardscrabble life in Realitos equipped Sáenz with knowledge of the difficulties Mexicans faced in Texas and a moral compass that helped him find his bearings. These explanations, however, fall short of providing a comprehensive understanding of Sáenz, even when only the merits of his diary are under consideration.

His prescient ability to see the war as an opportunity to advance the Mexican cause seems to defy satisfactory explanation. Accounting for the strength of his confidence about his righteous purpose is equally difficult. What made Sáenz strong enough to leave home, give up a relatively secure source of employment, and place himself in harm's way? Was it only chance that brought the fortuitous confluence of a war, with its democratizing influence in the United States, a minority community in search of social redemption, a band of brave and daring brothers in the battlefields of Europe, and a person of rare intellect, internal fortitude, and caring nature who could chronicle their experiences as a statement of righteous protest and visionary argument? It may never be possible to address everything of importance in Sáenz's life, nor to explain it fully and adequately. This in no way detracts from the indisputable fact that his contributions to history and leadership in his community are enormous. And this fact alone makes his diary worth reading.

Emilio Zamora

The 360th Infantry Regiment, 90th Division

Shown on the page facing the beginning of Sáenz's diary is the insignia of the 360th Infantry Regiment, 90th Division of the American Expeditionary Forces in 1919. Sáenz's note for the insignia is translated as follows:

WORLD WAR SOUVENIR

The postcard is by J. Luz Sáenz, Regimental Intelligence Office (R.I.O.) of the 360th Infantry Regiment, of the Texas and Oklahoma Division, after the major battles and while in Zeltingen, Germany, as the Army of Occupation of the American Expeditionary Forces in Europe in 1919.

The American soldiers of Mexican origin maintained the impressive martial reputation of our people in those horrific battles.

Sáenz also included a chronology of key dates for the regiment:

IMPORTANT CHRONOLOGY OF THE 360TH REGIMENT

1917 September. Assembled at Camp Travis, San Antonio
1918 June 6. Departed for Europe
　　　June 14. Embarked at New York on the *Olympic*
　　　June 21. Arrived at Southampton, England
　　　June 22. Crossed the English Channel on the *King Edward*
　　　June 23. Disembarked at Le Havre, France (Rest Camp No. I-A)
　　　From July 1 to August 18. Rouvres-sur-Aube (Discipline)
　　　From August 23 to October 10. Saint-Mihiel
　　　From October 16 to November 11. Verdun
　　　Armistice
　　　From December 2 to 6. Crossed Luxembourg
　　　From December 22 to May 17, 1919. By the Moselle in Germany
1919 May 28. Embarked at Saint-Nazaire, France
　　　June 7. Arrived at Boston
　　　June 17. Triumphant March in San Antonio
　　　June 21. Discharged at Camp Travis

Mexican Americans in the Great War

■

By
José de la Luz Sáenz
360th Infantry
Expeditionary Forces in France

LOS

MEXICO-AMERICANOS

en la
GRAN GUERRA

y su contingente en pró de la

DEMOCRACIA, LA HUMANIDAD Y LA JUSTICIA

por

J. LUZ SAENZ

Del Regimiento 360 de Infantería

FUERZAS EXPEDICIONARIAS EN FRANCIA

Preface

I wrote "My Personal Diary" as the near complete account of the lives of a special group of frontline soldiers who served among millions of others in the Allied army and shared in the misfortunes and dangers of the Great War. I especially wanted the Mexican-origin people to know and claim the deeds and suffering of the soldiers who defended the reputation and good name of *la raza* on the honor-testing battlefields of France.

History teaches that we forget and fail to repay the sacrifices of the men who fall in combat. It is a thousand times better for the veterans of the inevitable, destructive, and horrific wars that plague humanity to die forgotten than to have their sacrifice disregarded and unappreciated by the very people they defended in horrible battles far away from the safety and sweet tranquility of their homes.

The common American soldier continues to face misfortune, horror, ingratitude, indifference, and neglect. How could the humble Mexican Americans expect recognition and fairness in light of this hopeless and pervasive situation? Obviously, no one was going to record his glorious deeds and publish a reliable account. The "slackers" committed an unfortunate and regrettable mistake when they failed to answer the call from a nation in crisis and encouraged the public to think the rest of us did not want to make the sacrifice. We are glad and proud to know that our soldiers acted responsibly and bravely when the moment of truth arrived. It was wonderful to see them charging against enemy positions through "curtains of machine gun fire." As always, the Mexican American gave free expression to a daring and indomitable courage that he inherited from the stoic Aztec race.

The acts of heroism on the battlefields of the Great War were not reserved for one group of men. Everyone who received the order to make the sacrifice responded. The British, the Belgian, the Italian, the French, and the African also shared in the sacrifice. All of us were brave fighting men, subject to the same vicissitudes of military life, exposed to the same dangers, fighting together and defending *a common cause* during those terrible days of anguish and sorrow felt around the globe. Nevertheless, I have not addressed all experiences so men of other races can have the opportunity to narrate and judge us fairly, hoping they recognize the true heroism of men of honor.

Almost fifteen years have passed and no one has said, "This is what the Mexican American contributed during the war, this is how he conducted himself at the supreme hour of the bloody battles, and let this 'act' of recognition be our sincere tribute to them, if only to remember that they fell believing they were dying for a just and sacred cause."

We must reveal that truth. Today, more than ever, we must recognize their accomplishments so that other loyal citizens may be encouraged to join in the civic and military battles of the future.

Our people have formed a negative opinion of the current unfavorable circumstances. The wounds that many of our veterans carry in their souls are as serious as the ones they sustained on the battlefields and took to their graves. The veterans and their children have been wounded by the sad and disappointing failure to extend to them the just recognition of met responsibilities. Nothing less than the acknowledgment of their contributions can correct past mistakes and the long-standing prejudice against us. It will also provide a clear understanding of the true meaning of *loyalty*, the right of *citizenship*, and the love of *flag* and *country*.

Our unwavering loyalty in the desolate fields of Flanders, Château Thierry, Verdun, and Saint-Mihiel may serve us well. We expressed it at the most critical time, when we had to respond in the name of our people and help raise the morale of the dispirited Allies. We did this during the final push to rescue our civilization and restore the global peace that is necessary for establishing understanding and respect among the races, including our own.

The great American military lived up to the trust the world placed on it. Our soldiers took part in that glorious armada and they also lived up to their reputation as brave men. This is why we should be proud of the final Allied victory that removed the threat of the horrible world war. Our sacrifice was the last drop that made the cup run over. It made the armistice possible and offered us the opportunity to set the conditions for the end of the human hemorrhage . . . and it brought *peace!*

Without our help, the Allies would never have achieved victory. This will become more evident with the passage of time.

We never thought that ordinary soldiers like us should have to understand the cause of the war and why it started as it did. It was enough to hear the clamor for justice by the suffering humanity against imperial despotism and cruelty. We only had to witness the offense against the honor of nations. We are glad to have made the contribution of exposing our lives and sacrificing ourselves until we finished with the hostilities and achieved a clear and favorable conclusion to the war. Only time could tell if the treaties would bring lasting peace and that *justice* would prevail.

Those were the feelings and the spirit that filled our hearts. They emerged out of meeting our major responsibility to our *nation* during the horrendous hours of bloody battles.

My book does not pretend to be a work of art or a literary jewel, but it is a sincere and reliable account of my ideas, based on what I saw, what I did, and what I felt during the sixteen months when I answered my nation's call to duty. We are at peace now. Our country was once in danger, but it no longer faces the sinister and disquieting days, the difficult trials, the unimaginable anguish, and the terrifying uncertainty. The fear of universal ruin that enveloped everything and that seemed to be pulling us into the abyss faded away, and the brilliant rainbow of the sweet and coveted peace has returned.

We invoke memories that are like yesterday's deeply etched dreams and carefully set them aside for future use.

My favorite time to work on the diary was the twilight hours, usually with the reliable help of the flickering light of a paraffin candle. I wrote as the events unfolded, as the scenes that I observed were moving me. I wrote in the "barracks" where we enjoyed the gift of electrical light and at French "billets," far from clear danger but within earshot of the constant artillery rumble from the horrendous front. I wrote in "dugouts," our covered underground holes. Sometimes, I simply wrote with the sky as my cover, sometimes blue, sometimes covered with thick clouds yielding the unrelenting rain that often fell over France.

Although my ability may limit me, I wish to sketch true accounts of scenes we witnessed as we met our most sacred duty. I have done this while at Camp Travis, as we rode a Pullman train toward the port of departure at Hoboken, New Jersey, on our steamship voyage across the Atlantic, when we arrived in Great Britain, as we crossed the English Channel, upon our arrival in the glorious France, while in French towns and villages where we maintained ourselves in strict discipline, at the old and memorable battlefields and ruins from the times of the Crusades and of the Moors, in the fields and towns that had been laid to waste, amid the scattered bodies in battlefields cratered by powerful explosives, all through the difficult and weary marches along muddy roads on the way to German territory, as we bade farewell to Europe, during the public receptions in our country, while we waited for our discharge at Camp Travis, and, finally, during the joyful arrival at our homes.

We should not overlook why I sought to serve or the circumstances that explain my views and judgments that may appear to reflect my personal partialities, especially when I complain or indict people who did not treat me as the companion in arms that our shared responsibility required. I returned safe and sound to my family, and with the passage of time and the experience of living, I have forgotten the bitterness of that difficult life. I merely recall it as a chapter in my past.

May it please the heavens that the still-open, bleeding wounds call on humankind to rid itself of petty and personal resentments and that the memory of the war, the most destructive in our history, discourage the egotistical behavior that has a hold over nations.

Not long ago, we heard the nations of the world clamoring for peace. They were suffering, they complained of hunger, pestilence, misery, and the ravages of war. On the other hand, we have seen with our own eyes that as soon as the war ended and the spoils of victory were divided, nations rose up again, more arrogant, egotistical, prideful, and cunning than ever. The hope for better, permanent relations between nations fades away as haughty ideas enslave people again.

We learned to recognize the smell of fresh smoke from the powerful explosives, paid the bitter price of the supreme sacrifice, and saw at close range the destruction of modern war. We do not want more wars. Despite everything, wars will come again. Witness our restless youth with a spirit more eager for unknown adventures than our own ever were and be assured we will not be lacking for leaders who know how to manipulate human passions. We will once again see the laborer's son march alongside the young man of the "slums," clutching the rifle, leaping over the trenches, and braving the barbed wire and the asphyxiating gases as they are ordered, "over the top" and "forward, boys." Meanwhile, others will be enjoying life's pleasures and good fortune thousands of miles from the front, or they will curse the delayed victory or the war and its high cost. War! War! Future generations will continue to be spectators, tolerate the atrocities and barbarisms, and endorse the horrors and desolation. We expect justice for the soldiers who fell to make this world better, and we hope that history gathers their names and tells of their deeds with accurate reckoning. Those of us who despaired alongside the thousands of unknown and forgotten heroes will also have the moral responsibility to proclaim their acts of bravery and to do something to remember and honor their acts of self-denial. We will have to work at this until we reach our final hour, when we leap over our "last bulwark."

Prologue

Soon after the government announced registration, or the conscription of the fifth of June, we heard the mistaken views and interpretations circulating among our people. The alarm and mass confusion did great harm to the Mexican American community of Texas. Mexican Americans were certainly not the only ones who tried to evade registration, and we insist that they may have had good cause or at least a better reason than young men of other races. We are convinced that fear was not the cause during those confusing times, but a bad misunderstanding that has never been resolved. Without fear of erring much, two groups of citizens avoided or tried to evade military service in 1917 and 1918. Some were illiterate people who never attended schools in Texas, either because of their own failings or, frankly speaking, because they were never fully and equally accepted in the schools "for whites." They never had the opportunity to learn the meaning of patriotism, the sense of truly loving their flag and country. It is unreasonable to ask them to fight and die for something they do not understand. When the time to make a decision was upon us, it was too late to help them understand. The sense of duty to country begins when a person exercises independent reasoning. Everyone understands that this is the way we should engage life. We demonstrated it when we served in combat and survived. We gave ample proof of the long-standing martial qualities of the "American Race."

The second group of slackers included those few who knew enough to feel justly embittered (an understandable response to callous racial prejudice) about being denied the opportunities necessary to live like other deserving, self-respecting citizens in our nation. We vehemently disagreed with this view. That was not the time to air grievances and to try to dissuade grown people from continuing with their long-standing and hostile practices against us. These people have been unscrupulous politicians, small-minded citizens, and Mexican-hating individuals who have offended our racial pride, our dignity, and love of the homeland. They have also thought little about the consequences.

German or pro-German propaganda contributed to our distress during the recruiting days. German spies or sympathizers to the German cause laid the seeds of discord and encouraged disloyalty among Mexican Americans. This explains why many Mexicans and Mexican Americans left. Their escape to Mexico created two problems: the scarcity of farmworkers and accusations of disloyalty. It was impossible to make our own see the error of their ways. We were divided when we should have stood together, like we are known to do when we have a clear understanding of our patriotic duty.

I was teaching in Dittlinger, Comal County, on the memorable fifth of June. I did not register that day because I had done it a week earlier. Government officials advised us to register early, but not after the fifth. I confess that I acted in good faith when I picked up my registration forms before the fifth of June and the county secretary challenged me. He asked me a number of questions that I believe I answered correctly. I detected a marked irony and sarcasm in him during our short conversation. He asked, "Will you be afraid if sent to the trenches in France?" I answered, "I do not have a reason to be afraid. I know that I am expected to do this. Moreover, since it is a matter of honor to go and defend our star spangled banner, I believe that our Anglo compatriots, who always keep the best for themselves, would not deny us the same opportunity. If they are now accepting the sons of a race that they have always considered incapable of such noble sacrifice, then start counting me in." "You are talking too much," he concluded. I ended the conversation by stating, "You are the one who is asking too many questions."

So much hardship was heaped on us that few people noticed the large number of volunteers who presented themselves to fill the void left by the "slackers" of all races and colors. The public could not distinguish between the conscientious objectors and the people who did not fill out the confusing registration forms because they did not understand the requirements. Many people focused on some Mexican Americans who avoided military service and proceeded to judge the rest of us through the unjust lens of prejudice. How many of them have changed their minds? How many of them can now grant us justice, now that they have seen the obvious and important evidence in the telegram I reproduce below:

San Diego, Texas
April 30, 1917
General John J. Pershing
Commanding General
Fort Sam Houston, Texas

PLEASE TELEGRAPH THE APPROPRIATE OFFICIALS
TO ENLIST COMPANIES OF SPANISH-SPEAKING BOYS.

FELIPE GARCÍA[1]
Adjutant General, Headquarters[2]
Department of the South
Fort Sam Houston, Texas

May 1, 1917
Mr. Felipe García
San Diego, Texas

Dear Sir:

General Pershing has directed me to acknowledge receipt of your telegram of April 30th and to express his appreciation for the offer contained therein, but at present there is no requirement to enlist volunteer companies.

Your telegram will be placed on file and should the current law change, your offer will be given due consideration.

Very Sincerely Yours,

RALPH HARRISON
Lieutenant Colonel, General Secretary

This is an impressive response by one of our own just twenty-four days after the declaration of war against Germany. García not only offered to serve but also to organize entire companies of members of our *raza*, all volunteers. That is how some of us, the sons of the maligned Duval County, responded.

These were the circumstances when I realized that I would be among the "honorably selected." I stayed with my family during the month of June, after I had notified the post office clerk of my new address. I also notified the county judge and the sheriff and wrote them again from my new residence.

The first call was made during August and September, but I did not receive a notice. When November arrived, President Woodrow Wilson was making great offers to anyone who volunteered. I was given the opportunity—at an unfortunate moment—to find a way to detach myself from my civilian obligations so that I could defend the national honor, personal principles, ideas, or perhaps only someone else's capital, etc., but all for the nation.

I wrote Washington to offer my services and received a courteous and standard response expressing appreciation for my good intentions, but was

informed that I had been called in August and that they could not understand why I was not already in the military. What followed was very important. I was relieved that I could show that I was not responsible for the
mistake thanks to the early decision that I had made in notifying officials of
my change of address.

I filled out the dreaded questionnaire during the last days of December.
While others may have been dishonest in their responses to secure an exemption, some of us welcomed the opportunity to join the military. I received a
small card from the New Braunfels Draft Board on January 4, 1918, informing me that they had classified me Class "A" and first class. I received another
card on the twelfth ordering me to appear at New Braunfels for a physical
examination. A few days later, I learned that I was fit for military service.

FLORENCIO HERAS

Lencho, as we always called him, was another victim. Injustice, possibly
based on racial prejudice, dug its bestial claws on that poor and defenseless
man of the soil. He was unjustly forced into military service. In the first place,
Lencho was not the person they sought. Also, Lencho was a minor, as is evident in the following document that I copy:

Baptismal Certificate
Florencio Heras,
Son of Felipe Heras and Exiquia Conzález, born in Alice, Texas,
on the 9th day of April of 1898; baptized on the 24th of January of
1904, in accordance with the rites of the Roman Catholic Church,
at the Church of Saint Francis de Paula in San Diego, Texas, by the
Rev. S. P. Bard. Godparents: Eudoxio Villarreal and Anastasia García.
According to the Registry of this church, page 313—Book VI.
February 8, 1933
Rev. Fr. Eloy Suárez, O. P.

*Note: The date of February 8, 1933, refers to the date when the certificate was
released. It shows that Florencio Heras was barely nineteen years, ten months,
and eighteen days when he died on February 26, 1918, after having served in the
military for a good amount of time.*

Another Florencio Heras had lived in Benavides, but he had failed to
comply with the registration law and left for Mexico. Our government officials were either overzealous in their vigilance over military duty or they may

have wanted to collect the fifty dollars for every "slacker" they rounded up. They caught young Lencho during the early morning hours as he was frying some potatoes for breakfast.

His railroad boss, an Anglo and "a friend of the Mexicans," knew he was a minor but forced him to register by threatening to take away his job. Lencho had to work to support Gumersinda, his oldest sister who had raised him since he was a young boy. He worked at the Alfred railroad section.[3]

Someone had told him, "Lencho, the Americans do not like us. If you do not go to Mexico they will take you as a draftee even if you are under age. He never showed fear before the Germans in Europe, but he understood how easy it was for his fellow armed citizens to act unjustly. Lencho committed the high crime of joining the "slackers" and tried to leave for Mexico. These were unforgivable offenses to his enemies. They had the perfect excuse to wash their hands like Pontius Pilate and collect fifty dollars.

This is how the "Texan dragnet" reached the doors of his poor home as Lencho prepared his potatoes "a la française." He did not even have time to take the skillet off the stove, or to defend himself. The "rinches" placed two very good handcuffs on him and took him to Corpus Christi. He was still there when his brother Eugenio took him his baptismal record to see if this could help him. The "rinches" told him, "That piece of paper is worthless. What is this, everyone now wants to save himself with a baptismal certificate?"[4] They took him to Fort Worth and from there to our shores where he was placed on the ill-fated *Tuscania* that the Germans sank off the Irish coast.[5]

Lencho's life ended this way, a victim of fate and racial prejudice. Uncle Sam, true to his word, has been making restitution in the amount of $10,000 for a soldier lost in action. The death of the innocent, underage citizen, and the tyrannical abuse brought upon his poor, peaceful home, still has to be paid. An unrelenting voice cries out for justice.

Sixto Flores and another compatriot named Garza from Alice also died on the *Tuscania*.

As this was unfolding, I could see that things were turning serious. I decided that I would always remember this. The anti-Mexican views in Texas offended me, but I was hungry for adventure and accustomed to hard times. I welcomed anything, dared everything. How could this improve our situation? I did not know, I did not care to know, but I knew that in the midst of the ruinous world war it was necessary to show everyone that I was a true representative of our people.

I reported for my physical examination at New Braunfels. It was terribly cold at five in the morning when I had to take a passenger train from Leming. The hour-long wait seemed like a year. I was in deep thought during the one-hour trip to San Antonio. I was not riding for pleasure and the trip did not bring me peace of mind. My departure held unimaginable surprises. I was eating breakfast in San Antonio at fifteen past six.

I had time to see my sister and my little nephew—family members I also support—but I did not visit them because I did not want to alarm them.

I joined with a fellow traveler of German origin in San Antonio and discovered that he was also going to New Braunfels for his examination. We were the first to arrive at the post office, where we were examined. We were also the first to wait for word from the board.

I finished my business early and had enough time to visit some friends. I wanted to go to Dittlinger. Mr. Hermenegildo Luna, a good friend of mine, took me on his little express that he uses to take goods to his small store at "Las Caleras."[6] I ate at his good home and, like always, received the warmest attention from his family and friends who were from this place. I paid my respects to most of my friends and later visited the cherished school and the dear children I had taught during the previous school term.[7] I have given the best years of my life to the education of our children. I struggled much in Dittlinger and I could not help but feel sympathy for the children who are abandoned, unappreciated, ignored, and, worse, misunderstood. I was bitterly disappointed to hear that our people expected little from the school that year. Despite this, a flash of hope came to me. Everything would improve once we met the awaiting sacrifice. That was one of the reasons why we joined in the war effort. I thought the sacrifice would bring them a better and happier life.

My unexpected visit was so important. It was so full of possibilities for our future. At four in the afternoon, I took the fast train that runs from Houston to San Antonio. Mr. Rafael Cantú offered to see me off at the railroad station. I stayed in San Antonio that night until eleven and visited my sister and my little nephew Samuel. I shared all that had happened and then left for Leming.

The German who took the examination with me said he had secured an exemption because he had to help his parents with ranch work. The same board had decided I was fit for military service. I see no injustice since I volunteered to serve.

I was responsible for a small public school in the town of San Agustín in Atascosa County. I realized that I might serve and had notified the school board and my students' parents.[8]

On Friday, February 22, I received the famous card on behalf of the Honorable President Wilson which informed me of the high honor the nation was bestowing on me as a citizen. I was to defend it and follow the star spangled banner to France or any other part of the world where I might be sent. The message, as brief as it was significant and urgent, did not give me time to meet all my responsibilities with members of the school board who had entrusted me with the education of their children that year. My school closed without the customary ceremonies. I barely had time to prepare the following muddled farewell:

To My Students

My dear students: This is definitely our last day of school. You will start your vacation once I have gathered the texts that the government has supplied us. Rest, and have fun. I hope you enjoy the long period that follows. You will be free of classes and the required study.

I cannot say the same for me. I do not know what the future holds, but I can assure you that I will witness grand events, a thousand and one yet unknown sights, and I hope to return to tell you everything. Next Monday, at eleven in the morning, I will become part of the militia that will defend our country.

Until now, I have used pencil and pen to wage trying battles for the educational advancement of our people. You will soon hear that I am holding a rifle in the very trenches of France and upholding our people's pride for the glory and honor of our flag.

I do not know if you will have to follow me. I hope not. But if you do, I hope that my example helps you to be brave and strong enough to free yourself from everything that is dear on earth—the sweet peace, your homes, and your families.

I am not going on an excursion, I know that the life that awaits me will be difficult, the most demanding that I will have experienced, but I do not think it will be as difficult as Washington's crossing of the Delaware and his stay at Valley Forge. If it becomes just as difficult, so much the better, it will be a greater honor for our people. Long live Washington! Long live the star spangled banner! Long live our *raza!*

The need to answer my nation's call required that I leave my teaching position.

Saturday, February 23

I barely had enough time to submit the report of the school's closing and to secure my pay for the last days that I had worked. I said my good-byes to a few friends from Jourdanton and Pleasanton.

Sunday, February 24

Today was my last day at my San Agustín home. As expected, my departure saddened my family. The hours passed more quickly than usual despite my wishes to the contrary. I would have wanted to have the power of Jason to claim more hours on that day. I had a few instructions for my wife since I was also severing my family obligations. Our government was assuming them. We are only responsible for faithfully serving our country.

I left the responsibility of my children to the care of my loving companion who was enduring everything with stoic resignation. The supreme moment to leave finally arrived. No one can describe the deep sadness in our intimate moments, but I know that they are indelibly marked inside everyone who was to fight in the war. The survivors will always remember the farewells with tears of joy.

I gave my last embrace to my loved ones at two in the morning. My father-in-law accompanied me to the station at Leming where I boarded the train to New Braunfels.

The "Prologue" to my "My Personal Diary" includes everything that I consider important to describe the spirit with which I entered the military, which I could have avoided according to the conscription law.[9]

My Personal Diary

■

Historical notes
taken at the time of the events,
from February 25, 1918,
to June 21, 1919

Reporting at New Braunfels

Monday, February 25, 1918

The famed notice, the call from the nation, read, "Report to your Local Board in New Braunfels. The government declares you a soldier of the Great National Armada beginning at 11 a.m. on February 25." I met my obligation that day by reporting to the local board. By nine in the morning, I was at the post office where the recruits were to present themselves. I was the first one to arrive and asked about the others and was told they had not yet reported but that they had to be somewhere in town. I had learned that a great send-off was planned within the hour at the courthouse and headed for the place. Most of the German residents had already gathered. This was an interesting twist of fate. German Americans predominate in the surrounding area, and they belong to the same race we were going to fight. I am fortunate to see a race sacrificing to fight their own people, and I am going to serve on their side.

I heard several effusive and patriotic orations that praised the loyalty of the town's residents, almost all American citizens of German origin. I saw a friendly face among the orators, E. L. Davis from the University of Texas. He was clearly surprised and pleased to see me in the military. We should expect justice from men like him in the future. I told him that my decision to join the military must have surprised him because he was long accustomed to seeing me in another arena, advancing the intellectual, social, and political standing of our people in the schools of Texas. We have always thought of each other as good citizens and agree that we only needed this opportunity to once again demonstrate our civic loyalty. A fortuitous moment now subjected us to the most difficult test a free and self-conscious citizen could face. Onward!

The exhortations and words of praise for the Germans ended, and I did not hear one word directed at our people. Our presence was so insignificant.

I had been the only one to respond to the call. Another Mexican who was to have reported had been lured by the time-honored love for the fatherland that our elders instilled in us, and he left for Mexico. I hope everything goes well for him. Comal County contributed twenty-six men. The ceremony was not necessary to help us understand our obligations and how we were to behave on the way to San Antonio. Someone named Mittendorf was appointed the leader with the responsibility of presenting us at Camp Travis.

Our contingent included twenty-three Germans, two of English origin, and me, the only one of the American race. (I hope that no one objects to my use of the term *raza*. Everyone else can call us whatever they wish. Wells, for instance, calls us Amerindians.[1] Thanks. It is enough for the reader to note where I have been, under what circumstances, and who I am.) It does not matter that I am not in my cultural element, although I can now see that everything will change and we will all be treated as soldiers. Everyone was courteous.

They took us to a liquor store before we ate and gave us all we wanted to drink, as well as cigarettes. I refused the generous offer. This seemed strange to my companions who I think saw me as timid and fearful. How strange! I was thinking about something very different at that moment. People who know me would not have considered my behavior odd because they know that I have never taken up drinking or smoking.

The following are some thoughts that were racing through my mind. Our situation was a stroke of destiny, bringing us together to face the same misfortune. I now see that many of these Germans—I could call them selfish, arrogant, and greedy because of the way they treat our people—are as anguished as I am. Despite our shared misfortune, I felt brave and strong and without the need to show it. I cannot forget how unpatriotic these people have been when they have mistreated us and used the idea of loyalty as the yardstick with which to judge us. Many of them would have been incapable of putting aside their prejudice and treating me as their racial equal, but they now march besides me as we meet the most exalted duty before man. Now they have to show me that they are more loyal and worthy than me.

I have already stated that the opinion many foreigners have of us is unfortunate and even misguided. I was waiting at a tavern for the lunch hour when an old German approached me and asked me in Spanish, "Why didn't you leave for Mexico?" I wanted to instantly flatten him since I knew full well his intentions were not good and that he did not know whom he was addressing. I answered, "I do not have a reason for going to Mexico." "Many Mexicans have crossed into Mexico," he retorted. I continued, "I find nothing special or strange that Mexicans should go to Mexico, their homeland. They could not be in a better place. But if by saying Mexicans you mean us, the citizens of this country who are of Mexican origin and live as such, I for one can assure you most sincerely that we do not all think that way. Men from other races have also fallen short. But I want you to know that, unlike them, many of us have wanted to be men enough to disregard for a while or possibly forever all the abuse we receive daily from miserable whites who, unfortunately, are citizens of the great American nation. Again, I do not believe that all of this is a good reason for me to disregard my responsibility as a man. The flag that calls us to defend the nation, the flag under which we have been born, became men, and raised our children—we hold it high over the contemptible reptiles, the bad citizens. Their affronts have wounded us deeply, but not to the point of blinding us and encouraging us to ignore why we should heed the nation's calling. If we return determined to join the struggle for justice, we will wage it as before and with the same courage that we will show the despots of Europe." I leveled all of this and probably more at the German who tried to put something over on me, and I spoke in English. I did not want to respond in Spanish. I did not care if he did not understand, but I wanted the many others who were listening to know what I had said. I do not remember my tone, but I did notice that he seemed disoriented. He did not speak again or, more precisely, I did not give him a chance to say anything. I am sure he regretted challenging me the way he did. I cannot say he was afraid because the Germans in New Braunfels do not fear Mexicans. The old German walked away embarrassed, slipping through the crowd. Just as well. I did not need advice, especially from a German. Why did he not counsel his own, who clearly needed guidance at that time? Onlookers with big ears began to gather. Nothing had happened, just a German making full use of his farm Spanish and a Tejano using the language of Shakespeare.[2]

The government, that is, the people paid for our first meal. They will also pay for everything at the hotel on the corner to the west of the square. Its location explains why it is named Plaza Hotel. It is like many others around our big and rich state of Texas that hang their well-known sign at their entrances, "We don't serve Mexicans here." I had ceased being a Mexican, at least since eleven o'clock. An abundance of cordial behavior and a pleasant mood reigned over our meal. A person named Mr. Holstead gave us some containers with violets on behalf of his good wife. The liquor that my companions guzzled down is beginning to have its effect, and this was making for an increasingly lively scene. A young German named Werner suddenly approached me and said, "I speak a little Spanish, know Mexicans, and I call many of them my friends. I want us to start being good friends and to continue this during our military service." Since I take everyone as they come, I could not help but express my gratitude and reciprocate. I just cannot explain his strange behavior.

I sent my wife the following postcard after I ate.

> New Braunfels, Texas
> February 25, 1918
>
> My beloved wife:
> I arrived safe and sound at New Braunfels and just finished my first meal on Uncle Sam's tab. We will leave for San Antonio at 3:50 p.m. I will write all of you as soon as I know my new address. May God take care of my family.
>
> LUZ

We participated in an important program at the small town square at two in the afternoon. A man who may have been the mayor spoke to us in a pleasant manner from the small gazebo. They photographed us and told us when we would leave for the railroad station. Prior to this, we had walked to a booth where the ladies of the American Red Cross of New Braunfels gave us some comforters, or campaign bags, filled with items that we would absolutely need in the military.

It is impossible to describe the sad and moving scene when we left. The moment was solemn when my companions had to say good-bye to their loved ones. I had already gone through that ordeal, I knew what it meant. Millions can probably testify to what I say. None of my family members or the few friends I had in New Braunfels were there. Only two Mexican gentlemen, one I did not recognize, approached me with the usual "Good-bye, good cheer, and have a good trip." I had to show some appreciation because I knew that underneath the curt language, they were sincere and meant well.

When we were ordered to "march," I fell into formation and received a bag from one of the ladies from the Red Cross. I thanked her with all my heart, and away I went. When we arrived at the station, Mr. Adams, the sheriff of Comal County, told me in Spanish, "Be happy and say something." I responded in English that he should stop being pretentious, but because I knew whom I was dealing with, I added, "I have no reason to talk, but I want to assure you that my silence does not mean I am sad." He responded, "Oh, you speak good English." I then told him, "You said it. I only wish to express myself in my country's language." Anyone who thought I was obstinate was making a mistake. I simply did not feel comfortable, and the people around me did not inspire confidence or encourage me to be friendly.

I was responsible in everything else I was doing. However, I could not suddenly erase what I know about the German people from Comal County, as encouraging as the change from civilian to military life might be.

The train arrived and we barely had time for a quick good-bye before New Braunfels began to recede into the horizon. So many hearts were torn with pain, like the many others in villages, towns, and cities throughout the country.

Nothing special happened during our short trip. We made it quickly, in one hour, and barely had time to reminisce. I sat next to a Mexican man already in uniform. He had volunteered and thought he would be assigned to the air force. He spoke of the great opportunity we have in the military. I do not place much weight on this, but hope he is right. The soldier was Jesús Jiménez. I gave him the cigarettes I received at the station. I had no use for them. He transferred to our train on its return trip to Houston.

The train stopped before we reached San Antonio. The passenger cars were disconnected. Another engine was waiting for us and took us down a second line that had been built to transport troops to the center of the camps. The camps, Fort Sam Houston and Travis, were a brand new sight for us. Two large national flags above the barracks floated majestically with the wind. The movement was indescribable in this human honeycomb. Thousands and thousands of men were working everywhere. Some of the soldiers lived in good wooden barracks—the ones at Fort Sam Houston were constructed with expensive brick. Others lived in campaign tents made of good, thick, and water-resistant canvas. We stayed at Camp Travis.

As soon as we arrived, a sergeant who had been waiting ordered us to form a double column and, while we were in formation, marched us toward some distant barracks where we would undergo our first physical examination. We were ordered to "halt" before entering a building, and a tall, thin, and young black-mustachioed officer received us. He had a serious look and, worse than that, showed an exaggerated sense of military self-importance. All that arrogance, in my opinion, was unnecessary. We were nothing but "rookies." Despite this, he did not surprise us. We just thought he was offensive. The officer was more ridiculous than arrogant, and probably had been a bad, pretentious person as a civilian. He believed he was more powerful now that he was a person of importance. The fellow explained why he was inspecting us. Since the inspection did not measure up to his expectations, he scolded us. He did it so cruelly and without reason it felt like he was pouring boiling water over us. This gave us a bad early impression of military life. Whoever survives the great adventure will have to report this. After the inspection, which was nothing more than a farce, we went to our barracks where they fed us and gave us everything to make our bed. We selected metal cots and looked for a place to make our beds. They soon called us into formation. We made our mattress by filling our white canvas sacks with straw, and then we ate for the first time at Camp Travis. The night left us full of strange emotions. If we survive the campaign that starts today, we will probably remember this evening as a joyful one, although we would be suffering indignities.

Five soldiers in our barracks are ill, two have measles, two have tonsillitis, and one has indigestion. The problem with the first two has placed us under the strictest quarantine and close guard. I cannot sleep. The soldiers make so much noise. Some have been playing cards, others entertain themselves with dice, while still others sing or squawk. The cigarette smoke is the worst problem. Everyone except me shares in this pleasure. It makes me dizzy and nauseous. It was a horrible first night.

Tuesday, February 26

The sergeant's whistle, like the kind the city police use, woke us up early. He came into the barracks to tell us that we were to fall into formation in fifteen minutes. We did as ordered. Two officers were present. They called out our names and told us we were to continue filling the same places in morning formations or else face serious penalties. They called us into formation after breakfast and ordered us to clean the headquarters area. Some picked up pieces of paper and cigarette butts. Others had to clean the kitchen, while still others had to place the latrine and the shower area in order. I was with the last group.[3]

One of my first tasks was to figure out my address to receive mail. It is the following: 42nd Company, 11th Battalion, 165th Division Brigade.[4] I barely had time to write this letter:

42 Co., 11 Bn., 165 D. B.
Camp Travis, Texas
February 26, 1918

My dear wife:
I hope that all of you are doing well. I am fine, thanks to God. We arrived at the camp yesterday and were quickly placed in quarantine because two soldiers had German measles. They placed two guards over us during the day and two during the night. We cannot leave the barracks. This is good because they will not be taking us out to do physical exercises for at least two weeks. I will be ready for the

difficult and demanding tasks as I remain inside, only eating, bathing, and sleeping. We have nothing else to do but sweep and we even fight over the brooms because we get bored with being idle. I think I will like this life.

We get so excited with the many shiny rifles and the sound of the bugle, and this is not even taking into account the many balloons and the airplanes that flutter over us like vultures.

Tell me that all of you are doing well and I will be happy. You could come to San Antonio as soon as Aunt Barbarita is out of danger. Tell me everything that everyone has been doing. Mocha was well when I left her, poor thing. My Sam was happy waiting for me to take him to the ranch. I will take him when I return. Hellos for everyone.[5]

Luz

We cannot go anywhere or see much of anything since we are locked up. We entertain ourselves by hurling insults at the poor rookies who are arriving and passing by our barracks.

Wednesday, February 27

About an hour after breakfast, we received orders to clean the barracks, make our beds, clean the dining area, and the bathroom.

A German from New Braunfels works with the cooks. He is a good fellow, a new man. His name is Antón Venhauer. We arrived together.

Last night, some buddies from the northern part of Texas arrived at our barracks. One of them is always very sad. He seems ill since he does not speak with anyone, and he is always pensive. He looks frightened or seems to be afflicted by something related to fright.

We entertain ourselves with so many of the new recruits. Once off the train, they form two columns like we did once. They are in disarray and very badly dressed, just like when we arrived. We have come to call this kind of recruit a "rookie."

Some of them arrive with different types of colored caps, others with broad-brimmed "cowboy" hats or small head coverings associated with urban life, while still others wear "panamas." The poor laborers wear their little head coverings. Many of them carry the bags the ladies from the Red Cross gave them when they left their towns. The different streamers the men wear to signify their counties of origin are especially colorful, and in many cases very funny. The ribbons with the names of the local board and county come in all shapes and colors. Often, they simply carry cards or labels of all types, common and ordinary, like the ones that appear on railroad shipping bags for corn, beans, or potatoes. We really respect the insignias that identify us as government property. Some of us believe we should pin them on the lapels of our civilian coats.

It is our turn to entertain ourselves when we see these poor fellows arrive. We get our revenge with the same sing-song taunts and words of ridicule that were used on us.

I do not know how we came to use the word "rookies," since it means little squirrel. It may have to do with their sad countenance, or perhaps because their appearance changed so suddenly in this strange environment that is governed by rigid and odd rules so contrary to civilian life.

From the time a group of recruits arrives and reaches their barracks and, afterward, when they march in formation, the soldiers along the way yell cutting remarks at them. Here are some of them: "Where are you squirrels from?" "Throw away everything you have, it won't be long before you have to get rid of those shoes." It would be an understatement to say that we teased and bothered our victims. Many were drunk, and this made it funnier or encouraged more harassment because they made even better targets. This is the best way to endure a life that has become boring, monotonous, and sad. The change has come so quickly.

I helped clean the showers. We were so soaked we had to bathe.

Antón Venhauer has been a good friend. He has been on K.P., or kitchen duty, since we arrived. This brought good fortune to the men who were with him. We deserve whatever we can get from the kitchen. Few soldiers can say this.

Recruits from East Texas are filling up the barracks in front of us.

Thursday, February 28

One of the Germans who arrived with us really dislikes our new life and has said that he will not be with us for long. He claims to have sufficient cause for an exemption from military service or that someone with influence will most probably obtain his release.

After breakfast and following a few turns around the barracks picking up trash, we were ordered to fix the front of our building with a walkway or sidewalk. Some of us had to hike about 250 yards to get the stones; others put them in place.

We spent an afternoon doing this, all the while entertaining ourselves.

They say that things will get difficult when the quarantine ends, and this really discourages us because military life already leaves a lot to be desired, and to think that it could get worse. Whatever happens, we had a good day, or as some would say, we had it "pretty easy." To sum up, the quarantine at its best allows many of us to eat, bathe, and write letters, while others enjoy playing dice or cards.

The Brigade Station

Friday, March 1

We are in brigade station number 165 and I am in Company 42, of the 11th Battalion, the 180th Brigade, and the 90th Division. Two corporals, a sergeant, a second lieutenant, a first lieutenant, and a captain are responsible for our military review. I know Sergeant Rankin. He is a good person—gracious, friendly, and a long-standing member of the military, although he is still very young. The second lieutenant is of medium height. I still do not know his name, but he is very young and shows how well educated he is by the respectful way he treats us. The captain is named Johnson. You could not find a better person.

I can now appreciate the chance occurrence I had in the kitchen, or mess hall, this morning. Someone called us to "attention" while we ate breakfast, and the officer of the day asked if anyone knew how to type. No one responded, either because they did not know how or just did not wish to reply. When he asked for the third time, two raised their hands and then I followed.

They asked us to fill out insurance forms for the recruits. We were also to calculate the pay amounts the government would assign each family and the total that we were to set aside for them. We had to do this for all the soldiers in our company. This helped me understand how to prepare my own documents and to make sure that I receive all the benefits guaranteed to soldiers who faithfully meet their duty. The thousands of questions we asked the soldiers and the different cases I reviewed were enough for me to understand everything well and to fill out my forms properly. I realize that many poor fellows were not prepared to report what most benefited them.

Saturday, March 2

Two more Mexican buddies are with me now. I took care of their papers, the same as mine. They do not know the language well enough to fend for themselves, although they will be as good as the rest of the soldiers in other matters. One of them, Simón González, comes from Seguín, but he is from Martindale. He is young and from a very humble family. Simón is so uninformed that he understands little about what he is to do now. He is far, very far from knowing that as poor as he is, he is destined to fight until the end so that our people can hold our name high. Simón has a brother who is also in the military, and he leaves his elderly father, seventy years old and blind, all alone in Martindale.

José Leal is another of my buddies who shares our barracks. He is the type of Mexican who knows how to endure everything. José gives himself completely to the challenges of life. He is the personification of our people's well-known stoicism! José also lacks an education, but he is intelligent and his resolute disposition makes him appear indifferent to whatever destiny has in store for him. He leaves behind parents and siblings and a faithful girlfriend to whom he writes often and dedicates his time in the war. His family is from Seguín. Simón and José knew each other.

After I made sure they understood we are playing the last card in the game of life, I convinced José and Simón to leave their families all they will earn. I only keep three dollars from my monthly pay, an amount that is more than enough to keep me from being a burden on anyone. This will allow us to focus on what we have to do and to do it well. Our sacrifice is like the one made by Hernán Cortéz when he burned his ships at Veracruz.[1]

We continue under strict quarantine but went out for the first time this afternoon. We marched to the hospital for another physical examination. We were vaccinated and immunized. The shot was for typhoid. Several soldiers fainted as they were inoculated or when they saw that they were about to be vaccinated. Nerves fail men who think they are strong. We will remember the amusing scenes and difficulties during the horrible examination. We suffered that night from the pain of the inoculations.

Sunday, March 3

Our routine did not change although we were sore in the morning. We executed the same drills as before.

While we ate, an officer announced that we would fall into formation at two in the afternoon by the large hall area. We did as ordered and came together in the most complete silence and order. An officer spoke to us about the legal obligations we had assumed and how we should behave. He also spoke at length about his long military career. We now know that he was recently promoted to second lieutenant.

He is up in age, but he really seems to be sociable and every bit a gentleman. The officer finished by assuming a sense of military bearing and reading some articles from the military code of conduct.

Monday, March 4

Our arms still hurt. Today has been a boring and sad day. I felt nausea from the cigarette smoke and the loud noise. This is truly a military barrack. I spent a good amount of time talking to a buddy who had also been a public school teacher. We understood each other well and commiserated about our new life. We are determined to bear everything by making the best of things.

The "sad soldier" did not eat today, he seems very sick. I brought him coffee from the kitchen and later gave him some lemons. The good man offered to pay me but I declined. I only wanted to do my duty and be a friend. He was grateful and pleased. We are truly in a bad way when we cannot manage to scratch each other's backs.

We felt indescribable joy upon receiving our first letters from home.

LETTER FROM MY FATHER
Alice, Texas, March 1, 1918

My dear son:

I am glad that you are doing well. We are fine, thanks to God.

Son, you tell me that you are already in the military. The news does not surprise us. We knew that this day would come. You had already told us. I will ask God that he help you and that your service bring benefit to the government, that you act well, remain dedicated, and that you do not waver. Everything goes well with the man who does not do wrong. We pray to God that if you are to face danger that you survive in good spirits and that you return like a Pablo Martínez or a Zaragoza for the honor of our people.[2]

I have spoken to José and Ramón about whether they want to join you and they tell me they would be very glad to do it. They wish that I agreed, especially José who says he is proud to have a brother in the great American military. So, you are not alone in this world. You can count on the little "pomocas" and a Malinche who is "la Mocha."[3]

Son, do not fail to write as often as you can. I close,

Your father who loves you.

ROSALÍO SÁENZ

My dear wife:

I have not heard from you and I am worried because I did not leave all of you in good health. How is the ill person in the family coming along?

It may be a week before I can leave the camp. Make your plans. It would be good if you came to San Antonio. I regret that I cannot send you anything. The government's help, along with mine, will probably not arrive until April.

You have no reason to worry because I am in a safe place. Notice that I even typed my letter. I am our captain's "right hand man." As expected, not everyone is glad about this. No doubt, someone will want to take away my privileges. I would like to see them try!

You will receive more than fifty dollars. I am insured for ten thousand dollars. You may say that I am worth more than ten thousand dollars, but I doubt it. They will take care of me like a barbecued head, not because of my worth but because of the potential loss that I represent.[4]

Love to everyone and for my Adán

LUZ

Samuel and Adán:

I am going to tell you a story. In a small faraway town, an old man had two very good young boys. The old man, a good person too, was kind to the little ones and would tell them stories in the afternoon, after the work was done and before the sun would set, or when the moon was beginning to appear. He would tell them stories about boys who lived in other towns. He would talk to them about their favorite animals they played with. The children would listen very quietly to the old man. One day another old man arrived, the old man's grandfather. They call him Uncle Sam. He came to take the old man away to help him drive out or kill other old men who had been killing the sheep and destroying the crops that belonged to Uncle Sam. The first old man did not have a rifle, but Uncle Sam told him he had many, as well as money and beautiful clothing for the brave soldiers. The old man, brave as he was, told him that he would help him. One day, he left on a train that passed by the children's home. The children did not cry, and they stayed alone. How does that sound to you? When the old man arrived at one of Uncle Sam's many homes, he was well received. After feeding him, they dressed him in a military uniform, like the ones you see worn proudly on the city streets. If you look closely when you are walking these streets you can see the old man. If you do, tell him to tell you a story, he knows many. Oh! I forgot to tell you, when the old man arrived at Uncle Sam's house, he asked, "Do you want to send the little boys something to eat?" The old man answered, "No. I left them a few beans so that they may be well. Later, if they finish them and if you wish, you can send them more." Colorín . . . [5]

Good-bye!

My dear children were accustomed to hearing me tell a story, an anecdote, or a joke with a lesson every afternoon. I cannot do this anymore since I am leading another life elsewhere, but now and then, I will try to think of something and take the time to send them a story.

Tuesday, March 5

We welcomed an extraordinary event today. Formation was called at four. We were told of the exalted meaning of the uniform we were to wear and of the honor our country was bestowing upon us at a time when it was facing the threat of a terrible and powerful enemy. The grand and sublime image of *the Motherland and the future of my people* came to mind at that special and inspiring moment. They then gave us our new olive green uniforms. Our entire civilian appearance disappeared magically! The figure we strike is a sight to see. While the uniforms fit some well, they are loose on most of us. We find comfort in knowing that the uniform does not make the man, and we will be loyal when it comes time to defend the stars and stripes.

The novelty of wearing the uniform instantly rid us of the monotony somewhat. So many dreams passed through our warrior minds on that memorable afternoon!

I continue to work as a typist for the captain. I wrote some letters.

Wednesday, March 6

I have been oblivious to what may have happened today inside and outside our barracks. I have had a migraine headache or neuralgia and visited the military hospital where I was given a laxative powder. I had not left this place alone since we first arrived. The sergeant who is in charge of taking the daily sick list to the Medical Department accompanied me in the evening. The many sentinels who serve as guards stopped us often. Our sergeant had a passport that allowed him to pass without any problems. The trip seemed a strangely different experience, especially when we stopped in front of the hospital and discovered that so many other soldiers were waiting for the same reason. We were all in line, entering and exiting one by one.

Silhouettes of soldiers appeared everywhere. They were walking about with permission or carrying out a charge. We were the only ones who had to follow the sergeant like slaves or prisoners.

Thursday, March 7

I am very grateful to the captain and other officers for being kind enough to recommend me to my other superiors. I am mostly focused on doing everything that is expected of me. It will not be my fault if they do not know how to make good use of me, within the limits of my ability.

We finished filling out the insurance forms and extending other services to the soldiers in our company.

Friday, March 8

Today, Mr. Maximiliano González of Martindale came looking for his two sons, Filomeno and Simón. He is an elderly man who claims to be seventy years of age. He is almost sightless. He is actually blind. This is where we can see that the "fair law of the draft by public lottery" has failed and does not work as it was intended. The officers who enforce it commit serious errors and injustices, and they will probably go unpunished. They have deprived the old man of his two sons, his sole means of support, and the only loving family members he has in this world. The local board justified its clearly unfair action by noting that when his sons enter military service, the government would provide the father more money than he needs. They also point to the sons' difficult life as laborers. What a wretched finding! Although others may think he is ignorant and dim-witted, Mr. González is not so simpleminded that he cannot see how unfair they are with him. He says he is not asking for the money, although he needs it badly, but that he wishes for the care and protection that only his sons can provide him. He points out, for example, that receiving money without proper care would do more harm than good. He insists that his youngest son be freed. His son has cared for him the longest. His request, in our view and the thinking of many officers who have learned of the case, is more than *fair*. We believe that if he is refused it will be because he comes from a town where members of *our community* are treated unjustly. We also believe that our federal government will not know of these cases. They will be forgotten. How shameful!

The old man continues to insist that the money will never provide him the care and especially the love of a son (what better arguments!). Simón has been an obedient and dependable son. He has been mostly concerned with the care of his father since he began working as a farm laborer.

As I noted earlier, the captain is a fair man. He has given Mr. González some hope. After listening to him, he told us to take Simón to the mess hall to eat with us. Simón did this, and later the captain had him fill out some forms to request an exemption for Simón (I was the translator and I believe that I completed the task with the greatest care). Mr. González told us that he had no support after his sons left for the military, that he had lived almost entirely on charity, that he did not know anyone in San Antonio, and that he had given his last fifty cents to the young boy who had brought him to the camp. The captain had to send him to the Red Cross station since we could not take him to the city or to some other safe place. The Red Cross took care of him, at least for the moment. We gave him the little money we had.

I am glad to have translated and recounted this poor old man's case. His fight is the cause of the people and I have made it my own.

Saturday, March 9

They took us to the hospital to get inoculated again. I saw many friendly faces, including some Mexican friends from my town. They were among the many soldiers that were arriving. I did not have time to talk to them. We simply exchanged a few words so that we could locate each other later.

We witnessed the camp's great commotion and confusion while we waited a long while for our turn to enter the hospital. So many people had come, some in cars, others on foot. They all wanted to see their loved ones who were being recruited into the great American armada. Some of them were lucky to find them, while others, tired and covered with sweat, walked aimlessly through that confusing labyrinth the camp area has become. Many of the recruits who have located their family members and who are quarantined can only talk with them from a distance and always under the watchful eye of a posted sentinel. The others who are not quarantined or who have completed it, stroll happily through the streets with parents, brothers, sisters, girlfriends, and wives, etc., who are no doubt contemplating what we are going through. We long for the day when we can also be free to share in that pleasure.

The movement of people around the camp is intense, like in no other camp in the United States, or so they say. Groups of soldiers are everywhere, either carrying out a special order or some other assignment.

The pain from the inoculation is greater than before.

Sunday, March 10

Our Sundays are not much different from the other days of the week. It must be because we are quarantined. We did not have much to do today because of yesterday's inoculations and we have been yawning and in pain all day. My buddies enjoy themselves, or give themselves to deep thought, but without taking note of their surroundings. I have taken most of the day writing to my loved ones and to some friends who have written and asked for a quick reply.

The latest is that the haunting screams of one of our men awoke us last night. We first thought he might be having a nightmare. We then realized the problem was serious, and it became necessary to call the sergeant, who quickly went for a doctor. The doctor ordered that the soldier be taken to the hospital immediately.

Monday, March 11

Today, we learned that the sick recruit died last night of an epileptic seizure.

An officer reprimanded us early this morning because some of the men wake up too early and keep the others from sleeping. He set the hour for going to bed as well as for getting up in the morning. With God as my witness, we make thousands of mistakes because we are so new to this life. Patience, men in command, we will learn that there are deadlines for everything and that they benefit everyone. Little by little, we feel the iron hand of the military.

I feel sorry for my farmworker friends who are used to getting up at daybreak! Many of them were so accustomed to this that they would get up when the others were just going to bed. Everyone, including the recruits from the city who were used to waking up whenever they pleased, now have to abide by a sergeant's rude whistle that will shake up the slow and the sluggish. The farm boys will now have to remain long hours in their cots without anything to do but to summon sweet thoughts from home. The recruits from the city wake up like wobbly rats when the whistle calls.

I see no better solution to this than to follow one of our sayings, "We must get used to the sun that will rise, the wind that will blow, and the water that will flow." The wisdom of the ages will be of great help.[6]

Tuesday, March 12

Today, twenty-five of us bought small trunks; we'll use them to store our clothes and other items the government has given us. Each one cost $5.25.

I have discovered something that is interesting, but expected. I have begun to battle the horrible jealousy of a fellow soldier. He has been resentful since he noticed how the officers favor me. I had thought that some weak and small-minded person would eventually give in to this. He worries over the way they treat me. He takes this personally and wants to get rid of me. This is absurd and pedestrian. He may very well keep me from advancing, but this will not help him in his military career. If he could only understand that I am not seeking a position of importance, and that if I am ever appointed to one I want it to be because of my good work and not because of any kind of questionable intervention that would later discredit me.

March 12, 1918

My dear wife:

I received your letter last night. It made me very happy. I hope all of you continue to do well.

The captain is on his way and I have to stop writing and do some work. I finished the work that I had been assigned and continue with my letter. I am taking advantage of this typewriter that they will soon be taking away. I am too lazy to write by hand. They are coming for the typewriter.

Good-bye and may you all be happy,

LUZ

Wednesday, March 13

A vendor arrived with photographs of the camp. His kind does not sleep and knows how to exploit the silver mine that is the soldiers' money. Note this well, these are the false patriots. I bought a photo to send home, it captures our experiences well.

We continue to haul rocks for the sidewalk by the barrack. We brought them from a long distance in big wooden boxes that we made for the task. It was heavy work, but it was also a distraction and good exercise. We worked four to a box. The place with the rocks was far from the camp, about 200 yards distant, on the other side of the railroad tracks coming into the camp from the east.

The captain took me to the Personnel Department to complete my life insurance forms. I had to answer some questions the person in charge posed. He asked me if I filled in the questionnaire correctly, and I told him I did because I do not want to jeopardize my coverage. Although he spoke well of my work, I could see he did not believe me. I have done everything as expected. If I am not fit for service, let them exempt me.

I had no problem taking care of things, I was able to complete my insurance papers and guarantee myself full benefits.

Thursday, March 14

Today, while eating breakfast, we were ordered to prepare all our gear because we were moving to another place. We were to fall into formation and arrange our things. I found things entertaining as we presented ourselves for our first military assembly. We assembled our personal property as well as the government's belongings, including the many differently shaped and colored suitcases. We were like worker ants carrying trunks and grass-filled mats, moving without knowing where or why, we simply followed orders.

We put on an amusing display, heavily loaded like pack mules, and ended up at the other side of the railroad tracks, the last one on the east side of the camp, very near the arroyo, or the Salado River. We came across some campaign tents that had already been set up and put up our own since we are to live in them now. It was an unpleasant experience. We were beginning to like living in the barracks, despite everything, including the loss of our past privileges. We do not even have a kitchen, and the one that we may have to use is of poor quality. Our beds will be the same, except that we will now sleep in tents where we will surely suffer from the cold and the sun. Our gain will be the fresh air. We will eat a great deal of dirt with our food because the ground in this camp is sticky, and when it dries, the fine, unbearable dust is all around. All the food seems to be covered in salt and pepper, and to make matters worse we do not even have a table.

The landscape is beautiful. It is a vast plain that has been cleared for the training of the infantry and other troops. The tents easily accommodate five soldiers. We spent the rest of the morning setting up tents for the soldiers arriving later. My tent includes a carpenter named Cooper, a baker named Baccus, a railroad worker, and myself, a teacher.

The new captain is nothing like our previous one. His demeanor is very crude, and he has the body of a mastodon, makes full use of his authority, and is simply arrogant, despotic, and insolent. I imagine him to be one of those violent overseers I read about in books about slavery in another time, not ours. He is reddish, which makes him appear like the barbarous Huns of the past. He is clearly backcountry rough.

I was happy to see Second Lieutenant Curran Benton while waiting in line for lunch. He is a young friend from my childhood years and the son of a longtime teacher and friend from Corpus Christi. I do not know how Lieutenant Benton found out that I was here. I had not seen or heard from him in years. I put all of this behind me when we greeted. We disregarded military protocol and treated each other like we were in school. We only spoke briefly because we had to attend to duties. He gave me his address and we agreed to stay in touch. I will contact him as soon as the quarantine is lifted.

I forgot his address by the time he left, but I am sure it will be easy to get.

Friday, March 15

The new sergeant woke us up for formation with his whistle very early in the morning. That was our first reveille in all its glory. After calling the roll he made us march at a fast pace, "double quick," for about one hundred yards. A northern wind blew cold and hard and the exercise felt good. When we returned, we ate breakfast in the open air. This is now our mess hall.

We were ordered to tend to our tents, to line up our stakes, and to clean everything that could appear unsightly around them. Once I removed the rocks that were in the way, straightened things inside, and lined up the stakes, I went to the kitchen and converted a new wooden box into a washstand. I later bought a washbasin and put my name on it.

Since we do not have anything to do in the evenings, some of my Mexican buddies and I spend our time close to the latrine, which is a good distance from the tents. In order to get there we have to pass by the recruit training area. Many Mexicans live at this remote place. After our day's work, after we have eaten dinner and heard the names of the lucky ones who have received letters from home, after all of this daily routine, we go to places close to the Salado River that are always guarded by sentinels. We enjoy getting together to remember our past and to talk about what we expect in the future.

There, in the "drilling area," where we often find ourselves exhausted from the difficult training of the day, we get together at some point in the afternoon and even at night to remember a past that we may never enjoy again. At the end of the afternoon, when the sun has barely set and leaves behind an immense sea of reddish light that adorns the west, we gather to talk about our troubles, hopes, and dreams. These are beautiful moments that we will always treasure. Wherever we look, we can see the dark silhouettes of uniformed men, all with an earnest bearing, serious, and pensive. Over there, to the west, the lights of the great city of San Antonio de Béxar are barely visible.

Saturday, March 16

This has been a very hot day and we have really felt it during training. We do not know what we are going to do here without a place to bathe. The

Salado River is close, but we do not have permission to swim. Some men hope we may be allowed to go tomorrow.

Today, we received the last shot, and the vaccination to boot. After midday we did nothing. We only waited for the time when we are to go to the camp hospital.

My tent buddies received some nice packages from home. The sweets are good after the sparse meals we have been receiving since arriving at this place. I never had a taste for such things, but now I find myself wanting them. My buddies share their treats with me and I appreciate this. My family had offered to send me some sweets, but since we had been doing fine, I told them not to worry, that we did not need anything. Who could have foretold all of this? I was not the only one to underestimate the sudden and difficult changes we now face. Little by little we will learn to lighten the load and live better.

Sunday, March 17

Almost all of us woke up sick because of the shots and vaccination. The day went by quickly, I felt lazy and assumed that everyone felt the same way. The morning brought a northern wind that raised a lot of the dust we had loosened during the day. It is Sunday and we have nothing to do. Our circumstance does not encourage us to do anything.

I have been seeing airplanes all morning. They fly above our camp. Some of them have even landed where we train.

Many automobiles have been arriving since very early this morning, bringing relatives to visit the soldiers. They come with things. Many of the families bring food and eat with the men. We must remember that the quarantine is still in place and that the families cannot be near the soldiers. They have to stand ten feet from a line drawn by the sentinel who also guards the movement in and out of the camp. The cars line up alongside the road, and the soldiers talk with family members from inside and at some distance.

Many of the soldiers marched in a large military review in the afternoon. Several bands also participated. Since we could not join in, we were happy to see the review from a distance. The massive concentration of parading soldiers and their supervising officers was such a beautiful sight. More soldiers marched on their way to the baseball field where some played and others watched the national sport. Some of us have enjoyed the game so much in better times. They also had a band. We later saw them return in great spirits. They seemed to have really enjoyed themselves. All of these sights make our confined state more unbearable.

Our mail was delivered late in the afternoon. I received letters from some of my good friends and was happy to receive their good wishes. This made the rest of the day more agreeable, even though the monotony continued.

Monday, March 18

I typed ten letters for the redheaded captain. The short time I spent in his tent allowed me to see more closely the rough, cruel character of this arrogant military type. We could not get along and I found it necessary to tell him to look for someone else to do his work, for which I received no payment but much grief.

Many Indians from Oklahoma are staying in barracks near us. I had the good fortune of speaking with some and discovered that many have an impressive education and economic standing. They have shown us that they are true athletes, a racial ability they have preserved from the time of their ancestors and mine. They are clear about the part they are to play in the Great War. It largely parallels our own. We, the Mexican Americans, are going to war fully conscious of our decision and cherishing in our hearts the hope for a better future for our people who have been unjustly treated and scorned for so long.

We were told to line up our tent stakes after our meal. Later, we whitened them with lime. They assigned this work instead of training activities because the inoculations made many of the men feel out of sorts. Military discipline follows the Napoleonic code completely. It does not even allow a second for rest or thought because this is considered dangerous. The more the soldier's mind can be dulled the better. He will be less apt to conspire or protest against the tyranny that is forced upon him to obey and act as a machine. It would be better to deaden all reasoning and teach him to act by instinct.

It is incredible how much dust we eat with our meals. It rises out of the ground that we march on all week. These days of March bring strong and constant winds.

Tuesday, March 19

The captain called me to the officer's tent to type some letters. I had prepared several until it became necessary to use new carbon paper. The day was somewhat cold and humid, and the humidity soaked the papers. Immediately after I opened a small box with the carbon paper, the sheets above it curled up. The captain got angry because he thought it was my fault, and he tried to reprimand me. I had no choice but to show him that he was wrong. He destroyed the entire box of paper simply because the paper curled up. I refused to work after he told me I did not know how to handle the carbon paper. His violent behavior did not bother me. To the contrary, he freed me, for which I am grateful. I just brought him another man to do his work.

A few minutes later, I was training with my buddies.

We did a great deal of marching until midday, grew tired, and worked up an appetite. Once we ate, formation was called and we were told that whoever wanted to go swimming should bring his gear and soap. Most of us did. Only a few decided otherwise. Those who did not go continued with the training. Our march to the Salado River, the first one that we took since arriving, was very entertaining, pleasurable, and gratifying. Everyone was happy after the trip. The day was very hot and the water was cold.

The river has many good spots for swimming. The government has fixed up the entire river area for the soldiers.

Wednesday, March 20

We only marched until eleven and were called to the mess hall after lunch and given a physical examination. Uncovered above our waist, we passed by the examining doctors in the large tent. We wondered why they were doing this and were told that it was in preparation for our move to another camp or military group. Some of us took the news well because we are tired of the routine we have followed in the tent area. Others fear that we will be taken far from our families before we are able to take a day of liberty to go see them. In the end, we have no choice but to resign ourselves and accept what may come. The news has hit us like a bomb. We talk a great deal without knowing where all of this will end.

Thursday, March 21

We have not done anything else but supply ourselves with everything we need, that is, everything they brought to us. I find it interesting that they issue us everything we need. The soldiers mostly do what is expected of them. We understand that the government wants a military that acts as one, and that the officers are only interested in saying they have followed orders. That is why they give us parts of the uniform that do not match, which makes some of us appear ridiculous. This is a major problem in the military.

As I stated earlier, I have not been able to be of use to our captain. This is why I have decided it is best to only do my part as I am obligated to do it and to no longer volunteer as I would with someone who treated me better. This day has been very busy for the captain who has to prepare all our company reports for other officers. We also need many supplies, but the worst of it is the backlog of reports. The captain has been working hard all day and has made use of as many soldiers as possible to finish quickly. I did not help him when he sent for me. I prefer other duties. He came by in the afternoon to say he needed me and to go to his office.

A lot of work was pending when I arrived. As usual, the place was not without jealous characters who waste everything. My assignment did not go over well with some of my coworkers. Several of them wanted to show me that they knew more. It was so obvious that they bothered me. In the end, the captain told them, "Leave him alone, he knows this work better than all of you." I did not know how to take the compliment. He was giving me a great deal of praise or was being facetious. It could be one thing or the other. What I do know is that I was able to show them all that I knew the work and that I did it in record time.

A concert was held in the captain's tent in the evening. A band of black men who had come from a nearby camp performed the serenade. We had a good time while sitting on the ground and remembering moments from our civilian life.

Friday, March 22

We spent the whole day preparing to leave. The officers began to select the recruits who were to remain at Camp Travis and the ones who were to go to another military unit, that is, to other places different from ours. Carpenters, bakers, mechanics, and horsemen, etc., were selected out all day. Some of my buddies went with them while we were left to wait for new orders. We did not know what to think of this and were under strict orders not to say anything about our movements. If someone happened to know, he was prohibited from telling his family. When night fell, we were ordered to remain in our tents in case we were ordered to move immediately. We were told to remain awake, and here we were (it is eleven in the evening) waiting for orders.

Since this is a brigade camp, we have no doubts that many of us will have to go to different parts to complete the divisions that are forming. The 90th Division will be organized in Camp Travis. Its commander, General Henry T. Allen, appears anxious that the division be assembled to participate in the Great European War. This is why some of us hope to stay here.

Saturday, March 23

We waited almost half a night for orders to leave, but they did not come. Then they told us we could go to sleep. This is why we woke up somewhat drowsy, but we were always ready in line. Some of us figured that the transfers were for Fort Sill, Oklahoma. We believed that would be our destination. Of course, the orders could be revoked at any time. These measures were taken to confuse the enemy, who would want to know our troop movements. It is for our own good not to tell our family anything we know. It would be easy for them to spread the information that the thousands of enemy spies in this country are anxious to know. We should not forget that Germany continues to use its worldwide espionage system, its most powerful weapon.

Sunday, March 24

We had a beautiful morning and, as usual, automobiles began to arrive with families. This was a source of great joy since it would be the last time that many of the recruits would be receiving visitors. The rumors that we will soon leave this place continue and become more believable with time.

The order was given early in the day to prepare to march. We did not take long to get ready. The first morning hours passed while we waited for the order to move. The long wait was difficult. I had written my sister, my only relative in San Antonio, to visit me, but she did not. I lost hope of seeing her by the day's end. At that point, we received orders to begin preparing for our departure. The silent, serious, and bored men marched with some misgivings because they did not know where we were going.

I had the opportunity to see the different companies pass by as if they were in review. My attention was drawn to the platoons of serious and crest-fallen soldiers marching in tight formation. They marched past the front of my tent. Our company was the last one to deploy. It was already getting dark. We were part of the 9th Company, 3rd Battalion, of the 165th Division Brigade while in the tent encampment. The trucks transported our gear—our small trunks, our eternal blue bag, and the mattress with the blankets—and we carried the rest. We were worried that we did not know our destination. We were oblivious to everything during our march and thought we were really going to Oklahoma, but they began to divide us when we reached the barracks at old Camp Travis. A mere chance occurrence caused a mix-up that resulted in a gain for us. Our gear ended up in one place and we in another. They assigned all of us who are in the last platoon to general headquarters, lined us up in front of one of the barracks, and carried out the usual review to determine our occupations. They began to classify us according to what we reported.

It was late at night when we reached our quarters. Many of our buddies were already there. Since the first barrack had no room, we slept with the band of the 360th Infantry. After bathing, we ate and rested on this our first night of peace. We can finally hope for a few days of leave. The quarantine was lifted at that point. We will be assigned new officers.

H.Q. Co., 360th Inf., 90th Div.
Camp Travis, Texas
March 24, 1918

My Dear Wife:

I had not written because we were going to move and I did not know our destination. We are no longer quarantined. I am sorry I cannot go to see you. Marce is still dealing with life's challenges. I have told her that you are thinking of coming to San Antonio. José also wants to come to San Antonio to attend school.

Now that I have permission to leave, I have no money. They have not paid us yet. Your check will go to San Antonio.

I hope all of you take care of yourselves,

Luz

Camp Travis

Monday, March 25

We woke up appreciating our good fortune in the military. It seems that one of the soldier's best attributes is that he quickly forgets the difficulties of the past and resists fantasizing about the future, that is, if he wishes to occasionally enjoy some peace and quiet. Our future seems dim and we are subject to the whims of our superiors.

I met new buddies and said hello to old friends during breakfast. Two are from San Diego, past friends. . . . [missing text] . . . We got the haircut we needed so that we could appear decent and bought insignias for our collars, as well as some signal flags. I have pieced information together and figured out that I will be assigned to the R.I.O. What is that? I do not know?

Tuesday, March 26

We have spent the early hours of the day as usual. After midday they called formation and gave us our rifles. They did not prepare a ceremony for the presentation of the weapons. They will become inseparable companions during the most trying moments of our lives. I imagined something from the past at that moment—the way the Spartan mothers handed the armor to their sons as they left for war: "Return with it or on top of it." The declaration—typical of that martial race—was short but it had an exalted meaning. I imagined our flag as I thought of those words.

Filomeno González, son of the poor old Don Maximiliano González from Martindale and brother to Simón, came to visit me at the barracks. He has asked that I record his rifle number since he does not write or read in Spanish or English. His rifle number is 36336, and mine is 44981.

We spent the rest of the afternoon cleaning our rifles. They were very dirty on account of the oil that keeps them from rusting. By four o'clock our rifles were shiny and we eagerly took them to our first formation. I cannot describe the solemnity when we were told that our rifle training would begin tomorrow.

Every step we take is a new experience for us, it is also interesting, and this makes it bearable, but we do not ever forget that all of this has a purpose. The men who have been training for six months find it easy to perform all the rifle drills, and they even seem do them with pleasure. The maneuvers are difficult and overwhelming for the rest of us.

Wednesday, March 27

We began our training with the celebrated rifle. It was easy because we focused on learning the mechanics and names of the different parts. This lasted until twelve.

We did not train after our meal, and the officers began to pass out recreation passes or permissions to spend time in San Antonio. Almost all of them granted us leave until midnight. I do not know why, but they gave me a permanent pass, something that only the best-known soldiers deserve. They do this to discourage soldiers who may wish to desert.

I visited my home in San Antonio. Only my sister Marcelina and my little nephew Samuel were there. My wife and children are in Leming. My sister and I shared feelings that are difficult to describe. The great pleasure of seeing each other became one with the sadness of knowing I had little time to visit. The soldier, especially our own, enjoys many privileges during times of peace, but in a state of emergency like the present one, military discipline is necessary. This is why we will not be enjoying peacetime freedoms.

Since I am new to the military and love freedom, I am not in a position to appreciate much of what I consider the technical matters or procedures of the militia. Regarding the fulfillment of duty as men, I am prepared to make the ultimate sacrifice.

The time I spent at home was too brief, but I now enjoy the opportunity to visit my family often. I left for the camp after putting my little nephew to sleep, much like the magi did with his son in "The Thousand and One Nights." I promised my sister I would return the next Saturday.

I returned to camp with many fleeting thoughts. I thought of the sudden changes in my life during my walk through San Antonio. I passed the time in these streets when I prepared to be a teacher, when I visited the city, and when I needed relief from the pain of something terrible in my life. I again walk the streets, now that fate has suddenly made me a soldier in defense of one of humanity's most noble causes. In the middle of the military air that enveloped us, I crossed the city until I reached Fort Sam Houston and then my barracks where I barely slept that night.

Thursday, March 28

After breakfast, we were called to formation with shouldered rifles and marched at attention through many of the camp's streets. An officer named George marched at the front of our detachment. All along, he noted the names of the different important places we are to remember. We marched slowly, but since we were unaccustomed, it was difficult and tired us a great deal. Our fingers grew numb from holding our rifles so tightly.

By the early afternoon, they taught us to shoot targets, that is, to adjust our sights at various distances and in different positions. These activities continued until we had to prepare for the afternoon's review.

My oldest brother arrived at my home in San Antonio.

Friday, March 29

After marching for a while, the officers brought us to the barracks. We practiced the semaphore, or long distance signaling with flags. All of us have flags and insignia buttons. We have been told that anyone who does not have his buttons on his collar will be punished to the fullest extent of the law.

In front of our barrack, on the east side, a soldier put up some beautiful decorations to show his artistic skill and patriotism. The piece he created represents the symbolic insignia of the 360th regiment. It is a wooden structure bearing in relief the two intertwined swords of the cavalry, the two crossed rifles of the infantry, and the cannon of the artillery. An American eagle and the image of the great Wilson also appears. All of this is decorated with rocks covered with very white lime. Every time it rains, the lime is washed away and it becomes necessary to replace it.

The band also has its decorations and a presentable barrack. Small rocks on the side of the door that faces the south form the image of a lyre, while a bear, our mascot, appears on the other side. Our regiment's war yell is, "The bear jumped over the panther bluff, Hell's fire." It expresses our intent to humiliate the arrogant German.

Our mascot, a black bear, has his living quarters on the north side. It is a gigantic animal that is handled carefully when fed as well as when he undergoes medical treatment. He is bathed regularly now that it has been so hot. One man is always available for the daily care of the animal.

Saturday, March 30

Our training ended at twelve since it was Saturday. After lunch, and way before dinner, we prepared to go to town. This made us very happy. So many hopes danced in our minds! A good many recruits were waiting for their relatives, others their girlfriends, and still others were preparing for new romantic conquests. Military life has its dreams and fantasies, adventures and vicissitudes like other pursuits in life, or perhaps more than others.

As soon as I signed up, I left for home and saved my money like the poor soldier I am by walking to Fort Sam Houston. I then took a streetcar that was to take me directly to my house. I am always in deep thought when I do this. I cannot help but think about my future. Military life will take me to unexpected places as well as to others that I will seek and eventually reach. Life has allowed me to attain many of the things I have always wanted. I often dreamed as a youth that I would be enduring this life. Many history books have also inspired my spirit with hopes that will be realized once we make the sacrifice as Mexican soldiers. All the rattle and the tremendous technological might of this devastating war that visits suffering on most of the world cannot mean much without the social, intellectual, economic, moral, and political advancement of our people in Texas.

Sunday, March 31

I have been at the camp all morning despite the fact that it is Sunday. This is a day for rest or to take leave. Almost all of the soldiers from our company are in the city or visiting a nearby place. Many have secured permission to leave while others have families picking them up in their cars. After our meal, a buddy and I had been sitting under the shade of our barracks when we saw a family I knew. I was very happy because they were the first family to visit me. I had them wait so they could eat with us. After dinner, I went with them to the city and visited my home. My family was so happy. After a short visit, I said good-bye and returned to my barrack. I wish I could see them every day but my three dollars are not enough for the fare. I will have to spend many hours in my barrack that I would rather spend with them.

Monday, April 1

We follow the same regular routine. Things got serious when Colonel Casper Conrad and a major dropped by while we were doing physical exercises.

The colonel directed us for a short while, corrected some of our mistakes, and advised our trainers.

After breakfast, I went to an office where I have been working on orders from Chaplain Clarence Reese. I did not have much to do nor did the work tire me, the morning even seemed short. I returned to my quarters at eleven. Some soldiers were still doing signal exercises. My brother Eugenio and my little nephew Samuelito had come to visit and were waiting at my barrack. They ate with me and remained until it was nearly one when I had to return to work.

We can do no less than to praise our government for all it is doing to realize the true democratic ideals. The military shows great respect toward our visiting relatives, and it does not matter who they are, even if they are only friends or acquaintances. As long as they are visiting us, they are extended the same rights and privileges. We have not yet seen the horrible behavior of other races and other countries in their military barracks. May the people who visit, come back again. It is not unusual to see families sitting among the soldiers during the three meals of the day. This makes us feel united in the cause we are defending. It is gratifying.

Tuesday, April 2

We have much to be glad about in the military. Much of what is good comes from the strict adherence to orders. In civilian life we were free and sovereign but are now subject to the strictest of tyrannies. We have grown accustomed and even wake up without the help of the early reveille call. Many of us who were used to waking up very late and of our own free will are already up and ready by the time they give the first order. Somber expressions are evident at our first formation, as if we were alone and on our own. It seems as if no one wants to feel less important and is afraid to show that we were once in the habit of waking up late. The physical exercises come next, in the clean and refreshing air of the mornings. This gives added energy to our strong and healthy bodies. Then comes the breakfast; it is very rich and meets the expectations of the culinary arts and medical science. We eat with a great appetite. After that comes an hour of light work like fixing our beds and other equipment before we go out for training.

Pauses in the training allow some of us to rest. Others benefit from short conferences where they learn how to conduct themselves while waiting, resting, or deep in action. Sometimes, the classes are very interesting. At other times, they sap our spirit. To understand our occasional lack of interest, it is necessary to consider the sudden and radical change in our lives, as well as in the rushed training that prepares us for the slaughter. The urgency to send troops across the ocean explains the large number of recruits whose training is often inefficient. The pressure explains why we do not appreciate the training that is in our best interest and only see the things we want. The general discipline required for the major global campaign no doubt contributes to the many misunderstandings in our country.

Wednesday, April 3

The military drills, as rough as they are, are not so bad that they make us desperate—especially among those of us who have always known suffering, the sole basis for understanding the meaning of justice. Let the human drones complain, they have never appreciated the nobility of hard work and have always lived off the poor and uninformed. We pity them now. They are always frowning while in line. We hope that life in the military will show them how small-minded they have been.

Since I did not have anything to do after dinner, I bathed and went to our sleeping area to rest and to relieve the monotony and exhaustion from the training. Everything changed. Things seem to calm down after eight in the evening. The barracks are lit, but there is no noise. As far as movement is concerned, we only hear the "jitneys," or taxi cabs, that transport the soldiers to the city and back. I thought about this for a long time until it was time to sleep, the hour when the barrack lights start to go out. This made the silence that followed even more profound.

Thursday, April 4

We followed the usual routine and nothing new occurred today. I wrote my longtime friend, Mr. Velázquez,[1] the following letter:

Sr. Eulalio Velázquez
Kingsville, Texas

My Dear Sir and Friend:
I am happy to be writing this letter after a long lapse in time. Circumstances beyond my control are the cause.

With this letter you will clearly see that my life has almost completely changed, but the change has not been complete. I have only changed the way I live. I will continue to live with faith and confidence and will come out ahead with this new responsibility I have been given.

My sense of self-respect does not allow me to overlook in the least the good name of our forebears. I still remember the words of the writer who spoke under precarious circumstances but with the stoicism of our people, "The motherland is first."[2] How else are we to feel when the same blood runs through our veins?

The times are different and the causes are too, but we remain the same at this moment. Do you think it is wrong to call the United States "my adopted home" when it is the only MOTHERLAND that I can claim by birth and heritage?

You know that I have dedicated my life to the noble cause of progress for our people. I now believe that if it is not our primary responsibility, it is at least important enough that Mexican Americans do everything possible in pursuit of that ideal. I have also come to realize that many of our own have been wrong in avoiding military service.

We believe that the many people who could not read or write were innocent to a point. What poorly educated person could understand the weight of our obligation in light of the problems they suffer constantly? Others were merely expressing their deep resentment from the past.

We do not seek fame. We wish to be faithful to our duty that awaits us. We believe that we can stand tall next to the very best. May it be said that many of our own have fallen and continue to fall without bringing dishonor to our *raza*.

I write to you as someone who has always been concerned about our people's well-being. I have obviously observed the censor requirements in my letter. I will write now and then so that you may know of the gains we make here.

Do not feel obligated to respond, nor to print what I have said. Very few people are interested in these things. It is not worth the effort.

Send me your weekly once in a while; I need it.

As always, affectionately, your humble friend,

J.L.S.

The rain came down hard in the early afternoon. This gave the soldiers a rest. Most of them went to the city in search of pleasure. I could not go, but I accompanied Julián Martínez to his home. He only has a sister who is like his mother. Martínez is not married. We ate dinner for the second time because we are not accustomed to saying no and could not refuse the meal.

We enjoyed talking about so many things while playing the card game *malilla* until we had to leave to make curfew.

Friday, April 5

The Young Men's Christian Association (YMCA) offers important services to the soldiers, but the work is more show than real. It is a sectarian institution and it promotes a faith far beyond the country's protestant spirit. It wants to do much, but it seems to be badly organized with voids to fill and errors to correct. A large amount of money is collected for the organization, and it provides many valuable rewards to its directors.

The Regimental Intelligence Office, or R.I.O., is close to where I am presently working. That is where the mail is censored, especially the foreign-language correspondence.

I took the letter I had written to Mr. Velázquez to this department. My conversation with the officers was not cordial. When the lieutenant leveled some insults at me, I answered him with measured arguments in the form of backhanded quips. They had taken me for an ignorant and timid person. The majority of my Mexican buddies seem timid because they are poorly educated. They cannot defend themselves and accept their lot.

As expected, they did not like my response and became angry. Their insulting questions were no match for someone who understood their motive.

This was the last question the lieutenant asked me: "Is this letter written in Spanish or Mexican?" He asked this with the greatest sarcasm imaginable. "I wrote it. You have it in your hand, once you read it you will be able to tell," I answered. I could tell that the captain would have wanted to ask more questions. When I was leaving, the lieutenant said, "You can't get a thing out of this kind of greaser."[3] I retreated like a rattlesnake to its cave. I have thought about this a great deal. I regret that I did not respond as I wished. All in all, it is better that I meet my responsibility as a loyal soldier than to pay attention—at this time—to the nauseating spew of an abject and cowardly reptile. Onward.

I insist that he was an imbecile and that they were taking advantage of their positions. He thought he knew Spanish and demonstrated otherwise. He took my letter, read it awhile, and said, "It's fine."

Saturday, April 6

Another incident is worth noting. A lieutenant I later recognized as the chaplain of our regiment approached me while we were training with dummy rifles in place of the real ones we are to use in combat. He asked me several questions regarding my civilian life and education. Then he said, "Come with me, I have a small job for you." We went to the office of the Department of Information and Discharges. He introduced me to the office workers who gave me a cold reception. (You would think I was looking for trouble everywhere I went, and that was not the case. The reason is simple. My white buddies have never seen a Mexican like me challenging them over a job like this and their pride does not allow them to accept it.) The chaplain gave me a list of soldiers' names and their addresses. They appeared on cards that included the classification and other information that is noted when the recruit enlists. Really bad scribes had done the work (I refer to the calligraphy). My job was to figure out the writing. It looked like hieroglyphics in need of deciphering. I admit that I had never faced a more difficult challenge. The bad writing was impossible to decipher at first. The chaplain had left without explaining anything, and the cold reception I received from the men who could have treated me as a fellow worker kept me from asking for help. I was also too proud to bother them. Thanks to my isolation from everyone and my extensive teaching, writing, and reading experience with the unlettered, and after a good time of pondering the problem, I found a way to solve it. I began by figuring out the names of my *conraciales* and at some point I dealt with the others. I finished finding more than half of the names in less than an hour. This pleased the chaplain very much, but not my coworkers.

I now know that my very coworkers had been trying to identify the names for days and had failed. They fear that when I fill a position in the office one of them will have to go take the place of a foot soldier and undergo the difficult rifle training under the sun and wind. This is probably why I was not received well. I was ordered to type copies of the cards.

I only had few cards to complete at the end of the day and asked the chaplain if I needed to return the next morning. He informed me that I might be assigned permanently to the job. When I was about to finish, my fellow workers offered to help me in every way they could. I thanked them and told them they could depend on me if they wished.

Sunday, April 7

Today I met two more buddies that work here. They were not in the office yesterday. One is Italian and the other is German. I have been happier doing the more important work of an interpreter. I did it most of the day.

This is where people make claims when they feel they have been recruited unfairly. The cord that binds fathers, mothers, wives, and other relatives to the soldiers remains attached as they try to exempt their men from military service. Some men reject the honor of being privates in the army. I know that some people make just claims, and I have seen the importance of influence, including money, in securing an exemption. An attorney can easily pull apart an argument by a claimant and officers are known to give little weight to the complaints of the poor.

I waited eagerly for eleven o'clock so that I could visit home. The first "jitneys" were full and I had to wait a long while to get on one. These "busses" are packed with soldiers, the flower of the nation, as is often said. They are full of life and spreading happiness wherever they go. The men take cup after cup of life's honey. They will soon be taking drinks that are bitter with gall.

I spent the rest of the day at home, in complete peace. I did not go anywhere. Several acquaintances visited and asked me a thousand and one questions about my new life. Unlike Saturday, the day seemed very short. Since I was not familiar with the schedule of military life, I did not want to stay until the morning and said good-bye to my loved ones. It was not even nine and I was already in my barracks. There was much to see along the streets of the camp until the whole world grew silent when the bugle sounded the solemn taps. Everyone now had to sleep.

Monday, April 8

Our band played next to their barracks. While listening to the delightful pieces on that pleasant morning, I did paperwork on my Underwood typewriter for many of my buddies who have been transferred to other military units. Some have remained in our camp, the rest have had to leave for other parts of the union. The transfers are made according to a classification system that takes into account everyone's trade, occupation, and aptitude. This is how some divisions are being completed, after which they will ship across the ocean. I do not know my fate since I have expressed a preference for the 90th Division, which is composed of men from Texas and Oklahoma.

Tuesday, April 9

Simón González's father once again came to the office asking for exemptions. Poor old man, he tells us his sad story of hardships and all kinds of other sufferings. The attorney, who does not see the injustice, interrupts him, but he promises to do all that he can and sends him off. The poor old man comes to me and pleads that I explain everything to my superior, and he even thinks I am not interested in helping him. Poor man, he does not understand that we have the Great Wall of China before us. What is left for me to do for him or his son when I cannot do anything for myself?

I filled out some forms for Mr. González once again in accordance with military requirements, but nothing else seems possible. Justice does not dwell among us, and it is precisely because of this that we are to fight on the battlefields of that devastating war. The fight is necessary in Europe but here as well.

Wednesday, April 10

Once I finished my work, I retired to my barrack to wait for dinner. After we ate, the officer of the day announced that we were to fall in within an hour. We came to formation at the designated hour and marched to the great auditorium of the YMCA where we heard an interesting presentation on patriotism. A group of soldiers and some men from the city whose name I did not know presented several choral and musical performances.

The discipline shown by the different platoons that enter and exit the auditorium is a sight to see. Nothing was out of order. Every movement was made with a great deal of care and swiftness. I arrived at the barracks at nine, the hour of curfew. This is what thousands, or more precisely millions, of men in uniform are living at this very moment of great expectation in our nation. Imagine if you can, millions of men following the same daily routine, seeking the same purpose, eating the same food, waking up at the same hour, and many other things that we are obligated to do because our supreme destiny requires it.

Thursday, April 11

A beautiful sunny day, nothing extraordinary, very quiet, little work, the day was short.

After dinner, I visited the camp library. It contains a large number of volumes for the benefit and enjoyment of the men who are training to defend our country's essential principles of democracy and justice. I was able to see a variety of delightful and beautiful materials during my short visit. I registered so that I could have books to read during my hours of rest in the barrack. This time I selected a classic novel in Spanish, *José*, and an essay in English, "Will Power."[4]

When I reached my barrack, the soldiers were already falling into formation for another march. We went to the famous "sounding board," a type of open-air stage used to address a large number of troops. We had to march in front of the quarters of the commander general of the 90th Division, General Henry T. Allen. There he was, the old general, receiving demonstrations of respect from every military unit that passed before him. He appeared pleased, in a manner that was appropriate to his position. We were left to wonder or to guess his thoughts as he reviewed the passing units under his leadership. We were the fulfillment of his ardent desire to march to the front and fight the feared and very disciplined soldiers of the Kaiser.

Friday, April 12

We followed the usual routine today.

The staff of the YMCA showed a movie during the evening. It was very interesting. Afterward, I went to their study hall to write. A patriotic spirit reigned throughout the place. They give out a paper with a small, beautiful, and colored flag in the center. Another kind of paper that we can buy has the unit's emblem or the type of arms associated with this or that military group. The silence that hung over so many uniformed soldiers who were writing or reading was enough to bring on a deep sadness. This may be due to the profound and caring thoughts the soldier expresses as he writes his loved ones. Who among us can forget what we felt if we lived one hundred years on this earth?

Saturday, April 13

We rested in the afternoon. I wrote letters for many of my buddies, many who cannot read or write. The law that required the ability to read or write English in order to serve was a myth. It is easy to have an opinion on this matter. Here goes mine. When the sons of millionaires, sons of intellectuals—the cream of the powerful crop—saw that the law would exclude this large group, they must have said, "This law will exclude the 'greasers,' if not all, at least the majority, and many Negroes, and Indians as well and they are the very ones who have served and should continue to serve as cannon fodder. The more ignorant the man, the better suited he is for the bullets. And there were no misgivings or inconvenience in giving to the poor masses the HIGH HONOR of filling the most important of all positions, a place at the line of FIRE."

Some companions in arms and their brothers who do not even know how to write in their own language (Spanish) have discovered that I can help them in writing letters home. I went with several of them to the YMCA and wrote some letters. They bought me some refreshments later. The soldier may lose everything except his gratitude.

My role as a free scribe for my brothers puts me in a good position to examine their lives closely. Destiny has also dictated this.

I found out from an announcement in a hall of the Knights of Columbus that a daughter of President Wilson would sing tonight at the YMCA auditorium. Our regiment had not received the notice, but we were still allowed to attend and meet the great lady of the White House.[5]

While walking toward my barrack, I saw soldiers marching in formation and raising clouds of dust. When the endless snake of soldiers stopped to allow another group to enter the hall, I struck a conversation with some friends, and when I saw a space in one of the lines, I told myself, "This is my opportunity." I am destined to fill in for others. This is not the first time I take the liberty to fill in for someone else. That is how I entered the hall to meet Miss Wilson. The program was very pleasant. All of us sang several popular songs before the official program started.

When the curtain rose, Miss Wilson appeared in a beautiful suit of white silk. The soldiers received her loudly and heartily. (All of them were fully grown, with hair on chest, as any of our ancestors would have said.[6]) Miss Wilson wore an expensive ring, with a large, beautiful, and brilliant stone, on her left hand.

The ladies who accompanied her carried large containers holding flowers from our Texas gardens. Miss Wilson is not a raving beauty, nor even a gifted singer, but her modesty was enough to win the approval of the mass congregation of soldiers. Her prominent social standing also assured her success. The other young ladies followed with popular and trendy songs. We were not without songs or gracious young ladies who knew how to raise the temperature of the soldiers. The applause by the rough hands of the sons of Mars was so loud it was deafening. We must remember that this great military is composed of men of all social classes. We have a mix—all with the same uniform—of poor rural laborers, haughty millionaires, great intellectual luminaries, and others who do not know how to read or write.

Once the program ended, some ladies handed out flowers. We were so many that it was impossible for everyone to receive one. The companies began to file out in an orderly fashion. I left with the same company I had entered with. Once I was outside, I left the formation and returned to the hall where I found some soldiers who, like me, had nothing else to do but satisfy a primal curiosity. This was the time and occasion to shake the hand of the president's learned daughter. My Anglo-Saxon buddies did not know whether to call it a night or greet our important visitor. I reminded them of our responsibility and the chance to express our democratic spirit to her. They seem to have been waiting for someone to move them to action. We were not disappointed. She extended her hand in a very friendly and courteous manner, despite our coarse appearance and low military rank. We will never accept that our boldness was inappropriate.

Sunday, April 14

I spent another day at home. My entire family is pleased to see me meet the most important responsibility a citizen can make. They are proud that I should be wearing the uniform of the American armed forces. I ask them to continue feeling this same way when I reach the frontline trenches, over there in old Europe and face to face with the feared German. They tell me they are prepared for everything.

Monday, April 15

After dinner, we marched in formation to the "sounding board." This time Colonel Conrad was at the head of our regiment. All the regiments of the 90th Division were present with their respective bands. They came from different directions playing patriotic tunes. This lifted the troops' morale. Oh, this awakened martial spirit is so beautiful and enchanting! No wonder so many heroes have appeared in history. The same reasons under similar circumstances will necessarily give the same results.

We heard several speakers, and the bands played as if in a contest, some first and then others. We listened to the presentations and music while sitting down on the ground like children. I saw many fellow Mexicans that I had never seen before who were now also "Sammies."[7] After our return, I visited other barracks and friends. They all seem to accept their fate and are ready to sacrifice for the motherland and our people.

Tuesday, April 16

We received orders that those who had not received enough instruction on the use of the rifle or the different marching moves should return to their units. Once again, I was happy to go for my rifle. I welcome the opportunity to handle and use it. I would stay in the military until the last days of my life if it was less violent, savage, and criminal. I confess that I find it more attractive than the sedentary and competitive office work.

Our march was longer than previous ones. This tires us, sharpens our appetite, and will most probably give us a peaceful sleep.

We repeat: "Soldiers who do not work will never appreciate the pleasure of rest."

Wednesday, April 17

I did not feel well today, perhaps because of yesterday's fatigue. My head hurts and I feel sluggish. We did physical exercises and our superiors gave us short talks on military discipline. We appreciate this because all that is taught will no doubt serve a practical purpose.

I am glad to confirm that some of my comrades have moved up the ranks to positions of honor. This speaks well for our *raza*.

We marched until midday. After this, some soldiers played baseball while others went to the city. I am still not used to giving the required military salute to every officer I meet on the streets. One night, I crossed Houston Street while on a walk and saluted so many of them that they made me lose my way. I decided not to frequent the streets I have enjoyed under other circumstances and with free abandon. I had imagined something better with my uniform, and not the load of responsibilities that are impossible to avoid. It could not have been worse. The poor private does not have the time to see, examine, and enjoy anything new and interesting in the streets because he must always be alert and prepared for the appearance of an officer. I have decided to walk to Fort Sam Houston and from there take a streetcar to my home. That way I avoid the tiring challenge of being alert, looking for officers and hiding from them.

Thursday, April 18

Nothing extraordinary happened today. After reveille, we continued with our physical exercises, breakfast, the forced marches, practice in the use of the rifle, lunch, more marches and exercises, the cleaning in preparation for formation when we lower the flag, dinner, a short almost forced walk that was pointless and boring, taps, and the nightly rest. This is what we do every day.

Our troop is a collection of young men—the flower of the nation—so full of life and enthusiasm. Our men are a sight to see when formations require an orderly and clean appearance. The morning barely begins when our bugles break the silence with their sounds of reveille that put in motion the immense human beehive. The different regimental bands follow by blowing their martial sound into the air. At the end, the national anthem is played, and our flag undulates all day on its very tall mast and unfurls as it ascends majestically. Two sergeants perform this act religiously, raising it in the morning and lowering it at the end of the day.

Friday, April 19

We had another peaceful day. Since everything ends up being a required routine, we are always ready to think, daydream, or study anything after the work is done. I spend hours with my favorite pastime, studying or reading. I have already read several novels and other good books. I write frequently and receive letters from friends living in different places. This is important because it keeps me busy. I am determined to write about everything I see and feel in this demanding life. With this in mind, I tell my relatives to keep my letters because if I have the good fortune of returning, I will use them. If I do not return, they will serve as a remembrance of me.

I investigate and try to understand everything I witness or that I hear from some reliable source. I have much to write about when new changes or developments occur. I have not had much to write about recently because I have only observed the usual daily routines. I can only be a witness to the monotony of life that we are obligated to endure and the preparation for the great battles when we shall defend our national honor.

Saturday, April 20

I have felt so strange this morning. The first calls of reveille that awakened me seemed more beautiful than ever. While I heard them and was dressing to fall into formation, I thought a great deal about the men and the wars from other times. World history tells us of the great and fierce confrontations among people who have lived on this earth. My mind goes through the pages of history as if they were motion-picture films.

The physical exercises make my blood flow, and my excellent health gives me confidence and faith in everything that is to come. The sun was hotter than ever and it gave greater strength to everything on earth. Breakfast was to our complete liking. All the soldiers in the dining area radiated satisfaction.

Our government will never receive its due for the care and attention it has given to its military. Everything is the best of the best. The finest is set aside for the great national military. The best cooks and doctors inspect the food. Great care is taken, along with good hygiene. I do not know if things are like this in all the camps. Some soldiers may say otherwise. In Camp Travis, anyone who wishes to comment on the matter has to praise the government for its wise measures.

Sunday, April 21

We did not work today because it is a day of celebration for the "Texans."[8] The units that were to parade on the streets of San Antonio during the afternoon were selected early. They did not include my unit because we lack a great deal of discipline. Some friends insisted that I go with them, and since many men were missing, I was able to join the parade. I will never regret it. I asked my friends to teach me the basic orders and the different movements of the march. They quickly trained me until I felt ready.

April 21 is the greatest day in San Antonio. It stands out because of its importance in Texas history. I was fortunate to have witnessed on several occasions the military parades. I would never pass up the opportunity to participate in one of them, especially since I now have to the right to do it.

We marched from Camp Travis to the end of Avenue C, close to Houston Street. We waited a long time for the numerous floats, the groups of city officials, the police officers, firemen, etc. Finally, we began to move until we reached Houston Street. We then marched west toward Milam Plaza and then followed San Saba Street to Commerce and South Alamo. From there, we once again went to Avenue C. From there, we marched back to the camp.

I felt a stirring sensation as I held my rifle and marched to the fervent sounds of the bands and in step with the deeply resonant clamor and solemn calling of the warrior's drum. The thunderous applause from a crowd intoxicated with holy patriotism sharpened our senses, especially because we recognized the voices of our brothers, our parents, wives, girlfriends, and friends. Everything overwhelmed us in those moments. It was both overwhelming and sublime.

I had marched with other groups through the same streets on other occasions. I remember another parade like this one, the last one we organized during our 1914 convention of teachers.

This march has surely been one of the most trying ones because we had to move in formation, at attention, and carrying the rifle with great control. I was very tired when we returned to camp. After dinner and some rest, I began to write and ponder the transcendental importance of the parade. A letter to my good friend, the distinguished teacher William J. Knox, gave me the opportunity to comment on it.[9]

Sr. Prof. W. J. Knox
Navarro School
San Antonio, Texas

My dear *Profesor* and Friend

I take great pleasure in writing you. I do not doubt that my new undertaking has surprised you. Mr. Knox, I did not want to do less than anyone else in fulfilling the highest responsibility to our nation. I had already told you of this in a previous letter. You will probably receive it with this one. I have joined the army and am at your disposal, with the same trust in you as ever, though now with my new military spirit.

I just took part in a grand military parade in San Antonio. I remembered the times we marched as teachers of the children of our great nation. Now as then, the experience was a source of pride, and

I felt more than proud, I was fulfilled. No one understands better than you why I fight for the advancement of my *raza*. I believe that our participation in the so-called great world war has placed at our doors a great opportunity and we cannot pass it up.

I expect to return from France to continue my work where I left off. My desire has been to follow the shining path you have set.

There is no doubt that we will be victorious. Whether I return or not is no longer important, but I have faith in my return from this venture into the old world.

I expect to participate in the military parade tomorrow and will write you another letter if I do. I will march through the old streets of the historic San Antonio de Béxar as a soldier of the nation, just like we did not long ago as the humble teachers of the children of the nation. I will, with no less pride and satisfaction.

Please read this letter as well as others that I will write to the children of my *raza* who attend the Navarro School and that you so ably direct. I want them to know what their brothers in uniform are doing. We will wear it with honor during the supreme hours of our difficult trial for the well-being of all humanity.

Respectfully, your Friend,

Luz

Leming, Texas
April 20, 1918

Luz,

I hope that you are well, just as we are ourselves. We thank God. Our only wish is to see you. Our grandmother has been a little sick as a result of an accident. You know how she is. She cannot work but does not want to stay still. I have not been able to visit her, but my father and aunt did. Aunt Juanita is gravely ill and we fear that she may die.

You ask me when we plan to travel to San Antonio. We will go when you let me know that you will be visiting our home there. A few days ago our baby girl was sick, she is well now. She weighs twelve pounds. This thread that I am sending you measures her length. I am also sending you a lock of her hair.

I am saddened by what you say regarding our brother Eugenio. My brother Gregorio has had to work very hard on his land this year, and I have not seen him. My father is working with him.

This is all for now. We send you kisses and hugs, and greetings from dad and aunt. With the love of always,

Your wife,

MARÍA PETRA

My dear Mr. Knox:

I take great pleasure writing you this letter. Take note of my current location. This will tell you as sure as the light of day that I no longer mentor children in a faraway rural school. Now I can tell you with pride that "I am a soldier of our nation and ready to fight for her." These are my wishes. I make it very clear that in doing this I do no less but stand up for my dignity as a citizen of one of the greatest republics ever conceived that defends the honor and love we have for our families. Is this not right?

I have been in the service since February 25. My country's calling pulled me away from teaching the children of my *raza* and placed me where I can insure their honor, their racial pride, and a happier future. I am a man in arms, I will kill, I will help in killing, and I will do everything possible to save the nation.

It is impossible for anyone to know or even imagine what the soldier feels as he shoulders his rifle. Perhaps they can, when they are moved by the thousands of other enthusiastic spectators who applaud, scream, and discover their souls in the enthusiasm and sense of unity of the crowd—*the nation . . . the nation*!

The citizens who saw us march and give full expression to our valor and patriotism may entertain thoughts like these. The columns of soldiers, orderly, well kept, full of life, and happy, will soon charge the "impregnable" German fortifications. They will pass through the ancient theaters of war of the old world as the largest and best-prepared crusade of our times. The spectators cannot imagine how the same soldiers who paraded before them in full splendor today will return as the heroic, moving, and sad warriors that they will become. The survivors of the war will bring them the crowns of victory after restoring the peace for the people who cry and long for justice.

I repeat what I said in yesterday's letter. Please read them to the children of my *raza* and to people of other *razas*, to all the people of the world if possible, so that they can begin to know what we are doing, what we are thinking and so that they may understand the cause that will send some of their brothers back as dust or spirit. They will have fallen—with their country's uniform steeped in blood—to uphold our good name as a *raza*, to secure our rights, and to insist that they not deny us holy justice. They should continue studying with enthusiasm and dedication. This has been another reason for leaving the peace of sweet civilian life to join the military columns, the front lines of soldiers that soon, very soon, will make the major sacrifice for the national honor.

I remain, your caring and humble friend.

J. Luz Sáenz

Monday, April 22

I woke up somewhat tired and sore from yesterday's heavy march, all along remembering details of that memorable day of my life.

Rumors are beginning to circulate that our departure for France is near. I think it is still too early, but anything can happen because of the current circumstances. There is talk that groups will have to leave immediately, although we do not know who these may be or where they would go. The rumors that are circulating grab our attention, strike our interest, and give us food for thought since we all want to leave even if it is only to have something new to talk about.

I went home to prepare my loved ones so that no one is surprised if one day I happen to be among the soldiers selected for the much-anticipated journey, because "we already have a foot in the stirrup," as our grandparents would say.[10]

Tuesday, April 23

We still hear the echoed sounds of the twenty-first and cannot take in all the memories of that day. I look forward to a more propitious moment to write about this. We must think seriously about the part we are to play. I am certain that many of my Mexican brothers do not understand its importance. This necessarily means that our supreme sacrifice on behalf of the nation will not be appreciated or sufficiently recognized to contribute to the advancement of our future generations.

I assume the responsibility of engaging all the members of my *raza* and to urge them to be loyal in the fulfillment of our duty and to never betray the heroism for which we are known. I am taking notes that could easily turn into books regarding our actions and deportment in this great global tragedy. I am pleased to see many others seconding my call and rousing their spirit when they realize our situation. I find some who still refuse to make up their minds and who give themselves to the adventures of life, accepting whatever comes, and waiting indifferently for the imminent unfolding of the obvious and inevitable future. Our hope and desire is that what they learn in other lands will help them change, and that this will bring benefit to them and our people.

Wednesday, April 24

I often receive letters from my friends who commend my outlook and encourage me to continue moving forward. The letters are like new Moorish spurs that arouse my spirit and sustain me in the difficult struggle for my *raza*. None of the obstacles I am confronting daily cause me to deviate from my way of thinking and doubt success. Despite this violent present, I have ample reason to be hopeful for the men of all the *razas* of tomorrow.

Thursday, April 25

I had the pleasure of once again hearing the president's daughter sing. This time, her visit was better advertised, and the planning for her reception was more appropriate and complete. The officers poured out their affection and kindness. "Amazing, they understand English," says one of my sardonic Mexican friends. They received her with so many vases of expensive and beautiful flowers. We say once again, "it must be because they know English."[11]

The privates simply enjoyed themselves and applauded. This is the only way that people from below can render tribute to the ones above.

I did not want to pass the opportunity to ask my buddies what they thought of our distinguished visitor. They expressed many and wide-ranging opinions with their simple and sincere responses.

Friday, April 26

A Frenchman was among the officers who visited and trained us today. I could not tell his rank, but I was able to see the common soldier in him. I would say that he looks like a bird from back home that everyone knows as "woodpecker." He wears a well-fitted deep blue uniform with shiny black decorative material, shiny and fine "putees," and, finally, a bright red and black cape.[12] His constant movement makes the comparison more obvious. Later, I will explain why our military has so many "woodpeckers."

The officer trains the men on the use of the little 37.5 millimeter that arrived recently. We know it as the "one-pounder."

Two promising young Mexicans are among the recruits the Frenchman will train. They are Jesse Pérez, intelligent and of fair intellectual abilities, and Julián Martínez, who may lack schooling but is industrious and exhibits natural intelligence. They are from San Antonio.

Pablo López, from San Diego, has signed up for the squad that will use the feared trench mortars. These young men are among the few who demonstrate great devotion to military life. They take much pleasure in meeting their responsibilities. We expect much from them. I do not want to flatter them with this or much less detract from the great courage and the wonderful temperament of my other brothers who are part of the Great National Armada. We expect that they will know how to faithfully discharge their duties on this journey we are initiating.

Saturday, April 27

I worked until noon at the office of the sergeant major and went to the city in the afternoon. I spent the night or a good part of it with my sister and her little boy, Samuel. Samuelito loves me as if I were his father. His father died when he was born and I have given him the care he could never find elsewhere in this world. When it is time to leave, he accompanies me to the place where I take the streetcar. This afternoon he saw me off by stating, "I am going to visit you, so that I can see the bear." He refers to our regiment's mascot.

Sunday, April 28

I do not know why this Sunday seems more peaceful than others. The usual noise is gone, especially the sound of the cars with the many families visiting our barracks or the other vehicles on their way to the brigade station with the quarantined soldiers. Recruits are subject to a strict quarantine and examined with great care. This is where the recruit is introduced to the numerous medical procedures and the serious challenges to his morale that are to come.

I have spent my time inside today, reading and writing letters to my friends who insist that I explain what we are seeing and doing here. I do not know why this life of danger and difficult trials raises so much interest. I see that soldiers from other racial backgrounds are also asking for explanations. I am glad to give them, I really am. It is the best way to give expression to my imagination and to gather much of what I will want to say upon my return, if I happen to survive the slaughter.

Monday, April 29

I have been watching (it is ten in the morning) a group of soldiers for a while as they undergo strenuous training a short distance from the office where I work. I get irritated and my temperature rises as I witness and contemplate the moving scene before me.

A large number of government trucks with different responsibilities pass by, going in all directions. Although I am working, I can see and hear everything that passes near me. My work is a routine that requires very little thinking or concentration. I have a lot of time to think when on the typewriter. I have trained my fingers so that they do not require much effort as they make the typewriter go tick tock, tick tock.

Among my buddies from the brigade station that form part of the 90th Division, Eulogio Gómez and Eduardo Barrera have been assigned to mounted ordinance; Pepe González and Valente de la Rosa to the band; Filomeno González to the First Infantry Battalion; and Amado Cásares, Felipe Neri, Domingo Pacheco, and Juan Martínez to the combat engineering group. I was assigned to the R.I.O. of the General Headquarters of the 360th Infantry Regiment.

General Headquarters has ordered that all the soldiers be given the opportunity to apply for officers' school. I have inquired into this opportunity that is offered to the downtrodden on the condition that they are qualified. The general understanding is that this is not for Mexican soldiers. This may be the case, but I want to give it a try. I have asked a few officers for their opinion and while some recognize my right and encourage me, others frighten me by telling me about the difficult training and the many responsibilities involved. When it seemed that I had given up, I submitted my application telling them that I like the strict discipline and major responsibilities. I know my application will not get anywhere, but here it is:

Camp Travis, Texas, April 29, 1918
From: J. Luz Sáenz, Private, General Headquarters, 360th Infantry
To: Commander in Chief of the 90th Division
Subject: My application for officers' training school

I hereby apply for the Officers' School that will soon open for soldiers from this division.

My military service has been the following:

I joined the army two months ago. This is my entire military experience.

This has been my education:

(b) I completed the primary and secondary grades in the official school of Alice, Texas. I am a teacher and have a first class certificate from the state of Texas. I taught for eight consecutive years until I was accepted as a soldier. I speak and write Spanish, which is my native language, and have completed accounting and stenography in a commercial college.

I was born on May 17, 1888, in Realitos, Duval County, Texas, and I am an American citizen by birth, in the United States of America.

Signed: J. Luz Sáenz

First Signature _____

Second Signature _____

Note complete record, including officers' school, if any.

Note all the schools that you have attended.

If naturalized, note where you became a citizen

Endorsements for the Regiment commander or military department

Good-bye

Good-bye Juanita García
You are all that I love;
Good-bye town of Seguín
When will I see you again?

Good-bye Juanita García
You are all my hope's desire
Good-bye to all my friends,
Until I return from France.

Good-bye town of Seguín
My place of enlistment;
Good-bye Juanita García
I'm finally becoming a soldier.

Good-bye Juanita García
Good-bye my darling woman;
Pray to God in the heavens
That he grants my return.

With this I now say good-bye,
My most tender of farewells,
Good-bye Juanita García
I'm with the government now.

Good-bye town of Seguín,
Where I spent my youth;
Good-bye Juanita García
Until I return from France.

If my buddy S. Bustos did not write the song, he surely arranged it. He dedicates it to his unforgettable friend Amado Cásares from Seguín. Bustos left with a contingent of soldiers to Montgomery, Alabama, and Cásares remained with us. I will collect many of these sparks emerging out of the souls of the wounded, enamored, or contrite souls. I have not been able to collect any that describe our departure from our homes.

Tuesday, April 30

My other friends who work in the Office of Information and Discharges are intelligent, although I cannot tolerate their egotistical behavior and racial prejudice. I can tell they do not want me here because I was brought in to do much of the work they have not been able to do, arranging and preparing new office cards for the recruits. It could be that this misunderstanding is due to a difference in our civilian lives, to our different social customs, racial origins, to our manner of seeing things, to our individual sense of pride. We can only hope the unfortunate circumstances that have thrown us together in defense of a common cause will gradually make all of this disappear. I hope so, for the good of the cause!

My friends are always ready or getting ready to eat when I return from the office. Gómez, González, and Pérez always wait for me so that we can go together. They share their experiences while I give them the news I gathered from the office or the daily paper.

Five minutes before noon, the camp siren that announces fires and other major events goes off and, immediately, all of us, all the soldiers representing the entire nation, rise to attention. This is the most solemn, the most dignified way to honor the memory of the heroes who until now have fallen in battle over there, in the war that engulfs the world. This small act seems to invite profound and lofty thoughts among us because it will not be long before others do the same for us. Imagine this, the loud noise of 60,000 men and in full strength. At the moment when the distressing howl, wail, or moan of the siren parts the sky, everything stops, even the breathing. The many hearts in prayer for all of humanity are saddened by the pained lament of the siren that reaches the hearts of men who contemplate and cannot explain any other reason for the destruction of the world but *Human Pride*.

Wednesday, May 1

This has been a joyful day. My oldest brother and my little nephew visited me.

The difficult training continued as usual until midday.

I have already said that our meals are excellent. We are served in good amounts without being excessive or wasteful. A sergeant is in charge of each kitchen. Sergeants have to bring some skills, especially in the area of culinary arts, and they have to know a great deal of home economics. This also contributes to the excellent service. Cleanliness is evident in the serving utensils we use. The officer of the day visits the mess halls under him once or several times. Nothing could be done without strict military vigilance and discipline.

My brother, my little nephew, and I were so happy during our meal because we are gratified when we see the respect extended to relatives and friends when they visit. This is enough to fill us with pride and a heightened sense of responsibility. It also encourages us to entertain sweet hopes for the future. This is when we once again recognize that the sacrifice on behalf of our children is just.

After the meal, we went to the YMCA to write, to listen to music from a phonograph, etc. I then took my brother to the library and to the Knights of Columbus hall. We had a long conversation. I talked about my hopes and plans for the future. Since I do not know if I will die on a battlefield, I told him how my children are to be educated. My poor brother was so taken with what I said that he also wanted to enlist, but I insisted it was best for him and all the rest of us that he stay home because our families need him.

When it got dark, I accompanied them to the city and returned to the camp that very night. I took the streetcar from my house to the main post office, and then took a bus. Many wide-ranging thoughts raced through my mind while the bus speeded on its way. I felt the rush of memories of home, of all my family members and their future, of my hopes of surviving the war in Europe, and my wish to return to tell my story and the thousands of things that I will have witnessed.

The military atmosphere that I sensed as I reached my barracks seemed different, overwhelmed as I was by the deep silence and the intense darkness of the night. The faint light in the streets is barely enough for the sentinels, the eyes of the sleeping troops. A long while passed before I could calm down and sleep. I used the time to contemplate and philosophize over our present and approaching future. I was determined to accept my responsibility as a representative of my *raza* for whom much could be realized at the moment of trial. Sweet hopes, expectations, desires, . . . Enough!

655 S. Pecos St., or 1122 W. French Place
San Antonio, Texas, May 1, 1918

Mr. Sáenz,
My Dear Friend:
I was very glad to hear from you and surprised that you are in the military. I had not heard from you since last spring. I admire your noble purpose and feelings, and am proud to know that you have come to understand better than others the crisis that hangs over us and the whole world.

If there are more Mexican American soldiers in your neighborhood, that is, in the military and close by, you should teach them so that they are informed and know how to make the best impression possible. I am pleased that the Mexican American boys know how to respond to the call of our Nation. This is how they have done it in all our wars since 1836.

We want the best for the entire world. I hope that we, "The United States of the North," can contribute to the reconstruction of the weak nations that have been crushed and that we may be able to guarantee them "life and liberty so that they may build their happiness."

I am sure that you will gain a valuable education from your military experience. Your devotion to the highest of all responsibilities will bring you friendships and honor.

I will visit you soon.

Yours Affectionately, Your Loyal Servant,

(Signed) William J. Knox

p.s. Write me often, making careful note of your full address:

company, regiment, and place. You know that once you move, it will not be easy to know your whereabouts. Send me your regimental address. Request it from your superiors every day. I am sure that you will soon receive a position of trust and responsibility.

W. J. K.

Mr. W. J. Knox,
My Dear Friend:

Greetings! Are you well? I hope so.

You were no doubt surprised to find out that I am in the Great National Armada. How could I pass up this opportunity? It requires a supreme effort but it also allows me to realize the greatest wish of my life. I feared that I could not realize my dream in light of my great responsibility to my home and family. I only had to wait for the right moment, and here you have me now, showing off the dry olive green uniform.

Slowly but surely, I am taking advantage of every opportunity and completing all the required training. As my former teacher, you know my ability and my capacity to learn. I am anxious because they still have not explained "my obligation." I carry out every task and learn nothing. I poke here and poke there. I have been doing office work most of the time. However, as they say,

"Everything in its proper place, and even that which appears to be in the way, gives strength and sustains everything else."

My current address is: Hqs. Co. 360th Inf., 90th Division. You will not have problems finding me when you come. I work in the office of Information for Furloughs, close to my barrack. Come by this week if possible because we are going to Camp Bullis for target shooting the following week, and we will not return for weeks.

I spend most of my time at camp despite the fact that my family is in San Antonio. I visit the city once a week, although I would rather go every day. I will write you as often as I can.

Jesse Pérez, one of your former students, sends his regards. Do you remember him? He is in my company and he is already a private. Good-bye,

J. LUZ SÁENZ

Thursday, May 2

I walk to Ft. Sam Houston on most of my trips to the city. From there I take a streetcar to the west end. I bought a home in the area, near school number nine. I did not forget that my children needed schooling when I left for the war. I thought they should grow up close to a school since I did not know if I would return from the great campaign. If I fall in combat, Uncle Sam will have to assume this additional responsibility, and if I return, which would be best, I will continue as before. I have entered into a contract for the house with a citizen of German origin, well known as a miser of the first order. I fear that he will swindle me.

I took the streetcar to the post office this morning so I could ride on one of the jitneys that frequent the camp. I arrived very early, but many soldiers who had stayed in the city the previous night were also there and I had to wait a long time to find a place to sit in the streetcar. I reached the camp somewhat late. My friends were already up and ready to fall into formation. I barely had time to grab my rifle and take my place in line. Other soldiers who arrived with me were crafty and did not make formation, perhaps because they had been up all night and were hungover. The sergeant who checked attendance punished them with kitchen duty for the day. I have not yet done this work and would absolutely not want to do it because I have heard the tired men complain about it after their shifts.

I did light office work the rest of the day. I still do not know if my assignment is permanent or not and think I will soon have to do something different. I no longer doubt this.

I see that I will not receive much credit for my work. Others get credit for my underappreciated work and their files will reflect this. I can no longer hope for justice in the form of a promotion to sergeant. Waters now run so deep and dirty that we cannot operate with yesterday's trust and hope. I have implored our captain to transfer me to some other kind of work, and he has told me that I have to arrange this with my lieutenant. This really shuts the door tightly. The officer does not inspire trust. He seems very egotistical and arrogant. He has so unfairly put us through many bad moments that I have often searched for a good reason to disobey him.

Friday, May 3

After supper, Martínez and I visited his home. This handsome friend had lost his father and mother and lived under the care of his oldest sister. His family was cordial. I could tell how much his sister and nieces love him. We spent long hours enjoying our conversation and playing *malilla*.

Martínez's home is on the east side of the city of San Antonio, not very far from a big iron bridge on a road that turns into a major street. The high bridge has become famous in recent days because an Anglo couple died when their car crashed through a railing and landed with all of its passengers at the bottom of the arroyo.

We have had much rain lately and this increases our boredom in the barracks. The men smoke so much the lack of oxygen disgusts me to no end. I am left to visit my other friends in their barracks, which are nothing more than caves with men playing cards, dice, or doing their usual smoking. I put all of this out of my mind, however, once we lose ourselves in the memories of our sweet past or when we dream about the future. It seems that none of my buddies realize the imminent danger before us, and when we talk of France no one believes they will not return. Others are so optimistic they do not even think we will have to cross the ocean and get to know France. I think differently since I am better informed about what is happening over there. I do not say anything and urge them to be on their best behavior. I also try to make them understand that they are critical to a better future, especially the lucky ones who will return to tell the history of their deeds and report on how the others fell.

I am prepared. Once I fully understood the dangerous undertaking before me, I took proper leave of my family.

Profesor J. Luz Sáenz[13]

The May third issue of our "Notas de Kingsville" reported that Prof. Sáenz had volunteered to serve in the American military, which has been organized to cross the ocean and help the nations that form the entente. This is actually what has occurred.

Profesor Sáenz did not wait to be drafted but, knowing that registration would eventually take place, quickly presented himself before the recruiting office and declared that he would join the columns of the brave men preparing to cross the Atlantic to join with the Allies in the momentous and honorable fight. The war seeks the lofty and noble goal of finally and forever putting an end to the pride and foolishness of the soldiers of the Kaiser William. He is one of the most despotic and sanguinary tyrants. Free, conscientious, patriotic, and educated people detest him.

Profesor Sáenz is well known in South Texas. He has had the admirable responsibility of operating official schools for Mexican-origin children in many towns and cities. He has also published splendid newspaper articles that all Mexicans of sound judgment and serious bearing have received well and even enthusiastically.

Lastly, when necessary and fitting (and this has occurred on many occasions), *Profesor* Sáenz has taken to the rostrum and spoken with his able, eloquent, wise, and honest voice. He has done this on the days of eternal remembrance for the Mexican people, and to defend his *conraciales* when they have appealed to the always-just bar of public and informed opinion.

We commend Luz for his noble and virile response to the Teutonic despot. Our profound wish is that he affirms the name of his heroic race in the glorious France, the beloved Nation of the Immortal Victor Hugo, and that he returns to his family in Alice bearing the laurels of victory on his honorable brow.

AMADO GUTIÉRREZ

Saturday, May 4

The different military groups assembled in the afternoon into compact and well-formed units. We came together at the sounding board. The bands performed selected pieces, apparently competing for the favor of the officers who were present. It is interesting how each battalion is serious about defending their band. Everyone is told that his band is the best. The common soldier does not understand these schemes.

The official orator in the afternoon was a French officer whose rank I do not know. He spoke in very clear English and provided vivid descriptions of his poor nation, including the cruel and horrible slaughter of his countrymen who were made to suffer for simply pursuing the ideals other men favored. We will soon witness with our very eyes such scenes that will be of our own making.

The French officer called our attention to a French custom among the women. He told us that we should not expect them to accept us without first securing permission from parents and grandparents. He added that the soldier does not know how to enjoy his liquor, preferring to roll on the ground in a stupor. He finished by expounding on his vast experience in the trenches and his many wounds. The government obviously sent him to serve as an example. He did not say this, but it was understood. He is here as an instructor in the American military.

SINCERE CONGRATULATIONS

To the intelligent young ladies from Alice, Texas, Esther Pérez and Petra Escobedo.

Young ladies, you honor and inspire us, you raise our noble gaze as humble soldiers of the nation with your success (finishing high school).

Continue with your success as this will be a source of pride for you.

Your Mexican brothers

(Signed) Corporal Jesse Pérez
Private J. B. Martínez
" Pablo Pérez
" Eduardo B. Barrera
" Domingo Pacheco
" Eulogio Gómez
" Felipe Neri
" Amado Cásares
" J. Luz Sáenz

At the same time that we try to set an example, we call upon our own to make use of all that is good in civilian life.

Sunday, May 5

I am convinced that there is no justice or the adequate method or means to insure it in the Department of Information where soldiers are discharged if they have a good reason to be released. Mr. González and his son, whom I have already mentioned, came to the office today. They have come with the same concern. This time they have brought very good recommendations, but they lack the necessary influence or money to secure an exemption. The crafty individuals who have been exempted should have been receiving and cooling the hot German lead by now. The opinion of the Martindale board seems final. I believe that if we are going all the way to Europe to seek justice, we should guarantee it here first.

I visited José Leal in the afternoon and spent peaceful moments with him and other men of my *raza*. We then went to the YMCA where we had a good time writing letters to several friends who always ask us to respond quickly with a full account of our lives in the military.

Monday, May 6

I wrote more letters to family and friends.

My family is well, which makes me happy. Everyone seems very pleased that I wear the uniform because I tell them we are treated with respect and consideration. Despite everything, life is good, as long as we understand the meaning of war.

I may not be justified in complaining, but why deny what I always seem to be encountering in my career? I wish I did not have to deal with certain individuals, but they exist and are grist for my diary. It is obvious that the two races, the Anglo-Saxon and the Mexican American, misunderstand each other so much. Our military includes many soldiers from the north and west who only know our *raza* by what they see in films and hear from journalists who have never seen us or had anything to do with us. Worse still, Texans are especially prejudiced toward us. They do not know our worth or they choose to overlook our contributions to the United States. They actually deny them. My friend, Mr. Knox, has said in one of his letters, "You have participated in all the wars since 1836." We have contributed to all, or at least the most important ones. But how many people know the history of our *raza* like Mr. Knox? Very few know it because they are not interested in our social problems. This is why I have said, and many others already know it, that we must write a detailed account of our participation in this war. Who among us will have the good fortune of writing our epic story? They do not understand us, or they do not want to give us credit. We have offered what seems like a sacrifice in vain, in contrast to others who have tried to evade military service. Our willingness to serve and to want to learn everything and to do it quickly, places us under scrutiny and subject to doubt, distrust, and suspicion. These dark clouds dim our blue sky of hope. Upon added reflection, I say, we want light!! The sun is behind these dense and dark clouds! . . . !

When I focus on the deeds of my *raza*, I do not mean to minimize the praise my Anglo buddies, my brothers in misery, justly deserve. I have many good friends among them. They cannot but sympathize and agree with me when they understand the full extent of the problem.

Tuesday, May 7

I had to clean part of my uniform today to avoid a reprimand. The reviews are becoming more and more demanding every day and it is best to be prepared. Many soldiers have money and many clothes apart from what the government provides. They maintain them well because they pay for their care. This is not the case with those of us who do not have money and now and then have to do these small chores to avoid problems (this was my father's advice). We pay for the cleaning but get the uniform back in a week. This means we have to wear the other uniform the whole time. We often fail to keep our uniforms clean enough for the reviews while the rest of the men look so presentable.

Wednesday, May 8

I am pleased with my work in the office, probably because I am free from the heavy burden of training alongside other soldiers in the field. The days pass by so fast, probably because things are like in civilian life. I am exempt from the daily formations for physical exercise or rifle training and target shooting. I like to see these formations and to even join the exercises or other activities when they are not directed by the many imbecile and arrogant officers we have. My *raza's* character (I am Aztec through and through), as well as the past and current resentment against us, leads me to reject this Anglo attitude, even if it is expressed by someone with the silver bars of a captain. It is still too early, the wounds remain open, I cannot forget even if I wanted. On occasions such as these, I invoke the thought of our lofty purpose that has brought me here . . . to fulfill my duty as a good citizen and worthy parent, the model to my children.

Thursday, May 9

Two young Mexicans, José González from Falfurrias and Valente de la Rosa from Austin, are in our regiment's 360th Infantry band. Two Italians from Italy are also in the band. They joined our military because they were here when the war started. Our military is like a net; it catches all types of fish.

We continue to pass our time at the YMCA. The people in charge seem sincere in their concern for the soldier, or maybe they just want to keep their job. They do not cut costs in providing the soldiers what they need to pass the short time before they die.[14] An elderly man, a director of one of the many YMCA halls, seems to favor Mr. González. He comforts him and gives him hope.

Friday, May 10

I spoke at length with Pablo Pérez, a soldier in the trench mortar group. He is the kind of man we need for the advancement of our people. We would lose much if Pablo died in France. Like all young men who are full of life, his girlfriend has been his obsession since he joined. He confides in me and enjoys hearing phrases that I have picked up from books or that I have dreamed up for those dynamite letters I write. If the post office knew this, they would refuse to deliver the dangerous explosives. What more than a letter of love? His girlfriend is a beautiful young woman from a very good family. Pablo says that if he returns, the first thing he will do is marry her.

Pablo's family loves him very much and although they may not be wealthy, he can make a living without having to work for anyone.

Saturday, May 11

Jesse Pérez is another person who is well off and a worthy representative of our people. He has been raised in the better social surroundings of the city. His father has served as a "ranger," or federal officer, along the border for many years. This has been important for Jesse, especially because it has assured him fair treatment in the schools he has attended. He is assigned to the little 37.5-millimeter cannon, also known as a "one pounder." Its destructive power is as great as its shell is small. We expect much from the small gun in obliterating the machine gun nests. It can fire three kinds of ammunition. One of the shells is like a grenade, the other is a solid object used to bombard fortifications, and the third one delivers poisonous gases. Jesse is impressive with his well-proportioned body. He is not fat, not very tall, and very friendly, although serious. His Mexican features are obvious, although his disposition is all Anglo and his English is perfect because he has been raised among Anglos.

Jesse has asked that I convey his good wishes to Mr. Knox. He taught him as a child. This is how grateful our Mexican soldiers are with people who know how to touch their hearts. Mr. Knox has also taught teachers in classes I have attended year after year in San Antonio. This is where I have come to know this person with truly altruistic ideas that merit the love and respect of our people.

I am sure he will be happy to hear of my new position. Mr. Knox has taught our children for many years and has many close friends among the educated. He has just as many among the working people. He claims, "I am king there." I will ask him to visit us. I do not doubt that he will come; surely he will come.

Sunday, May 12

Eulogio Gómez from Bracketville is short, but he has a big heart. He is another one of those men who are unknown, poor, and without an education. Eulogio cannot be grateful to Texas for its schools. He speaks Spanish badly, his English is worse, but he marches in the columns that will make up the American army on its certain voyage on the high seas. I ask myself, what must be running through the minds of these men who do not know anything about their history and evolving racial identity and who have never been encouraged to think much about their civil and political rights. Will they truly feel obligated to give their lives for democracy, for humanity, for the rights of oppressed and destitute peoples, for justice, etc., etc.? If there is one thing that many of these poor souls understand it is the lack of interest and even the poor treatment and racial abuse directed against our people. They know this because they feel it themselves. Do you know why Eulogio joined? Because they told him, "Let's go fight like men against the 'Boches.'" He told them, "Let's go then." If they had spoken to him of ideas, rights, privileges, democracies, laurels, if they had told him that he was going to fight for the American flag, I am quite sure he would have said, "And what business do I have defending the flag of the 'gringos,' let them defend it, I will defend mine." The innocent blood of the Velázquez family is still fresh and warm. They were father and son, from Puente de Piedras, or Oakville.[15] The black and foul-smelling stains are still on the thorny cactus and the entrance to the corral. They cry out for justice and a better understanding between Anglo Americans and Mexican Americans.

They had just received the first notice from the government with the effusive and beautiful words impregnated with patriotism and calling Americans to military service. The Velázquez boys said, "They don't mean us." They asked their father, "Father, this says we are Americans and that we should go to war and fight until our death for the nation. What are we and which is our nation?" "You are Mexicans, yours is the nation of Juárez and Cuauhtémoc, and you are better dead than to register for service." I do not know what authority was asserted, but they decided to send armed officials to bring them in. The Velázquez boys remained firm in their conviction, based on a mistaken sense of Mexican identity. The old man and one of his sons fell at the entrance to the corral. They did not register for military service. The other son, after emptying his gun, was able to follow the arroyos and escape to Corpus Christi where he was arrested and taken to a military camp. He did not register yet he happily displays the uniform of the nation and bares his chest to the German bullets. He is left with the eternal agony and torment of crying over the death of his father and brother, but with the plain satisfaction that they fell refusing to sign something so complicated they did not understand.

Will we ever have understanding and justice? In Realitos authorities treated Mexicans like criminals and brought many of them in at gunpoint to register for military service, which they did not understand. The town became known for its large number of "slackers," Realitos of Duval County, Realitos my birthplace. I swear that if I had been there and if they had tried to drag me in the same way, I would have been the first "slacker," especially since I could not respond as the Velázquez men had.

As I was saying, it is good to see Eulogio content and ready to do his duty for the entire nation. What rewards await men like these if they return from the great crusade for humanity and democracy, and to make a better world?

Gómez's plain civilian life has given him the right to be assigned to a mounted detachment. His responsibility in combat will be to maintain contact with the different fighting groups in our regiment by way of written or oral messages.

His immediate superior, Sergeant Baton, appreciates him because he is really dependable and brave. I have already pointed out that he is determined and responsible, although he does not know how to read or write. We can already tell if a man is brave before we smell spent powder. Sergeant Baton has other English-speaking men under his command, but he especially trusts this humble brother of ours.

Gómez leaves a void in his home that is difficult to fill, but he knows how to "leave the plow" and, like Cincinnatus, can declare in the Mexican manner, "My homeland comes first." He will do well on the battlefields where dependability and bravery triumph.

Beautiful days have followed days of heavy rain. Those of us who do not have to go to the city are happy to be able to walk around the encampment in the afternoons and visit old friends or make new ones. The general appearance of camp is that of an ant colony. Many dry olive green uniforms appear until nine in the evening when the bugle calls us to retire.

Monday, May 13

Anyone who sees me regularly defending or praising members of my *raza* may think I am given to emotions or that I harbor ill will, but they do not see that when I speak about them, it is because no one will be truthful about their heroic deeds. I understand that when I am singing their praises the worth of their accomplishments will lose considerable meaning, especially in the eyes of people who dislike Mexican Americans. I do it because I am concerned and no one else is interested in assembling these historical notes for the future. I want to contribute something for that moment when someone may assume the responsibility of organizing and publishing this history.

We are not saying that all our Mexican soldiers are heroes simply because they are wearing the uniform. We have some that give themselves to personal pleasures, despair, pessimism, and even vice. The same thing happens to men of other races. They do not seem to care at all that this worldwide disaster has occurred and that it may never end.

Tuesday, May 14

Another day of routine ended in complete calm. No one noticed the disappearance of the astral king. The lovely and warm silver light of a beautiful moon of May, the beautiful moon of Texas, began to overtake the light of day. The night is suitable for thinking about many things and even for philosophizing about our insignificance and small worth in this world. The trumpet has just called for silence. Thousands of brave soldiers have obeyed the order as if under a spell. Everything has suddenly grown calm. The soft southern breeze has started to swell the waves of heat left by the hot sun that takes leave for arid lands. I feel the undulating warmth as I sit and observe from my cot, on the second floor of our barracks. The moon continues to rise quietly without any apparent bother from the refracted light of the sun. It seems to be spreading its majesty over our camp like an enchanted queen. Her sons of Mars wait for the dawn when they will rise to the rays of the warlike sun of May with their usual military equipment and other armaments. Their hope is that history will assemble within its pages all the major acts of bravery and convey this to other people who will inhabit this world.

Wednesday, May 15

I visited my home. My joy is boundless. Many profound thoughts follow as I find my way back to camp. I suddenly recall scenes from the past like in a movie, as the streetcar takes me through the busiest and most beautiful part of the city. My mind shifts to other worlds so effortlessly that what I see and hear before me seems like a dream that is also oblivious to thousands of other things. Many other soldiers join me in the streetcar, and they too lose themselves in deep meditation. Similar thoughts probably run through their minds. No one speaks until we reach the camp. They smoke a great deal; they say to pass the time. I do not smoke but do take my flights of fancy.

Our outlook is different when we are traveling to the city than when we are returning. Everything on the way there is indescribable, the noise, the shouting without reason, the mocking or honest laughter, conversations on every topic possible, the jokes, and the good humor.

Everything changes as soon as we reach the camp. The entire place smells and breathes military. The soldiers reign supreme, they give themselves to their own unique pleasures as they prepare for the grand bloody battles—smoking, playing, singing, swearing, and writing.

Thursday, May 16

We received orders that all the soldiers are to march at least two hours a day. Naturally, this was not going to sit well with us, but things did not change. Orders are orders. The hours we marched were exhausting. To make matters worse, we had one of those days of May that are memorable because of their hot sun and a slight breeze that feels like flames. The morning was hot and suffocating, we all sweated a good deal during the march.

We attended a scheduled class in the afternoon and then marched to the sounding board where we heard Colonel Conrad deliver an oration. The most significant part of the exercise was the orderly movement of the different groups. The rough edges of the recruit are disappearing little by little and the robot begins to emerge. The nearly sixty thousand soldiers who make up the division emerged from different directions to take their place in formation. Once Colonel Conrad gave the order, we sat down on the ground. The colonel and several majors advised us that our general deportment would determine the success of the crusade we are about to start on the other side of the ocean on behalf of our nation.

Once we begin to realize this responsibility, we will feel pride and understand the importance of the role we will have played. Destiny will tally the final result.

Friday, May 17

My birthday, I have been in this world thirty years. I decided to celebrate it at home and spent one of my happiest moments. I do not believe ever having another festive occasion like this or one that made such an impression on me. My brother and little nephew were once again with me at the camp. While noting the good quality of the food, our conversation turned to an observation that older war veterans make—there are no sweets on the front. We already understand that the war is not an outing in the country where people can pack what most pleases them. We hear that soldiers in war have eaten horses and other animals, practices that are scorned and despised in time of peace.

Once again, we had a good time at the Knights of Columbus hall. I wrote some letters and read out of a good book. They gave me another book to follow mass, as well as a religious object and a scapular. These gifts will remain with me during the deadly days that await me.

Saturday, May 18

It was hot today, quite fitting for the season. We did an especially forced march and I felt the physical exhaustion as well as the uplifting of the spirit. The body can suffer a great deal without bothering the spirit in the least. I had never felt my spirit in such a palpable way. When we could barely carry our rifles, when it seemed impossible to keep pace and remain in line, when even breathing was difficult, my thoughts would rise above all, and everything seemed small, even the very agony of the march. Under that all-consuming and roasting sun, I could see my buddies all sweaty, irritable, and grim, given to random but deep thoughts. We could only hear the dull cracking sound that our heavy loads and the cadence of our coarse, droning footsteps made on the ground.

The shoe of the private in military service is made of strong yet very soft leather, with many tacks that have big protruding heads and steel guards to protect the heel. The purpose is to minimize the wear as we march across the sharp rocks of the mountainous terrain. What follows is the cracking sound of mother earth as we march in formation.

Sunday, May 19

I went to say my farewells at Moore because we have good reason to believe our departure for another land is close at hand, possibly by way of the high seas. I spent time with special friends and family in Moore. I had a very happy day. The visit was too short and impromptu to be able to see all my old friends and students.

Moore is a small town with few people, it may not be considered very important, but I see it as an actual battlefield where I have often led fights over my major concern in civilian life—the education of people of my *raza*.

The business of outfitting us and completing the records for each soldier is so pressing that even the passes have been reduced to twenty-four hours. This prevented me from staying longer in Moore and going to Alice to see my father. He and some of my siblings are the only ones that have not seen me in uniform.

When the train arrived at five in the morning, I had to say good-bye to Moore and all its inhabitants, perhaps forever!

As soon as I got to San Antonio, I headed to the camp worrying that I would arrive late. Everything I had seen that day, the happiness I had experienced, was like a dream.

Monday, May 20

I woke up still thinking of Moore. The small humble town will stay in my memory for as long as I live. I was happy the whole day, it seemed so beautiful to me. I was so taken by my thoughts all day that I was oblivious to the many things I had to do. That is the nature of good fortune. While we are happy, the pain does not bother us. That may be why our suffering is so sharp and intense after waking up from such a sweet and romantic trance.

Tuesday, May 21

We marched around the camp and were once again told of the contents in each building. Many of us do not really know that our government extends benefits to its soldiers for their growth and development. Quick-thinking people who know how to make use of this become respectable individuals, all along benefiting themselves and their fellow citizens. Among the many buildings in camp, we find the great libraries where we educate and enjoy ourselves. All who are dedicated to studying can be found there. We also have various halls for rest and recreation, including theaters and places where we enjoy baseball. Everything is well equipped and available to everyone who knows how to make use of opportunities.

After our meal, the company received orders that we were to take a photograph so that an album of our regiment could be put together before the frenzied demands of the war began. I ordered two albums.

I again saw a German American soldier in the theater who had fallen ill as a result of the injections from the time we stayed in the tents. I thought he was dead since everyone had talked about this during our training in the field.

Wednesday, May 22

One who believes the private is only an unthinking robot fools himself. We can criticize our superiors, although this may be strictly prohibited in the military. We can say much in favor and against them, beginning with the corporals and sergeants. We know who lives up to his responsibilities and who does not care. Some officers are worthy of respect, while others only deserve contempt. The former are brave and gentlemanly, educated and just. The latter are simply foolish and arrogant, egotistical, vain, haughty, and make full use of the position their wealth secured for them—they could easily scare and run when the supreme hour arrives. We hope that for the sake of the nation this does not happen, even as they continue with their narrow-minded ways.

We had physical exercises at the strike of dawn. The bands were playing the best from their repertoire, and this encouraged us even more. If we ever return to tell of our difficult times in the military, we will first recall our impressions of these moments. Now I understand the momentary twinkle in the spent and sad eyes of the old disfigured veterans of past wars. Although the veterans faced misfortune in war, they now quickly and without thinking square off to salute the flag when they see the troops pass in formation flying the national banner. After this, they reenter the dark abandon set aside for old age.

From now on, our hearts will beat with pure joy every time we hear the sounds of the soldier's trumpet. We will feel this joy alongside the many thoughts of a glorious and hopeful past in the military.

We came to formation quicker and in a more orderly manner than usual. Colonel Conrad, Major Allen, and other officers reviewed our movements in the morning. The soldiers' spirit was overwhelming. The enthusiasm in the camp was indescribable. We could hear the sound of the bugle calling the orders of the day.

Thursday, May 23

After reading the day's orders in the morning, a large number of soldiers lined up to march to Camp Bullis for target shooting. Others went in trucks. Some of the soldiers returning from the exercise told us that it was difficult. Their sunburned faces and grimy appearance as well as their exhausted condition show this. I cannot describe the movement throughout the camp. A view from an airplane would be so beautiful. Platoons of soldiers are everywhere preparing their backpacks, while officers order others to march out.

Office workers like us who have it easy in the shade have not yet met this challenge, but our turn will come soon enough. Target shooting is required without exception. What soldier can consider himself complete without at least knowing how to shoot and to demonstrate this skill? What I most fear is that we will be among the soldiers who will have to march to the site. It takes thirty miles to get there and as many coming back. Let things come as they may! Onward, we are already in, what else can we do!

Friday, May 24

We were expecting it, this morning we were told that instead of going to the office, we were to prepare our backpacks for the field. Formation was called for seven o'clock; the trucks arrived later. Fifty soldiers boarded each truck and they took off for Camp Bullis.

A large number of trucks transported the troops. This was done quickly, as Uncle Sam's trucks travel fast. The trip was pleasant.

Camp Bullis is surrounded by tall hills or, better still, rocky peaks covered with fragrant cedars and other barbed vegetation, and different kinds of cacti. We have no barracks and every regiment has to supply its own tents. The encampments are located in a great clearing. The drainage system for the English-style privies is very hygienic, we even have a place to wash clothes, but there are no showers.

We had already set up our tents and put away our equipment by eleven. They immediately gave us each three hundred rifle cartridges and ordered that we change our uniform. They gave us the wide long johns of blue canvas and their accompanying jacket. Within fifteen minutes, we took on a less militaristic appearance and came to look like a railroad or prison work crew.

So much dust is raised in the short journey to the shooting range. The ground is already well trampled by the constant marching of the soldiers, and it is as dry as corn meal for the road.[16] The May sun was nearing its zenith at that moment and was placing its powerful rays on smoldering backs. We practiced shooting in a place that looks like an enormous pan. A giant bulwark about ten feet high stands to the east, next to a trench. The ditch protects the soldiers who set up our targets. We shot from different distances, in various positions, and according to different shooting rates. The soldiers who are in the trench tell us how many hits we made and how many we missed after each volley. They note this on a special card. This is how they can tell who is ready and who needs more practice. At that moment, no one knew that the faster we shot, the sooner we would be sent to France. No sir, we were more interested in a good shooting record.

The cartridges have very powerful powder that gives the rifle a strong kick. We shot until four in the afternoon. We did not eat and drank little because the water was so hot. When the time arrived to rest, we were very tired, hungry, and our arms were sore. We threw ourselves on the ground, but did not even feel it. We devoured the little food we were given and very quickly retired despite a beautiful and inviting moon that makes mothers cry.

Saturday, May 25

It is not hard to imagine how I woke up after yesterday's exhausting activities. We had little to eat and repeated yesterday's exercise. Necessity is the mother of invention. Some of us talked about what we could place on our shoulders to soften the rifle's kick. I thought about it, wet one of my towels, folded it well, and placed it on my shoulder underneath my clothes. This helped. I did not feel pain the entire day.

In the afternoon, Pérez invited Gómez and me to visit a cave he had discovered in the nearby hills. It was very late when we arrived and I insisted that no one risk entering since my buddies were beginning to show an animal-like curiosity that the field of psychology talks about. Crustaceans, or rattlesnakes, abound in these places. These are poisonous monsters, they do not attack but defend themselves and this has led to thousands of deaths.

During the walk in the country, we were able to appreciate the beauty of the landscape that surrounded us with beautiful woods of aromatic cedars. The small valleys were full of wildflowers whose fragrance reached us with the warm breeze that wafted over the petals and through their interiors. At this hour—it was seven in the evening—the beautiful silvery moon rose and completed a poetic picture deserving a place next to the master's works of art.

Sunday, May 26

We fired twice as many rounds today and, consequently, grew more tired and hungry. Despite this, we did not complete the day earlier than yesterday. Although life may be rough, we are getting used to it. After dinner, we took a walk down the narrow road between the rows of tents. We walked until we reached a large one known as the YMCA hall. The 36th Division band was there. They performed the "Marseillaise" and our national anthem that afternoon. I had never really listened to those sublime notes until now, played in the middle of forested hills before the very souls who could appreciate their true military and patriotic value.

My buddies and I had a spirited discussion after the concert. I shared what I know about the two hymns and something about the history of France and the United States, especially the part we are to play in the history of the "sister" nations during the war. I never get tired of urging them to meet their responsibilities as self-respecting men and brave soldiers. I insist that no other race surpasses ours in natural bravery and that under no circumstances should we diminish that ancestral heritage.

I saw Tomás Tunches, Francisco Alaníz, or Galavíz, and another young man named González, all of them from Alice. I was glad to greet them after hearing that they were surprised to see me in the military. Poor friends! They seemed to be saying, "Luz, you shouldn't be here, this is for us." "No, my friends, it isn't like that. I joined of my own free will and I hope I never regret it." They are pleased to hear me tell them how I joined and that every man needs to demonstrate his true worth. No one knows us, we have not had the time to show all that we can do, no one with good intentions leads us so that we may know this. We are now in the middle of it. Let us learn everything. We should make haste.

Among the soldiers who were there, I would have liked to have seen Manuel Salinas from Laredo, who I met in Moore.

Monday, May 27

This was another difficult day. We practiced at the firing range all day and did not eat. The sun was very hot. As midday neared, giant clouds gathered in the sky and the muggy climate seemed to announce a storm, one of those disturbances that have made the month of May so memorable. The artillery rounds grew more relentless, intense, and clear, and at that moment we imagined the sounds of the foreboding storm.

After dinner, I rested and relaxed by visiting old friends. We attended another concert at one of the YMCA halls and lost ourselves in our pasts. Memories of happy and sad days come to me as troubling visions that no longer have anything to do with my new life, but that try to encourage or terrorize me. Impossible! I go over them one by one with contempt.

My buddies, who are as miserable as me, try to occupy their minds, but it is hopeless. I see them walking, picking up a book, looking at it briefly and then throwing it away with disgust. They place records on the phonograph to the point of bothering everyone, they play cards without enjoying the game, they smoke and speak in a monotonous manner, or they yawn, and they do everything else that one does in anxious moments.

Tired over so much shooting, we retired early to our tents, but we could not rest well or sleep until we gave ourselves a towel bath.

Tuesday, March 28

We did not go to the firing range today. The officers gave us a pat on the back and announced that we were ready to face the German bullets of steel. They ordered us to march, and that is what we did all day. It was still early in the day when they told us to prepare our backpacks and wait for the trucks for our return to Camp Travis.

We were crowded and exposed to the dust and the sun the entire time, for a long while, until they told us, "You can go to sleep." Although these orders may be normal and probably necessary in the military, the lowly soldier finds nothing welcoming about them. Just look at their faces. This is when the soldier uses his crude language.

Should Mexican Americans, the poorest people in this global tragedy, join this struggle that is said to be for humanity, democracy, and justice? Yes, and it is no less lofty or necessary a cause than any our allies may have. We shall fight for our nation and for our *raza*; for our nation as we follow the symbolic flag of our birth and may our sacrifice serve the same purpose, for our *raza* as we fight for just recognition and for the racial pride of our martial tradition.

We should not be surprised that we are about to fight a despot and tyrant in the twentieth century. Our ancestors set the example for us. Our duty is to demonstrate that we are worthy of our heritage. In America, the continent, our people claim the just honor of rolling the first imperial head of a filibustering Kaiser down the foothills of the Sierra Madre, on a mountain named Campanas.[17]

Wednesday, May 29

We woke up to another morning at Camp Bullis after a night of waiting for the trucks. We never lost hope that they would arrive at any moment. The marked decline in food rations was making life more unpleasant and unbearable. All our field tents were folded and stacked up. The entire camp was no more than a pile of drab, dirty, and ugly things. Few soldiers spoke, and we presented a sullen appearance. We moved from here to there and from there to here without any purpose. The idle soldiers offered a good many hostile opinions. We grew more anxious with every truck that arrived, when they told us, "They are not yours." The soldiers who left were happy and forgot everything, while we were left grinding our teeth and listening to our rumbling stomachs.

Thursday, May 30

We waited until almost midday. Soon after the driver turned off the motor and as the truck was still moving, we scurried like ants, loading our things and helping others to load as fast as possible so that we could leave quickly. We did not eat, nor did we want to eat. The trip to San Antonio seemed long despite the fact that the trucks traveled fast. It felt like we had been gone for years and returned with such pleasure to our place of joyful pasts! Soon after arriving, we moved our familiar iron cots to their place, made our beds, put away our other belongings according to army regulations, went to the shower area, which was already full of impatient men, quickly shaved, put on new or clean clothes, and left the place as condemned men yearning for their liberty. Many of the men did not wait to eat at the camp but left immediately for the great city of noise and beauty to celebrate away the grief the sun and exercises had brought upon us at Camp Bullis.

After bathing and dressing, I noticed the striking effects of the sun on us. In just a few days, everyone had tanned and darkened, but the longing for social contact that bordered on insanity was even more noticeable. Nothing could keep the soldiers in camp. Veterans can appreciate this powerful desire to go to town better than a person who has never served. Oh, but the life and thoughts of these men who are full of strength and know they are destined for the slaughterhouse.

I visited my family and wanted nothing more than to hold them in my arms because our departure is no longer a vague possibility but a real likelihood. We only have a few days left in America.

Friday, May 31

I was instructed to write the name, company, regiment, etc. of each individual on his blue bag. These sacks are to be the trunks we will take with us across the Atlantic. We will pack our clothes and other campaign gear in them. While labeling the trunks, I found out that many soldiers are greatly mistaken that we will not be leaving for another six months. I also saw the importance of keeping soldiers in the dark about troop movements. They could easily reveal information that is so useful to German spies. The "Boches," as the Germans are called, are experts in the espionage business, and they seek to conquer the world with claims of self-defense.

Saturday, June 1

We were ordered to return the khaki canvas uniform in exchange for the one we will wear in France. The historic olive-colored uniform is made of pure wool. We were issued two uniforms and two sets of undergarments, an extra pair of shoes, food containers, and a first aid kit for the battlefield or in case of an accident. We needed to have all this prepared and ready for a general review, which should not be far off. The general in chief of the division will conduct the highly anticipated inspection.

After supper, as I was about to leave the barracks for a walk, I ran into our captain, who said, "Sáenz, I want to talk to you." He informed me in a harsh tone that the colonel leading our regiment to Europe needed a man with special qualities, and added, "I believe you are that person." I responded, "Captain, if you think I am that person and order me to do it, I have no choice but to obey. Give me the order." He then explained that I had to volunteer and that the assignment would allow me to avoid the harsh life of a private and earn the higher pay attached to the position. He added that the colonel was up in age, set in his ways, and that it would be wise to study him and learn his preferences. He reiterated that the position suited no one better, but that it all depended on my decision. We agreed that I would sleep on it and decide in the morning. I did not have to think about it much. A thousand thoughts crossed my mind with lightning speed. My heart rushed my entire blood supply to my head, I was confused, and I could not think. A storm had been unleashed in my mind, and deep down a slight voice was saying "no," "no," "no." What am I to do? I will have to first thank my superior for the attention he has given this humble man. Then, I will have to tell him, "No, I did not come to avoid the harsh life of a private, as long as it is an honorable one." If I am to be promoted or recognized, I want it to come to me differently. I have had moments when racial remarks have offended me, and I have exclaimed without thinking: "A thousand times a private than shine the colonel's boots." That very evening I informed my captain that I was declining the offer. "Suit yourself," he replied. I left thinking, "It was really my decision, my very own." The position should be given to someone who wants it. I will live by my convictions and continue as a private until the end.

Sunday, June 2

Our preparations continue and we no longer have time to visit the other barracks. Everything is chaotic and in a state of confusion, pandemonium, nothing is clear, nothing is understandable. What was orderly yesterday is the opposite today. We hear one order after another. A moment later each is pulled back or not carried through. The poor sergeants have had it rough today. They give us one thing then take it away only to give it back again. We are like blind men, just taking what we are given.

Many civilians search for family members without any luck because the soldiers have been moved to other barracks. This adds to the confusion, but there is no longer any doubt about what is to come. Trains are arriving with their long necklaces of Pullman cars. We will soon have to say farewell to everything and go to the slaughterhouse. Soldiers are starting to leave camp already. They go at night so we have no idea of their departure.

Monday, June 3

They continued to issue us clothing. We paraded in full review for the first time today. The parade passed in front of General Headquarters, in other words, our barracks. The bands played while the officers examined our equipment. Two officers were taking notes on everything they were seeing. At the same time, the troops were being inspected throughout the camp. This was a sight to see, so many men in uniform against the backdrop of equipment strewn about.

First Photo: Florencio Heras, of Alice, in the center. He died with the sinking of the *Tuscania*. Florencio deserves a monument to his memory. Second Photo: Sixto Flores, from Alice, another victim of the *Tuscania*. Third Photo: Felipe García, now living in Mission, made sergeant major in Camp Travis. Fourth Photo: Pablo Pérez of San Diego, a handsome American soldier of Mexican origin. Fifth Photo: Fortino Treviño, looking rugged in his trench uniform, slight but brave.

My brother Eugenio and sister Marcelina visited me and viewed our parade. This was the first time we paraded with our full gear of eighty-seven pounds. After the review, we received our pay. I could now spend an evening at home. I was so happy to tell my wife and little children of the preparations for the great voyage across the sea.

Tuesday, June 4

We had another parade at ten this morning. General Allen reviewed the troops. Our officers informed us that he was very happy with the mood in our division, which would include soldiers from the states of Oklahoma and Texas.

My wife, little children, and two siblings dined with me and were present for our review this afternoon. They quickly found out how tough military life is. My family witnessed how we can be treated, especially when incompetent and arrogant officers order us around. Several incidents underscored the difficulties privates face—the cannon fodder from time immemorial. My sixteen-year-old brother was left with a really bad impression when he observed the rough and insulting manner an officer used toward two poor soldiers who had not arranged their backpacks like he wanted. An example needed to be made, and it was their turn today. When will it be my turn? The officer jerked out the contents of the backpacks and ordered the two soldiers to pack them again.

I took my family to the YMCA after dinner. Once it got late, we said our good-byes, hoping to reunite in the city that very night. However, when I returned to camp, the order had already been given to deny passes to the city. No one left that night, except for a daring person here and there chancing it on his own.

I had a visit from old man Gus A. Graebner, with whom I have arranged housing for my family during my absence. He has really given me the run-around. The old man still does not have the contract ready, but I see that he is bent on finding out if I am going to the slaughter. I will not let him out of my sight. I do not trust him.

Wednesday, June 5

Daybreak found us ready to march wherever destiny may take us or, as the case may be, where man's fancy declares it. Several trains left last night. Engineers and carpenters have left on the first ones. We were read orders on how we should behave in transit. I realized the hour was very close when I heard this, so I ran to a nearby office where an old friend works. As fate would have

The gallant commander in chief of the expeditionary American forces in the Great World War, General John J. Pershing, and four of the great figures in the war. Mexican American soldiers will always remember our chief and companion in arms in defense of our homeland, as we followed our flag across the battlefields of Europe at war.

it, he is among the soldiers who will remain. I left him my trunk and asked that he send it home. He is King Hinnatt, from Alice. I really trust this fellow and know he will carry out my request.

We continued ridding ourselves of everything we cannot take to France. Outside and across our barracks, we have been piling up a lot of objects we have bought or received from family or friends. We were under orders to discard them. This was unavoidable. Since we have no time to send them home, they have to be added to the pile. Numerous civilians have appeared on the streets in animal-drawn carriages and automobiles, intent on taking the material and making use of it. The heap includes many new Texan hats, leggings, soap dishes, mirrors of all shapes and sizes, and even complete and valuable uniforms, undergarments, shoes, suitcases, ties, collars, and many other items we bought while in camp. The pile includes items we received from our homes. Everything is going!

Thursday, June 6, a memorable day in our lives

We rested and waited on our backpacks until three in the afternoon. At

The larger-than-life person and president in 1917, Woodrow Wilson, the learned and brave president who defended our national honor when he declared war against the despotic German empire.

that memorable and unforgettable hour, we picked up our bags and marched in formation to the Pullman cars that would transport us across the country to our port of embarkation. Sergeants were made responsible for the cars after groups of soldiers had been assigned to them. Guards were also stationed at the front and back of the cars and told not to let anyone in or out during the trip without an order from a superior officer.

At four, the engine's whistle blew and we bid a sad farewell to the camp where we had spent such pleasant and memorable times. Camp Travis is like a nest of tender memories. This is why parts of our souls may remain after we leave, perhaps forever. As the train sped up, the large, dark, and dusty hovels that served as our barracks retreated into the distance and our eyes glimpsed their last good-byes. The engine's whistle blew at every street crossing, sounding like sighs of sadness or groans of pain at our leaving. The engineer seemed to know how we felt and, with the use of blowing steam, sounded our farewells to San Antonio and our loved ones, to whom we were unable to give our final departing embrace.

By five in the afternoon, we had gone around the great city of San Antonio and were heading north to the station of the International and Great Northern. I passed three blocks from home. The train was traveling faster and the whistle blew more often. Either because I sought some kind of relief or simply moved involuntarily, I turned my eyes homeward. I saw little ones playing in the street and I waved good-bye to them, thinking they might be my own. I cannot be sure that they were my children, but whether mine or not, I am sure they were of my *raza*, and for them as for mine, I go to war!

Gómez, Barrera, and I have sworn an oath to stay together and not separate until destiny commands it.

We are traveling in a car named "Inverary." My friends have chosen the lower berth and I have taken the top one. At sundown, we passed by Dittlinger, a quarry worked by many men of my *raza*. This is where I taught or was in charge of their children's school for a year. That combination of work camp and community is another battlefield. I waged battles until I got the county to pay the teacher who taught our children. Those were the kinds of victories I sought in civilian life, opening the school doors for the workers' children. Now that I wear the warrior's uniform I hope to win other battles and bring justice to our people as we join an afflicted humanity that is calling for the sacrifice of conscious and freethinking men. This is exactly where the idea to pick up my rifle occurred to me. I was moved by the bad treatment many members of my *raza* face in these places where the Teutonic or German people predominates. Ingrates, they deny us equality and forget the thousand and one guarantees given to their ancestors when they settled these lands. Who brought them and what were the advantages and privileges extended to those colonists? The history is there; it does not lie. I believe that those of us who have offered to fight the Germans for being unjust and arrogant could start by setting an example of the many Iscariots, the bad citizens that we often come across in these parts.

I cannot forget the racist reaction by these people toward Mexicans when our marines landed in Veracruz.[18] They swore they were ready to spill their last drop of blood against the patriotic Mexicans. What must they be saying now that we want to finish with German savagery? We need Mexican patriotism now. If not, let the pro-German propaganda do its work around here. Mexican farmworkers are being told to leave for Mexico, and that they should not fight since Germany has nothing against Mexico. Our people are not without naive people who abandon the rich harvests when they hear this. Germany promises Mexico the return of Texas and who knows how many other things. Many uninformed Mexicans have left for Mexico, possibly expecting to return when Pancho Villa becomes the Kaiser of Texas.[19] This subterfuge will eventually come to light, including the many and assorted explanations by Mexican American slackers who never understood that the call of a nation in danger was just. Many of us are on our way to defend the dignity of our people at the supreme hour of battle against the soldiers of the Imperial Prince, son of William II.

We stopped for a few moments in New Braunfels, another one of those towns known for its prejudice against the humble Mexican worker. We learned from the crowd that many of our own are already ahead of us, among them *zurdo* and *picudo*.[20] We passed by Austin at night and were unable to view the capital of our imperial state of Texas, which I still do not know.

Some men try to sing popular tunes but fail to get a response and everyone ends up laughing. Popular songs abound, but they are not easy to remember. A few nights ago, some female friends I was visiting sang my favorite song, accompanied by the piano: "La plegaria de un niño a la hora del crepúsculo."[21] The Yankee spirit can be expressed in the sad parody I have made of a song that is practically an anthem.[22]

GOOD-BYE BROADWAY! HELLO FRANCE!

Good-bye New York town, good-bye Miss Liberty,
Your light of freedom will guide us across the sea,
Ev'ry soldier's sweetheart biding good-bye,
Ev'ry soldier's mother drying her eye.
Cheer up, we'll soon be there,
Singing this Yankee song.

Chorus

Good-bye Texas, Hello France, We're one million strong,
Good-bye sweethearts, wives and mothers,
It won't take us along,
Don't you worry while we're there,
It's for you that we're fighting too,
So, good-bye Texas, Hello France,
We're going to square our debt to you.

Viva Pershing! is the cry across the sea.
We're united in this fight for liberty,
France sent us a soldier, brave La Fayette
Whose deeds and fame we cannot forget.
Now that we have the chance
We'll pay our debt to France.

Friday, June 7

I cannot say anything about the cities we passed while we were asleep, but we were close to Corsicana by daybreak. We did not stop. Breakfast was served around nine and at ten we were entering the great city of Dallas. I could not sleep most of the night because I thought we might reach this commercial metropolis early in the morning and I wanted to see it.

The trip helps us appreciate the government's excellent arrangements to insure that the troops are fully supplied. We do not lift a finger. They serve us our meals and we sleep, entertain ourselves, and write, inside top-quality Pullman cars. I doubt that thousands of us would have stepped inside one of them if it had not been for destiny's hand.

If our food is not the best that we can want or expect, it is more than enough and of good quality and taste. Anyone who is not pleased with their miserable luck can complain all they want.

We reached the beautiful city of Greenville after lunch. They ordered us off and into formation, after which we marched on their wide and well-kept streets. We returned to the train and continued with our journey. The march gave us a good break because we had been sitting too long. Our bird's-eye view of Greenville was like a dream.

Saturday, June 8

We passed through Texarkana at five in the morning and then crossed into Arkansas. I saw a pretty little town called Smokey River. The sun appeared in a pale color like in my dream that night. Pine Bluffs is another lovely and picturesque town along the way. Later in the afternoon, we passed by a city where people were bidding a festive farewell to soldiers en route to meet the Grim Reaper, the one who lays waste to everything. We stayed on the train, but young ladies gave us bouquets of flowers during our brief stop.

The chaplain and I had a brief conversation about the history of the land we are traversing. We talked about precolonial times, far into the ashes of prehistoric times, to the ancient settlers of this entire region, before the Europeans had even imagined a New World.

I fell asleep but asked my friends to wake me up when we came to the "father of all rivers," the great, vast Mississippi. My dependable friends did not forget my request. They awakened me at the right time. I got off my berth at mid-river. Even though it was nighttime, I was able to appreciate the immense volume of water the river discharges daily into the Gulf of Mexico.

Sunday, June 9

We traveled all day without stopping. This denied me the opportunity to enjoy some of the beautiful and important towns along the way. I would have wanted to write a more complete account of our journey for my children. This diary will serve them well when they study geography and learn our route. We arrived in Cleveland, Ohio, around three thirty. The sight of the great American metropolis was a big letdown. I did not see anything I could compare with the beauty I had imagined. We now know that we were traveling through the worst parts of towns, the rail-yard areas. Is this not true? I have no idea why even the day and the general look of the city seemed unpleasant. The downcast sky accentuated the dark and filthy look of the buildings, which also revealed the ravages of time. The great amounts of smoke billowing out of the many factory stacks made the heavens gray. We had ten minutes to take leave of the train. With watch in hand, I ran five minutes to the downtown area and spent the remaining five minutes rushing back to the train. Many of us took this jaunt into the great city of Cleveland, a place of historical significance that is etched in my memory.

We went along the coast of lovely Lake Erie until we arrived in Buffalo, New York. We ate dinner as we passed by the shores of that poetic lake and contemplated the history of the region. The scenery was beautiful, as was this experience in my life. We went through the city of Buffalo that night and could see its beauty and size thanks to its bright lights. This was a reminder that electricity originates in the powerful volume of water the Niagara River discharges into Lake Ontario, all along forming the world-famous Niagara Falls. Everyone knows the use of electricity has declined since before the war as a result of government orders. The Anglo-Saxon girls kissed the soldiers farewell in Buffalo. Brave Anglo-Saxon girls! Those kisses would be the last for many of democracy's gallant soldiers who passed through Buffalo this evening.

Monday, June 10

We made daybreak in Utica. This reminds me of the geography lessons I have given our children on the great industries in these cities. Clearly, this is a railway hub of great importance. Afterward, we ascended slowly into the Allegheny Mountains, a part of the Appalachian region. When we reached the highest point, the train stopped and we ate. Imagine the beauty of the scenery that others have been enjoying. We took several minutes to contemplate the lovely vistas of those poetic mountains our men of letters have often described. Many little towns were located along the sides of the road. Their houses with red roofs contrasted beautifully with the vivid green fields and the periwinkle-colored mountains. Several streams of pure and crystalline water came down the sides of the mountains and disappeared in the farmlands of the small valleys. The farms in this mountainous region are not of great size but they are very fertile and beautiful. While eating, we were able to enjoy the clean, restorative environment. We had a great time.

We continued our trek into the mountains and through great tunnels. The train stopped for a moment at Norwich. A little girl riding on her father's shoulders bought several pastries from a vendor and gave them to us. We were very grateful to that little stranger and her father for their lovely kindness. She touched our hearts. The memory will remind me to never lament our sacrifice for the children, especially since I have also left mine behind.

This was the last town we passed by day. Norwich looks lovely and important from the train.

Tuesday, June 11

We continued across the state of New York. Everything is picturesque. We passed by many cities without stopping. It was nighttime when we took a break for a good while in Middletown. A woman among the people greeting us asked us if we were Indians. She did not even recognize the people from her own race, no doubt because everyone looked the same in the dark. I explained to her that we had all kinds and pointed out the slight differences between the Indians from Oklahoma and Mexican Americans from Texas. The lady stated with pride that she could trace her history to these parts before the coming of the whites and that we could still see the traces of the indigenous race in her face.

Two young boys, about twelve and fourteen years of age, asked for our names and begged that we write to them from France. We gladly promised to write. I am to write to Robert E. Hoey, 27 Albert Street, Middletown, New York.

From the Pullman Inverary, on my way to New York and France, in active duty for the Homeland, June 11, 1918

> My dear father:
> We continued on our way across the American Union toward the northeast until we reached Buffalo, N.Y. From there we headed to the Atlantic coast. At this moment we are surrounded by the Appalachian Mountains. I have enjoyed the panoramic views and taken pleasure in making use of my imagination. I am studying geography on a firsthand basis. The new sights distract our minds. May God keep all of you well and happy like me, and may my brothers take advantage of the opportunities I am sowing for them.
> With my regards, and in closing,
> Your son,
>
> LUZ

Wednesday, June 12

We traveled the entire night without sleeping, thinking we would reach New York. We did not make it. We kept an all night vigil over our backpacks that are at the ready and began to see the first houses of our nation's great metropolis at daybreak. At seven, we arrived at a train station on the bay of New York Harbor in Hoboken, New Jersey. We got off the train and boarded the steamer *Catskill*. The boat carried us across the mouth of the Hudson River until we disembarked on Long Island. From there, we took a train to Camp Mills, located on the great island that Henry Hudson discovered while on the ship named *Half Moon*.

We got on the train about eleven. The sleepless night and the lack of a meal, especially coffee, gave me a splitting headache that spoiled my arrival at

New York, the biggest city in the United States that could become the largest one in the world once the war is over. We made the short trip on a train that lacked basic services. I had some very difficult moments, including bilious nausea, all the way to our camp. An officer asked about my illness and I said it was not serious, that the trip had caused it. He gave orders to take my name and send me to the hospital. I insisted that all I needed was a short rest. I rested under a car and was awakened by a downpour. The rain was very cold but it made me feel better, although I must have looked pretty bad because my buddies showed concern. I marched to the military camp where we were to sleep for the night and helped my friends set up our tent. We were called for supper and I told them I was not going to eat anything that day. I laid down feeling all worn out but comfortable.

It was already getting dark when Gómez woke me up to say that we had been ordered to return some of the articles from Camp Travis in exchange for others. The new equipment we received included a steel helmet. It is an interesting piece of equipment, worn to protect us from projectiles and other blows. I wrote down these numbers: ZF38 for my helmet, 44981 for my rifle, and 77 for my backpack.

Rumors were circulating that we would remain in place for six months, and this is what some of the soldiers wrote to their loved ones. As far as I am concerned the stay could take years. Nothing pleased me on account of my headache, including the time we spent waiting in line to receive the new articles that were being issued. I went to bed weak but feeling much better. I did not care to know more about Camp Mills or New York. My poor health ruined any hope of acquainting myself with the city, at least for that day.

Thursday, June 13

The bugle woke us up earlier than usual, or the cloudy and cold morning may have made it appear that way. We were ordered to prepare our backpacks and bring down the tents and, much later, to receive more equipment. The roosters do not sing any more plainly! We did exactly as ordered and were later called to fall into formation for a march. A train took us to the other side of the bay and the *Washington* carried us to a large transatlantic vessel anchored at a pier. The ship has four stacks. It is the biggest I have ever seen.

Several ladies from the Red Cross gave each soldier an orange and a sandwich at the pier. They also gave us stamped postcards to mail home, which we gladly did. The cards informed our loved ones that we were in good health.

The ship was filled with soldiers by the time we arrived. The workers at the wharf were using huge cranes to hoist our equipment and the rest of the clothing into the ship's large storage areas. Everything followed strict orders. We began to situate ourselves in different locations, and once we had claimed our hammocks and placed our belongings in them, we started to walk through the different sections of the enormous ship, including areas that were off limits to the soldiers. We wanted to learn the name of the ship. Although I was not sure, rumors suggested that the steamship was the British Navy's *Olympic*. It was the largest ship of His Majesty King George V of England.

We were given a late call to eat. This was our first meal on the blue and salty sea that was prepared by His Majesty's British cooks. It was really strange, consisting of potatoes boiled in salted water, thick chunks of boiled horsemeat, and no bread or anything else. We were disgusted to no end but no one said much. The best option was to not eat. We were given the same rations at night but with an English tea that was of poor quality or very badly prepared. The few pieces of bread they gave us were rotten and had a very bad smell. We ground our teeth but did not know whom to blame. We realized that things were turning pretty grim.

We slept like cattle or hogs during our first night on the transatlantic vessel. It is impossible to say how many people are crammed into hammocks, doubled up and poorly fed. But we are at war and will have worse nights to talk about.

Friday, June 14

We again slept over the waters of the bay of New York. Our ship is so large we scarcely feel the rocking motion caused by the movement of the tidal waters. Since we have always been land bound, we are not really accustomed to fish, especially when it is poorly prepared. They may very well be serving us shark or *matalote*.[23]

At ten, they ordered us to close the ship's portholes, to keep away from the upper deck, and to avoid saying good-bye to anyone in port. We did not like the order but had to obey it. At eleven we started to feel and hear the heavy, groaning sound of the motors and the enormous chains pulling the anchors. Afterward, we heard the sound of the propeller's drag as it began to turn and felt the ship clearing its way into the salty waters. I went down to one of the uncovered portholes and took one last look at the beautiful city of New York. Millions of people were on the docks and on top of the buildings. I could see a large number of young women waving white handkerchiefs from the windows in the buildings where they worked. This made sense. The cream of the nation was joining the most important crusade of our time. How many will remain over there, how many will return? Are the blond office workers asking these questions? Could they know what was behind the round holes on the sides of the enormous transatlantic ship? Like imprisoned rats, thousands of patriotic eyes from our nation watched with intense emotion, with youth, with life, and eager for adventure.

I do not remember, but I am almost certain that a whistle signaled our departure. The emotions, coupled with thousands of thoughts racing through our minds, may have kept us from hearing it. This made our already ominous departure from America even more depressing.

We were far out when we were allowed to open the portholes and go deck side. I practically ran to the upper deck and found a place with a good view. We could still see thousands of men and women waving tender farewells with their tiny handkerchiefs as the great city's skyscrapers started getting smaller. We passed very close to the historic Statue of Liberty. My humble thoughts were transported back to unknown places as I observed the churning seawater wash against the blackish rock mass in the middle of the bay. The memorable words of a guillotined woman unexplainably came to me, "Liberty; Liberty! So much crime is committed in your name."[24] I began to calm down with these thoughts and everything returned to normal. The city grew smaller. All we could see for miles was the white statue, enveloped by the foam left by the keel of our steamer.

Two submarine chasers escorted us. They are known for their speed and guns. Submarines have little chance against these sharks of the sea. The submarine is a fearsome monster but too awkward to surface and discharge its terrible and destructive fire. The chasers, on the other hand, are swifter and can fire their better and more modern weapons more quickly. The ironclads can sink the submarines with one discharge from their guns because they are heavier. They are so fast the submarines cannot successfully submerge, shoot, or get away. The hope is that the chasers will finish with the Kaiser's fearsome offensive weapon. The steamships patrol ahead of us, circle our ship, go away and return like hunting dogs who scour the land and find tracks for their owners. They are beautifully camouflaged with random stripes of various colors to avoid being seen or recognized by the enemy and to take them by surprise. This allows them to surprise the enemy.

Saturday, June 15

Daybreak found us on the high seas of the majestic Atlantic Ocean. Nothing much happened during the day. We had a rainy afternoon. The sky was cloudy and the wind was cold and harsh. I spent most of the day on the deck observing the most sublime of God's work. Clearly, nothing can be better than this. I have stood at the front of the steamer, close to the two heavy anchors held by heavy chains. How much more will we experience before the creaking sound of the chains drop them and signal our arrival. *Solid Ground!*

The submarine chasers left yesterday at nightfall and we are now traveling on our own. We still see gulls on our trail picking up the garbage that is thrown overboard.

Sunday, June 16

Nothing remarkable happened today. Some of the soldiers' faces show how leaving home has affected their spirits. Here as in the train, we travel day and night, the only difference is that the ship does not follow a set route but zigzags to mislead the enemy. They say we are traveling 22 knots per hour, 24 hours a day.

Few gulls accompany us now. Soldiers who have already crossed the sea tell us that we will soon be left to ourselves.

The hours are long and tedious. We spend time on the ship's deck talking about the past. My fellow Mexicans ask me about our future. I find it very difficult to tell what is in store for us. I just tell them to be on their best behavior.

The sea has turned very rough and large swells of water are crashing against the side of the great ship. We have enjoyed seeing the crashing waves, which have caused so much damage to smaller ships.

This has been our first Sunday at sea.

Monday, June 17

Last night I had a beautiful dream of being at home. I experienced joy and felt a weariness that came from who knows where. The happy moments turn bad when we wake up and face austere circumstances. What could be more difficult than to entertain sweet dreams, as in times past, and to rid ourselves of them once we realize we can never enjoy them again?

Tuesday, June 18

It looks like it rained in Sayula. Our quiet protests have finally been answered.[25] We started to receive better food today and our cooks even took part in the preparation of our meals. The hope of restoring our stomach encourages us. Some say that one can die a better death on a full stomach.

We marched on deck "A," four men abreast. To get an idea of the great size of our ship, we marched four times around. We were ordered to fall into formation at one on deck "A." This was to be our first inspection at sea. The ship was heading due north and we assembled on the south side. About three hundred men came together in formation, four abreast. The day was calm and cold. We were ordered to take our clothes off. What a sight, so many athletic bodies in the prime of their life and in good health, in short, the flower of a great nation, aboard the largest English steamer and in the middle of the Atlantic Ocean. We were to undergo a physical examination but we were also displaying the vitality of a people who just now sends its first group of men to the great slaughter. The doctors examining us would almost instantly give their approval. At that precise moment, when we were relaxed and naked, the ship's horn gave out a dull and terrifying sound and we heard someone announce the "enemy," which meant a submarine or a fire! The confusion in the lower cabins is impossible to describe, but it was terrible. Most of the soldiers did not obey instructions, and this made any movement difficult and even dangerous. We feared the guard standing before us more than the submarine or the possible discharge. The guard was so afraid he fell to the floor, having some kind of a breakdown. Another officer who was running around giving orders was just as scared. Those of us who were naked in line remained calm, thinking it was all a drill and that everyone was acting ridiculous. No one thought of getting dressed because we were staying ready to dive into a cold, salty sea that was waiting to swallow us.

My buddy Fortino Treviño has given me an important, handy gift. The barber with whom he has formed a business and bought some "hair-cutting tools" had given him a little book with much helpful information for the foot soldier or the sailor. The book is a diary for writing down experiences in great detail and with good organization. I can make good use of it. It contains maps of the different fronts. An image of the English monarch, George V, faces the title page. The diary also includes many illustrations and explanatory notes on military life. Starting today, I am going to make use of the pages of this small book that I will call "My Personal Diary." I will enter everything of importance that I have already written about my military life.

Cruttinger is a young, good-looking, and fairly well educated Anglo-Saxon. He still has a long way to go before he can hold up to the rigors of the military. He always remembers his good mother and a girlfriend whose photo he cannot be without. His hammock is next to mine. We share conversations to pass away the hours, and he shares the sweets he regularly receives from home. We must not forget that men are fashioned out of boys.

On the Olympic, *June 18, 1918*

It is nighttime and I am sure that more than one soul trembles when he recalls today's simple exercise, which was meant to prepare us for a real submarine attack or the detonation of a floating bomb or some other explosive placed at the bottom of the sea. The many soldiers who do not give these training exercises the importance they deserve will be among the thousands who will drown like rats when this really occurs.

Wednesday, June 19

We follow the same routine. We get up, put our hammocks in order, go to breakfast, climb up to deck "A" to march with our rifles, and then move out to the main deck to chat or to pass the long hours of the day. The men with money buy things to eat from the canteens where everything is sold at high prices. This reminds me of the newspaper sellers and the fruit vendors in the American passenger trains. Maybe this only happens in the United States of the North.

A vulgar, dishonest, and mischievous Anglo-Saxon of about twenty-eight years of age sleeps among our crowded soldiers. They say he has married numerous times and promoted to sergeant on several occasions only to be demoted as often on account of his many vices. He is almost always doing K.P. or guard duty. He served as a squire to our mascot, the bear. Although he is very obedient to his superiors, officers always have to be around to insure his good behavior. Red, as he is known to the troops, today offered to sell us very delicious and inexpensive pies, for five cents less than at the canteen. We have no idea when he went into business with the King of England or opened up his pastry shop on board. We can say, however, that his inexpensive pies are also good, judging from the samples he has given us. Red says he buys them cheap. We could not care less about his purchase price because this could well be one of his many ruses on the high seas, like the burglaries or acts of piracy that occurred not long ago. Red already knows many tricks, but he can also learn or invent some new ones while at sea. We are curious to know how he secures the sweets, but it is enough that we save a nickel, this is a fair deal for impulsive soldiers.

Although our band was only meant to entertain our officers, they came down to the soldiers' deck and played for a while. The music seemed more beautiful than ever. We thought about our past, especially the loved ones we left on the other side of the ocean. They are becoming more distant with each passing day. This is really a demanding part of our destiny. How many millions of men must be sharing this with us? How many of us will die at the moment of truth? The survivors who remain to tell the truth will share the joy.

Thursday, June 20

It is impossible to know how many people are traveling on the ship. Some say the entire 90th Division is here, and if this is true, the numbers are large. We cannot believe this because the division is supposed to have close to sixty thousand men. Nonetheless, thousands of us are packed in here like sardines. Each soldier carries more than 87 pounds, on top of the weight of his person with uniform. We hear the ship also carries about three hundred horses, many machine guns, and heavy caliber, long-range cannon, some for shooting airplanes. We carry rifles, machine guns, one-pounders, mortars and Colt pistols, a month's supply of rations for us and for the horses, and enough charcoal for the trip, a month's worth for four stacks burning day and night. The ship has a crew of six hundred men. It is incredible that so much can fit in a shell like this, but one can better appreciate it when seeing how everything is organized and the enormous size of the ship. There are four decks above the water and so many more below. With all of this, the ship travels nonstop, day and night, at 22 knots per hour.

At daybreak, we noticed several submarine chasers escorting us. They do not come close and I cannot tell whether they are British or ours.

We took an extraordinary bath on the ship's deck. The English sailors told us we could bathe while they were washing the upper deck. The water was very cold but we were not going to miss the opportunity to say we bathed in the salty waves of the Atlantic before dying in the trenches of France.

Friday, June 21

We saw land at a distance this morning. An airplane later flew over us and sent signals to the ship's officers. We later saw a big observation balloon that seemed to be anchored to some rock buried in the sea or to a ship that was heading in that direction. I recorded the names of the submarine chasers today: F52, H6A, 48, 66, and 00. The land we have been observing since this morning is White Island, a good point of entry into Great Britain. We will be disembarking at Southampton. Its entrance has been planted with many mines for fear of German submarines. This, along with the low water depth and large size of our ship, has slowed us down. Since the sailors are English, they know the sea like their hands. We would be in trouble if they did not.

It must have been close to midday when we could no longer move forward because of the low tide. We had to wait for the high tide. Two gentlemen with embellished headgear came to our ship aboard two small steamers. They were English officers complying with some kind of protocol. They soon left.

We reached a great dock at 3:50 but did not disembark. The fog and smoke created a yellowish sunset as a backdrop to grayish clouds. We passed by Portsmouth. Several forts at a distance are guarding the entrance to the port. Many ships were already anchored while others were arriving or leaving the bay. It was a beautiful view of a port that was protected from sky and land. Everything was new to us.

I find it fascinating to observe the land that for many years I have known as Great Britain. I see her now. Praise God, who would have thought this! All I know about her history, legends, and culture comes to mind alongside the reality that I take in and contemplate.

Our steamship is anchored and we are ready. This is how we waited all night, but we did not disembark.

Saturday, June 22

We went ashore after lunch but not before observing some unpleasant scenes that unfolded on the dock the entire morning—an untold number of dirty women and children in tatters. We saw many young but thin and pale women, as well as many hopeless old ones, like the witches from the time of Robin Hood or the ones in William Shakespeare's immortal writings. The wretched people would approach the ship to beg. The soldiers would throw them their "hardtack," the American biscuits prepared without lard and salt, as well as cans of "cornwilly" or salmon. We cannot say this is a typical representation of the English people, in other words, we cannot judge an entire nation by a few poor citizens. They could be professional beggars—the children of misery—the kind we find among all peoples. We believe it just as unfair and insensitive when Anglo-Saxons judge our entire *raza* on the basis of indigent, uneducated, and vice-ridden people.

By ten, we had set foot on the land that is sacrosanct to the Anglo-Saxons and were told to seek cover under a warehouse that functioned as a workshop. This is to keep the enemy from knowing how many soldiers are coming from America and to insure a less hazardous passage across the English Channel. At eleven, we were given some very well written letters printed on rose paper. These were welcoming statements from the great English monarch to the humble soldiers of democracy. It was an invitation to visit the important, famous, and historic Windsor Castle—His Majesty's Royal Home. This seems like a fairy tale. The time has come for kings to shake the hands of humble shepherds, ordinary villagers! This unforgettable message also goes to the soldiers of my *raza*, the descendants of Benito Juárez, who in another era had the just fortitude to sentence the Austrian prince, the usurper of Mexico, to a firing squad! What a coincidence! These soldiers now come to give their lives, if necessary, to defeat an empire or several of them, and to help other crowns on the verge of falling, even as we speak. We find mother earth in such a predicament today! At any rate, we will have plenty of time to comply with such a special request from the noble monarch, His Majesty George V of England. For the moment, the trenches call us, from there we will attack the Germans until we force them to give back or abandon the land taken from the Belgians and the French. Can the world ever acknowledge that this is what the ground troops are to do, especially the Mexicans? The Germans call us masses of soldiers because they think they can *amasarnos*, or mold us, like dough.[26] We will remember this friendly invitation from the august English monarch as a special twist of irony.

We spent long tiring hours packed under a glass roof and then walked to the city, up to where the guards required passports. A letter they had given us was not enough. The understanding may have been that the invitation would be good once we swept away the last German from France. Any way you look at it, this is one of life's well-played jokes.

A small but well-armed battleship approached the dock at six in the afternoon. Three others followed. The transports will take us across the channel and leave us on the blessed ground of heroic France. We are leaving England without seeing anything, while the few people on the streets share nothing with us, nor do they care about our being here. They may be tired of the war and of seeing soldiers in uniform, or they may be failing to extend us some basic courtesies. We, who believed the spirit of the crusaders of King Richard the Lionheart still reigned, could not be more disappointed.

Several trains came for the wounded British soldiers who had been brought from the front. These scenes are not pleasant but neither should they make us weep. We ask every one of the returning soldiers, "What is the front like?" Many do not answer, possibly because they were not there and do not know what to say. The ones who respond say, "It's hell over there." What a way to talk to Europe's only hope. Let them say what they want, they are only seeing things for what they are now, not realizing that the entente will sink forever if the "tin soldiers" do not measure up.[27]

I boarded the *King Edward*. Only about four thousand men could fit. We stayed on deck as the waves rocked the anchored ship and the night fell upon us. We looked at England for the final time. She gave the appearance of an enormous cloud rising over the northern horizon. We could not see a single light due to the protective measures against submarines, zeppelins, and warplanes frequently found in these areas.

The steamship started moving at an impressive speed and we suddenly felt seasick. We had traveled for ten days and nights without the nausea, but now we feared the waves. What a horrible and disgusting night we had on account of our unsettled stomachs and the rolling sea! We fed the fish of the English Channel the supper of four thousand men. We were very cold on deck, and the smell was unbearable in our cabins. The ship's movement caused headaches and continuous vomiting. All this will make for a memorable trip in our otherwise ordinary lives. The soldiers piled on one another like sardines. Misery united them. The vomiting was so widespread that pale, somber, and sick faces were everywhere. The strange thing was that the time that we were sick passed without any cursing. Few men spoke and no one listened to the occasional song that seemed to appear out of nowhere. The repulsive and upsetting scene was unbearable. Thousands of soldiers were unable to exit the cabins and had to vomit inside. That is the way it was, thousands of soldiers either had a good supper that evening or they had plenty of coffee, hardtack, and salmon. Oh, the canned salmon! Who will ever forget it?

Several British soldiers who had been wounded at the front but had convalesced and recovered at a hospital in England accompanied us on the *King Edward*. They were returning to the trenches. They did not get sick. They are more accustomed to the kind of situation I just described. I have joined them in conversation. They describe unbelievable experiences to anyone who is interested in their stories of being on the front and in the trenches. We spoke at length about this. I asked so many questions they thought I did not believe everything they told me. With this, our conversation shifted to our lives in America, and this gave me the opportunity to talk their ears off since none of them have lived there. Some of the soldiers are Australian and others are from Great Britain. The amusing part in the conversation came when they asked me whether Mexicans and the Indians of Oklahoma still lived like savages. I decided to have a good time and told them that yes, the Indians of Oklahoma and the Mexicans had to leave behind our bows and arrows as well as our shields in order to carry rifles and wear uniforms. "And how did you become soldiers so soon?" one of them suddenly asked. I responded, "the Indians and Mexicans are soldiers by profession over there. Do your newspapers ever tell you of our continuous warring? We fight many of those wars for pleasure." I do not know if they took the hook. They only started to understand that I spoke in jest when I stated, "The Germans are going to have their hands full with all these Indians from America and if they get us angry, we will eat the ones we kill." We had a good time and if they did not believe everything I said to them, they at least know that they cannot pull the wool over my eyes in Europe.[28]

We were given postcards to sign and send home. This is what was printed on them:

> My Loved Ones in America:
> The steamship that carried us across the Atlantic arrived safely at
> a French port. Long live France.
>
> Luz

Sáenz with about fifty students of varying ages attending a segregated school in Moore, Texas. © 1910, Photo 8, Sáenz Papers, Nettie Lee Benson Latin American Collection, University of Texas Libraries, University of Texas at Austin.

Sáenz with more than seventy students of varying ages attending a Mexican school in San Agustín, or Moore, Texas. © 1915, Photo 6, Sáenz Papers, Nettie Lee Benson Latin American Collection, University of Texas Libraries, University of Texas at Austin.

BIRD'S-EYE VIEW OF CAMP TRAVIS, SAN ANTONIO, TEXAS.   222774

Bird's-eye view of Camp Travis, San Antonio, Texas. Reverse side of postcard from Sáenz to his father, Rosalío Sáenz, June 11, 1918. Postcard Collection, Sáenz Papers, Nettie Lee Benson Latin American Collection, University of Texas Libraries, University of Texas at Austin.

Rookies Drilling at Military Camp.

Rookies drilling at military camp, Camp Travis. Reverse side of postcard from Sáenz to nephew Sam, March 1918. Postcard Collection, Sáenz Papers, Nettie Lee Benson Latin American Collection, University of Texas Libraries, University of Texas at Austin.

▲ Sáenz with fellow faculty members at Benavides Public School, 1925–26 school year. Photo 24, Sáenz Papers, Nettie Lee Benson Latin American Collection, University of Texas Libraries, University of Texas at Austin.

▶ Sáenz as a delegate to the 1928 convention of the American Legion, San Antonio, Texas, 1928. Postcard Collection, Sáenz Papers, Nettie Lee Benson Latin American Collection, University of Texas Libraries, University of Texas at Austin.

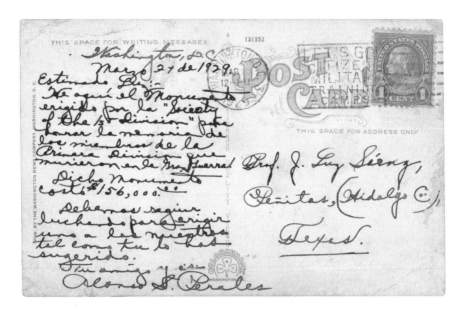

▲ Postcard note from Alonso S. Perales to Sáenz, referring to the idea of erecting a monument to Mexican World War I veterans, March 27, 1929. Postcard Collection, Sáenz Papers, Nettie Lee Benson Latin American Collection, University of Texas Libraries, University of Texas at Austin.

◄ Sáenz and "a group of my students," 1948. Photo 9, Sáenz Papers, Nettie Lee Benson Latin American Collection, University of Texas Libraries, University of Texas at Austin.

Sáenz and other unidentified persons listen attentively to Jose T. Canales speak in an auditorium, undated. Photo 20, Perales Papers, Nettie Lee Benson Latin American Collection, University of Texas Libraries, University of Texas at Austin.

A full auditorium of mostly Mexican men possibly listening to speakers, undated. Photo 22, Sáenz Papers, Nettie Lee Benson Latin American Collection, University of Texas Libraries, University of Texas at Austin.

France

Sunday, June 23

Last night's difficulties left us drained and with headaches. The *King Edward* looked more disgusting during the day than at night. Fog enveloped us and we were unable to tell when we had reached the French coast. I realized this at 7:45 in the morning, when the ship had already docked. Once on deck, I could tell what was before us. We were in the French waters of the Napoleons and Victor Hugo.

After offering a prayer to God for granting me the opportunity to see what I had dreamed since childhood, I felt a deep sense of fulfillment in my soul. We are here, in the middle of things. Reality is before us in bold form. We must meet our responsibility as more than an expression of our ideals, as a thorough accounting of ourselves to a world that has its eyes fixed on us. Long live the men of our *raza* in France, or may they die with honor.

The unfolding panorama of natural beauty is new to us. The rising and radiant sun salutes France as its people make the supreme sacrifice to secure their freedom from the yoke of the usurper's heavy boot. The sky is clear. Some old buildings are nearby. They are familiar because I have seen them in the old textbooks back home.

We disembarked at one of the docks at nine. The arrival of troops is such a common sight in France that our appearance was met by the coolest of receptions imaginable. It was enough for us to give up or go into a rage. We were expecting some kind of appreciation from the people we came to help liberate from the affront, tyranny, and violence of a tyrant who has the nation in its clutches. We are also here to pay a debt that some of our countrymen previously incurred, but this does not justify the lack of courtesy or appreciation. This does not mean we overlook other reasons for this situation. One explanation could be the unfortunate suffering caused by the war, which we will also feel very soon. We can see and understand this suffering. They have lost many men. Few homes have escaped losing someone in the Great War. That explains the sad and cold reception in England as well as in France. But I ask myself again, is this reason enough for the utter lack of sympathy toward us when we are here to make their cause our own? Or maybe it is none of this. They may be thinking we are acting in our own self-interest? Whatever the case, the very decision to join their side should be enough to expect a sign of friendship. There is more. Based on what I discovered from my conversations with the soldiers, people from England seem to be deeply jealous and distrustful of the Yankee soldier. They find themselves down, and we, the "tin soldiers," are their only hope; however, they remain very self-centered. They cannot reject us because they would be committing suicide or murder at the hands of the Germans who are hunting them down. They also fear that if the Allies win, the army from the new world will be credited with the victory. The truth of the matter is that envy has overtaken the hearts of the crusaders like in the past.

Since disembarking, we have come to feel the unusual circumstance that will surround us while in Europe. Let us prepare for this too.

Typical French scenes flashed before us. Very close to the dock, on both sides of the street, we see the posts of the French sentries. We also witness soldiers in heated conversations everywhere. The streets of Le Havre, which is the name of the port where we landed, are constructed with pieces of lumber like in early America. We walked across several streets and plazas and some people greeted us. A number of children begged for "sous," or cents. A child of about ten years of age who appeared to be well educated did not ask for "sous" and even seemed embarrassed that his friends would beg. The child approached us and after shaking our hands gave us some beautiful wild pansies from the bouquet he was carrying. I saved mine between the pages of the diary I am writing and will keep them as a reminder of the unknown child. I will learn his name some day.

The eastern section of Le Havre has a rest camp for soldiers arriving by water. Some say the English own it. We will rest here today and perhaps tonight as well. We had to walk up a narrow and serpentine street to get here. The king of Belgium, who reigned until recently, lived on the same street. The entire world has strong feelings for him because of the courage he displayed in defending his homeland against the rapacious and savage Teutonic monster. The entrance to his residence displays the Allies' flags in a beautiful flower vase and a Belgian flag that floats lazily on a short pole. A big cloth sign strung across the street reads, "Welcome American Soldiers."

I could not help but notice all the old buildings covered with plants and flowers and surrounded by garden walls full of exuberant vegetation that reflected the owner's capricious nature. The excellent French writers find material for their masterful works in these kinds of buildings.

Ever since this morning, we have been hearing the dull sounds of the artillery from the horrible battlefields toward the north. They sound like a distant storm approaching. Who can doubt their obvious presence when they are so close to us?

Airplanes have been flying over our camp, but they are ours or belong to the other Allies. These are the typical military scenes we witness every day.

Monday, June 24 (St. John's day)

I recalled, without any apparent reason, my community's tradition of running the cock on St. John's day. It was a special day of celebration for our elders.[1]

Last night was unforgettable. The camp is really a prison surrounded by a high wire fence to keep soldiers from getting out. The camp also has numerous guards who also discourage the soldiers from going to the city. Many women and an even larger number of boys and girls gather by the fence to beg for souvenirs or to sell something. They sell sweets, and some women in tatters even sell liquor to the soldiers. This is prohibited, but the women wrap the bottles with their robes and toss them into the fenced area while the guards make their rounds in the opposite direction. The soldiers pick the bottles up and throw what they believe covers the cost over the fence. The transaction is interesting. The little rascals and the less than saintly women fight over the money. They scratch, push, and scream when the coins hit the ground. We can testify to a generous amount of street cursing. We do not have to know French to know what is being said.

The sight is nothing more than one of the scenes immortalized by Victor Hugo in *Les Misérables*.

We were ordered to march at ten and quickly readied ourselves since we were tired of our imprisonment. We prefer to be at the front after our difficult night and the poor quality of food. Some fled to the city claiming that whatever punishment they receive cannot be worse than going to the slaughter and that anything was preferable to being locked up in here. They knew they would not be forgiven and are in jail now. They swear to have had a great time. What else can we say about the life we lead? They came back very drunk and tired, but very satisfied! Their behavior was not simply a case of insanity. It required nerves and a canny intelligence to avoid the guards and face the music. It was really an adventure. They were once sergeants but they are now privates. We applaud our buddies without following their example.

We began leaving the sad camp at 10:30 in the morning and marched through the same streets of Le Havre, saw the Belgian king's emblem, and saluted the flags of the Allies. We say farewell to these places as we march away, perhaps forever. We were not able to see other parts of the city, and this may also happen with the other cities we will cross. This is a reminder that we did not come to visit or to make friends but to defeat an enemy that has trampled the rights of humanity. We will have enough time to travel throughout Europe once we finish with this growing and horrendous tragedy that envelops us completely. This is a sad truth, but a truth nevertheless.

Meanwhile, we continue marching forward, eager and determined to face the supposedly formidable and invincible enemy and to demonstrate the bravery of the men of a free America.

We were already on the train by three in the afternoon. An interesting train! What a contrast to our own! Everything was small, and it had no amenities. Each of the cars that will carry us the entire trip had a sign that read: capacity 10 horses or 40 men (capacité 10 chevaux—40 hommes). This tells us that there is no difference between man and horse over here and that ten of the former are worth as much as forty of the latter in war.

Before bidding a farewell to the port, we turned to some typical scenes. I recognized the buildings, streets, and people from books I have read. The soldiers in uniform and the small groups of constables or civil police were also present. They are probably talking about the latest news from the front or our arrival. They may also be wondering about our comportment in the field of battle. Our sad appearance tells them little about how brave and victorious we will be at the decisive hour when many of us will die.

We left at four in trains with miniature engines and cars that were better suited for transporting beasts of burden than men. At any rate, we are in France and not far from the sounds of the front, where men are worth nothing and empty shoes abound by the thousands. Nothing will do us any good here, not even the Pullman cars of our country.

We could still see some of France during the day. I do not want to miss the opportunity when there is something to see. We did not pass by any important city, but did see many beautiful fields of wheat, sugar, and potatoes, as well as little villages where we heard the sharp screaming of children asking for souvenirs.

The train did not stop. We will pass by the historic city of Rouen on our way to Paris. I would love to visit this ancient city, which holds so many memories among the French. The night came quickly and we found ourselves preparing to sleep in the horse stalls that passed for railroad cars. My God, it is crowded! The best way to sleep is standing up.

Tuesday, July 25

Just as we thought, the train passed by Rouen and the outskirts of Paris last night. Little would have been served by staying awake since everything was dark. The French government had ordered that no one light a match, much less a lamp, after six in the evening. The sergeant of our stable-dormitory closed the door very early, leaving little room for air to circulate. We know that a law prohibits groups from congregating in the streets of the towns along the way and requires everyone to retire by sundown.

We traveled toward the south of France the entire night and woke up to a beautiful morning and a soft breeze. The newness of our surroundings made everything enjoyable. Our traveling conditions, however, kept us from fully appreciating everything on its own terms. Our outlook would have probably been completely different under better circumstances.

We have gone through important cities today, although I have not been able to find out their names because the trains do not stop for anything. We arrived in Troyes at four in the afternoon and got off at the next station. From there, we marched to Latrecy, located half a mile away from where we will be spending the night. In a small park covered by luxuriant trees, we pitched tents that only accommodate two soldiers each.

After setting our tents, we took to the streets like hungry dogs. Little or nothing was worth seeing. We made it from one end of town to the other in a few steps. Latrecy is a small village of humble farmers and laborers. Few people live here because most of them have gone to the populated centers where they can better serve their government. The villages only had items that munitions factories or other industrial workshops could not use.

The most notable sight that we came across on the street was a group of gypsies. They follow the armies like a band of crows to take whatever advantage they can. They were selling small items like sweet toasted chestnuts, pecans, and dried figs. Of course, everything was expensive. The busybodies are the consummate Jews. Since the soldiers have nowhere to spend what they have, they purchase everything. The buzzard-merchants soon run out of things to sell and are left with profits that barely fill their insatiable appetite.

Wednesday, June 26

Latrecy is one of those small towns that have escaped the ravages of war since the time of the Moors, when Charles Martel defeated them between Poitiers and Tours.[2] The remaining residents are a few decrepit old men and women, some children, and women who care for their properties. The rest are either at war or living in towns that offer more protection and a better livelihood. I had time to walk the short and narrow streets, visit a school that was closed down and a chapel where I prayed. I then had a conversation with a priest. I have struggled to make myself understood with the little French I know. I have not been able to buy a book to study French. I was at the church until 11:30. After a short rest in my tent, I surveyed our entire camp, thinking about how it looked to the people of the little town. At 2:30 I decided to climb a beautiful mountain a short distance to the east of the village. I went up through a number of vineyards and reached the summit without any difficulty. It is covered with beautiful pines and other trees, including many fragrant cedars. The ground was blanketed with soft green grass and it called me to take a siesta. I fell asleep while recalling delightful memories. I awoke and took a walk around the summit of the mountain where I found several worn pathways. Shortly after that, I heard the sound of airplanes flying overhead. They were very high and I could not tell whether they belonged to us, our Allies, or the enemy. My attention was especially drawn to the sound of the cannon nearby. I could even hear the whistling of the shells passing by at a low elevation. Not knowing if I was in danger, I went down to inquire and found out that our artillery was target shooting on both sides of the mountain and that the planes were directing the fire.

Thursday, June 27

Nothing important has occurred and the passing hours tire us because we have nothing to do. I went up the mountain again, this time with Gómez and Barrera. They had to return quickly because of orders. I stayed behind and spent hours in deep thought. Again, I took a siesta under the beautiful trees, observed the lovely views from the top, and heard our planes zooming over the mountain as they directed the artillery fire. I came down at suppertime. I will share this fast-moving day with my family when I return. I have so much faith in our victory that I believe our journey will be quick, up and back.

Friday, June 28

I remembered my mother while in church today, as this is the anniversary of her death. Then I took to the streets until I reached places where I enjoyed talking to the few people still in town. They are working hard harvesting hay in their fields and taking it to the stables. Most of them use heavy two-wheel carts that appear in the history books. This is how far behind they are from the rest of the world, all the while working slowly, talking, and having a good time. Both men and women wear the typical aprons. The women seem to walk comfortably in wooden shoes. They make a sound like the cattle with their hooves when they walk on hard or well-paved streets. They are a sight to behold as they make their long walks with ease. The workers tell me the hay season has been very good and they expect to fill their stables for the entire winter.

My dear wife:

I pray to God that all of you are well. I arrived safe and sound in France. Now I can really say I am in France. Too bad the censors do not allow us to say much. God grant us life and health and my return. You will then see me recounting with pride all the ups and downs of my ocean voyage while at war.

Do not worry about me, even if the letters take a long time to reach you.

Luz

Adán and Sam:

I really want to see you and tell you many wonderful stories about all the towns. Many children attend school just like you. I will not be able to see you today, tonight, or tomorrow morning, and maybe not for many mornings that may eventually become years. This matters little. The longer the time, the more I will want to see you, and the more that I will look forward to hearing everything you have been doing.

Be good and know that I always think of you.

Luz

My dear father:

We have finally reached heroic France, the home of the illustrious Victor Hugo. The mere act of being in this country of heroes reminds me that, by lineage, I also belong to a raza that is no less heroic. It is our *raza* that can rightfully claim pride—if we can call it so—for removing two filibustering emperors, one of them a close relative to the Kaiser, William II of Germany.[3] Our cause is just and we will be victorious.

Your son,

Luz

Saturday, June 29

They ordered us to fall in after lunch and get ready for a bath. We all took our soap, towels, and clothing and were glad to take the walk, which turned out to be a veritable outing.

We never would have imagined what occurred next. We were made to march at a fast pace for three miles until we reached a small bridge with a small, crystal clear and playful river flowing underneath. We were perspiring and exhausted in spite of the cool morning. The officers ordered us to halt and to immediately jump in the water. The first ones in screamed uncontrollably. They would say nothing and jump out quickly. Some never went back in. The water was very cold. Small pieces of ice were still hanging under the shade of the bridge. The bath ended very quickly since we could not stand the water that was as cold as it was clear.

The water was so crystalline that no one could have imagined the depth of the small river. It was four feet deep instead of the two or three we thought. We took a different route back and went through two little towns that appeared deserted. Despite this, we met very hospitable people during a short stop at one of the towns. The people insisted that we enjoy some refreshments. Some accepted the offer. When they took out their money to pay, the townspeople refused to accept it.

Sunday, June 30

I have been idle today and the time has passed slowly. We fell in around ten and marched to a vacant place close to the chapel. The chaplain of the regiment made use of a makeshift pulpit to worship the eternal Father in his own way and then preached a sermon on several topics. We sat on the ground during the service. The village priest was also present. Instead of sermonizing in the evangelical tradition, he criticized the religion and traditions of the residents of the village.

The townspeople dressed in their Sunday best. They really appreciate that our military is here. I spoke with several families to share experiences and improve my French vocabulary. I am interested in learning the language so I can know the people better. Some of my friends say I am wasting my time, and I tell them that I will be vindicated.[4]

I took a siesta at the usual hour. I miss the ones I used to take. The sun is unbearable in our small tents, so is the fine dust that settles in our lungs and the constant clatter of my fellow soldiers who have nothing better to do but make noise. Can anyone believe that so many people do not know how to make good use of their time? Knowing this is exactly what helps us take advantage of life's opportunities. The slaves to routine quickly despair and drag us down to the abyss.

We returned to the small towns of Memey and Vormy and their friendly people.

One of our soldiers of German descent shot himself in the foot as we were getting ready for the afternoon's rifle inspection. The unfortunate act was intentional because no one had orders to load their rifles. The pressure is mounting as word gets around that we are about to take our place at the line of fire. The poor soldier committed a serious mistake if he did it on purpose. He may have thought the injury would land him in a hospital, but this did not happen. A doctor showed up instantly, cleaned the wound, applied some ointment, wrapped some heavy bandages around the wound, and got him ready to serve. Shortly after that, he received his punishment, which was also a warning to the rest of us. He was assigned to guard duty for the entire night. Those of us who know what this means feel sorry for the poor soldier. May we always remember this lesson, "La guerre est la guerre."

Monday, July 1

We were ordered to prepare our backpacks this morning. This alarmed us because we did not know where we were going. I had seen the orders that we were to head for some little villages for some exercises and resupplying. I told my buddies but they did not believe me. They thought I was hiding the truth from them and that they were being sent to a front line. I told them not worry themselves to death, everything in due time, as our elders would say. Why do lies spread faster than the truth? It may be that the lie moves back and forth with the same rapidity as the wind that carries it, while the truth simply endures even as it faces the flames of hell. At any rate, someone had already put out the lie that I was mistaken and that we were going to the front. Some lies have taken such a hold of the soldier that he will take them to his grave.

We began to file out of the little town early in the morning to the sound of marching tunes played by our band members at the head of the line. Our flag was waving freely. The roads looked like white ribbons before we marched on them. They later gave the appearance of dark olive snakes. We marched from Latrecy to Rouvres four abreast, with our rifles on our shoulders and bayonets fixed. A breeze blew from the south, gentle enough to caress and unfurl our flag. It was impressive. The band director filled the air with sounds from his exquisite silver bugle that communicated orders and reminded us of our duty. This is the sound that leads responsible men to sacrifice everything. Our fallen men cannot feel the same way about their supreme sacrifice, buried as they are in the same trenches, for the same cause. We continued marching across vast prairies in silence or in meditation. Were we all seeing the same thing? Our flag was a few steps away and its beautiful colors stood out against the backdrop of France's grayish skies. It never looked more beautiful. I had never felt such affection until that moment when I imagined our country on the flag. And what is the meaning of homeland? My loved ones who I left across the sea and for whom I am following this flag and shall continue to follow until I either fall or triumph. From this moment on the flag represents everything to me in these foreign lands. If we fall, we will have been defending the honor of a *raza*, our homeland, and demonstrating by example to our children and fellow citizens how one dies in building a nation.

As the sky cleared up, the fatigue of the march and the weight of our packs on our backs made us feel the heat even more. We would walk an hour and rest for ten minutes. Our bugle would call us on, onward, onward! We finally reached the little town, Rouvres-sur-Aube, all dusty, thirsty, and hungry. The Aube is a tributary of the Seine, which passes through the heart of Paris. We had marched twelve kilometers. The townspeople are humble, generous, and very friendly. Large numbers of families live here, but few men are around because most are at war.

Barrera, Gómez, and I needed a place to sleep and claimed a shack used for storing hay for cattle. It was full of vermin, including a large number of spiders of all kinds and shapes. Ridding the place of the primal beings will be a major job for these three Sammies. After resting a bit, we went to the River Aube to bathe. The cold and clear waters seemed to call us. We later found out that bathing was not permitted at that spot, and we were so carefree doing it. Our life and thoughts returned to normal after the bath and a good steak dinner.

Tuesday, July 2

General Headquarters placed Sergeant Irwin in charge of our Intelligence Office. We took a beautiful road toward the west for rifle training in a vacant field. I set about studying in the afternoon with a book for learning French.

The officers as well as the troops behave themselves around French ladies, although it may still be too early for the soldiers to show their true character. The French women act very modestly. Girls between twelve and fourteen years of age tend the cattle in the neighboring fields. They leave with the cattle in the morning and return in the afternoon. The cows are going to make our lives difficult because they do not abide by our sense of cleanliness. They sleep exactly where we have to sweep in the mornings. As expected, the soldiers curse the cows and their owners, the government and lack of government.

Wednesday July 3

The lieutenant again took charge of our detachment on a day that was different from yesterday. I do not find this officer likeable; to the contrary, he bothers me and I am even hostile toward him. I have requested on several occasions to be transferred out but, unfortunately, I have not been successful. The captain has told me that it is up to the lieutenant to decide whether to transfer me or not. He rejects the request by saying I am better off here. I disagree.

We spent a good amount of time studying the manual of arms.[5] Our group includes some poor guys who have always worked under conditions that are very different from the rough and brutal military life. The poor souls could not handle their rifles as easily as the rest of us of humble backgrounds who are like oak trees; we have been thoroughly tested by the elements. We are ready to exploit misfortune itself. Who wins the wars? Is it really the ones who celebrate victory with speeches, drinks, and applause from thrilled audiences in smoke-filled rooms? No, clearly not. The people who can declare true victory are here, but they have to wait until days after the battles to treat their wounds and clean the dirty and ragged uniform they wore in the trenches.

We followed orders to march on the double, stop, lower weapons, and then continue moving forward. The movements had to be executed quickly and with precision. We were not able to move in unison because some soldiers were clumsy. They had the will but lacked the training. This irritated the officer to no end and, no matter how many times he repeated the order, some men continued to make mistakes. We were marching up and down a sloping foothill and only did the maneuver for a short while before we became exhausted. It was two in the afternoon and the sun was hotter than usual on that day, hour, and place. The soldiers became more tired and less able to execute orders. The officer grew angry with the poor inept soldiers, and we became irritated with him for being stupid and unjust. We could not understand why everyone should be punished when a few were at fault. At one point I found myself lowering my rifle in front of the officer, and I must have shown my displeasure with the way I did it because he came up to my face and said, "I can tell in your face what you want to tell me." "I am glad of it," I answered, without understanding why I had said it, but continued standing my ground. It was not long before I understood that I had made a mistake by talking back to an angry officer. All I could see at that moment was the unfairness, and I could have cared less about anything else. Moreover, the "I am glad of it" that I hurled at him was appropriate and courteous. I believe that we have come to Europe to defend our honor and not to accept humiliation, especially when it is unwarranted.

Thursday, July 4

This day is so different from yesterday! What cold weather! Today marks the independence of the thirteen original English colonies. The keystone of the United States of America was set in 1776. We had to use our thick wool coats all morning. It rained a little. Since it was a national holiday, we had no work responsibilities and took walks down the narrow streets and around the little town. The afternoon warmed up a bit but we did not take off our over-coats. A baseball game was scheduled for the afternoon between teams from General Headquarters and Company B of the 360th Infantry Battalion. The game was to be played on the field across from the famous château owned by a duke, in the northeastern part of the village. The château's importance, pic-turesque appearance, and history are best left for better-informed and skilled pens to describe than to a lowly private who only collects brief notes about the life he leads. I will note my observations on everything that involves us or that is important to us.

The mansion is typical of the French nobility. It is two stories high, with balconies, many furniture pieces, and of solid rock and brick construction and blue-slate roofing. Several attractive carriage houses are in the back, ready to be occupied by the guests' vehicles, of which there are many. The outside is white and it strikes a beautiful contrast with the surrounding dark green forest of tall pines and old juniper trees. A canal of crystalline water from the Aube River encircles it. A small lake or recreational pool of water with many aquatic plants accentuates its beauty. The roads that cross the park toward the castle are lovely. They are white, straight, and lined on both sides by tall and elegant trees, whose luxuriant branches meet on top and form a thick canopy. These roads are veritable boulevards. The park has about thirty acres and is fenced in by a thick seven-foot wall. The Aube River flows through the park and the canal runs outside. The view of the castle and the park is beautiful. I have not been inside the castle but Gómez and Barrera have visited it often and tell of its beauty and luxury.

Our colonel lives in the château. My buddies who often have to relay orders from General Headquarters are able to see the elegance of the place. I have seen the duke several times and he does not strike me as very old. He always seems to be worrying about something and dresses modestly, and even poorly and plain. He wears civilian clothing with the "putees" worn by French soldiers. His son, who is around twenty, often accompanies him. The son has spent his time talking and walking with some French ladies who may be related to him. We do not know why he does not join the military, probably because he is physically weak, and even rickety and effeminate. The few families I have observed have left me with an unfavorable opinion of the nobility. I believe they represent a social class that degenerates over time. They could not survive the front lines of the imperiled homeland nor do they encourage us to ever want to have their waxen-colored skin (lacking blood), straight hair, and delicate hands that are only useful in the vice-ridden singing cafés. They may be the ones who govern France's destiny and enlighten the world, but they fail to measure up because of their poor physical condition and lack of intelligence. The Hugos, Flammarions, Gambettas, and Napoleons did not emerge from this class.[6] The nobility cannot avoid one thing: worrying about the future. Will their titles continue to have relevance?

The baseball game took place in front of the historic castle. It was lively in spite of the cold weather and the constant drizzle. Our band played some special pieces and transported our minds to places beyond the seas. Company B was winning decisively until the critical moment when one of our own, Felipe Neri, came up to bat with two men on base. The pitcher almost broke Felipe's rib with a bad pitch, but Neri did not let go of the bat. Later, he took a tremendous swing and hit the ball into the river. His home run brought in three runs and tied the game until it ended.

I had a conversation with friends I had not seen in a while and others I met during the game. Several of us stayed after the game for a band concert. I had the pleasure of chatting with Fidel Gleim, a fairly well educated young man of German and Mexican descent from a well-to-do family. We left very late in the afternoon by way of the beautiful avenues leading to the charming château. We had such a good time that we will have to share this with our children once we return to the homeland.

Friday, July 5

We were assigned to dig a ditch for a toilet and latrine. Some of us gathered to burn dry weeds to keep the mosquitoes away and avoid illness and death. We came to fight; we do not want to die from insect bites.

I was told to pick up my orders for guard duty at ten. I prepared my rifle and went to my assigned post at the entrance to the great park by the château. I could not have asked for a better place. I was to prevent vandalism and the use of the park as a restroom. My station was beside a beautiful juniper tree that cast a lovely shade next to the canal. I would have preferred to use the place for a good nap rather than guard duty. A beautiful panorama surrounded me. I could see the castle surrounded by trees. The view of the walkways reminded me of one of Corot's classic paintings.[7] The sun could scarcely find an opening through the thick canopy. A moonlit evening would have been ideal for couples in love. How many times must they have said to each other the "I love you until I die" in such a romantic setting, under the shade of the juniper and pine trees! How often must the gurgling and chattering sound of children and the happy murmurings of young happy ladies have been heard in place of the deathly silence that now surrounds us! Life, the sweet life of bygone days!

All of this makes me think why I have been allowed to be here, as I contemplate my surroundings that appear as if in a dream. At that point I understand the infinite power of the hidden Hand that weaves our destinies on Earth.

The cheerful birds that were lightly moving the tree branches and at times almost landing on me and a little lone fish that hardly moved the water to signal life produced the only sounds and movements that interrupted my long hours of meditation. Only one officer went into the park the whole day, and he was on his way to the castle to see the colonel. A military salute, and that was all. The officer of the day came to relieve me at four and I left for supper and my rest. This was my first day on guard duty since I joined the military.

Sr. Eulalio Velázquez
El Paso, Texas

My dear friend:
I am finally in France, heroic France, the cradle of democracy and liberty. The immortal, the colossal and beloved son of France, Victor Hugo, is always on my mind as I march across this sacred land. I had never been more inspired than when I hear the "Marseillaise," France's national anthem. I constantly recall pages and pages of history and the immortal motto—Liberty, equality, and fraternity. I am awed by such human greatness.

I am following my flag and listening to my conscience. I am eager to do my part in the great tragedy. We may not be as disciplined as the sons of Germany, but we are committed to fight for what is only understood by the sons of democracy—Liberty.

The soldiers of my *raza*, the noble Aztec *raza*, do not falter. We may not all survive this war, but we expect that our descendants will acknowledge and receive recognition for our contributions.

Mr. Velázquez, I lack the complete mastery of the language of this country that could help me better understand what I see. I do not believe that I will have a difficult time learning French since it is easy to master and I am motivated. The call of the homeland is the only thing that gets in the way.

I want to tell you about an interesting experience that I believe important, at least to our people.

Since I know that people of Aztec origin are to play an important role in the war as soldiers, I suggested that they tattoo on their chests the legendary symbol of our *raza*, the Aztec Eagle devouring the serpent. I recently learned that the sons of the irredentist Poland carry on their chests a similar symbol—a white Eagle.

What a noble and heroic lesson from these liberty-loving people. Cordially

J. L. S,

Censored by Prescott Williams, Lieutenant from the 360th infantry.

Saturday, July 6

We left Camp Travis a month ago. We cannot deny the distance and disheartening absence from our country, friends, and families. Will we be gone forever? No one knows. One of two possibilities can occur. We came to kill or die. Are the things we have observed during the last thirty days believable? Everything has left such deep impressions that we can play them back in our minds like a movie.

My loved ones sent me a photograph of my little ones and me. It was taken three days before I left for Europe.

Sunday, July 7

I thought about going to mass but we were ordered to march so I had to pray to God on the road. We headed for a small mountainside area located to the northeast. The purpose of the exercise was not clear since we must have marched around five kilometers and then returned. It was already suppertime when we returned to Rouvres. I was assigned guard duty at 5:30. This time, I was to guard the gasoline without having to walk around the area. My replacement came every two hours. I should note that when I speak of long hours, we have to remember my time spent as a guard. I did nothing; I only thought, just thought and thought. I stood guard for twelve hours during a twenty-four-hour period.

Monday, July 8

Nothing new has happened. I had to continue guard duty today because it is a twenty-four-hour job with intervals of two hours of watch and two of rest. I was unable to sleep very well last night and have had a very bad headache. This means I cannot pay much attention to everything around me. My buddies who are carrying out similar assignments also carry a long face, but we are like the animals in the fable, "no one complains for fear of the lion."[8]

The afternoon was meant for sad memories. Our surroundings influence our mood and bring on thoughts from the past. Soldiers have dreadful moments that sadden their lives.

Tuesday, July 9

We marched five kilometers to Gurgy-le-Ville in raincoats, as it was raining. The march could have been more pleasant but for the bad weather. The rain fell with no wind. This made the march more difficult. Once we reached the village, they ordered us to fall into formation and then dismissed us for fifteen minutes of rest. We had little time to walk around, so the best we could do was to rest. They called us back into formation a short while later. The troops have an interesting look. Everyone is soaked and wrapped up in a raincoat. We look like wet mice, no more, no less. Despite this, we returned happy and in a good mood. We may have finally grown accustomed to the changes brought on by military life and the capricious acts of men against men.

When we returned, I set about to write a long letter to my friends about the adventure in France that we experience as an army in training. At suppertime I saw that the assignment board listed the people who were to be doing K.P. duty. Since my name was on the list, I went to find out when I was scheduled to start. This is also a twenty-four-hour job, except that we do not rest as much as in guard duty. Time passes quickly, or slowly, depending on how one gets along with the kitchen sergeant. Friends who have done the honorable work, like washing pots and peeling potatoes, have told me this. I set out to make the best of it. It could not be the worst thing to do in the military.

Wednesday, July 10

This was my first day on K.P. duty, and I cannot complain like the others. To the contrary, I feel great and look forward to doing it again. The soldiers who complain may be working like turtles. The work is much easier than the

rifle maneuvers, nothing like the forced marches, and it does not come close
to the demands of twenty-four-hour guard duty.

Fidel Gleim, my coworker, is also doing K.P. for the first time. We are
green to the task, but are willing and able to learn everything about being a
soldier whose life floats according to the will of the wind. We were to bring
water for the kitchen in large eight-gallon containers and a few smaller ones.
I forgot to note that we were wearing blue denims and hats with a three-
pointed shape. We had to bring the water from the public fountain and had
a good time talking with the French ladies who were getting water for their
homes. I have learned many French words and can construct my own sentences and carry short conversations. I can now translate the French newspapers, a job that I gladly do for free for my friends who buy them so that
I can tell them the news. French is easier to read than to speak because of
the pronunciation. Fidel knows it better since he studied it at a university in
the United States. Of course, regarding matters of courtesy, we went beyond
the call of duty and let the ladies get their water first. We were acting out of
personal convenience.

The fountain is also a place for washing. A number of soldiers are washing
their clothes there. Some do not behave like they should with the women and
even take advantage of their unfortunate situation. It looks bad although it is
not the worst that one can expect from members of an army. It is good that
we are new to the military profession, but we will soon behave like veterans
of many other wars.

We also cut meat, peeled potatoes, cleaned pots, served our brothers in
misery, and helped out as much as we could, as much as was possible. We did
so well the sergeant was pleased with us.

Since the sergeant cannot write English well, he made me his confidant
and begged me to write a letter to his tender Dulcinea.[9] This was right up
my alley and I wanted to please my superior—an odd thought. I drew on
the rules of grammar and style I could still recall because I had come to believe this kind of writing was from a different world. I made full use of the
language of love. This brought me good returns. I had spent most of the day
preparing the letter. The good sergeant wanted to pay me but I absolutely
refused. You have to sacrifice something when you are a common soldier. He
gave me the keys to the pantry and we took care of ourselves, in a reasonable
and responsible manner.

After work, we went swimming in the Aube River and later visited the
church, where we had a lively conversation with the priest. His last name is
Moura. We hear he is of German descent but French to the bone.

Thursday, July 11

We marched toward the hills in the west. At nine in the morning, we engaged in bayonet practice for forty-five minutes and trained on how to hide from the enemy when facing danger. The instruction was very interesting. It was difficult finding the people who were hiding. We used all the intelligence we could muster to camouflage ourselves with our uniform, the dry grass, the dead leaves, and the color of the earth.

We had "wigwag" training, or long-distance communications with flags, in the afternoon. Strenuous marching followed. I was too tired to visit my friends that night so I stayed in studying French and some material out of the French newspapers. One could say that French has become my language, and if someone doubts this, let them ask the platoons of soldiers who visit my rat hole every afternoon to hear me read the news and to report to them of our advances and victories against the Germans.

Friday, July 12

We marched this morning until we figured the average distance we could cover per minute. We also studied our general orders, which are indispensable for guard duty and our safe movement in and out of camp. Officers also trained us in signaling over long distances.

After our morning flag signaling, we scouted the nearby woods of Rouvres and the mountain to the west. We enjoyed the lessons. I like to learn something new, especially when the wide world and nature are my text. This is not the case with the rigid manual of arms that stunts all thinking and only serves to turn man into robot. I think the general idea is that the less the private thinks, the better he will be able to carry out his barbaric assignments, which later become his feats of valor. This leads me to conclude that if I am subjected to these kinds of rules, I will never stand out as a private. I maintain that I will be in a better condition to do well by keeping my clear-thinking abilities. I have confidence in my own reasoning and do not need to turn into a machine.

We saw a movie this evening at the YMCA tent. I had a good time, as I was distracted from the life we are leading.

Saturday, July 13

I received letters from the United States at eight in the morning. One was from Mr. Juan F. Guajardo, from Natalia, Texas, who requests, among other things, that we hold high the name of our *raza*. My brothers, Eugenio and

José, call on me to do the same. They say they are more convinced than ever about our loyalty. I tell my buddies about the small request I often receive and urge them to prepare themselves and avoid getting caught without the lard when it comes time to prepare the food.

We hardly worked this afternoon, we only marched to the neighboring hills and returned as if on a stroll, singing and happy, and hungry as ever. If our food had been poisoned, all of us would have died.

We still had some sunlight after supper and used the opportunity to take a leisurely walk down the dusty streets of Rouvres. The few liquor establishments in town are the soldiers' preferred gathering places. I visited one of the businesses to buy material for my writing. I came across my old buddies Barrera and Gómez and they immediately offered me the traditional drink, beer. I drank a glass because I did not want to slight my friends, but I really do not think much of it.

Soldiers are crammed into these businesses. They are drinking and smoking or else they are simply making a great deal of noise. Of course, a little bit of everything is taking place. Some are playing cards with great interest in their bets. Others are simply passing the time and enjoying some peace. They do not even worry about the hand they get because the idea is not to win. Two soldiers in the corner look like they have had too much to drink. Their awkward manner shows it. They seem to be giving themselves to conversations about their distant homes and their profound sadness. Some do not even talk, smoke, or drink, but are lost in their thoughts. Finally, the soldiers who are arriving act so determined to drink one would think the beer is running out. They shove and force their way inside to arrogantly demand service. The money, after all, is flowing. Everyone wants to spend his money and snug up to the wine. The poor (or, better still, rich) barmaids do not seem bothered. It is best that they do not understand what we are saying. We have paid for their friendly service with our patronage. Their welcoming ways are part of their job and we have paid for it.

Sunday, July 14

Today was France's great day. We observed the national holiday in honor of the heroes of the Bastille who fell fighting for the liberty of all people. A makeshift platform was erected in the small town square of Rouvres, and several of our officers gave eloquent speeches. The large number of soldiers who gathered heard our band play beautifully, as it usually does. The townspeople also came in large numbers, but they benefited little if at all from the speeches because they were in English and few of them understood.

This really turned out to be a response to what occurred earlier this morning. Father Moura gave a beautiful sermon with great oratorical skill. He invoked very pleasant memories of heroes from the past and spoke about people who are sacrificing for their nation and humanity. He also gave high praise to members of the American military for their conduct, bravery, and selflessness and for coming to pay a debt. Americans had come to offer their lives for the freedom of France, the same way that France had offered the lives of its own people for the freedom of the United States of America. Of course, he said all this in French and very few understood it.

The soldiers are beginning to appreciate the importance of speaking more than one language. They think I am a paragon of wisdom when French, Anglos, and Mexican Americans surround me to discuss the news of the war. All of them would like to know what is being said. The French may be talking to me and explaining something and before I can figure out what they are saying, some uncouth Anglo-Saxon insists on knowing what was said and I tell him. Meanwhile, Mexicans who do not understand French or English also want explanations. I oblige everyone. Of course, this is insane since everyone wants to know the same thing and does not want to hear it from someone else. They want it to come from me. I find it amusing when some Frenchmen and I are having a conversation and switch to a topic unrelated to the war. My buddies, who do not understand, blindly follow the talking but do not hear the heart of the conversation. When they tire from waiting, they ask me, "and what else," expecting that by then I will have much to share. They become disappointed when they discover the conversation has strayed from the trenches. It saddens me to see them distance themselves. Many of them have never understood the part they are playing or where they are playing it. They do not know where they are, how they came across the ocean, or the direction to the north. They just follow the crowd and the crowd follows the leaders and that is all. What are these men going to recount at home when they do not even understand the days they have lived?

I visited the forests, streets, and agricultural fields in the afternoon. After taking a bath I returned to our small village, the place where we train as the great army that will defend humankind and democracy, as well as the wealth of the Rockefellers, the Morgans, and others.

Monday, July 15

My buddy Varela gave me a novel, *El placer*, by Gabriele D'Annunzio. This is the first work in Spanish that I have read in Europe. I do not find the subject matter to my liking and would have preferred a more respectable theme, a different subject, and some other author. I wonder why I dislike that Italian luminary.[10]

We did a strenuous seven-and-a-half-kilometer march this morning to a village named Andeferre and returned tired and with blistered feet. Many soldiers went to the hospital. I also had problems with my feet but decided not to go to the hospital because I do not like the care they give the poor souls who go there. Their treatment is worse than the condition they treat. The officers often suspect that the soldiers are feigning their illness. I applied one of our home remedies when we went to the Aube for a swim. I inserted a thread through the blister and left the thread inside to drain it. I was soon ready for the next expedition, just like the muleteer's donkeys that only have to roll about before they are ready to move on again.[11]

Tuesday, July 16

We reconnoitered some more today, entered Rouvres as scouts, and pretended that the village could not be trusted. The lead squad went ahead and we followed a short distance away as its main point of contact, all well trained to communicate with the main body. I walked very carefully as a point man on the sidewalks edging the houses. When I reached the water fountain, I had to move in closer on the sidewalk. The humidity had made the area very slippery and my famous mountain-climbing "hobnail" shoes failed me.[12] I slipped, fell on the hard pavement, and rolled into the gully. I almost broke my ribs but, like a good soldier, held my rifle tightly as I slid on my back. I laughed to myself uncontrollably and made so much noise on entering the German town that I recalled the squawking geese that long ago saved Rome.[13]

I had a long talk this afternoon with a soldier of Polish descent who I met the day we were leaving Camp Travis. The young soldier, a good kid, left his family in St. Paul, Minnesota. His life is much like mine, including his pain and suffering as well as his desire that his *raza*, who long ago lost everything, take its place among the free people of the world. When he talks to me about the great and outstanding men of irredentist Poland, he gets inspired and proud. When I tell him my story, he concludes that I am right. Many men, many *razas*, many opinions and ambitions, a lot of good, a lot of bad, this is the army.

Wednesday, July 17

Some of the squads had to march to some unknown destination today. I was not ordered to go anywhere and stayed behind with my buddies to clean the streets. Clearing the dung of French cattle is not a dishonorable task since it will prepare us to sweep the Germans away. The work is not so difficult that we cannot take in our surroundings. I first notice the sad and difficult life the townspeople lead. It may be mostly due to this miserable war, but the daily scenes I see are the same ones their men of letters have described throughout history. I believe that people, like the trees, have their own countenance and whosoever takes it away ends their lives as well. These people are indestructible and will have to endure if the more-refined and highly civilized people expect to survive. I am not an artist, but wish I were so I could now and then render something of those in the village that we will long remember, if we live that long.

The streets are very narrow and sinuous. This works against the orderly arrangement of the buildings, which were built along the streets or trails a long time ago. The buildings are scattered and crisscross laterally, diagonally, and across. They all hug the street, making it unnecessary to build fences like in communities in America. They are constructed of great white stones and have large, rough, and crudely hewed beams inside. They sacrifice aesthetics for usefulness.

The interiors are well kept because French women are industrious and clean. The few fences that exist are made of stone, and the streets are not very clean. The source of water for public use is a stream that comes from some hill or mountain. The water enters the villages by way of drainage pipes that appear safe since the townspeople have used them for generations without any chemicals. Two scenes on the streets are forever impressed in our minds: French women carrying out their domestic chores and the eternal two-wheeled wagons with their constant creaking sound. Every home has its fruit trees and a garden, the indispensable source of life for French families.

Thursday, July 18

I sent many letters to my loved ones yesterday.

We did not receive marching orders because of the threatening rain this morning. We were told to draw maps of Rouvres-sur-Aube and its surroundings when we fell into formation. This was a really slow day, we learned very little. Strangely, our officer was very generous, jovial, and talkative today.

A few of us Aztecs gathered in the afternoon. We recalled the invincible Indian of San Pablo de Guelatao and his many sacrifices that are worth emulating.[14] We also acknowledged the difference in time and circumstance. He fought against the tyranny of a French despot while we come to offer our lives so that the freedom of the French survives the autocracy of the German Kaiser. How the times and motives change!

Friday, July 19

I was assigned to guard the sleeping areas. I slept, washed my clothes, shaved, wrote letters, read French and Spanish, and mended my clothes. I enjoyed being alone and without any worries. We are left with few moments like this, and that is why I am grateful for them. This is a good time to recall the past and ponder the future. I stayed all day in my manger-shack. When my friends returned in the afternoon, I told them what I had done and they shared what they had seen during the march. I wish I had been with them and they wanted to stay with me. That is the nature of life! An eternal contradiction!

Saturday, July 20

At 4:45 this morning, the bugle sounded and ordered us to prepare for a long march. We finished breakfast and readied ourselves with our light backpacks by six. How beautiful to see an army at this hour and in this state! Naturally, all the men were happy. We started marching at 7:30. (I should note that I always know the exact time because of my pocket watch, a gift from my kind brother. It is an interesting watch that serves as a calendar and even tells the phases of the moon and temperature.) The day was beautiful and sunny and the breeze was warm.

I was ordered to accompany Lieutenant George on a mission upon reaching the village of Colmiers. We were to survey the topography of the area and report in writing.

We went ahead and took shortcuts. The trip was beautiful and interesting, but it was especially enjoyable because we were not held to rigid military rules. Lieutenant George shared parts of his interesting life and I spoke of mine. We enjoyed the work because we had studied geography and learned about nature as civilians. He has also been a schoolteacher. The villages of Colmiers de Haute, Salfenager Foret de la Faye, and Grancey-le-Château were beautiful, especially Foret de la Faye, which we crossed on a lovely road. We stopped every moment we saw an attractive site. The forest of very tall and shapely trees, which were destined for the mill, reminded me of the imaginary woods where little Red Riding Hood came across the wolf. The lieutenant laughed when I shared this with him

We ate our lunch at eleven, in the middle of the shady French forest. We arrived at the beautiful castle of Grancey-le-Château shortly before twelve and waited for the troops. They began arriving an hour later. By that time, the lieutenant and I were rested and ready for the return trip.

We were given fifteen minutes for lunch and then we marched back through another route with different villages and fields. When we arrived at a small town, which served as a railway center, it was already four o'clock in the afternoon and we were quite tired. A large number of trucks were waiting to take us to Rouvres. The soldiers who arrived first immediately got on one. When our truck made a sudden stop another one came so close behind us it pressed against the leg of Miles Massenburg and almost broke it. One of the soldiers immediately grabbed the first aid kit and bandaged him. It was not that big a deal. He was more scared than anything.

We arrived at Rouvres at seven. It was suppertime and we ate heartily. We spent the rest of the night talking about the events of the day.

Sunday, July 21

We had a peaceful day. I was somewhat tired this morning because of yesterday's march. The rest of the soldiers apparently felt the same. Everything seemed to be moving at a slow or lazy pace. I went to mass after lunch and even the sermon seemed solemn to me.

In the afternoon, I went to the beautiful spot to the west of the castle where we bathed. It is delightful. The water is crystalline, like all the streams we have seen around here. The beautiful pool is surrounded by trees planted according to man's whim. The current turns into a charming cascade, its water falling into a pool about fifty feet in diameter and ten feet deep. The water is so clear and calm we can see stones of different colors at the bottom. We have had a good rest. Swimming is the best medicine for restoring the spirit when exhausted, bored, or discouraged. It gives us new life.

José González, the band's second bugler, is one of the best swimmers. We enjoy watching him execute different maneuvers in the water, on the surface, or on his way to the bottom of the stream. We are content with fording the stream and diving for stones in the cold water. We are in the middle of summer and it seems the same as always.

Pablo and I decided to take a stroll around the village after the swim, and we spoke to our heart's delight about home and friends.

The days are passing by quickly and it will not be long before we are called to the front lines. The Germans are apparently gearing up for action now that they realize help from America is underway. The Germans are apparently convinced that what happened at Château-Thierry was not a chance occurrence but that American forces did their job. This happened shortly after midday, on July 2, when a marine brigade was ordered to occupy a position in support of French forces. They did not expect action, nor did we, but the prince of the

German crown decided to push the French back. He thought the fifty-mile march to Paris would be a stroll and threw the best of his troops against the French, who resisted tenaciously, but they knew it was impossible to stop the charging Fritz. He was sweeping down on them. Our men were on the way to their positions when the storm overtook them. In the middle of the chaos, large numbers of French soldiers retreated any way they could, the ones who could. The Germans were charging hard. Our soldiers were not retreating because they had orders to occupy a certain position and to remain there. When the French passed by on their way to the rear, the Germans met up with our ground troops who had reached some wheat fields. Some of the soldiers got off the trucks and took whatever cover they could find, in the fields, by the road, and behind the stalks. Many of them engaged the enemy from the trucks because the Germans arrived so suddenly, determined to fight. Luckily, our soldiers had their machine guns and ammunition. They stopped the Germans and made them retreat every time they charged. The town of Château-Thierry was left like shriveled leather. The third time our soldiers took charge, the Germans realized it was the Sammies who were shooting at them and they stopped attacking. They were thoroughly de feated. Our soldiers simply wanted to tear into them. The news traveled from one front to another and many did not believe it. We had no better witnesses than the Germans themselves. They tell the story. This is why we say we could soon be sent into the wheat fields to fight the Germans. Those marines have committed us. Are we men or not?

Monday, July 22

Many soldiers still need training in target shooting. We trained with automatic Colt pistols today but preferred to use our rifles. We practiced long-distance signaling and changing into our masks as quickly as possible to avoid the asphyxiating gases. Officers also gave us instruction on the military use of topographical maps.

Tuesday, July 23

We continued with target shooting and gas mask and signaling training. I was called by the General Headquarters soon after midday and learned that we were to prepare for a march to a quiet front. How long have they told us this story? We are even beginning to think they are lying to us.

I could not find my friends when I returned and had no idea where they might be. I stayed stuck in place with nothing to do.

Wednesday, July 24

I was called again to the office. The sergeants think of me when a difficult task has gotten them in trouble. I wonder if they really find me useful, I just know this is not fair. If I do not merit the rank necessary for an assignment in the office, I should not be sent there. I figure that some of them are incompetent and they are in the office because of the kind of "pull" that is well known in the army. I can prove to them that on the many occasions they have called me, the problem is not that they have more work than they can handle. They just cannot do the work. How can I make everyone know that they are incompetent if they take credit for all the work I do for them? That is how freeloaders sit around and earn their rank insignias. They are professional bootlickers.

I read some news about the war after supper. A great deal of activity is occurring near Château-Thierry, the place where some days ago our soldiers stood out. Many of us wish we had been in the battle and are eager to test ourselves against the Germans. We welcome the orders, and I think our wishes will now be fulfilled.

Thursday, July 25

I had another day with nothing to do and was left in charge of guarding my barrack. I followed the same routine the rest of the day, readying my clothing, reading, writing, shaving, reading French, and entering more and more notes in my diary.

This is not the first day I have been assigned to stay behind to care for equipment that no one is to touch. I ask myself, why is so much kindness directed at me? Do my friends not deserve days of rest too? On some occasions I have asked them what they do. They have teased me by saying they are attending a training school. Why do they not take me too? I belong to this detachment by orders of General Headquarters. Someone told me and it seems true, my job is to train others to take my place.

Two soldiers are really interested in my office position, and they are trying hard to get it. I have told them I do not seek the position or any other. I just want to fulfill my duty wherever I am assigned. I have made several requests for a transfer to another group and have been denied. I can only chalk this up to bad faith among some of the superiors. Racial prejudice is notorious between Anglo-Saxons and Mexican Americans and would get worse if the latter were promoted.

Friday, July 26

This morning, we did a force march to the other side of Arbot, a small town about five kilometers south of Rouvres. We returned at one in the afternoon. They paid us after the meal in French currency, war money. This reminded me of the bills the Republic of Mexico issued during the time of Carranza.[15] The soldiers acted silly after getting paid. Berner, the carpenter, and our Polish friend outdid themselves. They gave themselves to drinking a lot of the white and red juice that people in these parts call "les bon vins."

We have also been issued wool leggings and the famous chapeau, a funny hat that turns us into roosters with cropped crests.

We continue to hear news about the "heated" front. This excites us and leads my fellow Mexicans to say in unison, "Bring it on"!!

Saturday, July 27

It has been raining all day and we have passed the time practicing our signaling in a big, old dilapidated house. The little village looks sad, occupied as it is by so many soldiers. Everything looks gray and stark, the cold, occasional rain falls silently, and the soldiers walk across the streets wrapped in raincoats. They look like dark bulking figures moving from place to place as if searching for a place to hide. Loud laughter rolls out of some homes where highly spirited soldiers are drinking a great amount of the famous white and red French wine. Once the vinegar takes its effect on the stomach, their memories bring on laughter, singing, or screaming. Others do not speak and lose themselves in their thoughts, as if dreaming while awake. Others play dice.

Sunday, July 28

We had such a beautiful day! The sun was pleasingly bright. It offered a sharp contrast to yesterday. I went to mass and visited some Mexican friends in Arbot after lunch. Gómez accompanied me. The endless white road adorned with its majestic trees seemed more agreeable than when we had to march over it. The town is similar to Rouvres. Its residents and the life they lead is the same. We ate supper with our friends, who were very kind to us. I should point out, even though this may not be the appropriate thing to say, my fellow Mexicans treat me with much respect. I am grateful especially since I have just started being helpful to them. Many of them see me as their confidant. I write letters for them in Spanish as well as in English.

Our Mexican friends did not want us to return by ourselves so several of them accompanied us to Rouvres, five kilometers away. The fellowship that has grown among our own is beautiful. It will be even more wonderful if we continue it when we return. Our band was playing in the park by the castle when we reached Rouvres. We had a good time while in conversation. I wanted them to share their experiences, impressions, and opinions about what we will be doing in a few days. They all expect to return to America. I remind them that the survivors will have to hold their heads up high with confidence and pride, and that their sense of importance should come from our excellent deportment in combat. They promise to remember this for the sake of our honor. I tell them I am recording all of this and that I will share it with our people upon my return. I add that our *raza* must know how we faced the great crusade of all times on behalf of humankind. Our brothers returned to Arbot very late that night.

Monday, July 29

We did physical exercises until three then took a cold bath. I had a good time with Sergeant X. This is one great hulk of a man, hunched somewhat, and shaped like a gorilla, but he is noble and kind. Those who know him say he is a brave man. There is no reason to doubt this; he shows it. He is just a typical farmer or cowboy, crude and with a rustic upbringing. While no one in civilian life would have dared to lay a finger on this hulking man, we make him the butt of endless pranks. He just laughs and takes it with the patience of a donkey. He may be forgiving because he has pity on us. It is impossible to get inside the heads of the men of diverse walks of life who serve under the stars and stripes.

I went to one of the YMCA halls that evening to hear a talk on "Our Loyalty."

THAT GOOD BEAR
(For my children)

Do you remember the good bear? The one with the very tidy shed at the camp where you visited me and had a good time? The good bear never showed anger against anyone or for any reason because he was good and gentle, but one day he became so angry he looked enraged. You may remember that he was a good little animal and that all he did was eat and sleep on the fine mattress of soft hay the sons of Uncle Sam made for him. Well, if you had seen him that particular day, you would not have recognized him. He did not look like the same bear. Since you do not know why he acted that way, I am going to tell you. I will first tell you that Uncle Sam no longer gets angry when we speak as we please. He also knows that you are good little children. You should know that the good bear had many little cubs—a cub is a small bear—and that he had hid and taken care of them in a hollow tree. The little cubs never hurt anyone either. But Uncle Kaiser lived close to the tree. He was a wicked and bad old person who was quick to anger and made the neighbors tremble. Well, one day this bad old man saw one of the little clubs playing in a large pool of water near the forest where they lived. He chased them away with a stick. The cubs did not return for many days. When the little bears figured that the old man was no longer around, they returned to the swimming hole. They were swimming when the old man appeared with his rifle. He had been waiting for them. And do you know what he did to them? Well, he drowned the smaller ones who were not able to get away quickly. When the good bear learned this, he became so furious and so angry that he broke his chain and began running through the forest screaming: "THE BEAR WENT OVER THE PANTHER BLUFF" (the bear does not fear the blustering panther). And when he jumped over the mountain ledges he would scream even louder: "HELL'S FIRE AND FUZZY-O" (the devil's horns and infernal fire)! I am sending you a drawing by one of my friends of the bear running over the rugged terrain and through the forest. You can see him in the postcard. Do you think he looks like the good bear you saw at Camp Travis sleeping on his mattress? What do you think?

J. L. S.

From France, preparing for the great battles.

Tuesday, July 30

I was left to guard my sleeping area once again and my friends left for more training. I have already said I do not like this, but I do the best I can. I have been reading French, writing letters, and editing some of my notes. I have time to think about every single moment of my short military service of five months. I spent the entire day in my shack thinking about all I have experienced. I enjoyed reliving things and entered them in my diary as reminiscences for my family.

I roamed the streets after supper mostly to ponder things, to gain a fresh view of this village that I have seen during the day, at night, by sunlight, by moonlight, in darkness, while celebrating and when fatigued, in my good and bad moments, alone and with others, happy and sad, voluntarily and against my will, and with and without a purpose. I was not going anywhere special today and came up to a YMCA tent. I found out that some British musicians were going to put on a concert that evening.

The entire ensemble consisted of a handsome couple. She was a lovely young woman, healthy, beautiful, and full of enthusiasm. He was her young companion. We could say that they were made for each other. The singer and the violinist were visiting British camps and bringing happiness to the poor souls. The government gave them permission to meet this noble purpose. We were lucky to have seen them because they arrived very late and were not able to stay until the next day. We had not heard anything like this for such a long time that we no longer thought it could ever be heard anywhere. This helped us appreciate the true meaning of art. They were real artists. The selections were varied and happy and consisted of songs, ditties, and violin playing. It was very enjoyable. Food for the soul!

> My dear wife:
> I am so pleased to write you this letter. May God take care of everyone.
>
> I wanted to write you in Spanish but the censors keep us from writing in anything other than English. As you know, I have had to write in English when traveling through America by train and when crossing the sea. Do not be surprised if I start writing in French since I now know the language. I am not exaggerating when I say that I will also steal the language from the "Boches." But I will not do this until we defeat them.
>
> I was very bothered that my letters had to be censored, that others would read them before you. That is why I left out so many things and my letters lacked feeling. They now tell us, "You can write in whatever language you wish, with the understanding that the ones in English will arrive first." This is why I will be writing to you in English and Spanish. I do not know why it has to be that way because this question of languages does not matter to me. No one writes my letters for me and you do not ask anyone to read them to you. So, what do you think?
>
> Do not worry that I am gone. It does little good. Duty demands my sacrifice, the sacrifice that embodies the love I have for all of you and the joy that I expect to have with you some day. Everything is meant to make my children happy.

Resign yourselves to things. I wish all of you happiness until my return.

Luz

Wednesday, July 31

I was ordered to join the cleaning and digging detail. It did not last long and we remained inactive the rest of the day. I even had time to study a good amount of French. I think I have made much progress in learning the language. I am already able to carry on extended conversations on any subject. My buddies buy me the paper so I can read them the news. They have seen me making progress and cannot believe I did not know the language at all.

I washed my clothes and then returned some books that the good Father Moura had loaned me. I read on a variety of subjects as well as on topics of general interest.

Thursday, August 1

Everyone had to sweep the streets for fifteen minutes. We were so critical of the people in the village and their cattle when we first arrived, but as the days have passed and we have done the work, we now view it as natural or as something we were meant to do. We clean the streets at the same time the cowgirls (the French shepherd girls) take their cows to the hills, and we have often swept the same place two and three times. The cattle do not understand. If they do, they do not care. They leave their marks on the cleanest surfaces and encourage the soldiers to give free rein to their profanity, which is as common as it is plentiful. The poor cowgirls worry a great deal and really wish the cattle behaved differently, but the cows could care less about the Yankee soldiers. We must remind everyone that our job is to sweep away the Germans and that we should start this now. That is all.

I bring up the cowgirls because there really is no one else but the poor and badly dressed young women who care for these animals. The soldiers do not mind being in the towns that are only inhabited by women. The only thing to lament is the large army of bachelors that are to be served. I have to say something that faithfully captures what we are seeing. We must remember that we have also left towns with wives, sisters, daughters, etc. Who will respect them if we do not set the example here?

I went through the clothes the soldiers returned and sorted out the ones that are in good condition. Afterward, I typed. I was sad to learn that my friends, the sappers, were ordered to march to some unknown place. We are starting to break apart.

We Demonstrate That We Are Worthy
Of Occupying A Place At The Front,
In The Fight For Liberty And Justice[16]

(This is how my letter appeared in *La Prensa* while we waited for the moment and the orders to march to the front, when everything was ready, when we had written our last statements, and when all that remained was the supreme hour of sacrifice. I wrote it from Rouvres-sur-Aube, Haute-de-Marne, France.)

An eloquent letter from the battlefront; an American soldier of Mexican descent speaks enthusiastically of France and the cause he set out to join.

The small things, the everyday events that generally go unnoticed by most people, occasionally move us deeply, and we try not to show it or even admit it to ourselves.

We wonder, all surprised and bothered, why we feel this way and ask, how is it that someone can affect us so easily?

The point is that we cannot suppress the feeling nor can we avoid showing it. This is what our reporter discovered yesterday when he received a seemingly inconsequential missive, a letter from a soldier fighting the Germans at the battlefront.

A Letter From The Front

The following inscription appears in a red triangle, on one of the corners of a square yellow envelope: American YMCA. The barely legible postmarks appear next to the signatures of the censors and the numbers that identify military groups, divisions, etc.

The letter is written in pencil at the very front where the fighting is taking place. It comes from a place where millions of men are fighting, some in pursuit of a noble ideal, while others for the sake of a misunderstood purpose. The letter originates in the land of sacrifice and heroism. The hand that wrote it has kept a firm grip on a rifle while in combat.

The reporter was enthralled when he began reading what José de la Luz Sáenz, one of the soldiers of Mexican origin in France with the great American army, wrote the editor of *La Prensa*.

The letter is clear and eloquent in its sheer simplicity. A fully formed and uncomplicated soul writes it. He is so absorbed by the great spectacle of the war. The writer is inspired by the spirit that drives the French, American, and English legions against the invading hordes that recreate on a peaceful and florid day the dreadful venture of the barbarians of Alaric and Attila.

The almost literal translation of the letter written in English follows:

SACRED FRANCE

With my country's flag before me, destiny has brought me to France, the cradle of liberty. Every foothill, every valley, every village represents a page in history that gives these people the unequaled right to be proud.

We could learn so much if we knew this language. It is so much like our Spanish and I believe I will soon learn the language and have the means to learn about these great people.

We cannot know everything that is important about the French, unless we engage them in an intimate way.

The French have been more hospitable than we had expected. In short, one must see the people and allow oneself to appreciate their moral strength.

It is obvious that these men have been born to fight for their survival. Their history demonstrates this.

They are clearly and sincerely hopeful about the outcome of the war. They also feel indebted to America for the obvious support we have given their cause.

SOLDIERS OF LATIN DESCENT

Mr. Lozano, this is still not the time to speak at length about the record of the Texas-Mexican boys who follow the American flag.

I take the liberty to say that many of them have already fallen and others are in combat. A large number of them are also waiting in training camps for the moment when they can demonstrate that we deserve a place among the soldiers who fall on the battlefields defending an ideal that we, the sons and daughters of liberty, believe is genuine and sacred. Send us some copies of *La Prensa*. As always, your friend,

J. LUZ SÁENZ

FAITH IN THE IDEAL

This is what the letter said in its four pages with small lettering, written hurriedly between bugle calls and officers' orders. The letter says more than can be expressed with words. Each line, idea, and simple and laconic phrases express an immense faith in victory, a thorough and complete sense of the righteousness of the Allied cause, and a divine-like enthusiasm that always accompanies the moments of victory.

The writer has dedicated the best years of his life to becoming a better person and helping others to do the same.

He has been a public school teacher in Texas for many years and everyone knows that few people have worked harder than he in educating our *raza* in this part of the United States.

When duty took him into the military, he had already been recognized for his work in the schools of New Braunfels, Moore, Leming, Alice, and Cotulla.

Friday, August 2

We marched toward Gurgy, three kilometers to the west, and stacked our rifles when we arrived at nine in the morning. We hardly ever do this operation but it looks beautiful and I remember seeing it in books. This makes us feel like soldiers through and through. Our imagination knows no bounds and we take in the whole of Europe. We are proud to know that we too are warriors in these historic battlefields.

We turned in most of our spare clothing by the afternoon to be ready to move to the front at a moment's notice. We cannot tell our families any of this. Our movements are hidden from the enemy. This tells us we are not far off from seeing fire and blood. (I am taking these notes in shorthand. No one else will be able to decipher them.)

Saturday, August 3

The lieutenant took the rest of my buddies to training and I stayed behind like before but under the command of another lieutenant who will train us. This officer lacks military bearing and is not arrogant like the others. He also seems dim-witted. We have heard that he was a sergeant until a few days ago. They also say he is brave and responsible. The lieutenant has just come from the hospital where he was treated for a wound. He was not wounded at the front, but somewhere close to it.

We did target practice with our rifles and pistols again.

When we returned, I heard of a celebration involving English artists that was to take place at the "Château-Thierry." The gathering was for the officers. The rest of us are only supposed to know about it. We know the better morsels go to the lions.

Sunday, August 4

I went to mass at eight. It was well attended by the townspeople, and more soldiers than usual were present. After the services, Pablo and I took another stroll through the foothills. Note that I lead the life of a private like the rest of the soldiers. I was not the only one who took these walks.

We had a good time observing the four small towns from the highest hill. Our conversation invariably turned to family and home. We wrote letters when we returned. I have already noted that I write the love letters for my buddies.

I was told during lunch to do guard duty for the second time, so I spent the rest of the day preparing for my assignment. I left my rifle ready and shining, my clothes as prepared as one could expect, and the rest of the equipment in the best possible shape.

I assumed my post after our assembly at the park by the castle, at the town's mill. The changing of the guard was striking and serious. The soldiers who carry the flag, conduct the military rifle salute, and change the guard with the rhythm of the music before the serious gaze of the officers in charge. The soldier I am replacing completes his duty by giving us the orders he carried out and sharing the secret password. The responsibilities of a sentinel are among the most important in the military. I expect to say more about this on some other occasion.

Monday, August 5

I was at my post on the little bridge over the Aube when morning came. I have two more hours to think, and think some more. The sentinels do their guard duty like faithful canines while everyone sleeps. We are at war and a good distance away from the front; however, we learn to be vigilant so that we can find the barbarian descendants of Attila's hordes who are planning to conquer the world, if allowed and granted the importance they give themselves. We are constantly told of the Kaiser's clever and intelligent soldiers. We will find out soon enough if the lion is as tough as they say he is and if he can handle the soldiers of my *raza* who are known for dying without any hesitation.

This is not empty talk, much less bragging. We know of moments in history when large numbers of hats belonging to courageous Europeans were littered on the foothills of the Sierra Madre. And if we are to believe our elders, the blue blood of a prince from these parts was splattered over an old volcanic stone wall in Querétaro in 1867.

My most demanding responsibility was to present arms to the officers who passed by, especially the officer of the day or the commander of our regiment. If this was to happen, I was to inform the sergeant of the guards to prepare for an inspection. No officer came by until ten. Shortly afterward, I began to see the troops in formation and the sergeants' presentation of the flag. I will have to perform this drill that I have enjoyed seeing others execute. I continued thinking about what I would do in different situations I could face. Our army began marching. Our star spangled banner waved in the open air at the head of the march. The sight was impressive. I was filled with emotion, especially enthusiasm, when our troops presented arms to our nation's flag.

The large formations of soldiers marched uniformly and at attention behind the flag. The marching sound of the troops with heavy loads on their shoulders plus the deathly silence they observed grew monotonous, and I began to give myself to thoughts of the scenes I had just observed. I suddenly saw Colonel Howard Price's car approaching at high speed. Everything happened so quickly I completely forgot my responsibilities. Before I knew it he was before me saying something I did not understand. I do not know how I did it, but I then presented arms as expected but forgot to call the sergeant of the guards. I was not reprimanded, although I thought I would be. When the troops returned in the afternoon, I was more alert and faithfully met my responsibilities.

After my guard duty and supper, Pablo and I read parts of *Romeo and Juliet*.

Tuesday, August 6

It rained a great deal all morning and we stayed in our stables until noon. No one complains about our lodging any more. The sons of Wall Street and some other braggarts, the poor farmworkers, the proud Anglo-Saxons as well as the humble Mexican Americans are all adjusting to this miserable life. This is a prelude to the greatest and most cruel sacrifices for freedom.

We went to target practice this afternoon and discharged twenty rounds with our rifles while wearing our masks. It is hard to believe how one man or the opinion of many can make someone do something. An ordinary little man who somehow reached the rank of officer, probably in some college where money counts, now curses, mistreats, and even humiliates hundreds of grown men armed to the teeth and ready to face the greatest and best equipped brutes on earth. This may seem like an exaggeration but it is true, and if people doubt this, let them ask "my brave" comrades in arms.

We received little news from the front today.

Wednesday, August 7

We found ourselves enveloped in calmness this morning. Aside from the sounds of reveille that woke us, everything was peaceful and we seemed to be far from the front where millions of men are fighting for the sake of other men.

I was called to the Intelligence Office during the exercise period. This was odd since I did not think I belonged there anymore. I felt that the order was more of a humiliation than a privilege. I have already explained why I feel this way. We participated in a military maneuver. This gives us a good idea about what awaits us at the front. The maneuver tires us but adds variety to the daily routine. Now I can appreciate how terrible this life must be for old and tired men. The army needs brave men with nothing to tie them down.

Thursday, August 8

We were awakened very early after barely sleeping two hours and spent the rest of the night preparing for an important maneuver. The day was very hot and our packs were especially heavy. We took one of our longest walks, close to thirty-five kilometers. We had never marched at such a fast pace. Many soldiers dropped from fatigue. The sergeants had been ordered to treat the poor devils roughly and they did what they were told. *Dura lex, sed lex.*[17]

Friday, August 9

We did another forced march toward the east today and got soaked since we did not bring our raincoats. This is how we are beginning to get a taste of the full sense of military life. It was interesting that the large number of soldiers were soaked to the bone but seemed to bear it with pride. Once in a while you could hear someone singing one of our popular songs, which quickly resonated in the hearts of men who seemed to have been waiting for someone to sing. Some of us were deep in thought despite the rain that fell hard and cold. When we returned, a buddy and I went swimming in one of the ponds by the Aube River located in a park in the town of La Motte. We practiced using the prismatic compass after supper.

Saturday, August 10

We continued making calculations with the compass this morning. The process is not at all foreign to me. I could have done better than the rest of the boys who have never done this before, but I could not stand the lieutenant's unfair treatment and had to talk back to him in a harsh and serious tone. Our assignment was to sketch a certain hill that was before us and then do some calculations. Some of my buddies did not understand any of this, yet the officer would say nothing about the muddled and blotched work they turned in for review. This bothered our "small tyrant" and he decided to take it out on me. This is why I reacted. He did not respond. I was ready for anything.

I went to a concert presented by an Italian violinist and a French singer during the evening. The performance brought on fond memories that helped me lighten the effects of the miserable experiences of the day.

Sunday, August 11

I went to mass in the morning after our usual chores and returned to write to my loved ones. I especially enjoyed a letter from my dear father. He always tells me to faithfully discharge my duties and not to dishonor the bravery of our indigenous blood. He describes beautiful scenes from home that I reread and enjoy as the reliable accounts they are. I know them because they are etched in my mind.

I washed my clothes to prepare for the marches or maneuvers that we are now executing often. We do this in preparation for the solemn trial that will end this war once and for all. We receive many reports that keep us informed of the advances both sides make as they pursue victory. But nothing in history can compare with the massive preparations we are taking now. We can see that the fight will be dreadful, the loss of human life will be immense, but victory will surely be ours. We are by no means showing blind optimism.

I enjoyed the last hours of the day strolling through the park in La Motte.

Monday, August 12

Our work was easy and enjoyable this morning. We practiced signaling and learned to communicate orders by telephone and lights in an abandoned garden on the outskirts of Rouvres.

In the afternoon, we were ordered to sew our explorer insignias on the left cuff of our coats. It is a green stripe, three inches long and half an inch wide and it has to be placed two inches from the edge of the cuff. The color was selected in memory of the traditional English custom of honoring the men of Sherwood Forest and their legendary hero, Robin Hood.

Tuesday, August 13

We followed yesterday's order by sewing the green stripe on our coats, and we felt proud. The human heart is so weak! How many of us will lose the piece of cloth and feel sorry for ourselves? How many of us will have met the responsibility it implies? How many will have been faithful to the symbol?

Anyone who sees one of the ten men who make up the Intelligence Office could say, "There goes one of the chosen ones in intelligence who will be the eyes of the regiment during the horrible hours." Is there a greater source of pride? Pride, whatever for?

Wednesday, August 14

We did not exercise today. I learned that the opening in the Intelligence Office is for the position of scribe, secretary, interpreter, stenographer, and artist, in other words, nothing but a simple petty clerk. Some day, I will be proud to say I served in that position. We did map reading, but it lasted until eleven in the morning and then we studied the surrounding topography. This type of work is more interesting and fair.

Thursday, August 15

We left for Chameroy at eight and after a light march of three hours arrived a little tired but in time to eat with the soldiers stationed there. We enjoyed sharing the meal with them. They seemed to be happy to have us.

We traced maps from three in the afternoon until eleven at night and improved the longer we worked at it. All this work is in preparation for a big military review tomorrow. I find it interesting and instructive to see how they plan a military campaign. I suppose everything will be more interesting when the action starts and our nerves are subjected to the pressure. Looking forward to this may sound gruesome, but this is war. It helps us forget the suffering of others as well as our own.

I have asked a good number of my buddies whether they really want to witness all the destruction and cruelty of war. They tell me they do and that this is the reason we came. This is our general feeling. We are already in the field of battle and I do not think this is simple bravado. What would the people who bear ill will toward my *raza* say now that they see these men who they thought would not embrace the national cause because they did not want to fill out a questionnaire or did not understand why they were being called Americans and asked to put on the uniform? I repeat, what would they say now that they see them so willingly take on the Germans who were ravaging Europe and seriously intending to leap across the ocean and into America?

Friday, August 16

I worked until eleven o'clock last night and woke up late. It was so dark I did not feel like venturing out to look for a good place to sleep. This little town has no room for the arriving troops. Gómez, Barrera, and I went into a small garden and set up our bedding under a small tree. When the bugle call awakened us at six we realized we had been sleeping under a fruit tree. Its fruit was green in color and similar in size to an apple. We did not pay much attention to it and went to breakfast, leaving behind our gear under the tree. We found soldiers eating the fruit when we returned. It was a plum tree of good quality. The plums were ripe although their color was green. We did not eat any other kind of dessert because the plums were so good.

I next went to General Headquarters. The attack against Rochet Ville began at eight. It was beautiful to see so many men moving forward to the front over grassy fields the summer had turned yellow. The attack had lasted one hour when our command post moved, at nine. The mock combat ended at twelve. We witnessed many interesting things. Many of our men were oblivious to the purpose of the exercise, just as they will be when the fighting actually occurs. They were exposed to the imaginary dangers that existed everywhere in that front. We ate at one and slept for a few minutes. Then we continued preparing for our return. The colonel got into his good vehicle and the other officers did the same. The private was left to march—a common practice in war. We were a band of soldiers, and acted as the group that we were intended to be when we were presented with the opportunity to play a joke on a fellow soldier driving a Red Cross ambulance. He had orders to take our gear but did not know what they meant by gear. When he inquired, we lost no time in replying that the load included us. The soldier swallowed the bait. Many people are mistaken into thinking we enjoy some privileges because they see us in the colonel's office. We are "intelligent" enough to keep quiet and take advantage of an opportunity that saved us many miles of difficult marching. We arrived early and had enough time to bathe and get dressed for formation before the other soldiers arrived. We were fresh when it came time to inspect our feet. The doctor doing the inspection suspected something but he did not say anything. We got away with it. It is never too late to learn to use one's wits.

Saturday, August 17

We had a beautiful morning. We took in our clean, peaceful surroundings and contemplated yesterday's experiences. I dreamed that I was home last night and I enjoyed myself so much I still feel happy. I will be happier if the dream becomes a reality some day. I am sure my fellow soldiers also have their sweet dreams.

After breakfast we began packing our copying equipment in boxes that are to be well marked and sent to the front a few days ahead of our arrival. We were issued rations for the long campaign, and we also got paid. We washed clothes and bathed as we prepared for the march to the assigned front where we will be baptized in fire and death. I went up to my friends Pablo and Julián in the afternoon and told them that our march to the front was no longer a probability but a reality. I urged them to write to their families and to be ready for whatever the future held in store for us. I shared with them my method for getting ready and they liked it. With this in mind, we went to confession and took Holy Communion in the morning. I began writing a very long farewell letter to my family, expressing my final wishes in case I fell in the field of honor.

FINAL LETTER TO MY WIFE

My dear wife: This is my last letter to you. This moment had to arrive sooner or later. It is here. Cry for me, I can understand this since we know how much you care for me and are recalling the difficult and happy times in our lives. You are also concerned about my children growing up as orphans. While you wait for the calm that is to come, know that my sacrifice was necessary and more than necessary, it was honorable. It was a thousand times honorable to have fallen for the inalienable rights of humankind and the future well-being of our children. You may think that they had everything with me there, but that is not the case. As long as the horrible and long-standing prejudice continues in Texas against our *raza*, our happiness will never be complete. I would not have been a man had I fled the draft to avoid the scorn where I was born and expected to die. The fight for the rights of the oppressed gives us the opportunity to claim justice for the humiliations and difficulties we often face because we carry the indelible characteristics of our *raza*. Our purpose is to demonstrate our dignity as a people before the whole world. It is necessary to fall where the best have died, and you can be sure that I will have fallen as a man of worth.

Our children's future is secure. Watch over them. Do not neglect their education for this will mean that you will have fulfilled the most important wish from your husband who loved you very much and sacrificed everything for all of you.

I have written this letter in absolute peace, long before I saw the horrors of war and its appalling devastation. I have decided to write this letter because I may be among the soldiers who will have fallen before the action starts. As you will see, I will leave this letter and other mementos with my trusted confessor and priest so that he can send them to you two months after the human carnage has ended.

(I wrote this on the eighteenth)

You and the rest of the family would not believe how happy I am as I march to the front (we will leave this very afternoon or tomorrow). I bid my farewell to this world after receiving the sacraments in the morning. Only you, my family, will be in my thoughts when the final moment comes.

Good-bye.

To My Children

My dear children: One day you will be able to understand this letter. You will see the responsibility I have left you, to maintain your honor as good citizens and members of our family. Your father knew how to die for this in the great world war.

To My Father

My dear Father: I have fallen, as all good sons should fall, to bring honor and pride to our nation and families. You can rest assured that your son never faltered in demonstrating the strong ancestral qualities of his people.

To My *Raza*

Do not forget that we have fallen fighting with the sole purpose of holding our good name high. Living without the rights of free men is not living. We are demonstrating once and for all that we are good enough to fight for those rights so that society extends them to us in the future. We will no longer be responsible if you do not educate your children after the war. Educate them until they are fully aware of their obligations and rights as good citizens. Do this so we can rest in peace. Our blood has joined the dust and ashes of all the warriors who have fallen on the holy ground of a liberated France.

To Our Government

We always had faith in our government's good intentions to insure equal rights for all its citizens. If in life we complained or protested against bad government, it is because local officials continue to be a problem. Our sacrifice in battle is the final act of protest against the wretched citizens who have been unable to free themselves of the racial prejudice against our people. Texas has many towns with this obvious hostile attitude that denies us all consideration, including the schooling of our children. This problem has been responsible for the "slackers" who left for Mexico.

We firmly believe the tragedy of the war will change many of the hostile attitudes we saw before the war and we hope that our sacrifice brings us the justice and recognition we deserve.

This will have come at a very high price but it is necessary and we pay it gladly. It has always been necessary to overcome the arrogance of self-serving and tyrannical men.

We only expect justice as we fall in battle. As far as we are concerned, we have demonstrated the worth of our *raza*. We hope that fellow citizens of all racial backgrounds follow this highly noble example in the United States and that they will no longer have to face the problem of war, but faithfully manage the challenges of peace.

Sunday, August 18

Another beautiful day, everything is peaceful and quiet. Everyone in town attended mass in their Sunday best. Sergeant Kelleher, Gleim, two soldiers, and I received the sacraments at six in the morning. We entertained such sweet memories during the inspirational ceremony!

After lunch, I packed everything that I could not take to the front. I placed items like correspondence, diary, final letter, keepsakes for my children, some books, etc. in the pouch the Red Cross in New Braunfels had given me. I took the pouch to Father Moura and gave him the little money I had so that he could send me some books to the front. I also asked him to mail my pouch home two months after the end of the war in case he had not received a letter from me. If I write him, he is to send it to me to the address in my letter. The pouch now has the address it needs if it is to go to America.

The lieutenant in charge of our detail ordered us to go to his place at nine and pack all the supplies we are to take to the front. I was assigned the marking of the boxes for the office supplies.

Our friend, the lieutenant, is staying in a humble home belonging to an old woman, who looks sad but is very tidy. The house is located to the west, on the last street of Rouvres. This street passes by the church and the western end of the château.

Once the office supplies were in order, we returned to our quarters where we found that all the boys were ready. They had rid themselves of everything they could not take to the front. We had orders not to take anything the government had not issued us. We had to throw away so many valued things. These are military regulations. Sergeant Irwin will be in charge of our detail. He was already following orders he had received. I prepared my backpack while some soldiers filled their canteens with water. I did not fill mine because I remembered that we are not allowed to drink during these marches.

Everyone was ready and standing by his equipment at one. The grateful people of Rouvres were present and bidding us farewell. They treated our departure differently. We simply saw it as something new in our military lives. They have said good-bye to many armies annihilated by the Germans. Why could the same thing not happen to us? They saw the possibilities, while we only felt uncertainty. They know that many of us will never return. Their tears show it.

Our military band began to play a march from across the public school and a courthouse located in something like a square with a public fountain. Our splendid army began marching to the rhythm of the music. The flag and regimental banner followed. The French people paid tribute to the flag, some by bursting out with all manner of enthusiasm, others by simply removing their hats.

We left by way of a very beautiful road. A poor soul fell from exhaustion and the heat of the sun just as we were leaving Rouvres. He was coming from some distant place. The harsh demands of the military forced him to continue marching without hesitation. We saw some of our soldiers in the villages we passed through. The final hours of our march were very difficult because we were already so tired. We had marched at a quick pace.

We were told to set camp and put up our small tents about half a kilometer from the Latrecy station, in a wheat field that had just been harvested. Barrera and I shared a tent. We slept under lovely moonlight on makeshift mattresses made of wheat stubble. At sunset we had a beautiful panoramic view of the village of Latrecy-la-Ville, its mountains, church, and other buildings. I found out that part of the army had left the station this very day at three in the morning.

Monday, August 19

A good number of buddies left for the front very early in the day. The sound of the bugle woke us up in the middle of the wheat field. What a beautiful sight to behold that early, cool morning—so many soldiers in the ready and quickly breaking camp! We ate our light breakfast with gusto and received letters and good news from home. I receive much correspondence because I write to many people. I am rarely without letters. This makes my boring life bearable.

We remained in place until twelve when we were ordered to go to the station where the "miniature" locomotive was waiting with its long line of "toy" cars displaying the familiar sign "10 chevaux, 40 hommes." Forty of us, with equipment and all, were assigned to a somewhat uncomfortable place in one of the cars. We boarded at three, and the Lilliputian engine blew its whistle and we said our final farewell to Latrecy and its surroundings at 3:45.

The sun began to set slowly as we traveled over the tracks with that little engine whistling at every station. We passed by several villages without stopping. I could not make out many of their names. We passed by the town of Chamont as darkness fell. The General Headquarters of our 90th Division, composed of soldiers from Texas and Oklahoma, is located here.

Tuesday, August 20

We traveled all night until we reached Toul at sunrise. This is a lovely town with much military activity. I can see many hospitals for the wounded—a bad omen—as well as stockpiles of munitions and food. We got off for a short while at the station. What a difference between these train stations and ours in America! We had time to get coffee in one of the Red Cross's canteens. The train continued on its march until we reached the side of a mountain where the Dungermain fortification is located. A village was located at the foot of the mountain. Small groups of us went about setting ourselves up in horse stables. The village has very narrow and poorly laid out streets. The roads that head out in all directions are very beautiful and well constructed. They are like white ribbons that seem to wind until they end here.

After setting up my lodging, I took to the streets to observe and study everything. My buddies bought all the papers sold in town and brought them to me so that I could read the war news to them. More and more, I see the importance of knowing several languages. No one questions my translations anymore and everything I say is taken as an article of faith. The best thing in all of this is what I charge them for the translations, which is nothing at all. They often bring me copies of the same documents thinking they are different. They also test me when I translate for them among the French women. The soldiers who hear me speak just stand there observing the impression I make on the women. We are pleased with our progress and the news we get from the French people in their own language. I sometimes leave the French trying to figure out what I said, but they understand me.

At ten, I decided to climb the very important fortification on the mountain. I saw many placements with cannon of all calibers protected by barbed wire. I also discovered mulberries in the barbed wire, they were tasty and I ate to my heart's content. It was already twelve when I came down. My friends were very interested in my find. I made my second visit with them.

We were ordered to retire to our stables very early because of a possible night raid, a common occurrence in Toul. One of the sergeants, the kind who acts brave with the unfortunate soldiers who cannot defend themselves against superiors, was in charge of warning us if this occurred. We did not have to wait long. It was still light when we began to hear the roar of engines in the air. They were German "bombers" that have caused so much fear during this war. The sergeant was ridiculously funny when he told the soldiers to take cover. Even the poor French families who were still walking the streets could tell from the screams that our sergeant was scared. The townspeople continued with their daily routine as if there was no danger. This was enough to embarrass us because of the noisy display our very brave sergeant made. He wanted to impress everyone, but the soldiers mocked and ignored him. A Frenchman asked me what the noise was all about and I explained things somewhat by telling him we were ordered to withdraw to our sleeping quarters as soon as possible. A short while later we heard our cannon opening fire and the thunderous explosions that made the ground shudder and rumble. We thought they were probably bombs from the airplanes. We can see the lights from the rockets on the mountainside that are used to send signals. I think the communications are between the French.

Nothing new happened in the evening in spite of the scare the sergeant gave us. A fellow soldier who had consumed too much wine decided to go outside but injured himself when the airplane alarm was sounded. Our stable was completely dark. Also, the ladder in the chicken coop was very old and rotten. When the soldier tried to climb down, he slid and injured himself. He almost broke his ribs before reaching the front.

Wednesday, August 21

We had a beautiful sunny and slightly warm morning after a night of nervous tension. We could hear the booming roar of the cannon at the front from the place where we were eating breakfast. The bellowing of these metal monsters is like a distant enraged sea or an approaching storm. Our conversation during breakfast turned to last night's raid and the scare we gave the French women who must have thought the Boches were upon us.

Enemy planes flew over us at a high altitude while some of our own appeared later. I went up to the fort again. This time, I reached the barbed wire and large trenches that defend it. A large ditch that can be filled with water in a matter of minutes to impede the enemy's movement encircles the cannon emplacement that the airplanes have been bombing. A drawbridge provides access to the artillery. This brings to mind the castles of the Middle Ages and the bloody battles fought with big knives and swords around those forts, which obviously continue to be used today. We stepped down into an underground area protected by a strong, heavy metal-solid door. We could see two big and strong German prisoners through the bars. They were sullen and looked threatening and they looked at us with interest but without saying a word. I told one of my buddies: "There you have an example of the kind of soldiers who have made the entire world cower before them. They do not impress me. Their well-built bodies would make good targets for our guns. Their fame and greatness is due to their strict discipline and excellent weapons. This also should not frighten the descendants of the Indian from Guelatao who confronted the first cannon and flintlocks with slings and clubs. We can also recall the armies or, better yet, the rabble that Father Hidalgo placed in front of the soldiers of Castile, and the barefoot and hungry troops that Zaragoza led to defend Guadalupe and Loreto against soldiers who had stood out in Magenta and Solferino."[18] Let's not forget this, my friends, "The lion has always appeared more ferocious than he really is."

A French guard told us we could not go any farther so we went back and took a walk around the foot of the mountain. I counted eleven observation balloons located a good distance away. The balloons were far apart from one another and might well mark the dividing line of the front. What we once imagined was slowly turning into a harsh reality. Without a doubt, the greatest war of all time is being fought on the other side of those balloons.

As we walked down a path to the village, we came across one of the boys from the band who was absorbed in the act of cutting his hair. Brave soldiers can set themselves down to do anything anywhere. He set up his shop in the middle of a vineyard, under the sun, and in the open air. An old bench served as his furniture, and nature—in all her splendor—served as his decorated backdrop. We shaved and then wrote letters to our faraway homes. It is a shame that we cannot say anything about what we are seeing. I note this down hoping I may live to share it with my children and someone else's children. Who else would be interested in what the poor soldiers of my people or of other races are going through? Their race—white or black—will not matter when they are forgotten or unappreciated. If they are foot soldiers, are they already among the unknown? They follow the strict application of the law. It is necessary that they die for their nation, that they fall defending their flag, and that they do not falter in bringing credit and pride to their race. At any rate, what better honor than to die for democracy and humanity while paying our debt to France?

Some sergeants asked me to type some orders, the same ones the men of our regiment were to follow during our march to the front. The orders were given that very afternoon and our preparations began. When night fell, we were ordered to fall into formation and begin our march. We moved in silence while a good number of trucks waited half a kilometer away to transport us to the front. The dark trucks projected quite a silhouette as they moved across the distant horizon, carrying their precious cargo of human flesh to the slaughterhouse. The dark night hung heavy over the earth. Only a slight reflection from the stars lit our way.

The convoy left by nine, breaking the silence with the engines' snorting sounds. The moon was rising as we passed by the last streets of Toul. The signaling lights from the German strongholds were visible at a distance. The lights came hard and fast, in different colors and sizes. They all carried messages. This is the way we will be sending our own in the dark of night. I will be doing this when we reach the field of battle. There you have it, the war with all its challenges.

Even though we traveled by truck, the trip was very difficult because we were standing up. It was very uncomfortable. Our trucks moved fast and kicked up thick clouds of dust on the white roads. They left us about half a kilometer from a village called Villers-en-Haye. I had a lovely moonlit view of the village ruins. The big houses of solid stone were full of holes left by the German artillery. Everything was quiet and deserted; no civilian soul was around. Once in a while, a French soldier passed by carrying out some order. Thousands of men were sleeping behind the walls or out in the open. The whole place looked like a cemetery.

We entered the village at a slow pace and did not find a place to set camp until it was almost morning. We ended up in a big long house with many wire cots. The building may have recently served as a front-line hospital. It is now a place of rest for the soldiers heading for the front or returning from it. When I speak of the front, I mean the last trenches, the first in the line of fire, which is not far from here. From here on out, everything is a battlefield.

Thursday, August 22

I woke up very late this morning and went to breakfast. We could see a barrage of heavy artillery fire that the German batteries directed at some of our airplanes. We then saw three of our airplanes way up in the sky in a firefight with three German planes. We are in the war's danger zone and these incidents are to be our constant companions. We are obviously excited since this is the first real aerial combat we have seen.

They set up our kitchen in an orchard with a good harvest of yellow and dark plums, very big and very sweet. That was our dessert in spite of being told not to eat anything like that at the front. After breakfast, we bathed in a river separating Villers-en-Haye from Griescourt. Soldiers from another American division are camped in Griescourt, and they have YMCA and Salvation Army halls. We had a good time talking and sharing information about life in the last trenches. We continue with our primal curiosity.

We received orders at nightfall to march to the actual front, to the line of fire, where millions of souls have recently been meeting their end. We quickly prepared for the march. The moon has been rising late; this is why our first hours were dark, as dark as the memories we will have of this war. We began marching to the front slowly and quietly. At one point, we rested and then became confused when we moved. Some soldiers had been separated from the group. I lost contact with Gómez and Barrera, my comrades-in-misery, and joined the soldiers who were moving toward the line of fire. Our division marched forward while another one left to make room for us. We marched in silence and they passed us all happy and loud. We took frequent breaks to give our men time to get situated in the first trenches and heard the sound of a German plane coming our way when we reached the top of a hill. An observation balloon was nearby and this is what the plane may have been seeking. When the plane fired at the balloon, it was forced to land immediately. We had been ordered to hit the ground and we remained in that position. The ominous bird put our nerves on edge when it flew over our heads.

I arrived at Jezainville with the main body, not knowing the whereabouts of my friends. This was the second village enemy fire had destroyed. It has been exposed to German artillery for four years. Complete confusion reigned in that place. We looked for a place to camp while others were moving out. They were as lost as we were. A large group of soldiers was assembled in a small square that had a public fountain. We witnessed this in the dark. Our second battalion immediately took its place in the trenches of the first line of fire. The third battalion occupied the trench of resistance, and our first assumed the rear guard.[19]

I did not take long to find out that my friends were a kilometer behind me, where our command post was located. I had no choice but to find a place to sleep. I found the kitchen sergeant and our supply sergeant in the first dilapidated shack I entered. The house had more soldiers than could be comfortably accommodated. I had not seen anything so disgusting. The French soldiers who had stayed there had turned the place into a dung heap. We discovered that the French army practiced poor hygiene. They may have been so tired of fighting they cared little about health issues. There is nothing worse than war!

I was getting ready to leave when I met up with Martínez. I did not recognize him because he was wearing his gas mask. This is probably the only way to tolerate the stench of human dung. Martínez told me of an unoccupied room that no one wanted simply because it was empty. I discovered that it was one thousand times better than all the rest. Others followed me and we slept well and peacefully, lulled by the cannon's booming noise, which is not as frightening as they say. I ask my fellow Mexicans and myself, can we maintain this cold-blooded outlook at the supreme moment when we attack the enemy's trenches? Oh, this is terrible! My friends tell me they cannot wait for that moment. I do not look forward to it, but I am ready.

Friday, August 23

We got up, went to breakfast, and ate well. I then started looking for ways to join up with my friends. Truthfully, I was not very interested in being with them because I had not been told where we would be assigned. Also, I was in the front lines and had more freedom here than under the command of an unfair officer.

I noticed a group of soldiers examining a recently captured German machine gun and a bomb that had failed to detonate. I continued walking and took my time exploring the town, including a church damaged by cannon fire. I went up a hill that guarded the town and reached the communication trenches that led me to the first line of fire. My friends were there, ready for orders to "go over the top." Everything was quiet; no one was firing. The German ramparts were visible even though we had to traverse many open trenches and barbed wire to reach them. The Moselle River is to the right and several elevated places that are suited for artillery placements are evident on both sides. This was my first visit to the front line and my first view of the enemy. Everything looks so natural that I cannot imagine that at any moment all this could change into a crater with pieces of men flying everywhere, and the clamoring sound of wounded men all around us, and the stench of the blood-soaked ground.

Someone jolted me out of my self-absorption with the news that officers were looking for me. I dropped what I was doing and headed for Jezainville where I found the soldier who had been sent for me. He told me rudely that the colonel was calling for me and to follow him.

Soldiers like this messenger are easy to describe. They are only concerned with acting rude. He angered me so much I had to level a serious threat against him, although I could not match his strength. He never told me where we were going. He just wanted to get me angry. I was carrying a full load and he had nothing. Whenever it suited his fancy, he would enter into a conversation with someone to waste time and make me wait for him. I resorted to the language of the soldier when I ran out of things to say. This made him pay more attention.

The command post was a kilometer behind us, close to a quarry, in a good bunker reinforced with metal, sticks, and dirt. I came across Colonel Price when I entered the first dugout. He had a bunch of papers in his hand. As soon as he saw me, he asked, "Do you speak French?" "No, sir," I answered. The colonel continued pacing and chewing on his customary Cuban cigar but without saying a word. I continued to wait for more orders. Finally, he gave me the papers and said, "Can you tell me what this says?" I took the papers and looked them over. They were in French, very poorly written, and with many spelling errors. I responded, "Colonel, sir, I do not speak French but I can tell you in English what the poor writing says." "Well, that's what I want," he said, and added, "Can you type?" And since I replied in the affirmative, I was given the task of typing ten copies of the translations. I quickly did this and was then told to wait until four in the afternoon when the wireless communication usually arrives from Paris. The wireless messages from America come in the morning. I did not say anything but thought to myself, "I can stay in this well-fortified place until the end of time."

Once I went over the events of the day, I concluded that the interpreter was no one other than the soldier who went for me. When the documents overwhelmed him and he discovered he could not do the job, he looked for someone else to do the work. I do not know who told him that I knew French. I could not have told the colonel that I spoke French when I had never studied it and much less if I had known that a Creole from New Orleans who claimed the language as his native tongue could not do the work now being assigned to me. At any rate, I am now serving in this position, but not because I wanted it this way.

What can my friends say now? They mocked and teased me when I studied French. They would ask if speaking French to the Germans would stop their bullets, and they said whatever else they thought might bother me. Well, my French is good and the bantering will not affect me. My work is much more interesting than theirs. It will allow me to stay abreast of whatever is happening at the different fronts and in America. I am pleased with the way things are shaping up.

The copies I made were sent to the different groups in our division, the artillery, machine guns, etc. They will have to accept what I was able to decipher from the rubbish I was given. An explanation at this point would be appropriate: The papers were badly written. French telegraph operators are not very good writers even with a fully equipped office. They are even less able here, in the open air where we have to use the knee instead of fine mahogany tables and the pencil without an eraser. We also have to work in humid conditions and under the light of dim paraffin candles instead of the incandescent bulb. We must add that they are copying a nonnative language and that the Germans insert whatever words come to mind—a wise move on their part—to muddle the meaning of the wireless message. We are told that the Germans have very fine telegraphic equipment. Our operators reduce the messages to scribble because they write down everything they hear. The result is that even the native speakers have problems understanding them. This is the material I have to decipher. I would have preferred that others had paved the way for me. The many years I taught students who could not read nor even WRITE, and the millions of cases of horrible penmanship that I have had to translate helped me figure things out.

Soldiers who have been educated are beginning to fail us. What hope could I have without an education? We are in the thick of things and have no choice but to make the effort. I relaxed the rest of the day. When night came, I made my bed on a dilapidated porch covered by a thin sheet of metal that offered some protection from the rain and dew. I could have slept in a dugout close to another one by the colonel's office, but it was very humid and it had a bad odor from an unknown source. It was very dirty and dark. I even imagined it full of white lice that seem harmless but capable of causing major diseases or plagues that destroy armies. They are also very annoying and disgusting.

We were two kilometers from the line of fire. The continuous artillery fire from both sides can be heard clearly. Several French cannon of various sizes are nearby. I have seen them fire now and then, but not continuously. A heavy one roars occasionally. The soldiers move it from one position to another. They do this to confuse the enemy, who is trying to pinpoint its location. The smaller 75-millimeter cannon fires at a higher rate. A few minutes ago, we heard the terrifying sound of a large German projectile that detonated some distance from our dugout. A soldier by the door of our dugout dove under a table. We thought he was playing but afterward understood his reaction. He went into a cold sweat and lost his nerve. It is still too soon to know everything that is happening.

Sergeant Irwin is in charge of our squadron. He is a good person and fills me in on things. He asks me for help when he does not understand something and admits that he lacks much of what I have learned from the books. He does not have an education but is fair, and I have promised to help him in all I can. Sergeant Irwin is brave and intelligent and does not have much use for military airs. He is very funny and entertains us with his funny jokes.

Saturday, August 24

The morning was beautiful. I started cleaning the typewriter after breakfast. I can see that I will now use this weapon to battle the subjects of William II. I use its keys to relay orders to the artillerymen so they can blow up the enemy's stockpiles of munitions, the shipments of supplies that are reaching their trenches, and the known positions of the fearsome soldiers who harass us. After all is said and done, they are of flesh and blood and, like everyone else, fall under rifle or machine gun fire.

Since typewriting will not be difficult and because I want to do as good a job as possible, I have memorized a list that I prepared of some of the most frequently used abbreviations, some technical terms, and other useful words. Necessity sharpens the intellect. Learn this lesson my children, you can never learn enough while you are young. What you learn, however, learn well and without conceit. Aside from the heavy load the government has placed on my shoulders, I am carrying a bilingual dictionary by Arturo Cuyas, a book on shorthand, and another one on learning French. I have already noted the jokes I have endured because of it. Now that I am in a hole thirty feet under the ground, I can tell my friends that the books literally helped me build a protective trench around me. The German shells do not understand French or Spanish, but they have shown how one man's failure required a replacement and the officers thought of me. Studying won out. This has been a source of satisfaction because I have used my limited Spanish in censorship. Now I can say that my knowledge of French pulled me out of the first line of fire. It did not remove me completely from danger. The risk is everywhere on the front, but I came to fill a position that is more difficult than carrying a rifle. Millions carry rifles but few can make the typewriter keys click and send orders in Spanish, English, or French. I say this with confidence. The officers will have to accept whatever I say until a trained interpreter takes my place. Meanwhile, it is important that I stay abreast of the great battlefields and events from other parts of the world that are not at war.

My buddies look for me in the evenings so that I can tell them the news from around the world. I cannot tell them everything, only what is available to them in the press. Some of them look to sleep close to me with that purpose in mind. This includes some of our soldiers of German descent. Under other circumstances, they would have rejected my help and tried to insult me.

We had a heavy rainstorm early in the day. This is the first we have seen in Europe. I wrote letters to my love ones.

Sunday, August 25

A powerful German bomber flew over us at two in the morning. The panic this unexpected nocturnal visitor caused was terrible. We heard it from afar. The night was still after the rain when we heard the motor's rough, muffled humming sound. We were struck with fear and acted like we were asleep. Our only protection consisted of zinc sheets that any piece of shrapnel could pierce. The few seconds the plane flew over us seemed like long, terrible years. It dropped three bombs, which caused other frightening explosions. The night's darkness made everything seem worse. One of the bombs exploded sixty yards away and left a big crater on a road intersection. The other two fell farther away. We did not suffer losses, but the experience was etched in our minds.

We heard many discharges from our cannon during the metal bird's flight. A few minutes later, the Germans opened considerable fire with their heavy guns. I can say that this was our first baptism under fire. Many shells passed over our heads, filling the air with terrifying and deadly howling sounds. The blasts tore through the darkness much like thunder follows lightning. We observed a great deal of aerial activity.

I have no idea how many casualties the Germans may have caused. We are responsible for some of them. A lieutenant who was training some sergeants on the use of hand grenades killed himself and a sergeant this morning when one of the grenades exploded above his head. One of our sentinels killed a fellow soldier because he did not recognize him and opened fire. He was clearly nervous from the planes of the night before.

Monday, August 26

Today was a really peaceful day. Some French artillerymen are deploying their cannon a short distance from our encampment. They covered them with branches from the forest and fired some test shots toward the northeast. The blasts shook the entire area and shattered glass in the dugout. Peace followed. This is how the day ended.

Tuesday, August 27

We could say that this day has been peaceful again despite more aerial activity. We have noticed that almost all of the airplanes belong to the enemy. This front is officially considered a quiet area, but we do not see anything calm about it. The enemy has not stopped harassing our men.

My work is easy and gives me time to study French and shorthand. I have been observing some of our troops in small-scale maneuvers.

Wednesday, August 28

Airplanes were engaged in a terrible dogfight at ten in the morning. A German plane was bent on destroying our observation balloons. Its pilot squandered his skill and valor. A number of machine guns and cannon protected a balloon that was near us. It was pulled down in time and escaped the plane's fire. Two of our airplanes shot down the German, but not before he had destroyed three balloons.

I bathed in the afternoon in a small stream a short distance from our position. I then went to Jezainville and bought eggs, sweets, etc. We were hard-pressed to find anything to buy and could not figure out what to do with our free time.

Thursday, August 29

Nothing special occurred today. Three large shells fell close by us when we were eating. They may have been targeting our kitchens or our planes flying over the enemy trenches. This gave us a good scare and kept us from enjoying our meal as before. The fear of losing one's life and the appetite for food are intimately related.

Friday, August 30

Gómez, Barrera, and I made breakfast the way we like it. The cooks did not want to give us any grease but they relented when we argued with them. We ate the dozen eggs I bought yesterday. The only thing Barrera missed in the breakfast that we gave him was the "chilipitín" pepper from the Tío Quemado creek in Duval County.

A French priest who is my friend came to our office today. He seems to be getting the cold shoulder from our officers. His English is very good and he is here in service to our army. I helped take his luggage to Jezainville.

Saturday, August 31

I had more sweet dreams of home last night. This is the third time I see myself at home but always with the strong desire to return to the front.

My buddies who are returning from the front line tell me of their troubles and escapades. The only danger they have faced is the poison gases. They are very dirty and now have to wash their clothes and bathe.

Barrera had a tough, dangerous experience yesterday afternoon. A lieutenant had ordered that he take him close to the front on horseback. He wanted to visit the line of fire, and Barrera took him to a small forest near a stockpile of rifle ammunition. Barrera stayed under some metal roofing with the horses while the officer walked through the trenches. The Germans quickly discovered the horses and began firing poison gas shells. Barrera immediately put masks on himself and the horses. He waited for the officer all afternoon and night. As soon as the gassing started, the officer had climbed on a motorcycle and left and had said nothing about Barrera.

We did not know what was happening. The lieutenant asked me in the afternoon and again this morning if I had seen Barrera. I answered that I had not. Barrera stayed in place until dawn, until he could no longer stand the hunger and came in for breakfast. He was still thinking of returning to wait for the lieutenant until he found out the officer was here. The lieutenant never asked him anything. We do not believe this officer was up to the task and deserves to be reprimanded. Obviously, the best part of the story was that Barrera had not died while taking care of a stupid person.[20]

Sunday, September 1

This morning was cooler than usual. I wrote letters home. I sometimes witness cases that finally grant us just recognition. My Mexican brothers are also optimistic. I do not doubt their word since I trust the way they carry themselves. Military life is still a new experience. It is a source of pleasure and pride for us. We are not far from showing loyalty to its fullest. If we complain at times it is because injustices never end. We are not alarmed by military life, nor do we see death as an obstacle. We knew that the trenches would not be a cakewalk from the moment we enlisted.

I wrote my father a long letter after the church service.

Monday, September 2

This is Labor Day, which is widely observed in America. The day was peaceful until the noon hour. Twelve large projectiles hit the little town of Montaville. Our scouts discovered fifty horses, and we informed the French artillerymen who were to the right. They bombed them until none were left alive. One of the ugliest, most difficult scenes is unfolding before our eyes. Man, with all his advantages and innovations of war, is merciless in the destruction of poor and defenseless animals. All of this is sad but inevitable in war. Every day we agree more with whoever said, "War is Hell."

The terrible 150-millimeter cannon began to bomb our position as it was getting dark. It was a horrible day for the soldiers. The shells were flying over our heads, howling like souls from hell.

Tuesday, September 3

A daring German plane made four low passes over us. Our machine guns fired but the plane escaped unscathed.

A sentinel wounded another soldier. They are becoming a source of embarrassment. It seems that they do not wait for the soldiers' identifying response because they fear the German soldiers and open fire.

The night began with a horrendous bombing on Jezainville. The little town has been a target for the German artillery for more than four years. If not for the mountain that surrounds and protects the town, it would have been destroyed a long time ago.

Wednesday, September 4

The days begin so serene and peaceful one could overlook that humankind's enemy is so close. After our baptism by fire, our nerves are no longer rattled as before. We do not even mention the bombings, which have intensified with each passing day.

We witnessed a great deal of aerial activity today although the planes flew at a high altitude. At night, they bombarded us with numerous gas shells that landed a distance away, but we really felt them. The gases permeate the air we breathe.

Thursday, September 5

The morning was very hot, but my work was fairly easy. Several colonels visited our office and a sergeant and I went to Blenode. We heard the zooming sound of four large exploding bombs that fell on the town's houses. They cut through the air with a shrilling sound and left a plume of black smoke rising from the old and now shattered rooftops. This was followed by the blast's "J-u-u-á-c!" Pieces of slate and wood flew all around. Some of the soldiers who happened to be in the area ran; others stood still, either because they were unharmed or had made a stupid mistake. We went looking for a motorcycle but when we located one, the sergeant got on it and left me on foot. This was all right because I was able to visit the towns on the other side of the Moselle River.

Interestingly, the German soldiers were not far downstream from the French soldiers who were also bathing.

I received letters from home and I was glad to answer them.

Friday, September 6

The dawn came with very heavy rains. One of the soldiers in our company named Nelson, who is with the Red Cross, does not believe in war as a matter of conscience. Officials denied him an exemption because they believed that he was trying to evade military service. He has been openly predicting for some time that the war will end soon. No one takes him seriously even though we share his good wishes. According to Nelson, the war will end today at three in the afternoon.

Last night's intense cannonade has continued all day. Many French troops, as well as tanks and vehicles with munitions, have been going to the front. The day closed with rain and heavy and unrelenting cannon fire. Our soldiers are a sight to see when they return all muddied and wet, but with a stoic bearing of free Americans.

Officers publicly commended my work today. This made some weak individuals envious of me.

Saturday, September 7

We have been answering the German cannon fire at the rate of two for one since last night. The artillery duel has continued all day. The machine guns have also stood out with their destructive work. They do not shoot for the sake of shooting. When these turkeys cluck, someone is nearing their nest. All this action is due to the continuous movement of French troops down the line of fire on the right. The Germans are the ones who are scared now.

Something tells us we should expect an evil storm at the nearby front. Death is present because men have sown it. Who can blame God's law when we do not obey it?

I have continued working as a translator of the French wireless communications. I translated a communiqué of 390 words today and can say I did a good job because no one has said otherwise.

Sunday, September 8

It continued raining and I almost did not go out to eat. I stayed inside my cave. Our entire existence is monotonous, all gray, and with drenching rain. My buddies complete this sad picture with their soaked and dirty uniforms. I believe the rain comes down when we fight. Once the serious fighting begins, it starts to rain and rain. This is good for us because the rain keeps the gases from spreading. It presses the gases down into the ground and weakens their effect. God helps us with this.

I bathed in very cold water and wrote letters. The heavy cannonade continued but the shells have no longer landed close enough to rattle our nerves. We consider the distant roaring sounds an indispensable part of our daily routine, much like the din of our great factories.

Monday, September 9

The artillery fire continues as usual. Our buddies from the First Battalion who were holding the front line were relieved and sent to the rear guard. They came to bathe and wash their clothes after spending several days smelling like burned gunpowder. They are beginning to say that war is hell. It could be that they are repeating a popular saying or that conditions may really be looking like hell.

Tuesday, September 10

Last night's artillery duel was more intense. I went to Jezainville for no special reason, simply to pass the time. I took in the scenery. It is very beautiful in spite of everything. I really wish I could walk all those hills that are now armed to the teeth and full of men who are ready to fight. I would have enjoyed another walk and a view of the enemy's territory with one of the powerful telescopes. A dark veil covers the area they call "no man's land."

When I reached the YMCA tent, I learned that a German shell had just killed one of our soldiers waiting in line to buy some sweets. "His time was up," some say. I say, "No, we are all already living on borrowed time." The truth is that he is among the many who will not be able to participate in the festivities we have prepared for the Germans. They have made us feel like we were jumping rope for them, we will now steamroll them.

Fellow fallen soldier: may your soul rest in eternal peace while ours continue to suffer the sorrows of the war and others yet to come.

Wednesday, September 11

The rain continues. We were ordered to prepare for a march to a position closer to the action so we can see and participate in the revelry. We spent most of the day packing our gear. I packed my books with some misgivings because the load I am carrying is too heavy. It includes rations, munitions, and everything else that makes up a complete pack.

We are not happy to leave this protected hiding place for the open field. This reminds me of Hans Andersen and his long-suffering patience, "Perhaps the end is near."[21] Sergeant Schwarz and I went ahead to our new command post at 6:30 in the evening. We had to pass by Jezainville where we were to meet our fellow office workers. We saved time because we did not have to march with the main body. We followed a trail through a beautiful forest of tall trees. The rain began to come down more heavily and the night grew darker. Our load was very heavy. The temperature was not cold but we still wore our raincoats. This made us sweat. Breathing was difficult.

I described the events leading to the fifteenth in a letter to *La Prensa*. I could not say everything at that time, but now I can. I have expanded that letter with details that I could not write.

This is my letter as it appeared in *La Prensa*:

HOW OUR OWN FIGHT IN FRANCE[22]
The brave boys who carry Mexican blood in their veins are fighting and dying, and holding high the name of our *raza*.

We received a letter from the front yesterday. José de la Luz Sáenz, a soldier of Mexican origin who fights for liberty under the stars and stripes, wrote it at the very battlefield where the greatest tragedy of all times is being played out. We saw the young teacher of Texas children as he went off to war with such high-minded enthusiasm. Today he shares his profound thoughts, the moving images that the war has engraved in his spirit.

The account is interesting, rich with emotion, color, and truth. It reads so completely different from the dry message of a cablegram and directs our spirit to a glorious terrain that, not unlike the sands of Marathon, will go down in history for its cries of bloody battles, the clashing of spears, and the shouts of victory that announce the dawn of a new life.[23]

We have not added anything to the letter. Doing so would have taken away its freshness and intensity. We would have desecrated it.

We offer it to our readers exactly as we received it:

I am completely, or rather fully content in the trenches during my few hours of respite from the continuous fighting. I am happy and satisfied with the way things have turned out. You may have already read of our total victory against the men of Kaiser Wilhelm by the time this letter reaches you. At any rate, I remember your long-standing understanding and consideration of me and wish to send you my latest thoughts regarding our contributions in this awesome crusade.

This could take volumes and volumes of writing. I truly regret my inability to offer a full and complete account of my spiritual growth in this war. It has inspired me greatly.

Because of my lack of ability, I will limit myself to sharing a few thoughts of our glorious advance.

This is how the diary of J. Luz Sáenz begins, written during moments of rest during the fighting, in the open field of battle, while Teutonic grenades are exploding everywhere and the immense blue skies that outlined the strange silhouettes of birds of steel that man has used to rob from our feathered friends the dominion over unreachable summits. The author writes from the same battlefields where millions of men in the flower of their youth are recording with their blood the most glorious moment in the history of mankind. They are forging the brave and serene soul of the world of tomorrow with their sacrifice.

Wednesday Night, September 11

I do not have to say anything about the intelligent and careful preparation that went into this raid, which has given our troops one of the most glorious and well-deserved victories. Anyone who is even slightly informed about these things can appreciate this.

A continuous movement of men toward the front occurred the previous night. Thousands and thousands of them came from all parts on foot, on horseback, in trucks, and even on motorcycles and tanks. The large number of marching soldiers and the war machines that advanced purposefully to the line of fire crammed the roads and byways. We could hear the constant sound of trucks carrying food and munitions, tanks closing in on their positions, and tractors transporting the heavy cannon from warships for use on land.

The night was especially dark and with heavy rain. A tempest was over us, delaying our glorious day, the great moment of victory for our cause. I left our command post and went to the small town of Jezainville, a distance of one kilometer. This is where I joined Sergeant Hal A. Irwin (today he sleeps the eternal sleep of heroes deep in his tomb, in the very field of battle). He was a brave companion, full of enthusiasm and faith. Five or six of us went to our new command post, the one we would be occupying during the assault.

We put aside our fatigue as we listened to our sergeant's lively conversation during the five-kilometer walk. He told us that some day we would share with our children and grandchildren the memory of this amazing adventure, that we would tell of the important part we are playing in this conflict, the greatest war in history (today, we are realizing the beautiful, prophetic vision of our good friend Irwin).

We arrived at Montaville after crossing a foothill. Things started to get more serious. German grenades started exploding close to the village around nine in the evening. This is how the enemy was welcoming us. Much as I try, it is impossible to describe my profound feelings during these terrible moments. I had heard a lot about the bursts of machine gun fire and its horrifying effects, which we now felt all around us. They never slowed me down.

The grenades were falling about fifty meters from us. The light of the explosions helped us to see our way. So many of us rolled down the foot of the hill when the grenades exploded! And yet the light from these same grenades helped us see in the dark.

A sergeant who acted as our guide got so far ahead of us that we lost contact. Our march became more difficult when we lost our way and had to climb the slippery and sticky clay on the side of a hill. I had to use my rifle as a cane to climb the hill. This is how I reached the side of another hill where the historic Le Prete forest begins. This was the location of our command post. We stayed in well-protected foxholes that somebody had dug out. The office of our colonel, the commander of our regiment, is near our foxholes.

Dispatches were arriving in quick succession bringing news from the different fighting units at the front. All of them had followed orders and were more than ready to advance. By this time (around eleven at night) everyone knew the reason why so many men were readying for battle while so near to the enemy. I knew that "the ZERO hour" would arrive at six in the morning. This was the supreme moment when we would jump over the ramparts and attack the enemy lines. It was the right time to demonstrate our manly courage. You could see the excited, quiet, and somber faces, as well as the serious and determined ones. Oh how those hours of unavoidable misfortune awakened such deep empathy among the men! The waiting was awful; it was agony itself.

Thursday, September 12

We must have had about two hours of restless sleep when a horrific noise shook the ground and awakened us. Our artillery had just directed its terrible fire on the enemy, the famous "barrage" that history will recount. How many tons of explosives—including shrapnel and poisonous gases—did we fire in such a short period of time? I could not guess the number, but I am sure there were many. The rapid, incessant, and horrible artillery fire that shook everything around us continued until ten in the morning. Intermittent fire lasted the rest of the day.

We took over fifteen thousand German prisoners as well as a great quantity of war supplies. Fifteen thousand captives mean that many rifles will no longer fire. How many must have been completely put out of action?

Our line of fire advanced beyond our objective, quickly and with only a slight loss of men.

This is the way that we attacked: As planned, the order was given to go "over the top" at six in the morning, leap over the trenches, and bare our chests against the fire of the enemy who was well prepared with all kinds of firepower, including rifles, pistols, bayonets, machine guns, mortars, small artillery, and hand grenades, all with powerful explosives. Our men defied death as they jumped over the trenches with great trepidation. The assault included infantry and machine gun squadrons, alongside automatic rifles, tanks, and the trench mortars—very powerful and terribly effective at a short distance—and many light, fast-moving, and rapid-firing cannon.

Our men were incredible as they ran over the enemy trenches, taking many prisoners and occupying positions of great strategic value. Our brave men presented an impressive sight when wave after wave of them entered the battlefield under a rain of explosives that left the kind of devastation we associate with the cyclones and tornados in Texas. Neither the shrapnel that filled the air nor the poisonous gas grenades slowed them down. They continued moving forward amid the whistling sound of the bullets and shrapnel, the sudden shouts of fellow soldiers, the screams of the wounded, and the sight of fallen comrades. They moved over a terrain dotted with rain-filled craters that the artillery was constantly creating. This is how we pushed our line beyond the point we had been assigned. We were exhausted, hungry, wounded, and gassed, but we had achieved our first victory.

The first two prisoners we brought to the office for a debriefing caused quite a stir. All of us wanted to hear what they had to say. They looked unsightly in their very German-style uniforms, rough and rugged boots, long mustaches, and helmets that gave them a ferocious look handed down by Alaric and Attila. My humble companion Gómez escorted the two wild men of the trenches who had learned to kill in so many savage and modern ways. He took them to the prisoner concentration camp at the point of his bayonet. One of them was very rebellious or very German. The other one was different, probably because he was younger and wanted to live. He gave us good information.

Friday, September 13

We witnessed a dogfight as our advance continued. One of our planes shot down a German plane nearby. It was an exhilarating sight. We saw one of the planes chasing the other with its machine guns firing away. They produced the rattling sound we hear in carnivals. Shortly after that, we saw black smoke coming from one of the sides of the German plane and figured the gas tank must have ignited. The plane nosedived with a winding motion like a wounded bird. One of the pilots—we do not know if he was dead or alive—fell from the sky like a lifeless leaf from a dried-up tree, spinning and spinning until he smashed into Mother Earth. We could not find the words to condemn the war and the pride that brought it upon us when we witnessed the unfortunate Christian spinning in the air without any hope whatsoever of saving himself.

Saturday, September 14

The scene that we had witnessed was the conversation of the day. Luis Rodríguez, one of our brave brothers from Losoya, Texas, and a follower of the Kaiser were impaled in each other's bayonets. If this is not the best reason to be proud of Mexicans (this is akin to worshipping the savage nature of armed men) we cannot think of a better one. These two human lions found each other while on scouting patrols. What happened when they met? No one knows. We do not believe they took the time to exchange pleasantries or words of any kind. They only had one thought: Fulfill the call of duty. The clashing sounds of the bayonet's steel followed, along with three cries of agony, and the dark mantle of the night covered them in silence. This entire drama took place in the dark and in the most profound state of silence. The German had sustained two bayonet wounds, the Mexican only one. They ended up leaning against each other in a narrow trench. The night's rain worked its miracle by washing the blood that could have made the usually unsightly scene more horrendous. They still looked alive as if they were in good health and with the full vigor of life. They had barely released their grip over their rifles that propped them up. All their blood collected at their feet. It would soon turn into mud, worms, stench, and murky matter. A fatal end!

The airplanes were in serious combat the entire morning. They later retired to their bases to be resupplied with ammunition and gasoline or to tend to repairs that cannot be done while in the air.

Many gas victims have arrived. This is one of the most sad and horrible results of war. Some of the boys tell me that many soldiers throw away most of their equipment during combat in order to lighten their load and enjoy some freedom of movement. Wearing the gas mask and carrying the rest of the load is oppressive because breathing becomes very difficult. The poisonous gases give you a few seconds to hold your breath until the mask is in place. Doing this on the battlefield where death is all around requires steady nerves that are difficult to maintain. We put up with hunger, exhaustion, and the rain, but the lack of clean air is impossible to tolerate. Men seem resigned to die, and even welcome it when a shell hits them and we cannot stop the hemorrhage. On the other hand, dying slowly from the poison in our lungs and the loss of our minds is horrible. Watching the wretched scene of victims agonizing, drooling, purplish, and feverish is just as bad.

Sunday, September 15

This was a day of mourning for our detachment, the Intelligence Corps of the 360th. Death took our brave, popular Sergeant Irwin at ten in the morning. He saved entire battalions on several occasions and was trying to save a company of soldiers in enemy territory when he fell. When Sergeant Irwin found himself too far away to contact us, he decided to save the last two buddies by jumping out of his foxhole and into the open field. The artillery opened fire from different directions and a shell that landed nearby killed him. An enormous fragment tore into the left side of his thorax. When soldiers rendered him aid, he could only say "take me to the hospital." They dragged him to a small foxhole where he died and was buried. May he rest in peace and serve as the best example of sacrificing oneself for the nation.

Something else happened that was no less heroic. We had been having difficulties with a machine gun that was firing out of a well-fortified pillbox. The impressive fortification allowed the machine gun to cut down all the soldiers who tried to move past it. One of our sergeants was ordered to remove the entrenched German who had been engaging entire armies. The sergeant asked a Mexican private to accompany him. Moisés Carrejo of Laredo, Texas, received the honor. These are the kind of moments that can immortalize a man. A serious and singular decision followed as it became necessary to sacrifice soldiers' lives. We had no time to occupy ourselves with anything else. Who were the lucky ones? The nearby soldiers. Did they fail? Never! They removed their heavy load and crawled on their stomachs with their pistols drawn. There was no other way to climb or come down the hill. They moved halfway up with Carrejo in front and exposed themselves to German fire. They climbed a little higher. The German did not go any farther. Carrejo understood that the danger was the same whether he advanced or retreated so he continued crawling until he reached the top of the hill and the machine gun. The German soldier did not notice him and continued to concentrate on our advancing troops, who more than ever tried to draw his attention. Carrejo had time to move closer, and with nerves of steel, got near the German soldier and jumped on him. He shot the German in the neck and threw him, dead as could be, into the bottom of the trench.

The German had stopped our advance by himself. He thought he was safe, but did not understand fearsome Aztec courage. It was also obvious that a Colt pistol could silence a German soldier behind a modern machine gun in an invincible pillbox.

The day ended with the impressive advance of French forces toward the front, as well as the movement of our large cannon that are getting close and ready to crush Fritz. Life has become more difficult for the artillerymen who have to drag these enormous monsters over muddy terrain. There is no other way. According to the information secured from one of the prisoners, which is corroborated by others, the Germans are making a forced retreat. We have also been taking Austrian prisoners.

One of our great cannon was deployed fifty yards from our position. Its first practice discharge blew out the glass windows in our dugout.

Our army suffered few losses. They are insignificant when we consider what we have done, including the large number of prisoners and material that we have captured. According to some of the high-ranking prisoners, they never expected our sudden attack. We even caught them asleep. When the bombing started, they had no other recourse but to retreat to their quarters and wait for our deadly artillery and advancing troops. The little resistance they offered meant they had given up. They surprised us. Their willingness to surrender unconditionally also showed a low morale.

The real resistance came from the German artillery. They continue to fire from Metz.

On this day, our fearsome American eagle has flown with triumphant pride over the palace of Kaiser Wilhelm II of Germany.

Monday, September 16

Our artillery, machine guns, and infantry continue their intense firing. We did not prepare an intelligence report this afternoon. I cannot explain it, but I believe our men's forward movement has been so quick it is impossible to locate the different command posts. Call it what you will, strategic retreat or something else, the Germans are on the run. Once in a while they resist with their truck-mounted artillery, a weak attempt to protect their infantry.

I wrote home and did nothing while outside the entire day. This is my first Sixteenth of September at war. Today is the solemn day for our people in Mexico. The martial spirit of my people speaks . . . "The spirit shall speak for my *raza*!"[24]

Tuesday, September 17

We did not advance today and everything was normal as far as the war was concerned. Everyone who had money was allowed to telegraph home with the news that things have gone well against the Germans, the same ones who were supposed to sweep us away as if they were using a broom. In the end, we brushed them off with our bullets and bayonets. They themselves say this.

I had no money to communicate with my family; they will have to continue agonizing over me. I am glad that Providence has not called me and allowed me to continue with my military duties, "I'm fine with my bad luck."

Wednesday, September 18

Nothing new has transpired as another day passes and brings us closer to our end. We have stopped moving forward and all we are able to do now is repeat a thousand and one times our impressions over our first baptism of blood. They are so deeply etched we will remember them as if they happened yesterday even if we live one hundred years.

I received the sad news that my good friend Pablo Pérez was killed during our last battle. I do not doubt it but I also pray to God that this is not true since his passing has not been confirmed.

I received a letter from Crispín, my brother.

Thursday, September 19

It was rainy and cold today. I had a splitting headache and soon after finishing my report, I went to my foxhole and slept soundly until this morning. I am glad that I have suffered headaches as often as when I was in civilian life. Because of this, I can tolerate the life of the sons of Mars.

How Carrejo and Four Others Died

Friday, September 20

woke up very early, washed, and went to the office, feeling good but somewhat weak after yesterday's migraine. The barrage was heavy at Le Prete Forest yesterday. Our command post is located on its edge. If this is such a peaceful sector, then why do the cords and other regalia on the soldiers' uniforms burn the way they do? What we do know is that we are providing critical help in the great Saint-Mihiel campaign to secure the territory the Germans grabbed from France four years ago. And we did it in just a few days of fighting. Everything was done so quickly the enemy never discovered our covert preparations. We can truthfully say that we gave them a taste of their own medicine.

The days followed their normal course. The nervous excitement normally felt in the front trenches ended as we advanced against the tenacious enemy. The capture of the German machine gun was already old news. It was necessary to find new adventures. Oh, but how life in the line of fire offers opportunities for a thousand adventures! Death is at every turn. We are so used to it we no longer fear it.

Company M's trench zigzagged by the side of a small hill. The area had a lush vineyard loaded with delicious fruit. We dug the trenches without giving much thought to the fact that the land had been used for nurturing wheat, vineyards, and gardens.

I should note that we ate well in the front trenches after an advance. The food was good and included a variety of items. For breakfast, they gave us good hot coffee with canned milk, oatmeal, bacon, butter, syrup, and hard American biscuits. For lunch (at four in the afternoon), we had beans cooked in bacon, corn, salmon, beefsteak, hash, plums, and the unforgettable cornwillie (corned beef hash made of bull or dog meat). Everything was delicious and served in generous amounts, but our friends and brothers in misery, Moisés Carrejo from Laredo, Canuto Farías from Beeville, Cayetano González from Tuleta, Max Hinojosa from Falfurrias, and Andrés Rosales from El Paso, were not satisfied and looked for the opportunity to also eat the "forbidden grapes." We had strict orders not to eat any fruit or vegetable on the battlefields, but all it took was for one of the boys to say, "Last one to climb and get grapes is a . . . !" The five men jumped like panthers out of the trenches and practically landed under the barrels of the German cannon. My Mexican brothers had been eating together for a few days all the while talking about their adventures and revisiting pleasant memories from their distant homes. The actions of these fearless men put their fellow soldiers in danger when the German fired his artillery at them. The whole world trembled when someone mentioned the German artillery and its engineers. The Mexicans were the only ones who dared to mock those despicable Boches. The evidence was there. Our brave soldiers!

They repeated their regular grape-picking excursion at four. The Germans were more successful with their fire this time. They had been so embarrassed at not being able to demonstrate the technical knowledge they acquired in military school. A huge bomb landed in the very trenches where the boys were eating. After the horrible explosion and in the middle of a thick cloud of dark and stinking smoke, we found a disgusting mass covered under dirt, three Mexican Americans and two German Americans. That is how Carrejo and his inseparable companions fell. Max and Andrés survived to tell the story. Their names, like those of all humble soldiers, are destined to be quickly forgotten in the dark shadows of oblivion. They died demonstrating unrestrained valor for the lofty principles of our cause. They deserve the eternal gratitude of our people!

Saturday, September 21

I typed quite a bit today because a prisoner we captured last night gave us much valuable information. I had to make several copies of the report so the people responsible for examining this kind of information can decide on its merits.

The duel between the heavy-caliber cannon lasted all night. We did not suffer many deaths on our front.

Sunday, September 22

The German cannon shelled our positions heavily all night until dawn. Our compatriots who remained in the states—exempt from duty or in military service but without the chance of ever coming here—will miss the greatest adventure of our time. They will not have crouched or curled up by the sides of the trenches, in water-soaked foxholes, and, worst of all, they will not have faced the continuous explosion of shells inching closer to their positions. Even drunks cannot sleep in these conditions. Some soldiers insist that they sleep well, but they give themselves away before the day is over when they give an account of what transpired during the night. We really wish a night like ours for fellow citizens who sleep in soft beds until the morning, just one, so that they can appreciate the difficult, bad, horrible, and dangerous moments faced by the many soldiers who will not return to claim credit or tally dues. If they had seen the appearance of the soldiers in their trenches at daybreak and if they had understood the look, then we could heal the world and make it a true paradise for democracy.

We have not heard anything about our losses in the last battle. Sometimes it is better not to know and to feign ignorance. The French have been moving more trucks and 75 millimeter guns to the front. Several of the cannon of the US Marines have passed by and others have been deployed near our position.

I have been so concerned that I had not realized this was Sunday.

According to our way of thinking, the French should be given credit for their courage. The poor private only has one uniform, a blanket, rifle, and bayonet, and is poorly fed. I have seen their daily rations. They consist of raw potatoes, a liter of white wine, and a piece of bread, the famous "pain de guerre." Those of us who are familiar with it know that it is not appetizing, especially when we are at war and facing an enemy. The bread is made with wheat bran. If it has flour, it usually contains very little and is of very poor quality. Many people insist it is mostly made of sawdust from a soft and fragrant tree growing in the mountains. Like any fresh bread, it smells good when it is hot out of the oven, but once it gets cold and hard, it feels like wood. We have seen hundreds or thousands of soldiers that look like they are whittling wood when slicing or cutting pieces of bread with a pocketknife. Even under these conditions, however, the French soldier is the first one to attack the enemy trenches while singing the "Marseillaise." The thousands of white crosses with a tricolor at their center speak of the many who have fallen before the powerful salvos from the vicious and violent Germans.

I have moved into an old house and Gómez and Barrera have joined me. I enter into some serious conversations with some Frenchmen who are also staying with us and have come to feel comfortable exchanging views in their language. All of them have been serving for more than two years and are tired of the war, but they are willing to fight until they throw the Germans out of France. They tell me their people are very grateful for our help in the war. They believe that final victory will come within days.

Our first cold front hit us today, reminding us that we are not at home and that winter approaches. Winter will make our lives a thousand times worse. We have heard rumors that General John J. Pershing, the commander in chief of the American forces, will know how to make use of our sterling troops and favorable weather to lead the supreme offensive that will squash the Germans.

Monday, September 23

Two prisoners we took today provided the necessary information for our artillerymen to wipe out a good number of the enemy's positions.

Could yesterday's occurrence have been superstition or a premonition? When my buddies announced it was suppertime, I was typing and focusing on my office work. Gómez said, "let's go to supper," and I sensed a loss of nerve and it felt stranger than fear itself, but I was able to control my emotions. The soldiers began to get their utensils. I did not want to say anything about what had come over me. No one may have noticed what was happening and I had no reason to worry, as I was more than thirty feet below ground and well protected. Also, we were not fighting but on a break. I felt something strange and unexplainable. I told my good friend Gómez, "please get my supper; I want to finish this job." He did not think twice, picked up my lunch container, jumped out of the foxhole and quickly returned with my food. I ate and continued working, without thinking or feeling anything again. This occurred yesterday at four. Today, supper was announced at the same time and we went to eat as usual. Everyone got in line and offered his lunch box to show that he was ready to be served. We all followed the routine. While in line, we heard the braying mule sound of a heavy-caliber shell flying through the air. There is little time to find shelter when you hear the sound. We barely had time to fall to the ground and fill up a small nearby ditch with our bodies. All this took place in a fraction of a second. We fell hard to the ground and felt a tremor run through our faces. The heavy shell landed at the end of the line, where we had formed the line for supper. It shook the ground and took our breath away. The enormous shell tore into the ground. One can well imagine our anxious moments as we waited for the explosion that was to follow and tell us if we were to live or die. We held our breath during those terrible seconds. Soon enough, someone said, "This one failed Fritz." We returned to the land of the living, got up, and set about examining the monster of death that had landed in lifeless form next to our supper line. It measured around four feet in length and eleven or twelve inches in diameter. We had scarcely shaken off the cold sweat that comes at times like these, when someone blurted, "If it had exploded, neither kitchen nor cooks would have survived!" What about us? It was obvious that we would have been the first ones to be flung to faraway places. We could have landed back on Mother Earth as useless matter or as an incapacitated lot destined to join the home guard and civilian life.

As expected, the soldiers continued talking and offering opinions about the incident. When my turn came, I described my experience from the previous day and asked my buddies to be candid with their thoughts. I asked them if they thought that what I had felt was real and not a dream and whether it was related or not to what just occurred. That was my challenge to them. Some said nothing and became somewhat pensive. Others believed what I said and corroborated my story with their own. We also had cynics, as one would expect in such a big army with men of so many races who think differently.

I had another interesting experience today. Someone stole my underwear, which I had washed yesterday. This is the first time this has happened. Our soldiers are so well provisioned they never have to resort to stealing clothes. This problem may be due to soldiers throwing their clothes away to avoid carrying a heavy load during the marches. Some even discard their food rations and then complain about not having enough to eat. This is really unfair to our government. Each man is fully equipped with two complete uniforms of wool, three changes of underwear (two of light material and three heavy, sometimes all three are the heavy kind), four pairs of socks, wool shirts (many of us have three), and an extra pair of heavy shoes. Why steal?

Tuesday, September 24

We had another serious artillery duel last night. Three airplanes flew over us and directed machine gun fire on our positions. Some were flying at a low altitude and dropping propaganda materials. Our artillery responded with heavy fire but could not bring down any of them. The printed materials were written in English and announced that the war was about to end, that Germany was stronger than ever. Their posturing made us laugh instead of striking us with fear.

I received letters from home and felt very happy.

One of the big guns that are to be used against heavy fortifications passed by on its way to the front around ten this morning. Twelve large, strong horses and twenty muscular soldiers pulled it over roads mangled by the shells that are constantly exploding over them. We witnessed their difficult lives. The men and horses were exhausted from the difficult march. They had just entered Le Prete Forest, about four hundred yards from our position, when we heard a tremendous explosion that shook the entire area. A shell had landed on all the unfortunate men and animals as they positioned the monstrous cannon to do damage on "our fellow man." The lesson is this: "Do to your neighbor what he wishes for you and if you can do a little more, the better." A messenger brought us the news. We went to see the "glorious" scene as soon as we could. This is the way we should describe these kinds of situations. If others deserve crowns and flowers, these soldiers should receive the palms of glory with roots and all. It is necessary to praise them with something immediately. Otherwise, oblivion will consume them. Neither horse nor soldier survived, and the steel monster became useless! A more horrible sight cannot be imagined. The torn, darkened, foul-smelling, and newly exposed human flesh of so many men in the full bloom of life was mixed with the equally fresh horse remains that smelled of burned blood and gunpowder! Oh, war, we are still alive to witness with our very eyes what you have been, are, and will continue to be until the end of time!

Wednesday, September 25

Much aerial activity occurred today. One of our responsibilities is to use big telescopes to identify the types of airplanes flying over us. We have little difficulty seeing the marks underneath their wings.

The news that we are to prepare for a move to a new front hit us like a bomb. This means another offensive. More blood will be spilled. We left everything in place as if we were to return. The order stated, "You might return."

We left our command post at six in the afternoon, sixty men from the R.I.O, some zappers, messengers, and the signal corps, the ones who look after the phones. The maps and other orders were given to some sergeants who were to take us to our new command post. They were not to share the orders with the lowly privates. This was not the worst of it. The problem was that the sergeants lost their way because they did not understand the geographic marks on the maps. When we were about to reach our destination—at eight—we lost our way while walking on very narrow roads in the middle of a dense forest. The soldiers and the other sergeants who were with our platoon had nothing to say, we simply continued to move forward.

Barrera, the unforgettable soldier from San Diego, was the only one on horseback. He had other horses in tow. The horses were for some officers who were to ride them back. His packhorse carried a sack of barley and gas masks for all the horses. We must remember that even the poor animals share in the miseries of this war. It was interesting to see the troops walking with no definite idea or plan, very tired, surrounded by thick fog, and facing the entrenched Germans nearby. We were soaked with sweat; we walked as quietly as possible. No one talked even though we were not told to be quiet. We only heard the tired and uneven marching sound of men and animals.

We moved like this until eleven. We would walk forward, read the map to find our way back, and end up in the same spot. We knew we were lost. It was then that we began to hear the impolite chatter from the angry, tired, and frustrated soldiers. Their words were not kind, although they did not bear ill will. Their language was simply the most natural expression by desperate soldiers sensing imminent danger. The Germans began directing a terrible barrage at us that immediately triggered a response from our artillery. The duel would not have been unusual, except that it reminded us of our position in the middle of "no man's land." The shells crisscrossed over our heads and emptied their dreaded shrapnel on us. They accomplished what they set out to do. The shelling made our march more difficult and even made it tougher to find our way back through the thick forest. The shells were so numerous and they exploded so often that they practically lighted up the bare trees. We would have preferred to march under the cover of darkness. When it became obvious that we could not find our way out of the forest, we were ordered to seek shelter in a foxhole. The incessant bombing lasted for a good while. We could hear the shells howling as they flew over us, in much the same way that souls must scream in eternal hell. It is no exaggeration to say that the different caliber fire was so intense that many shells met in midair and exploded, raining shrapnel over us. The destruction of the forest was dreadful. No one spoke. Everyone was quiet as we took in everything. It was like a dream that could not be believed. Once in a great while someone would say something but we would not respond. That was not the time for conversation. The heavy hand of destiny had made us unwilling spectators. We were all eyes and ears, observing and hearing everything. I had the nagging feeling that I thought was shared by everyone, that it was a shame to lose our lives under such tragic circumstances.

The situation may be serious, but we are not about to stop recording experiences we will remember after the storm has passed. The events will lose their sense of urgency and even seem amusing once we recall them calmly and far removed from this place. Sergeant Baton insisted that we continue to move forward. Other sergeants disagreed. We had neither voice nor vote and had to obey. Danger was all around us and it made no difference if we moved or not. We have one life to lose and feel that it has been dangling for some time from our saddle straps. We would occasionally move from one foxhole to another. Each could accommodate four men in the act of firing. We were following Sergeant Baton. We recognize his bravery and decisiveness, and he has treated us better than other superiors. It is best to be with people we trust during the fighting and when the end arrives. The rest of the soldiers had settled so well into their foxholes that the earth seemed to have swallowed them. One of the sergeants made an effort to get his men together and move forward, but no one responded.

While moving between the foxholes, Gómez, Barrera, and I became so busy with the instruments we were carrying that I forgot my rifle, and I did not miss it until a good while later. This shows that we were still lacking in the art of war and, like Juan A. Mateos's warriors, we had a long way before we made "the rifle and our saddle a part of us."[1] I returned for my rifle, leaving everything behind, including my buddies. I found many foxholes with rifles. The devil's ground was strewn with weapons, but I wanted mine. I could not see or recognize anything in the darkness, except for the flashes of the exploding shells. The trees were falling and this made the search more difficult. Finally, I found it. I relaxed and returned with no problems. I was not worried about anything because I had done well in finding my rifle. Later, I wondered why I had not taken another rifle since they were all the same, had the same owner, and served an identical purpose. I did not think about those things.

When I found my friends, they made me the butt of their jokes. They said I had been a good soldier and that my rifle had come first before my life.

Sergeant Baton finally decided to go out in search of our command post, which had been our objective all along. Fewer than a dozen men joined him. Barrera would not leave his two horses. If the march was difficult for the foot soldiers, it was harder for Barrera and his horses. The flashes of light from exploding shells showed Barrera struggling with the animals, which also seemed to be losing their nerve. He had to find a way to move with his horses, with death always looming over him. He could not abandon them. They had become a part of him. The foul smell of so many gases and spent shells made the place unbearable and nauseating. It felt like Dante's inferno.

Some of our soldiers were spouting an infernal language with free abandon. They cursed when it would have been best to reach out to God in prayer. Man is capable of everything!

We had an important and dangerous experience while all of this was going on. Shining objects appeared by the branches that had fallen from the broken and stripped trees and near the many craters left by the exploding shells. The dew had turned into rain, soaking everything, while the flashes of light from the explosions revealed a row of helmets. We first thought they were French and knew they were not ours. When we checked out the area, we heard someone shout "Stop" as we neared the helmets. We could not tell if the command was for us or the soldiers we had discovered, but quickly realized it was directed at what turned out to be a patrol of six Germans who were scouting no man's land, and that an American colonel had shouted the command. He was also lost in the confusion and was looking for his post. One of our messengers was with him. They saved us from falling into the clutches of the Germans they took prisoner. The head of the German patrol was a high-ranking officer. We did not know his rank, but discovered that he knew enough English to be understood. He told us the patrol was bent on taking us prisoners, but they had not noticed that someone had come up behind them while they were waiting to ambush us. We made them prisoners but that had resulted from the fact that they were lost and wandering through no man's land. The Germans were taken to the concentration camp and we continued on our way.

The capture of a German colonel and his squad by an American colonel lost in no man's land and accompanied only by a messenger sounds more like a movie than the real thing. We must not forget, however, that everything that took place in that wretched land will never be completely understood. The things that occurred are impossible to faithfully reproduce in a movie. During the rainy nights and the terrible attacks and counterattacks, it was not uncommon to find good-sized platoons of wandering, shocked, disconcerted, desperate, and lost soldiers who welcomed being captured. This is how the remarkable case of Luis C. Gutiérrez of Losoya, Texas, occurred.

We quickened our pace and reached the first position in the front that we had previously occupied. The animals had to stay behind because it was impossible to march with them. Barrera stayed with them. Gómez and I regretted the parting of ways but it could not be helped. We came to a fortification that had served as a German command post a few days earlier. Little can be said about these structures but that the Germans thought them impenetrable and that they would only occupy them until the end of the war. They had them for four years, equipped with all the modern conveniences, and the assurance that the French would never take them. The structures included trenches with well-arranged halls and paved floors, cement walls, and a roof that offered good protection. Many had protective iron sheets, steel rails taken as spoils from the French, cement, and a lot of dirt. They were well supplied with furniture stolen from French homes and had all that was needed to live comfortably in the trenches, including electric lights, musical instruments like pianos, etc., and much beer. They may not have had much food, but they had plenty to drink. They were making good use of the area they had taken. Germans have always believed they owned everything taken by force. This is why they have even cut timber and, on many occasions, sent it home. They would do this with other things of value like machinery for their factories, trains, etc. We later came across one of those fortifications and made it our command post. The place had a good roof although it was open in the direction of the enemy. We are sleeping in one of the French trenches with an exit facing away from our troops. We had just retired and were feeling the warmth of our bed when we heard a voice: "Up and over the top!" Many of the soldiers who did not usually discard their backpacks and slept by simply leaning against them were better prepared to answer the call than the rest of us who were already in bed. We have different ways of thinking. If we slept, we were in a better condition to continue. If we did not sleep, they would get the best of us. Our bodies are weak when we do not sleep or rest. This is obvious, but we are told, *forward*! And forward we go!

A Horrible Night in "No Man's Land"

Thursday, September 26

We were on the move in the early morning. Gas shells fell on all the wooded areas, and the odor seeping out of the crater-marked ground was horrible and asphyxiating. The destruction of the great trees was also shocking. The powerful explosives from the heavy artillery uprooted them. The moon appeared at the first light of day while the sky was still full of stars and the dew over the plants in the woods and valleys brought the temperature down. This is what we saw of the countryside as we crossed it on our way to our destination.

We arrived at the actual command post at six in the morning after a search of twelve hours in the brambles, where death was suspended over us. I had not really done all I could for the soldiers because the order had been a secret and I could not reveal any of it. I knew the plan of action given to our sergeants because I had worked on it all day. I had marked many of the positions that appeared on the small rough sketch. Our adventure actually took me on an unexpected, unwanted, and unforgettable visit to the feared no man's land. Fortunately, we made the journey and we were now ready for whatever was to follow. How many of our soldiers have fallen during this fight and are not able to say this?

The lack of sleep, along with gas, left me with a serious headache, but I was fortunate to get my hands on a small solid alcohol stove. It was very useful, and I demonstrated this by quickly making myself a cup of coffee. My buddies teased me when I got it, but were later amazed at its usefulness. Making coffee in such difficult circumstances requires an explanation so no one may think I am exaggerating. Other soldiers could have done the same, and if they did not, it may have been entirely their fault. The reader may remember that I included the "condiment can" among my food utensils. The can has compartments. Since I have not had food to carry, I fill one half with sugar and the other with coffee. Who can doubt me when I say I have often avoided the headaches caused by the lack of coffee in the morning? On occasions when the morning finds us on our feet, I am glad to be able to chew on a spoonful of coffee with a bit of sugar. I also carry salt and pepper in the container, and during the hard, trying moments when I have nothing else but a can of tomatoes, everyone should know that I do not stay hungry for long. Many soldiers have been less prepared and have suffered the long moments of "growling stomachs."

Other soldiers used the "magical stove" on that morning. They can attest to its worth. Oh good God, so much misery, and we do not understand why! The hot coffee with our reliable "hardtack" biscuits hit the spot and revived exhausted, hungry, and drowsy soldiers. This is not the first time I have avoided going without in such difficult circumstances. I have also sought out my readings, conversations and, especially, recollections from my past.

The command post was at the foot of a hill that overlooked an entire beautiful valley with a meandering creek of crystalline water. Our post faced memorable hill 121, where so many German cannon were located.

Our command post was a true fortification, constructed with attention to detail by someone who understood how well it could defy death. It was one of the famous "pillboxes." The thick walls were made of Roman cement and its roof of heavy zinc plates, a layer of weighty steel rails, and a complete cover of dirt. These are the kinds of posts that typically include small cannon and machine guns. The fort oversaw most of the terrain that we had crossed without the benefit of cover. A large number of trenches stretched along the side of the hill. Many of our men fell during the night and are continuing to fall in these trenches. We had a hard time hearing the moans of injured soldiers. They were cold, hungry, thirsty, in pain, and weak from the loss of blood and untreated injuries. They asked for water and medical attention, but we could do nothing. What will our fate be if injured in battle! Under these circumstances, we would rather die. This weighed heavily on us. We were very sad and disheartened, but had to meet our military responsibilities. Like last night, the bombardment continues today. The German engineers knew the location of our post, they understood its importance, and their cannon fired with great accuracy. The shells exploded over us and we could hear the bullets and shrapnel whistle and buzz through the air. The shells had obvious bad intentions, and they rained shrapnel over the trees that surrounded us. As foot soldiers we preferred the open air and sat outside our foxholes to hear and see, to witness all these things. I had nothing else to do but to put my observations in writing, and here they are.

Many of our machine guns were placed alongside the hill. They would occasionally discharge heavy volleys while the infantry fired in quick succession. The Germans answered with heavy cannon fire that filled the air with deadly shrapnel.

Enemy artillery fire surprised and surrounded Company M of the 3rd Infantry Battalion at the same time that our men were firing on a German emplacement. The company was nearly wiped out. The few soldiers who survived will always remember this. Other companies replaced them until we were able to secure the post. The horrible trail of dead and wounded soldiers was visible along the side of the hill. Our men died as real heroes because they were not just carrying out an order, they were also sacrificing themselves as they provided cover to thousands and thousands of men. This is war. And what about those who die? They remain unknown.

We held our positions until after the noon hour when we were ordered to return to our old command post close to Monteville. We retreated with our rifles at the ready. The enemy did not stop shelling us as we made our way without taking time to defend ourselves. We moved through some well-covered trenches. Sometimes we had to take to the open field where we made good targets for the German cannon. Their artillery fired on us knowing that we could not respond effectively. Soldiers were walking everywhere without any form of organization. We were not falling apart, much less defeated, but everyone was doing as they pleased.

We had a difficult time moving through a good number of places because the Germans had marked them well. It was extremely dangerous.

Some of our wounded and gassed soldiers found refuge in an enormous crater left by an enemy bomb. They were trying to avoid the dangerous shells. A short while later, another group of soldiers slipped in with them. At that very moment, the bloodthirsty Fritz fired another bomb that landed on what looked like a trap set by hunters. The bomb disintegrated all of them. This was one of the most horrendous sights we saw with our own eyes and felt with our souls. The Germans must have been celebrating it as one of their biggest victories. To pay back is like returning a favor.

Gómez, Barrera, and I continued to move at short intervals. I asked them if it was possible to avoid a shell by the sound it made. The question gave them an opportunity to claim expert knowledge on the subject. They agreed that the sound could be the warning to escape. Gómez and Barrera have seen more explosions than most soldiers. (This is because they have been crossing the dangerous battlefields as couriers since we reached the front. The cold, rain, and danger matter little to them. Also, they cannot expect replacements because the other messengers usually hide in their foxholes and do not respond when called.) I thought the shells were somewhat considerate in announcing their arrival. They advised me that "when you hear the whizzing, immediately fall to the ground, into some ditch on either side of the road to avoid the shrapnel and shell fragments." I took their counsel in good faith. Soon after that, I heard the piercing braying sound of a big one tearing above our heads. No sooner had my friends warned, "Here comes one," than I quickly threw myself on the ground with a loud thud. I landed in a small ditch by the side of the road. They laughed uncontrollably at the joke they had played on me. The shell was exploding two miles away at the very moment I took cover. I caught on too late but promised I would make them pay. I can say this because I have the advantage of being older.

By the afternoon, I finally understood that by the time we hear the strident bellowing of one of those infernal monsters, the danger has passed. We were held up temporarily in Villers-en-Frey because the little town was being heavily bombarded with deadly accuracy. One of the hardest hit areas was the road we were on. While on the road, I had the opportunity to closely observe the effects of the enemy's barrage. I saw explosions everywhere. A black trail of smoke first rises from the ground, followed by a heavy shaking of everything around us and, almost at the same time, lightning and the deafening explosions that shred the shells into shrapnel and tear into the bowels of the earth. Afterward, we could hear the fragments and the shrapnel, garbage, and great clumps of ground or dust flying through the air. The explosions followed one after another. The shells fell everywhere. This explains why the soldiers killed by the explosions do not even hear the thunderous sound.

Our friend, Sergeant Kruger, miraculously survived an incident he will never forget. He was walking ahead of us when we suddenly saw the flash of lightning and a deadly plume of smoke nearby. We were shaken instantly. There was no time for anyone to fall to the ground. Sergeant Kruger tottered a bit, righted himself, and continued marching. We had heard a dull sound and quickly began examining soldiers close to us to see if someone had been hit by the shrapnel. We went up to the sergeant and asked, "Are you okay Sergeant?" He answered, "I don't feel an injury although I felt something hit me." We continued walking, and a short time later he took off his backpack to satisfy his curiosity. We began to look at the backpack and discovered a hole about two inches long and one inch wide. The clothes showed signs of the trajectory of the metal. We found a shell fragment in the pocket of the backpack and in a can of the famous corned beef. The piece of metal is now his best souvenir because it came close to his body and almost caused his death. We could not believe it. We have often come close to being killed. This time, we must credit a can of meat for saving the life of an American sergeant.

The lack of sleep, the march, and the gases made us lightheaded by the time we reached our post. I had a bad headache and could not find anyone to receive my report. I did not feel like eating supper and quickly moved into my nest. I went out like a light.

Friday, September 27

The rest helped me recover. I woke up very early and went to my post to do the first translation of the day. The report was brief but interesting. No reason was given for yesterday's sacrifice. These experiences will be muted in history.

I wrote some letters home.

I received a letter from a young woman in Cotulla who was my student many years ago. A letter from her was what I least expected. She must be an attractive woman by now. She shared some colorful stories about the town and the friends I left behind. Her letter brought back memories from a seemingly distant past.

I made a new friend today. He is one of the aides to a French lieutenant who serves as a liaison with our colonel and speaks Spanish fluently. The soldier was born and raised in Argentina and has properties there. He tells me that when the war began he brought his family to France so he could serve his country. He complains about how the war is dragging on, but is determined to fight until he dies or we win. We understand each other so well and engage in long conversations over a number of topics. This helps us momentarily forget the smell of spent powder and the gases of war. His name is Macelin Andreus and he is with the 6th Company of the 162nd Infantry Regiment.

Roy Martin, another friend, has come from the front lines to give me a souvenir he found in a trench where he sleeps. It is a lovely French book of poems on fishing and agriculture. He thought the book was important because it contains an infinite number of beautiful illustrations. The book's subject matter is obviously of little importance to a frontline soldier. I nevertheless appreciate the present because it expresses Martin's kindness and his regard for me. I will take care of it and send it home along with other souvenirs I have collected. I regret that I might have to leave many things behind, including the book from Martin, especially if we continue moving so quickly to other fronts.

Gómez, Barrera, and I have found a good way to keep busy during the long nights. I should note that our latitude gives us shorter days than in Texas. This means we have longer nights to think and to think some more.

They enjoy the short stories, anecdotes, tales, and jokes I tell them. Since this is my strong point, I am able to entertain them until we are ready to go to sleep. We fix our beds—or rat's nests—early in the morning in the big dilapidated house by the hill. For four years, the house has taken in many soldiers of different social and racial backgrounds on their way to the front. How many soldiers who have slept here must now be enjoying their eternal rest! Paraffin candles provide lighting. They may be weak but they are better than the San Antonio lights on Houston Street. Other soldiers and the three Frenchmen are also quartered in this shack. The others play cards or dice and write. We spend hours longing for other times and places with our stories. Rainy nights make us happy because they help us forget the horrors of this cursed war.

Saturday, September 28

Something interesting occurred in our sector today. A German soldier of Polish descent deserted with the idea of surrendering to our army. He kept waving a white handkerchief so that we would take him prisoner. Our soldiers, however, were on to the cunning and crafty Germans who were known for being deceitful. This time, the deserter did not receive the benefit of the doubt. The soldiers of the 3rd Battalion were the first to fire, until he fell. He barely had enough time to show his good intentions when he was taken prisoner. He said he had decided to come to our side because he was tired of a war that was being fought for Prussian tyranny. The prisoner sounded credible when he asked for a map to show us where most of the enemy's artillery was located. Our doctors cared for him as much as they could, but it was all in vain. He had several wounds in his lungs and died shortly thereafter. The information he gave was very useful in our subsequent operations.

We felt good after a second day of rest and only have yesterday's bitter memories to replay in our minds.

Sunday, September 29

I was awakened very early and ordered to make carbon copies of the information the Polish German deserter provided yesterday. The report notes that the wretched soldier did not only want to escape, but also that he would have been glad to join us in our cause. He was an artillery sergeant with the 33rd Regiment.

My Dear Wife:

I was very happy to receive your last letter. I have been well and have been receiving frequent letters from all of you. Know that as long as we are in this crusade, we do not belong to one another. We are the children of our nation until we achieve victory or die. Let us thank God for his kindness toward us. Share everything in your letters. I am not in need of anything except the sight of all of you and since this is not possible, I want nothing now. I have not bought anything with the little they pay me here. If this continues, I will become rich. Keep the clippings of some of my letters that appear in *La Prensa*.

I close, yours always,

Luz

Marce:

I am very happy to reply to your letter. Everything is well with me.

Do not leave our home. You are needed there as much as in the war. I always think of the baby "chicks" I left behind and I never lose hope of seeing them again.

I sent Eugenio and some other persons an account of something I witnessed here not long ago. We have really dealt a blow to the pride of the German Kaiser during the last few days. If we continue like this, he will have to twist his arrogant moustache and finally sue for peace.

As always,

Your brother who loves all of you,

Luz

Monday, September 30

Our ground fire shot up a German plane. This was the only major distraction of the day, the kind of death-defying incident that helps us pass the time. This reminds me of the Romans during those cruel days when their great circus was in its heyday, when it offered the best entertainment for carefree audiences. They amused themselves with bloody fights between men, beasts, and even men and beasts. They were a bloodthirsty people who were oblivious to the suffering of others. It may not be long before we can say the same about us, that is, if we are made to continue with this spectacle.

The day was more than boring, cold, and cloudy. Dark clouds passed over us. The sky may be so taken aback by our cruel, savage behavior that it places a heavy black shroud between us and the divine blue firmament.

Tuesday, October 1

I found out that the French soldiers left yesterday. They were ordered to their units. This means that the big offensive, maybe the final one, is not far off. Wishing a positive outcome from our next encounter is useless. We have seen enough to know what we are saying.

We were so pleased to have received official word that Bulgaria has abandoned the ranks of the enemy. They are like King David when he cast his harp because he could no longer carry the load. We heard that Bulgaria had to surrender *unconditionally* because they felt alone and could not get the help they expected from Germany and Austria. The pieces are falling! Oh, barbarous nation with so many human forms of beasts, you are heartless and capable of the most horrendous and bloody crimes! God's justice finally triumphs over you!

This is very important for our cause and is the best kind of victory we could have secured. It will bring us great benefits. What may these be? We cannot know at this time.

Thursday, October 2

I received letters from home and felt boundless joy. Several other friends also wrote. My good friend, Mr. Knox, sent some clippings from *La Prensa*, including a letter I had sent the paper. He encourages me to continue writing so that Mexicans know how we are representing them here. I will do it with pleasure. I also received a copy of *El Latino-Americano* from my old and dear friend, Mr. Amado Gutiérrez.

I did a lot of French translations today.

I received some returned letters that did not reach their destination because of incomplete addresses. We also have to thank our government for this, for the good way it handles our correspondence, for which we pay nothing.

I went to Monteville in the afternoon. After the one-mile trip, I examined the place closely and revisited the horrible night of September 11. I stopped at several places to look at the battlefield and replayed all the important scenes that were fresh on my mind.

The dull thunder of cannon fire can be heard a short distance away. I took a few minutes to observe our artillerymen and to listen to the roar of the cannon as they deliver their explosives on enemy positions. I then watched some French soldiers handling a 75-millimeter cannon. They were directing their fire toward the north.

I went to our general quarters while at Monteville, picked up some information, and talked with some of my old buddies. Later, I walked through the village to take stock of the damage that the artillery had carried out over the years. The rain started to come down hard, giving me a different sense of the town's old and wrecked buildings. I visited buildings that had served as schools, one for the boys and another for the girls. Our soldiers now use them as barracks. I also dropped in on the church. It was abandoned and as sad as the surrounding graves. So many memories came to me as I contemplated the silence. The place is quiet but rich in history! These are the same sights we have witnessed in the histories of the world.

I bought some sweets and continued with my run through the little town, which I will remember for as long as I live.

Before reaching the post, I saw soldiers positioning another one of our big guns. Some Frenchmen were also preparing to pound on the Germans with a fearsome howitzer. These are the kind of cannon that deliver a 5-foot tall, 16½-inch diameter shell weighing 2,100 pounds. They can wear down the nerves. The monsters will roar tonight and watch over us as they silence the enemy's cannon. I was tired but content after my depressing visit to Monteville.

Thursday, October 3

Early today, I translated the French wireless with the news that peace is approaching. Several French officers who were visiting our colonel read my translation. The colonel asked them, "Is this job done well?" They looked at it and responded, "Magnifique, Magnifique," which was immensely satisfying to me. I never would have thought it was a good translation but it was the best I could do under the circumstances. Their generous response will make my translations go smoother. In other words, I will be more confident and work with greater ease.

Friday, October 4

We dedicated our morning to preparing for what seemed to be a quick departure from this place. The feeling is that we had been in this peaceful sector long enough and that we have to relieve our brothers who are truly in "an active sector and front."

About two in the afternoon, a small French tank passed close by our position on the road to the front. This gave me the opportunity to examine closely the powerful war machine that will make a major contribution to our final triumph. It looked exactly like a slow tortoise—it has an impenetrable scaly shell of burnished steel with four people inside representing its brain. They are armed to the teeth like pirates and carry the best and most modern rifles and machine guns, hand bombs, telescopes, and plenty of food and war supplies.

I had an interesting and pleasant dream last night. Chalk it up to frayed nerves (as some believe) or a premonition of what is to come (as others believe), but I saw my father. He came to me when I was sleeping and, without saying anything, gave me a good-bye kiss on the forehead. When I awoke, I continued enjoying the pleasant sensation that had been brought on by a troubled nervous system. Although I knew this had been a dream, I could see that I needed something. I needed my father's blessing and that was all I required as we prepared for another dangerous trip, an uncertain but necessary one for the sake of my family and nation.

Saturday, October 5

We were issued uniforms and other winter clothes today. This means we will be ready for the great offensives and battles of winter.

One of the patrols that normally go out into "no man's land" lost two soldiers last night when they came across a German scouting patrol in the field of death. This is what happened: one of our lieutenants was ordered to reconnoiter a trench in the area. We knew that German soldiers fired at us from the trench every morning but remained inactive the rest of the day. The officer formed a patrol that included members of my *raza,* Francisco Hernández and Agapito Salinas. The night was dark when the odyssey began. Their assignment was to inspect the trench. The order was a death sentence but it was also typical of the commands we carried out on the front. Their route posed serious problems because of the extensive barbed wire and numerous craters along the way. They had to follow this path and cross a stream that was not deep enough to drown in but that posed a formidable challenge. The sappers had blazed the only trail possible up to the little creek and placed a tree across it as a bridge. The entire patrol crossed. The men walked at intervals and each had a white handkerchief on his back so that they could recognize each other. As the soldiers walked like cats, quietly up a hill and near the trench, they failed to hear four Germans coming their way with a powerful machine gun and enough fire power to make some noise, perhaps all night long. When they were almost on top of the enemy, one of our men yelled, "Germans." Our soldiers immediately opened up with their automatic rifles. Afterward, someone yelled, "Let's go." No one wants to admit it now, but someone called out the retreat. One eyewitness said they ran like deer. No one tried to cross the difficult bridge because it could only take one person at a time. They all jumped in the water and forded the stream. Upon their return, they appeared disorderly and were carrying on about how they had discovered the Germans and how they had sent them on their way. The officer reacted as expected, "Of course we knew the Germans were there. We sent you to gather more information, what can you tell us about the trench?" They responded, "We didn't make it to the place. That's the problem." The officer ordered them to "Get back immediately before the Germans take the trench and prevent you from reaching it, and see what you can find inside." The unlucky but brave men built up the necessary courage to return. They went back the same way they came, without saying a word. The rest of us watched nervously. This time they were successful and secured the needed information. They confirmed that the running skirmish had resulted in the killing of four Germans who were carrying the heavy machine gun they now paraded like a trophy. The result is what counts and this was a good one.

I bathed in the morning and washed my clothes because of the lice that are beginning to infest us. They abound in the trenches that have housed so many men without the time to clean themselves. It is impossible to escape this plague because we are forced to occupy places frequented by soldiers infested with lice. The French and German soldiers are covered with these pests because they have been in the field of battle for so long and do not have the necessary clothes and soap. I checked my underclothes today and found two fat, crystalline, and black-striped lice. I immediately went to the kitchen, asked for soap, and boiled all my clothes, including the ones in my backpack and what I was wearing. I also moved to another sleeping area.

Our German prisoners have given up killing the lice. We often see them lying down or sitting in the sun, shirtless, and even without their undershirts. I guess they are not meant to kill, kill, and kill lice but prefer to reflect on when they killed, killed, and killed human beings. These scenes are cause for pity, anger, and disgust, but they are unavoidable and we may have to witness even worse behavior.

Another Frenchman, a young soldier, came to serve as an orderly for a French officer who is assigned to our commander. He makes many things out of the copper and bronze shells, including cigarette lighters with flint stones and gasoline. The smokers find the gadgets useful. The decorative designs he places on these little boxes are truly artistic. He makes some in the shape of closed books, others as open books, and still others carry elegant patterns of saints. He does all this by hand. I have lengthy conversations with him in French. He praises me when I show progress in his native tongue. I only see kindness in him that I may not be worthy of receiving.

Sunday, October 6

I had barely exited my nest when I realized that a good number of my fellow soldiers were impatiently waiting to question me about the news or rumor that was spreading like wildfire, that the prideful Germans were asking for a truce or armistice. The general feeling is that peace will be difficult to reach unless serious initiatives are taken. Moreover, the allies insist on the liberation of Poland and the Balkan countries, which the Germans have not been willing to accept. We do not know how they feel about it now.

I continue facing racial conflicts. I will not give up, I will not submit as long as I can wield the sword.

Monday, October 7

It rained quite a bit last night. I read carefully the peace proposals our president offered the enemy and the German chancellor. I see nothing that bodes well for the peace that we want without a serious and bloody encounter between us and the Kaiser's soldiers. We all know that German soldiers are dispirited and lack military morale, but their pride is still too great to accept defeat.

The German bombardment was very intense the rest of the day.

The sun finally came out at sundown, favoring us with a wonderful vista of natural beauty.

It rarely happens, but we were very happy in the office today. I cannot explain it.

I was ordered to go to Monteville and secure some office supplies since we had run out. I brought some of my books for my reading pleasure. I traveled by myself and had the time to savor everything I saw.

I found my loyal friend Gómez at General Headquarters and spoke with him for a good while. On my way back, I enjoyed how the fall and its cold rains were turning the nearby forest into a beautiful sight. It is taking on a thousand hues. The trees are beginning to shed the leaves that protected them from the burning rays of the summer sun and are preparing for the slower pace of winter. I was overjoyed with the splendid panorama of autumn before me. My position in the field has allowed me to see enemy shells explode in the middle of these forests, scattering into the air thousands of leaves of every color and uprooting and destroying many trees. The beautiful yellow and red leaves fly through the air like a frightened mass of butterflies, confused by the dirt, shells, and the metal fragments with their buzzing sound of death. Even the poor and defenseless trees that adorn Mother Nature suffer man's barbarity! This is civilization in the twentieth century and these are our scientific advancements, man's most arrogant source of pride!

Wednesday, October 9

Frost covered the ground last night and the sky was overcast like when a snow storm is about to come. I typed a lot today. We have witnessed a great deal of aerial activity, ours and the enemy's. The enemy shoots our planes and we shoot theirs. We have spent the day watching men serve as targets. This is a spectacle for soldiers who have so much time on their hands. We will enter the arena soon enough so that others can enjoy themselves, ridicule us, or derive some other earthly pleasure at our expense. It seems that the purpose of all this aerial activity is to secure reliable information on military positions and the other elements of war by both sides.

We received orders to pack our things and prepare to leave. What is our destination? We are not sure and can only expect that it will be some front where our mettle will be tested. Much is made of our division, not the least of which is that our soldiers long to show what they can do. Our limited experience tells us that the only way to force the surrender of a weakened enemy is to hit him hard and we will do that.

We are more than confident of our advantage in the quantity of war material and food supplies. Also, who can doubt our abilities next to any other men? The sooner we start moving, the better it will be for our suffering humankind.

We should ask some questions. What reward should we expect as we prepare to sacrifice? What awaits us when the supreme hour arrives? What will be best, to fall in the field of battle or survive the war? The soldiers who die will have made payment in full. The rest of us will return home to pay the debt incurred during the great slaughter.

Our replacements seem very capable. They have come to learn as much as they can so they can take our place after we are gone. We should note that all of them outrank us. I once again see the obvious injustice. I am a plain foot soldier, and I have served in a position that a private first class was unable to carry out and that, according to current military law, only commissioned officers are entitled to fill. If I am not able to serve in that position, why assign me the responsibilities that belong to someone else? And if I am capable of doing the job, why not promote me in rank, not for self-serving reasons, but for the sake of fairness?

A German plane outmaneuvered our artillery. The pilot demonstrated impressive abilities and undeniable valor or a disregard for his own life, all in service to his nation. He was a brave German! The moment will come when we too will demonstrate our loyalty and show that the German is not better than we are.

Thursday, October 10

We have just informed our replacements about our obligations and all that we have done while on the front. We let them do the work today. The captain who is to replace me prepared his report and translated the wireless message. A work mate of mine, an Anglo-Saxon, behaved terribly. He tried to make me look bad before our replacements, but my work spoke for itself and he got a well-deserved reprimand.

It was cold during the first hours of the morning when we received orders to move out. A group of more than twenty-five planes flew by on the way to the front. I felt moved as I gave Mousson one last look. I have used the telescope on so many occasions to view the beautiful statue of the heroine Joan of Arc at the town's high point, as well as the unforgettable Bois de le Prete, the Moselle River, and the chapel of Jezainville. We bid our most tender farewell, perhaps forever.

Our march to Jezainville began around six in the afternoon. We carried all our belongings; they were heavy loads. We set out in closed column formation while our replacements marched into the area in the same manner. We found out that the 7th Division was replacing us. The walk to Jezainville was strenuous since we were still trying to catch up with the 1st Battalion. By the time we reached our destination, the 1st Battalion had left. We had to continue the chase. We spent a few minutes with some of our buddies from the 345th Machine Gun Regiment. We were all muddy and exhausted the evening we arrived at the village named Villers-en-Haye, on the other side of Griescourt. The place was packed with soldiers, and all of them were strangers. It all seemed like a dream in the midst of that great assembly of people we did not know.

We could not find a house so we had to sleep in the open, under a dark and cold sky.

Toul, Choloy, and Rampondt

Friday, October 11

We met with some countrymen of German descent whom we had known as civilians and ate a sorry breakfast of cold meat and dry crackers. We had not yet caught up with the 1st Battalion. As far as we can tell, they left yesterday morning for Toul. We began our march to Toul after breakfast. Onward to Toul, again. The four of us who stuck together said little, only what was necessary. There was reason for our bad mood. I had a very bad headache and was tired due to sleepless nights, the cold, and hunger, but especially because of the lack of coffee.

We were fortunate to come across a truck heading in the same direction. We got on the truck, but sadly, it turned in a different direction, so we had to get off and continue on foot. A short while later, another truck appeared that was traveling to Toul. We boarded it and went on our way.

While on the march, we had time to take in the beautiful roads and the territory we had crossed at night on our way to the front. We could hear the cannon from a greater distance than on the previous occasion when we were here. We had forced the stubborn Germans to retreat a good distance. In several cases, we had pushed them back as far as the trenches on their own soil, something many of them would have thought impossible.

The last truck we boarded dropped us off at a lovely village close to the historic town of Toul. The general discomfort my headache caused and the pressing need to reach our regiment kept me from visiting the surrounding historic villages.

The command post was set up at Choloy. The rest of the units are located in the nearby villages. Once I located the post, I wandered through the narrow, muddy streets brimming with the commotion of war. Some men arrived while others left. French soldiers were running in all directions. The civilians were engaged in their various routines.

After a long conversation with Gómez and Barrera, they took me to their hiding place, a large stable on the outskirts of town. I claimed a spot I liked, next door to the kitchen. We are going to sleep where they store hay for the cattle. Everything is forgiven and forgotten as we build up our love for the war.

The entire day was very cloudy and the skies threatened a downpour; however, our troubles were over, at least for the moment. A soldier's woes are not eternal! Take courage, those of you who will be in the next war. I inquired about my responsibilities and was told that all I had to do was rest, which was fine by me. I immediately headed for my pile of grass and prepared my sleeping nest. My friends are going to have a difficult time finding me to read them the French papers with news from the front and the world, especially the reports on the peace initiatives. This is what we really care about.

Saturday, October 12

We received welcomed news about the war at a time when many are reporting an imminent peace. The *Journal* reports that the Kaiser is meeting with all his royalty to talk about concluding the war. Rumors are already going around that the Kaiser has abdicated his throne. I get a kick out of my buddies who are anxious about hearing the news from me. I also find it heartwarming. Only those of us "who are feeling the heat of the fire" can understand what this means "for the men whose lives hang by a thread." We are glad things are getting hotter for the Kaiser. My friends are always buying newspapers for me to read. I just arrived and already my stable looks like a veritable mess of papers. Think about it, an unending line of soldiers coming in and going out, all of them with the one thought in mind. Our sleeping area is so dark I have a difficult time finding my way. The light of a weak paraffin candle that always burns near my bed attracts them like a swarm of captivated butterflies. Groups of soldiers are always waiting for me to read them the news. I do not charge my poor friends because I am just as curious as they are. Oh, how misery is able to turn us into brothers! It would be so good to inject this feeling on our uncaring citizens! My friends buy me papers and candles without my asking. Several French soldiers who sleep with us join in and help me share the news. They do not speak English and I cannot say that I can speak French, but they understand me and are impressed with my abilities. One of them is well educated and smart and has good manners. This is why I like exchanging views with him. The others are charlatans and uncouth. Whenever I talk with the more sensible one, the others just look on without protesting. These are the lovely scenes from our everyday life.

We visited the delousing station. They disinfected us like cattle with brooms dipped in foul-smelling water, after which we bathed. We are sacrificing decency, false modesty, and discretion for health, and may destiny continue finding its way. This brings to mind our buddy Francisco de Hoyos. They allowed him to keep his mustache. He looks like a happy follower of Confucius. We disinfected our clothes, an easier task. We placed them in large cylinders and steamed them until the wool began to wrinkle. Once we wear them, our looks say everything. We look like sheep with our well-formed curls. As our fellow Mexican soldiers say, "Someone will sooner or later search for our horns."[1] At any rate, we were happy to return to our nest of hay with a lighter load and fewer pests.

I saw my friends from the 2nd Battalion as I was waiting my turn at the delousing station. No one can escape it. Everything around us mostly has the sad, unattractive, desolate, and monotonous appearance of war. Only a soldier can tolerate this.

Sunday, October 13

We had a beautiful day after a heavy rain and low temperatures. The rumors and news about peace continue to arrive. The soldiers do not speak, nor are they interested in anything else. My buddies are always stopping me to see if I have heard anything new. This keeps me from leaving my rat hole and moving about freely to become acquainted with the town, its people, language, and customs. They are not satisfied with the little I know. I feel as though they want me to say that "The war is over, let's go home." They think I am hiding something, that I am keeping things from them. What simple-mindedness, no one wants this more than me, and I would scream it at the top of my lungs if true! Of course, the soldiers say more than what appears in the papers. After all, they can add to the news at will. Some are not happy with my translations because they have already heard so much more through the rumor mill. Their buddies add details that do not appear in the press. The idea of peace is building among everyone. The news in a telegram that arrived late today hit us like a bombshell. It reported that Germany had accepted President's Wilson famous fourteen points for peace. The *Herald* confirmed this. We can hardly believe the good news although we want it with all our hearts. Oh, the sweetness of peace! Millions of souls would agree with me?

I find it interesting that after the press has confirmed the news of peace, my buddies doubt it and few of them are as happy of its possibility as before. What more do they want?

I saw all my Mexican friends except Julián Martínez. Pablo Pérez is in a French hospital. I learned the details about how he was gassed at Saint-Mihiel. As the Germans were about to move, they noticed the movement of our troops and fired a barrage of gas shells. One of them hit the foxhole hiding Pérez and his buddies. We had heard the more disturbing story that Pablo had died. We were happy to hear this was not so.

We passed the day like the revolutionary Pablo Martínez in the work of Juan A. Mateos. We read news about the war in our hideout while a rainstorm passed over us. Only the ghosts were missing because we already have plenty of old, ugly, and abandoned hovels like the bishop's quarters that Mateos describes.[2]

Sergeant Schwarz and I were told during supper to pack our things. We were anxious because the order surely means we are being sent to the trenches in the line of fire. We especially feared we would be sent to do battle against Hindenburg's formidable line of trenches. If this is true, we are going up against the network of trenches that are so impregnable only prisoners of war can cross them. We will test the bravery of the German soldiers who are considered demigods. This is saying much, but we know that men are being born daily who can go beyond those who have fallen before them. These are men of courage and with no less intelligence than Hindenburg.

We spent most of the night packing our things. With every article we put away, we bundled memories and would say, as Hans Andersen once did, "The end may be near."[3]

Monday, October 14

Our customary good mood reigned during breakfast because man may forget everything except that he is human with basic needs. Someone once noted this truth, "Everything in the world is a lie; only hunger is real."[4] This explains why we are glad to feed the monster gnawing in our gut. Meanwhile, our final hour has not yet arrived, as it has for many of our buddies who have fallen. The soldiers have their utensils and are sitting on the ground where they usually eat and engage in conversation. The full-blown laughter was a sight to behold.

During breakfast, a friend informed me that my lieutenant, a man I believe has treated me somewhat unfairly, was very ill, perhaps with the flu. On hearing this, I thought about our important sense of fellowship and took him something to eat at his room. His fever was very high. I suppose my visit took him by surprise, but he was courteous and friendly. He drank the coffee with great pleasure but was not interested in the rest of his breakfast. I offered to help and he asked that I help him get up. He thanked me; I said good-bye and went on with my daily routine.

The certainty of peace appears to be going the way of soap bubbles. The papers are no longer saying anything.

Our band played, and we were happy for this because we had not heard them since August 19. This could be the last time we enjoy them.

Tuesday, October 15

The day began with a heavy rain that made the muddy streets worse. The bugle called on the 3rd Battalion to fall in with a sound that has impressed us so much during these unforgettable times. We were tired of being stuck in our nests and took to the streets to see the few places worth seeing. Most of the soldiers gather where liquor is sold. The tobacco smoke in those places is unbearable. I prefer to walk the streets even when it is raining. I walk through the town, studying everything, and then I return to my rabbit's den to write and read, or to chat with the French.

Valente de la Rosa brought us the sad news that José "Pepe" González, the band's second bugler, had died of pneumonia in the hospital and that he was to be buried right away. De la Rosa, Gómez, and I left immediately to see if we could make it to the funeral. We walked through roads, meadows, and sown fields until we reached the makeshift cemetery for fallen soldiers in Toul. Everything was well arranged. Each grave had a white cross and stood out only by the number on an aluminum tag. The soldiers wear this tag around their neck when they are alive. They actually wear two. One is affixed to the blanket containing the remains and the other is sent to Washington for identification and to inform the family of the deceased. By the time we arrived, our friend's remains were already resting under the wet and cold ground. All we could do was stand at attention next to the grave of our companion who was such a friend during the good and bad times. We prayed that he rest in peace and that his sacrifice not be in vain.

On our return to town, we found some news on the kitchen bulletin board. The orders stated: (1) be up by 4 a.m.; (2) breakfast at 5 a.m.; (3) march at 7 a.m. These are familiar orders. They mean our day is near. After supper I wrote a letter to José González's bereaving father

A. E. F. in France
360th Inf., 90th Div.
October 15, 1918
Falfurrias, Texas

Mr. Doroteo González

The government must have already informed you of your son's death. You do not know me, but it is not improper for me to write you especially since I was so close to your departed son. May you find in this sad letter the message that should be received by every single parent who has lost sons in this global crusade for the rights of our suffering humankind, a war in which many Mexicans are fighting and representing our people with pride.

Your son succumbed while in the clutches of the cruel pneumonia he contracted because he was exposed to the elements in the field of battle. He fell as all the brave should fall, defending nation, home, and family.

Several of us went to his funeral hoping to reach the burial of his remains, but we did not arrive on time. Nevertheless, we offered a prayer by his grave, beseeching the Supreme Being that these sacrifices not have been in vain, but that they contribute to the betterment of our poorly understood and even less appreciated *raza*.

Mr. González, we trust that after a period of bitter pain you will be able to finally accept his passing. Know that your son was not the first nor will he be the last member of our *raza* to sacrifice his life. We who are still alive are also committed to fulfill our serious responsibility to the nation.

You and your dear family should know that if we fall in battle, we hope with all our hearts that one of our own survives and knows that he is to inform our parents about how we carried ourselves to the very end.

We share your loss at the same time we praise the comportment of our comrade who knew how to bear all the miseries so that he could fulfill his duty as a brave citizen.

Sincerely,

J. LUZ SÁENZ

Wednesday, October 16

Yesterday's orders were followed to the letter. We had eaten breakfast, readied our backpacks, and prepared for the long march by 7 a.m. As soon as the trucks arrived, twenty men started boarding each of the Fords.

I began the very cold day with a serious headache.

The trucks drove without a stop and completed the trip quickly. We ate at a small picturesque, squalid, and seemingly abandoned town. The buildings did not show damage from artillery fire. I was not able to write down the names of the other towns we passed. On the other hand, my headache did not encourage me to note down anything. It was very late when we arrived at the outskirts of Rampondt, where we were to spend the night. Our trucks dropped us off and continued on their way to deliver food and war provisions to the soldiers at the next front. The town is small but a very important rail center. We are southeast of the great Verdun front. As expected, I saw many French soldiers.

We had to march about a mile on roads that were knee-deep in mud in order to reach Rampondt. The shack where we are staying barely provides cover from the rain. We do not know how long we will stay in this town, but I do not think it will be much more because of the great movement of men and supplies to the front. This means we are needed there. We finally reached a place where the poor and the nameless are needed and will not be rejected because of race or color!

Our shack is located at the foot of a hill. We have been using the surrounding trees for fuel and have made mattresses out of some bales of hay meant for horses but that we also use to keep dry on the wet ground. This is where Gómez, Barrera, and I will sleep. Other soldiers are also with us. We pass the time as usual, talking, telling jokes, singing, and reading. The other fellows play dice and cards, and they brag about what they did or had in civilian life. They exaggerate so much that they almost always end up quarreling. This becomes another form of free entertainment for us. They cannot understand and benefit from what we do or say because they only speak one language.

We can hear the distant rumbling of the constant bombardment at the wretched front. It sounds like a huge mill with large stones grinding human flesh. The front cannot be far because the trucks are coming and going, one after the other, and fast.

The Field of Battle in France

My Dear Wife,

I am doing well and hope that it is God's Will that all of you are doing well too. I am sending you a certificate. Visit the Red Cross so that someone can better explain how to use it. If you are able and would like to send me something, do it as soon as possible so that I can receive it by Christmas. I would prefer some thick socks. Although I must admit that we have enough of them, I also have to say that we spend many days in damp places, as well as in mud, and even in water itself. Changing socks is a great relief these days. Many soldiers throw away their socks at night and are left with only wet ones to wear day and night. This has caused many deaths due to pneumonia. I do not care for excuses, when death calls on me I want it to come straight and swift.

Loving all of you forever,

Luz

Thursday, October 17

We barely ate breakfast because our kitchen is not here and the ones that are in the area have very limited rations for the soldiers. Jesse Pérez and I had a good time talking about our experiences. I saw several of the boys from Alice, the town where "I came to be a man," as our elders say. Running into them brought back many pleasant memories.

Some of the fellows in our sleeping area say they do not like the place and they leave, but new people keep arriving. We have the best spot in the shack. This may be why we do not say anything and are comfortable with everything, like the shrewd rabbit of lore.

I went out in the afternoon to explore a beautiful forest to the northeast where one can catch a beautiful panoramic view of the area. A large number of wheat fields have been planted on the hill. This makes the mesa even more beautiful, surrounded as it is by trees destined for the mill. Although the day was peaceful and cold, the view was grand, but for some reason it also brought me profound sadness. We will come to appreciate the area's entire natural beauty as we become accustomed to its unavoidable gray appearance. The rail traffic is intense and noisy. The noise caused by the constant movement of trucks to and from the front also tells us much of the strategic importance of this place.

Friday, October 18

The serious pain I had last night kept me from sleeping well. I hardly had an appetite this morning. The sun was in full splendor and the view of the town and its surroundings seemed even more beautiful from our shack on top of the hill. The town is full of activity. Today's traffic is greater than yesterday. A good number of planes have been flying over us today. We hear that German airplanes will raid the town and, as a consequence, have been ordered to turn in early and keep all lights out.

I received a letter from my brother Eugenio telling me that everything is going well. I answered his letter and others I have received.

We have discovered many rats and lice in this place. They are an enemy and are feared as much as the Germans. The reason for the rats could be the large number of warehouses with food. The lice are brought in by the soldiers who have been moving between our position and the front. The lice are so numerous that even the rats carry them.

The night arrives, and while this should be a time of quiet and rest, we begin to hear the sound of cannon fire in a constant duel to the death. We are not far from that horrible fight, a mirror image of hell.

Saturday, October 19

I have been in a bad mood today. A fellow soldier insulted me in a cowardly way, but I did not allow him to drag me down to his level. Before moving on, I am going to investigate why he would act that way. Fortunately, we are in the right place to resolve this.

I had nothing to do this afternoon so I spent some time in the quiet and dark forest. I enjoyed thinking about the past and musing about the future, not caring about the uncertainty of the moment because it does not bother me anymore.

My good friend Amado Cásares, who was with the sappers, has joined the band just as we had asked him to do a long time ago. This pleases us because he is in a better position to be treated fairly and appreciated for his artistic skills. His poor physical condition puts him in a disadvantage as a foot soldier, but he is brave and has intellectual qualities that are worth noting.

Sunday, October 20

I woke up late and barely made it for breakfast. I then went to the office to copy a note for Lieutenant Williams. While there, I was given poor materials to complete a task and received little credit for my work. I wrote some letters describing how we live in these surroundings.

We participated in a review and were read a speech by our division's commander in chief. We learned that we were moving to the most feared front near Verdun to destroy Hindenburg's unassailable trenches. We also heard that our nation was expecting every one of us to fulfill our highest duty as brave soldiers and that our nation's pride and future depended on how we did at the front. The sound of the words was so beautiful because they represented *The Truth*! Who would have thought this! "The future of the nation" depends on these humble men who will probably be forgotten. As soldiers who have left loved ones behind, we will make the ultimate sacrifice for them. Our chests are filled with pride and we burn with the desire to triumph or die in glory for our children.

The newspapers brought some very promising news regarding the Anglo-Belgian victory over the Germans.

Lieutenant George is not feeling well. Some of us are also ill but we do not want to be placed on the infirmary list while we can still fight. This is what we the Mexicans have decided. If we are to fall, we want to die on the battlefield and not in a hospital.

Monday, October 21

Nothing out of the ordinary happened during our first hours of the day. I worked a good while in the office and had time to wash my handkerchiefs and towels. The sun began shining beautifully by ten, although the day remained cold.

The preparations have started. This means we are about to move to the front. The rumors are setting off the soldiers like a disturbed ant colony. If it was not for the misfortune that hangs over the poor—the cannon fodder—we could acknowledge the beauty in the spirit of the men about to face death.

The evening was moonlit and clear. Several planes of possible German origin flew over us on the way to the central part of France. The sound of their motors is different from the French and American airplanes. Our survival instinct teaches us many things.

Moving across the Rubble
of the Battlefield to Reach the Enemy
and Occupy the Line of Fire
Montfaucon and Dead Man's Hill

Tuesday, October 22

We had breakfast very early and quickly prepared for the march to the well-known Verdun front. Along the way we passed by several small towns in ruins. I took down the names of Nixeville, Dombasle en-Argonne, Recicourt, Avocourt, Melancourt, and Montfaucon. Only their names survived. Our sappers were demolishing some structures damaged by artillery fire and using the stones from the ruins to fix the roads. The remains of the once-beautiful towns are being put to good use since the rubble is in our way and we need roads to remove the enemy from the fortifications they refuse to vacate. The Germans left incredible destruction as they tried to take Verdun, located on our right and over the river Meuse. The names of towns like Avocourt only appear on boards lying in the ruins. Some of our engineers who have been in the thick of things near Montfaucon have told us of horrible scenes. We have more than their verbal reports to know what happened. The devastation by the artillery is everywhere. The entire field is yellow or green as a result of the gases. Large quantities of rations, ammunition, and pieces of weapons are all over the place. Backpacks are also strewn on the ground and denuded forests have been turned into pieces of wood and debris. We found shells of every caliber and large piles of unused ammunition that suggest a large number of artillery emplacements. We were met by a mist of unbearable smell that may be due to the fetid blood of man and beast lying here and there, scattered and unburied. A friend pointed out the remaining corners of a great building. This is all that was left of a Catholic church. A great crucifix was practically intact next to what had been the altar. It seems the very bombs recognized the importance that much of humankind gives this religious symbol. Anyone who was not a witness may doubt me but

241

thousands of soldiers passed by here in their difficult march and can attest to what I saw. The corners of the building had served as the last refuge for companies of German machine gunners. We found large piles of their discharged cartridges and many used and unused clips. Nine machine guns were piled up in one corner. This can provide a better sense of the kind of damage one emplacement can inflict on a column in the open. What kind of terrible massacre must have taken place here? The memorable "Dead Man's Hill" was a short distance away. We will never know exactly how many men from both sides lost their lives here. We also saw with our own eyes the equally famous "Hill No. 304." Thousands of lives were lost by this foothill too. Whoever took the hill could never be sure they would hold it for long; the fighting was bloody and constant, as was the human loss. An American officer has been credited with using his own wits to hold it. He had several ten-inch cannon fire on the hill to dig out a new trench, which gave our soldiers greater protection. We removed the enemy with brute force from his "unassailable fortifications."

There is no denying that this entire place still reeks of human blood, and one can almost hear the groans and moans of dying soldiers. We spent the night in the open, on the west side of the Montfaucon forest. Everything was wet, the ground was spewing water, maybe blood, and finding a place to sleep was not easy. We found a big dugout with water, filled it with thick poles that are abundant in the area, and then covered them with heavy sheets of steel we had found. We rested on some sheets and covered ourselves with still others to protect us from the constant rain. Soldiers have been enduring these wretched conditions for four long years. Humankind longs for the day when peace can reign again.

Wednesday, October 23

In spite of it all, we woke up well rested and ate cold rations for breakfast in our foxhole. Misery and misfortune makes brothers of even the wild beasts! Too bad this does not last!

Nothing indicated that we were to move, so we set out for a nearby field that was teeming with soldiers ready to fight on top of the remains of the dead. I should say forest instead of field because not too long ago this was a beautiful area of precious woods. It is now a mess of scattered branches and lifeless trees. Some thick trunks are sticking out of the ground while others have been uprooted by the explosives. We could not walk around much less explore the area. How much worse must it have been during the terrible battles! Great

God, how can men survive all this! The harsh terrain slowed us down and required that we be on guard and careful. Some soldiers dug foxholes for sleeping while others prepared them for fighting. Some were dug by the Germans who destroyed the woods while defending their positions. They had abandoned them when they retreated, or fled, which is the same thing. The French and Americans also used the foxholes, until the rain rendered them useless. This does not mean we would not use them in an emergency. Life is so sweet! So many soldiers who slept in these holes are now abiding in eternal sleep, beyond the ire of man! To think that many of us will be among them!

We were notified during the lunch hour to prepare to march by 3:30 p.m. We did as we were told but were made to wait. We were waiting at five. Shells began to fall over the entire forest. The Germans had obviously detected our position. The shells seemed to have been fired with no particular target in mind, although some of them hit their mark. We lost some of our soldiers. It was a shame that we did not have an opportunity to see them tear into the Germans. We just cannot afford anything less; we are practically on top of the Germans.

We started our difficult march through the brambles at sundown. The roads were not visible and the bridges had been blown away by dynamite or artillery fire. As soon as night fell, we heard the sound of enemy planes dropping their terrible bombs, but we continued moving into the fire.

We saw a dogfight in the dark of night. The powerful searchlights from both sides gave the adversaries some help. The spectacle was unusual and the newness of it attracted our attention. As soon as the white beams of light found their target, the guns would fire from the ground. We came to fear the darkness even more as the forest, once silent as a tomb, awakened with frightened birds making a cackle of deafening proportions. We could see the sparks every time a plane was hit.

We walked slowly and very close to one another to avoid losing sight of the main body. We had no problem as long as we were the only group moving forward. However, we lost our way when we met up with soldiers who were returning from the front in complete disarray.

We passed by some towns in ruins that looked more unsightly against the shadows of the night. The roads were camouflaged. Our march lasted past midnight, until we reached the side of a hill where we were allowed to sleep. Some soldiers put up tents while the rest of us made our bedding on the ground and quickly fell into a deep sleep.

Thursday, October 24

We woke up well rested after the sun had risen. Officers ordered us to go into the nearby forest, between the villages of Cierges and Nantillais. By ten in the morning, we discovered that our kitchen was near Nantillais. After the lunch hour, I visited the battlefield; gear belonging to soldiers who had fallen during the fighting was scattered all over. Many 75 millimeter cannon were all around, but in pieces. I also saw several German "juiz-bangs." We named the shells after the sound that they make. The Germans had also left some guns when they made their "hot" retreat and destroyed others with dynamite or with the cannon's shells. This last act was the easiest for them. They covered the mouths of the cannon and fired them. We discovered huge emplacements in the forest. Some of the cannon were never used while many multicaliber mortars remained in place. We found large deposits of ordnance all over the place.

I saw a detachment of our marines positioning a ten-inch monster, the kind that had been firing at the Kaiser. They moved the cannon with their brute strength because we no longer had horses or engines. The marines loaded and fired the cannon, and then they cleaned them with silk rags. The shells were heavy and several strong men had to handle them with the help of a lever or crane designed for the job.

I continued with my walk through the area where fierce battles had been fought a few days or, perhaps, hours ago. We are very close to the front. Every now and then misdirected shells with bad intentions hit our rest area. We are lending support to the first line of fire. When the soldiers in front of us tire or their forces are depleted, we have to take their place. This is not the place to be, at the head of the line.

The ground has been so overturned we may very well discover bodies that need proper burial. The artillery fire that has killed them has only covered them with loose dirt.

About ten o'clock, Gómez told me about some good places to sleep and I went looking for them. They were close to Nantillais and not far from our regiment's command post. This night, we will sleep in a trench that once belonged to the Germans.

I have a headache and an upset stomach, like many other soldiers around here.

Around four, we saw two German planes pursuing one of our own. They were so close we could see they were striking our plane. Our plane was not returning fire, as far as we could tell. It landed a short distance from our command post. The German planes flew to a higher elevation and toward their country. Since we did not see anyone get out of the plane, a few of us had nothing better to do than to investigate. We discovered that the pilot and machine gunner were dead. The pilot was the last to die, having had enough life left to land his plane in good order. We doubt the Germans knew they had killed the French crew. The courageous Frenchmen had harassed the enemy and returned to the bosom of their homeland after the deadly chase!

Friday, October 25

We endured a horrible cannonade the entire night. Much of it included gas. The huge craters and pieces of metal embedded in the ground tell us that some of the guns were high caliber. We will always remember the enemy's pyrotechnic demonstrations, which they offered free of charge.

The disgusting diarrhea is beginning to set up camp among the soldiers. It has many causes. The most common is exposure to the cold and humidity, but also the gas-contaminated food, especially the bread. Whatever the case, many soldiers were sick last night. I only slept a few minutes and was able to see many of the shells that exploded in our area.

My stomach was more upset this morning and my headache kept me from eating anything. My good friend Major Farris gave me some medication, which helped. I appreciate my loyal companions for showing concern and providing me with food. I accepted the food so they did not think I was slighting them.

I have been seeing a great deal of movement of soldiers and war machines to the front. The sun has not set and we are already hearing the crackling sounds of exploding German grenades raining everywhere. A very dangerous night awaits us.

Five Days and Nights in a Foxhole in Romagne

Saturday, October 26

I awoke feeling much better but not completely well. I am not hungry and fear I have to inform the doctors of my condition and that they will send me to some hospital. I feel very weak but would regret missing this battle, which is supposed to be terrible.

I received orders to accompany Sergeant Schwarz in search of a command post for our colonel. I prepared my backpack, bid my friends farewell, and set out to look for the sergeant. I hope to see my buddies soon unless a shell comes between us. I am going where many shells are dropping. No doubt about that.

I was concerned about our assignment because we were expected to complete it alone and on foot, but things turned out differently. We were assigned a Ford truck because Lieutenant Williams was accompanying us. The short ride gave us the opportunity to witness the usual littered equipment belonging to soldiers who had fought and possibly died. We also saw other fresh battlefield signs of fights to the death. Cannon, rifles, and machine gun ammunition, as well as blankets, clothing, and entire backpacks belonging to the enemy and our soldiers were scattered all over the place. They had also discarded hats and shoes. Despite everything, we were pleased to see that our soldiers had forced the enemy out of their invincible trenches. At what price? We do not know and this matters little since we have achieved an honorable victory. We also saw unburied German corpses before arriving at our destination. Many of them were decomposing. When someone pointed out a dead German soldier on the road, our officer replied, "I couldn't care less if there were ten thousand of them in the same condition." We said nothing. Men reason in so many different ways.

A heavy artillery bombardment began when we reached Romagne. All we could see was roofing material flying all over and solid rock walls collapsing. The slamming sound of the explosions was like a sack of metal dropping from high above. This was followed by the whistling sound of metal shards flying out of the black smoke. We said nothing as we found cover in the gutted buildings and waited for the final moment. I do not know if we feel fear, rage, or simply desperation as we witness the destruction by a seemingly invincible enemy. The bullets did not all miss their mark. Many found their targets among us, as we huddled together.

Many of our artillery emplacements and machine gun squadrons were outside the village, but they were silent as ordered. Some soldiers drank wine from their canteens to drown their sorrow and fear. This means that death is very close, although we are still not in actual combat. Real combat, as someone has accurately noted, is like hell on earth.

Our officer accompanied us until we reached a little village. The sergeant and I were told to move on. We waited for a pause in the bombing and then went our way. We finally reached the train station, the place we are to hold for our colonel. It has a solid foundation that can clearly help to fortify our position. The interior walls are massive and well-built with metal and cement. It currently houses a Red Cross hospital that we need to relocate before we use the structure. There was nothing to keep us from sleeping there. As soon as nightfall arrived, we began to witness the agony of war. The wounded started to arrive, and since the operating room was next door, we heard screams that were loud enough to keep a drunk awake. Whether we wanted to or not, we had to witness everything as our bed was at the entrance of the hospital.

Sunday, October 27

We woke up alive and well, and for this I thanked the heavens. We may have made it through the night, but we did not sleep well. The sergeant and I had to share a bed due to the lack of space. Even in the middle of such calamity, we cannot keep from being selfish and self-absorbed. While preparing our bed, the sergeant said, "This is the first time I will be sleeping with a stranger." I quickly responded, "Misfortune has forced me to lie down with many Germans." The sergeant is of German descent. We looked for something to eat at eight o'clock and got a clearer sense of last night's bombardment. A soldier who had sought refuge with us but could not find room decided to make his bed outside, by the hospital's entrance. A shell took his life. His body did not move one inch. The strong smell of gas was everywhere. All of this was enough to ruin our appetite. The bombing left dead, wounded, and gassed soldiers in its wake.

We ate breakfast in a kitchen with another detachment that did not have to feed us. Artillery fire continued throughout the day, especially during our meals. The poor cooks make the best targets for the Germans because the smoke from their stoves gives them away, regardless of their location. The other poor souls who take food to the soldiers in the trenches are hounded by artillery fire until they are killed, gassed, or drop the food. The Germans enjoy seeing our soldiers running and trying to escape the shells. Juan Salinas of Edinburg has managed to escape injury for days because God is great. They open fire on him every time he delivers food. He has dropped a lot of it to save his skin. Today, he drenched himself with coffee as he was approaching one of the trenches. He told me about his baths of "cornwilly" and beans. The poor fellow has no other defense than that of a humble little mouse. This is war, and that is the price you have to pay.

Monday, October 28

We received unwelcomed news today, but since our opinion matters little, we have to take everything as it comes. A colonel from the 89th Division took over the place we were holding for our colonel. When the sergeant informed him that Colonel Price had selected the place, he responded, "I can select it too." The conversation ended and we went looking for "another little mesquite," like that rooster in the song.

I selected a place under some great heaps of lumber the Germans had brought from France after their invasion. The shelling had not damaged the wet lumber much. When the sergeant realized what I wanted to do, he boasted, "It's not necessary to go so far, death can find you anywhere."

We took shelter at the railroad station. Its roof is poorly constructed with wood that can only protect us against the rain and cold weather. It has several holes and does not offer good cover. We miraculously escaped a German barrage this afternoon while gathering straw for our mattresses. We are a short distance from the front where the Germans can easily spot us. Several shells landed on the railroad tracks. The explosion destroyed the heavy steel tracks and showered us with shrapnel.

A heavy bombardment began in the early evening. It seemed to intensify as the night progressed. Some large gas projectiles hit our area and then a heavy caliber shell exploded, shook the entire ground, and spread the gases all over the place. In the thick of things, the sergeant told me, "We should look for a more secure place." I let him know that I too could posture by saying,

"It's not necessary, death can find you anywhere." We had a difficult time all night and had to wear our gas masks until daybreak.

Tuesday, October 29

Last night was the worst I have experienced. We survived because God is great and merciful. It was late when we went for breakfast. As I noted previously, we had a hard time getting food from the kitchen because we do not belong to its detachment and the lieutenant did not leave orders for us to be fed. They had food available for us only because men are dying all the time.

We had just crossed over a small stream and joined a serving line about thirty yards away when a grenade blew up the makeshift bridge. A second grenade wounded two buddies waiting in line. They were taken to the hospital immediately. The rest of us lost our appetite, but we must eat to live, and later die, if that is our lot.

I could not eat there, but filled my lunch box and took it to my trench. After my nerves calmed down and my stomach improved, I ate and quickly forgot the moving scene. I may become a victim in similar circumstances to come.

Wednesday, October 30

The morning was very cold after a night of heavy frost. We ate breakfast late and almost froze waiting in line for two hours. Everything was covered with frost and a light wind burned our feet and ears. It was so cold last night we did not even think of taking off our shoes. The cannon fire was continuous but the gases were not too bad. They are worse when it is cold and dry. The rain cleans the air.

(Whoever reads this book will tire of the monotony in our lives and, honestly, this is more taxing for the soldiers than the very action that could cause their deaths. Reader, do not forget this and listen to us patiently until this book is concluded.)

We finally buried a German soldier who had been dead since we arrived fifteen days ago. Poor soul, he asks nothing so we pay him no heed. He was already decomposing. We simply do not have the time to do right by the dead. We cast aside all concerns or ethical considerations as we try to save our skin. In the beginning, fresh blood caused us nausea, a dead body horrified us and, if we came across a corpse, we avoid it. Blood no longer smells and we walk over the dead when we need to cover more ground. Humanitarian obligations go out the window when we face the enemy in combat, and many of the living are half-dead.

The soldiers have been setting up a good many artillery emplacements today, including 77-millimeter guns and other heavy cannon. A ten-inch caliber was positioned by one of the kitchens. Its first salvo shook the entire area. These are the sounds that unsettle steady nerves. Several French artillery positions to our left have been heavily battered, and this has left many dead and wounded. The wounded are brought to this hospital while the dead are buried on the spot. How lovely, now the entire area is a cemetery!

I have been observing everything up close because I have nothing to do and being anywhere else is just as dangerous. The grenades that have been killing and wounding the French soldiers are exploding so close to me their fragments and shrapnel are whizzing past my head. I wish I had a good telescope to study the area and understand everything that is happening on their side and our own since I have nothing else to do but await my fate.

Many enemy planes have been flying close to us today. They have been under heavy fire from our machine guns and our special antiaircraft cannon. None of the Germans have been brought down. One of the planes flew low and dropped a large amount of propaganda material in English. They say the war is coming to an end because Germany is stronger than ever and the Allies will suffer a complete defeat if they continue to depend on a nation whose troops have no military discipline whatsoever. They refer to the United States as a transplanted version of European civilization that lacks a historical beginning of its own. Instead of discouraging us, they have strengthened our resolve. This is not the first time they have tried to scare us with their bluster. We are here to find out for ourselves, we want to see the entire German might.

Since very early this morning and until very late this evening, columns of well-armed and fully-equipped soldiers have been marching to the front. They are taking their place on the first line that begins here. We can see the German fortifications. I have never been this close to the barbaric Huns, the descendants of Alaric and Attila. They deny the relation, but it applies and it is useless to keep rejecting it. The generations to come will know them by these names.

A good number of machines of war have been passing by, including French tanks. Every small hill is fortified with artillery, and large stores of munitions of all types and calibers are everywhere. I feel sorry for the poor fellows who cart munitions and bread during the night. They get as close as possible and hurl the bread onto canvases and sometimes the grass. Some of them are Mexicans. They tell me of their forays into "no man's land" or whatever places they manage to reach. They suffer many hardships with Uncle Sam's two-wheeled, mule-drawn carts. Everything tells us the assault is going to be one of the most terrible. Many tears will be shed in America, but may God make them the last. Let there be a secure, sound, and lasting peace.

My brief, unexpected encounter with the front has been very useful. I could not have seen what I have witnessed under other circumstances. I can do as I please because I have no one to order me around at this time. We were sent here to take possession of the place under the station. Another officer took it and we are left without anything to do but wait for Colonel Price and our regiment. Many of my buddies have passed by and asked what I am doing. They laugh when I tell them I do not know and that I have been without anything to do for a few days. I have made good use of my many moments of inactivity in the middle of this terribly dangerous situation.

The villages of Romagne and Bantheville are full of soldiers. You cannot stick a pin anywhere without touching a soldier. The movement of men as well as trucks, cars, tanks, and beasts of burden is evident on all the roads, paths, and the general area. I am especially struck by the limited movement among the Germans. They only seem to be occupied with figuring out where we settle down to bother us at night. We are like an army of pygmies moving closer into the clutches of the waiting monster. The men look like ants moving their war machines closer and closer. It is nine and we have barely heard an exploding enemy shell. Our cannon have only fired test shots. The sides of the hills look like they are covered with spotted cats. This is what the cannon look like with their camouflaged disguises of dyed sacks, branches, and other creations used to fool the other side. Bombs appear to have fallen throughout during the previous nights. Only our place has escaped. Who knows what will happen tonight!

Thursday, October 31

The shells fell on us hard after nine last night; this did not bother us and we slept soundly. We have the same view as before, except that we are seeing greater destruction and more material scattered about. Many wounded and gassed soldiers have arrived, more artillery pieces have been set up, and additional troops have been assigned to the woods, our first line of fire. Many machine guns, trench mortars, and kitchen detachments are also taking their place at this line. Who says our cooks do not know the front? The order finally arrived, as we knew it would. At sunrise we are to storm Hindenburg's trenches. This has caused such a sensation! It is chilling to think about what will occur tomorrow, during the attack and afterward. These are the moments when men have faltered and opted for suicide or completely lost their senses. This will test the mettle of the descendants of Xicotencatl and Cuauhtémoc.[1]

We were told by one o'clock that we would march to the first line of fire and set up our command post. Unbelievable, we are so close to the Hindenburg line! Who would have thought our ground troops, the "tin" soldiers, could do this to the demigods of war? I walked by myself to the place we were to spend the evening. I moved slowly, observing everything around me. If this had not been the field of death, I would have said everything was beautiful and interesting. The forests, like our newly formed ant hill of men, are resting and preparing to make the ultimate sacrifice. Some of the soldiers were simply leaning on their backpacks while others were lying on them, but all of them were in their foxholes, taking shelter from the machine gun fire. It was as if they were waiting to be told to hug the ground. Some of them talked while others said nothing and looked sleepy. I was talking with some of them when a grenade landed in a foxhole with two of my buddies. Nothing was left of them. Pieces—ribs and shoes with feet and all—went flying and landed in some nearby trees. The stench of human blood and spent powder was dizzying.

I had a conversation with Simón González while in his foxhole. I advised him to carry himself well and to be brave in combat. He answered, "Don't worry, Sáenz, González will always conduct himself like a man while fighting the Germans."

Poor fellow, he had been the victim of the cruelest injustice! The death of his poor and blind elderly father was mostly due to the decision by the Martindale draft board to take the only two sons who could support him during the last days of his life. I remember what that grief-stricken and tearful father told me the last time I saw him: "The Anglos on the board told me that my sons will provide me more money as soldiers than as civilians and that if they die the government will give me even more. But I tell them I do not want the money, I need to be cared for and who better than my sons to do it? I just want one, the youngest, my Simón. He has been helping me these last few years and can do it until I die. The money I will receive from them will bring me more problems. What can I do as a blind man and without understanding much of this? They do not want to understand me. Money can make many things possible, but it cannot match a child's affection." The old man knew what he was talking about. We had just arrived in France and he had not yet received his first payment from his sons when he succumbed to hunger, loneliness, and the unbearable pain of losing his sons. I said goodbye to González and my other buddies and returned to my foxhole.

I will probably never again see what I witnessed today. Soon after my arrival, I was ordered to look for my buddies, the scouts. They had stayed behind with much of the equipment. I went by myself again and, because of this, I selected the way that suited me the best. I was looking all around and approaching the point where I was to take another road. All this took place in the forest across from Bantheville. I saw some Red Cross trucks with a doctor and Red Cross assistants at the intersection picking up the wounded who had fallen in the area. Some of the wounded soldiers were lying on the ground while others seemed dead and had just been brought in on stretchers. At that moment a bomb landed and took the dead, the wounded, and the living. It was a horrific but typical war scene. Our nerves hardly get excited any more. I approached to offer help but they did not need it. The survivors had no scratches. The others were in no condition to receive help.

I met up with my friends close to the station at Romagne. Sergeant Kelleher, Massenburg, Gersbach, and Schulze were carrying a heavy load and I arrived in time to help. After they lit up their cigarettes and the sergeant his eternal pipe, we began our march, keeping some distance between each other. The Germans saw us right away and began firing at us. I was marching ahead as the guide and carrying a heavy telescope and other boxes. We approached our position and were about to take the small road that led away from Bantheville when Colonel Price appeared with a French officer in a blue uniform. The officer was very tall and known for his courage as a "daredevil," or a soldier who does not fear the devil himself. They took the same road and walked in the same direction as us. I had no choice but to follow Colonel Price who was walking purposefully and rapidly with the "daredevil" behind him. I kept up with them in spite of my heavy load.

The Germans had no problems recognizing the colonel. They did not need the "daredevil" to give him away. The two silver eagles proudly displayed on his shoulders were sufficient. The gigantic Frenchman was also visible, and he was not making an effort to keep a distance from the colonel, who was in a big hurry and I believe was sporting the usual cigarette in his mouth. The Germans opened heavy fire with their "juiz-bangs." We heard the shells exploding on both sides of the road. The shelling lasted a few minutes, but it seemed like years. All we heard was the deadly screeching sound of the projectiles going "j-u-i-z-z-z-b-a-n-g," "j-u-i-z-z-z-b-a-n-g"! We moved quickly, ducking every now and then as we heard the whizzing sounds of the grenades as they passed by and exploded nearby on the ground. Our colonel did not bat an eye and just kept moving faster. Without thinking, I also moved faster and my companions did the same. A sheer sense of duty was moving me forward. No one ordered me to stop and I did not know if I was going to end up in the German foxholes. I simply kept moving. Finally, one of my buddies behind me yelled out what I was waiting to hear, "stop." I did not wait to be told twice and immediately found cover from the shrapnel. My friends would later tell me, "Why didn't you stop, were you not afraid?" I told them, "You will be expected to report, two men were in charge. Speaking for myself, who in the world would care to note anything about me, including that I was afraid?"

We learned of the terrible barrage that was being planned for Hindenburg's impregnable trenches once we arrived at our position. We no longer felt the names or types of German trenches mattered because our soldiers have demolished them everywhere they have attacked. It is our turn to attack the rest of the trenches, which are occupied by the cream of the German army. Our soldiers will jump "over the top" and we have no choice but to overrun the Germans if they continue fighting. Gómez, Barrera, and I were told that we would be moving tomorrow at ten. I took the opportunity to explore the destruction in the woods where everything had been turned into rubble. I also saw the mire that forced the Germans to abandon their ordnance. They did not take everything. Much of it could not be moved owing to the rough terrain and our "hot" advance. They left much of their ammunition behind, not because they have a lot to spare but because they were more interested in coming out alive. The many things they left in the foxholes meant they fled in a hurry or they died underneath the mounds that are now their graves.

I grew tired and joined my friends to prepare my bedding for the night. A constant rain began to fall on the battlefield. The clouds swelled quickly and the ground turned dark. Readers will remember this—especially if they were witnesses—that the dense fog turned into a light rain that managed to get everything wet. Nor can they forget the platoons of soldiers in good spirits and smoking wherever they could. They were talking, huddled in foxholes, or lying on their backpacks, but drenched from the rain. Stepping on that eternal mud was as familiar as the dull sound of the exploding grenades over the wet and sticky ground.

I found some foxholes in good shape and far from our command post, but we decided not to use them. Gómez showed me one a short distance away, but it was very wet. It also did not make sense to dig into the difficult clay soil for one night of sleep. Barrera, who was as tired as I, was sick of the sticky mud and we were not in any mood for the pick and shovel work. Gómez did not feel this way. As soon as he finished his assignment, he started digging with much enthusiasm. He embarrassed us, a rare reaction for a soldier. I had the idea of building a strong barricade and went to a nearby rifle and machine gun ammunition dump to collect as many boxes as possible. The boxes had been emptied when the ammunition was handed out for the attack. The boxes are of thick wood and have a sheet metal box inside. They are bigger than the ones used for packaging our rationed tomatoes. I filled the boxes with dirt and placed them around the foxhole, stacked two rows high. I then piled some long poles on top with several strips of canvas to protect us from the rain.

We took special care to prepare our beds, perhaps for the last time. The powerful mortars have started to rain on us. This is the only effective weapon when the enemy gets very close. The last thing we did—at my suggestion— was to secure a place to sleep by digging a hole underneath a small tree, which had been shattered into pieces. We built the hole to shelter our heads and then emptied the backpacks and prepared our beds as if we were to remain in place for the rest of the war. I even took my shoes off, as if we were one hundred miles from danger. My excuse is that there are moments when living may not be worth much. Bloody conflicts between single-minded men are horrible, and this is certainly the place to win medals.

We went to bed early. The artillery fire was becoming more intense and our side began to suffer losses. Things worsened as the night wore on. It is impossible to believe that man, the weak insect he is, can bear such terrible trials! Last night we witnessed horrible scenes that can break the hardiest spirit. Despite it all, we survived! Oh great God! The following tells it all. In the middle of a series of powerful explosions that tore through the skies in quick succession, an incendiary shell landed near us, blew off our sergeant's feet, and instantly set fire to some Bengal signaling flares. The red flaring light did nothing but increase the Dantean horror. All we could see were fear-possessed eyes and faces. The explosion left a man floundering on the ground, and several wounded soldiers were crying out nearby, but no one could make sense of the infernal red fire. Without thinking, Sergeant Bater shoveled wet dirt on the fire and put it out immediately. The Germans would have finished with us if they had continued firing. Our injured sergeant endured a very crude surgery before he was taken to the hospital. We have to thank Sergeant Darnell for rescuing him. He did it with courage and a strength borne out of a hardscrabble civilian life. We could have used painkillers or chloroform and the other accoutrements of modern medicine. The man of iron took it all, supporting himself on the shoulders of two of his friends while smoking a cigarette. The legs were amputated; his feet had already been blown away by the explosion. He did not complain nor did his face show signs of pain. A bolt of pain reached his brain and then he smiled. This is how the sapper sergeant fell. We hope he lives so that he can continue as a living example of courage.

Our barrage started before eleven and relieved our nerves, which were already worn out due to the lack of sleep. It was not easy to fall asleep or remain calm after four or five hours of lying down knowing that bodies were being blown away and that we were facing the same possible fate. I can still hear the loud whistling sound of the infernal shells that climbed two hundred yards into the sky and came down as if looking for a human being to obliterate. Thousands of explosives were raining down on our position. As soon as our barrage began, the enemy grew silent, and we began to breathe more easily.

We saw many clear signs of God's mercy last night. This should be enough to make the ignorant and small-minded humans mend their ways. We will see what happens, if we can survive this.

How We Destroyed Hindenburg's Impregnable Trenches

Friday, November 1

Daylight found us alive and well, but we did not get up until late. We will never forget what we saw last night. A shell landed on the few branches of the splintered tree with the roots that covered our heads. The explosion destroyed our little fort, and big pieces of shrapnel dug into the boxes that then fell on us. This happened while Barrera was on his feet. A splinter slightly bigger than a needle struck him on the back of his neck, reminding us that we were not free of danger. Of course, Gómez and I had a good scare because we thought we had lost our friend. While Gómez stood guard, a huge shell had landed close to the foxhole where Barrera and I were sleeping. We do not know how many minutes we were unconscious. Although we were fine, we did not realize until Gómez woke us up that we were covered in dirt. The explosion had killed soldiers sleeping next to us.

We had expected the sight that was before us in the morning. Large numbers of German prisoners began arriving. The wretched men looked relieved because they had managed to survive. What more could one expect? The prisoners included old men, young ones, and even younger boys. One of their artillery officers was drunk and could hardly walk. The others were ready to answer questions. They discovered that we did not hate them like soldiers of other races would have. We do not harbor significant resentment because we have not been subject to the outrageous actions they have taken on the Poles, French, Belgians, Italians, and British.

It broke our hearts to see this part of the war. Many of our wounded soldiers were arriving without having received any medical treatment. Many had bled all night and were very weak. One of them took off his jacket and shirt to show us two wounds on his back that reached all the way to his chest. Although the wounds were not critical, they were very dangerous. Another soldier was missing his entire lower jaw. The others had missing feet and supported themselves on the shoulders of their companions, as Sergeant Darnell had done. Several had head, arm, and leg wounds. They have suffered all this and maybe more at the hands of the Germans, who were trained to wage the cruelest war in the history of man. The point, however, is that the lowly private bears it all, or the worst of it. Moreover, he is not the cause of these infernal wars that are pounding mankind. Demented human race, you exalt the martial spirit instead of suppressing it!

A group of German artillerymen confessed that they had never seen anything like our cannon fire and that the barrage did not give them time to find a foxhole. Their commander had disappeared into his foxhole to drink wine and avoid the inevitable pain of death. He had ordered them to do as they pleased. They waited to die or be taken prisoners by our soldiers. This is corroborated by the large number of men who gave up without a fight. They say their only hope for survival was to fall into our hands. They were really scared of the British and the French. Why? What had they done to those people? Behold the history with its bloody pages that they wrote in Belgium and northern France. They understand everything all too well and, consequently, fear these aggrieved peoples.

Soon thereafter, our brothers charged the enemy positions. A line of machine guns next to us had been directing heavy fire since around five in the morning. The firing suddenly stopped and we heard the clear and distinct voice of the officers, "Over the top and forward." What a terrible order. We were to jump out bare chested and into the clutches of death, to attack an enemy that was barricaded in his impregnable trenches, and to brave the curtains of machine gun and rifle fire and all the other modern inventions of war. Our advance was noticeable as the enemy's fire declined and their major hellish offensive lost steam. We also noticed that their cannon grew increasingly silent, mostly because our own guns were hitting their mark. The cannon from hell that had fired on us all night were being silenced, perhaps forever. May God make this true! Our soldiers carried out the glorious offensive against a thousand obstacles. The selfless act of our zealous youth made everything possible. Von Hindenburg's trenches were either destroyed or seized. Victory was ours. Nothing could deny our complete success. Germany will have to surrender.

I was ordered to get some water in the afternoon and left for the kitchen and the stream at Romagne. I had crossed the crystal-clear stream on several previous occasions. I was now able to see what had transpired the night before. What was the full measure of our formidable attack? Several of our patrols were picking up the dead and burying them. A few German soldiers were helping them. I approached a pit being filled with the dead who were to be covered with dirt. The soldiers wrapped the bodies in blankets and placed dog tags on them. Many of the bodies were mangled and unrecognizable. Others could not be pieced together. Parts from different bodies were going to be buried together. Who could take issue with this? They will have to remain here until they are exhumed at the end of the war and buried in a better place. What better place for burial than the fields of honor they defended? I believe that we have the legal right to take our own to America, although the expenses will prevent it. It would be best if the government used the money to help the widows and orphaned children.

Another detachment was gathering the backpacks of the dead. It is difficult to see so many of these backpacks without their owners, the same soldiers we engaged in conversation with yesterday afternoon. Once we arrived at Romagne, I recognized the place that Sergeant Schwarz and I shared for five nights. Artillery fire had blown the roof away. Out of curiosity, I checked for the ruinous signs of war and, sure enough, I found some. The soldiers who had taken our place the night we left had died. Their lifeless bodies were resting where we had slept five nights in a row, one in each bed. No one can imagine how I felt when I saw this. I thought that others could have witnessed the same scene with us as the victims. I wanted to investigate further and entered the sleeping area; the door was open. The place was such a mess. Garbage and objects of all kinds were scattered next to the dirt and rocks and the black soot from the explosion. All of this covered the dead and made them barely recognizable. The bodies were not in pieces and little blood was showing. They may have died from the blasts of the exploding shells. They were blackened from the horror-causing smoke of the explosions. Deeply pained and saddened, I left that place of rubble and misery.

Our artillery force is large and moves fast toward the front. We are occupying more German ground and have to fortify the positions we have overtaken to discourage counterattacks. The Germans have shown that they can also move quickly. On some occasions, our soldiers have been unable to catch up with them.

Our office has not moved. According to Barrera and Gómez, the messengers maintain contact between the command post and its forward-moving units. They now have to run longer distances with their messages.

I should provide some background on these humble men—all friends and brothers—with whom I share the misery of war.

Eulogio Gómez left his parents and brothers in Brackettville. I know nothing about his past, but a buddy knew him as a civilian and speaks well of him and his family. He is like many of our men who come into this world without noise or fanfare and grow up alone without anyone ever taking notice of them, except for people who are close to them. They belong to our great nation but are never recognized as such until misfortune and calamity come knocking on their doors.

Society finally decided that the descriptor "100 percent American" could be extended to races that had been thought unworthy of such consideration. This occurred with the arrival of the devastating threat of the Great War, when it became necessary to send men as cannon fodder, when studies determined that only citizens should be sent to fight, and when it became known that 95 percent of them would probably never return.

We were all to act like *Americans*, but some people sought easy jobs in government and business in order to stay in the United States. No one seemed to be claiming the honor of serving on the front lines, but we needed men to meet this responsibility. Where would they come from? At that point, they remembered the uneducated and ignored masses that are stuck in the agricultural fields of the South where "cotton is king" (king of slaves). Everyone should recall that newspapers published copies of a law claiming that people who could not read, write, or speak the national language would not be bothered to go overseas. We were happy to hear this, and many of us thought justice would finally prevail because many of our people do not meet these qualifications. They were not to blame for this; our schools had denied them equal access.

In many towns, racial prejudice is solely responsible for denying our children the opportunity to attend a school. Instead of teaching them love of country, they have injured their racial sensibilities. They became resentful, and this explains their behavior.

For one reason or another, society concluded that the more ignorant the soldier, the better for him to face the bullets. This is why hundreds, perhaps thousands, of poor men of our *raza* are wearing the good uniform of our nation and are in the line of fire in the trenches. More than that, they have been serving *with honor*.

Gómez could not read or write Spanish or English, nor could he even write his name. I had him order a book from New York so that I could teach him enough to write brief letters in Spanish to his parents during our rest breaks in the Saint-Mihiel sector. He has told me that, "As far as schooling is concerned, I owe nothing to our native state." He did not know anything about geography, not even that it existed. Gómez, nevertheless, carries out assignments that require some knowledge of geography. It is so demanding that even soldiers who have studied it have made mistakes. Gómez is so adept he does not need a compass to find the hiding places of the officers of our regiment.

I asked Gómez how he avoided getting lost like the other messengers during our advances across so much barbed wire. The "runners," or messengers, were always losing their way when we moved forward. Many of them were clever and hid in foxholes to avoid danger. Gómez was the only one who never got lost or went missing during the critical moments of the fighting. When he was not running messages, Gómez could be found at the colonel's office awaiting orders. He explained in his uncomplicated manner how he avoided getting lost in the constantly changing battlefield. (We know of the changing terrain because our planes are always taking aerial photos of the battlefield.) He pointed out that, "When I go from here to there, I place small stakes along the way until I get to the place I am going, and, when I return, I remove them." I then asked, "Why do you remove them, could you not use them again?" "No," he replied, "that would be a mistake. Since the command posts are always changing, I have to do a lot of moving, and I would be in real trouble if I were to come across some of those old stakes. You see, I really do not know where I am going. I find the command posts after walking for a long time." Everyone should know this intimate part of the life of the small fair-skinned Gómez. As God is my witness, this small man is very important. Many others have been so frightened they have lost their way. Since I am always dealing with maps of our operations (this is another responsibility I have despite my rank of private), I have asked him about some important places at the front. Based on his responses, I know that he has exposed himself to grave danger many times, often without knowing it. Sergeant Baton is his friend and hails from the same hometown. The sergeant treats him well because he knows him.

Eduardo B. Barrera is from San Diego. I do not know anything about his family except that he left his good mother behind. Barrera has good insurance coverage. If he dies in battle, the insurance may not make her happy or help her adjust to his passing, but it would allow her to live well for the rest of her life. I think that Barrera has a small ranch. At any rate, Barrera's mother will be in better shape than most. Barrera obviously lacked influence in his hometown. If Barrera had the same "pull" as others, he would not have been sent to the trenches. He never thought of leaving for Mexico or seeking citizenship in that country. We have rebuked the men who did this to avoid the weight of the backpack and the delight of breathing gases on an empty stomach.

Barrera immersed himself in a country school. This is how he learned to write his name and write letters that our mothers do not understand but figure out with "sweet" tears in their eyes. Barrera is kind and passive and he has a country boy demeanor with a farmworker appearance that wins him friends wherever he goes. He knows how to ride a horse. This is why he has been assigned to a cavalry unit. Under other circumstances, Barrera would never have done what we have seen him do, assuming the awesome responsibility of "fighting to the death." He is not as sharp as Gómez, but he is not less responsible or unwilling to meet his responsibility, even to the point of risking his life if necessary. He has been brave and resolute.

I have studied this humble man very closely and with much interest. My hope is that if he returns to civilian life, the difficulties and the despair we have faced in the new and old world may serve him well. I have no doubt that he will build a happy home and that he will devote himself completely to it, and that if he has children, he will zealously guard their education. We have already said that when the next world war comes, we do not want our children to follow our footsteps because we are illiterate or cannot understand the whites.

San Antonio, Texas
October 1918

Mr. Sáenz:

I was so happy to receive your letter of September 16. *La Prensa* published one of your letters. Your eyewitness account was amazing. I read it to my brother's family. Do you know Lieutenant Jorge P. Knox of the 538th Infantry? He is my nephew. The war looks like it is going well from here. The allies are winning everywhere.

Thousands of new soldiers are still being recruited here. The influenza has hit pretty hard. Many people have died. We appreciate and do not forget the sacrifice and devotion of "our soldiers." Many Mexican Texans are at the battlefront. The uniform suits them well and I believe that in the future they will be able to better appreciate their homeland and thoroughly understand the meaning of their flag. This is going to be an education for all of you. You will learn a great lesson about "world issues," "an appreciation for the world," and "patriotism."

You have displayed a very noble outlook and we appreciate you for that.

Look for Lieutenant George P. Knox, Intelligence Department officer with Colonel Kavannaugh's general staff.

Sincerely,

W. J. Knox

P.S. May you return safe and sound to enjoy the honors extended to active duty soldiers.

Simón González and Others

Saturday, November 2

We had a more restful sleep last night and woke up in a better mood, thank God.

This is the day Catholics honor their dead. We saw large numbers of soldiers fall in battle. My God! What has become of *Christianity*? We cannot calculate the losses on both sides. I cannot help but think that millions of mothers are on their knees at this moment imploring God for the dead and for us the living.

We have been preparing today's general offensive; we expect it to be our decisive blow against the enemy. The fighting is intense all along a front more than 150 miles long. We have been taking thousands of prisoners, including very young and very old soldiers. They are all thoroughly exhausted from the demands of the war and present a pathetic picture. They look awful, although they are also happy to have survived the fighting and entertain the sweet hope of seeing their loved ones. We have heard that we will no longer exchange prisoners. This will discourage taking more prisoners and help us avoid shedding more blood.

The wireless brought us the good news that the Kaiser has abdicated his imperial crown. His crown got so "hot" he could no longer keep it on his august head. The worst of it is that he will have to find refuge in a neutral country. This will be unfortunate because it keeps us from completing our mission. Someone will be denied the great reward for the Kaiser's head. Good pilots and captains go to the bottom with their ships, but the Kaiser has been a bad leader who has merely tried to save his skin. What hope does he have while alive? To be the recipient of the civilized world's loathing? Will he have the same fate as the sad and famous crown prince Franz Ferdinand? What awaits the Kaiser? Suicide, if he had any shame. The blood that was shed at Verdun clamors for justice against this bloody barbarian. The same wireless message informs us that the no less barbaric Turks have also surrendered unconditionally. The messages were received and decoded on the battlefield when the fighting was at its height, when death was waving its inexorable scythe over our heads, when life had become so difficult and uncertain that very little mattered. The news should have lifted our spirits, but it had little effect on us because of what we have seen and are seeing now. It is tempting to see the news as a strategic invention with military value. My friends had been so eager to hear this news, but they no longer get excited. I translated it into French and am the first among the troops to hear about it along the entire front. I pray to God the news is confirmed for the good of all mankind.

Our 90th Division has suffered many losses while assuming the major responsibility in this sector. They calculate that we have registered a 40 percent loss of dead or wounded soldiers. The figures seem overstated but I keep seeing the battlefields littered with the unburied bodies and other soldiers who continue to fall. The brutal consolation is that the enemy has suffered more because they are seeing losses while fighting on the entire front against all the Allies. What a slaughter! How many men must have lost their lives just yesterday and today? Our line is advancing evenly. The Germans are not stopping us anywhere. This is horrible for a people who have invited the rage of God and man. The wireless also informs us the Germans are retreating so fast we cannot catch up with them. We are using planes that are continuously returning for more bombs to drop on the units of German soldiers that are scattering all around. Our pilots tell us that most of the "Boches" are not carrying their weapons and that they are running. They say the Germans are only resisting with truck-mounted artillery and that all they need are wings on their feet to make a flying retreat.

It is one in the afternoon and we have been ordered to march and join the advancing line of fire ahead. Food rations and ammunition are already being handed out. The threat of rain might bring us bad weather. A large number of soldiers are resting on their backpacks and waiting for their marching orders. I see nothing but unwavering courage in all their faces as they wait to move out in a few minutes. I should make special mention of one of my buddies. He is Feliciano Carter from El Paso, a bright soldier who has little or no education. He took out his small knife while we were resting, grabbed a piece of wood from the bottom of a box for canned tomatoes, and began to whittle the shape of an American soldier. His problems, worries, and the fear of dying were far removed as he focused on his art, his unrealized dream. Carter was carving the soldier while thousands, perhaps millions of men were only thinking of the possibility of death. What was his purpose? He wanted to carve a souvenir. It was the most perfect work of art when one considers the place, the material, the tools, and the terrible circumstances.

As soon as the officers gave out their order to "fall in," the sudden muffled sounds of military gear cut through the silence as each soldier adjusted his backpack and picked up his rifle. Carter approached me and said, "Sáenz, I didn't have enough wood to include the rifle that I have made for other carved soldiers, but keep it as a souvenir from your friend." After receiving the little wooden soldier, I responded, "I will definitely keep it. The souvenir will bring back memories, most of which fade away with time."

Carter's work of art needs to be seen to be appreciated, but my observations in this diary must suffice. It is also necessary to have carried the unbearable load of our backpacks and to have advanced through "no man's land" as we attacked the enemy or pursued them over well-defended trenches to understand how well the wooden soldier reflects our feelings and appearance.

The wooden soldier's helmet is hung low over the head to shade his view so he can scan the position of the enemy who is lying in wait for the best moment to fire at him. The mask that protects him against the poisonous gases is on his chest and ready for any danger or emergency. His small water canteen, which spells survival during the supreme hours of the offensive, appears on his right side, by the hip and very close at hand. Our inner garments and other utensils for shaving, writing, etc. are in the upper part of the backpack. It includes the three rolled blankets which become our bed and a uniform wrapped in waterproof tent material that we use to shelter us from the rain while on the march. He carries the famous campaign shoes (hobnails) on top of the backpack. A small magazine of one hundred rifle cartridges and a dozen hand grenades are attached to his belt and another one hundred cartridges for his rifle on a bandolier across his chest. My soldier only needs two large cans of tomatoes, another one of devil's meat (cornwilly), or hash, and a rifle swung across his shoulder in the position of attention with five cartridges inside its magazine and a fixed bayonet. Anyone who has carried an entire load on his back can imagine the wooden soldier at a moment of critical importance, at the well-known Verdun front. He strikes the same pose as we did when we forced the fearsome German soldiers from their *hardly* impregnable trenches.

The sky was gray when we marched through the field of uncovered bodies. Artillery shells were still landing everywhere. It was rare to find a foxhole without dead soldiers, our own or theirs. I have been especially struck by the fact that our dead are mostly lying on their stomachs while the Germans are on their backs. Many of the bodies are in pieces. I remember a German body in this condition as we neared Aincreville. His steel helmet only contained a head connected to the windpipe and lungs and heart. This may have been a gruesome sight under other circumstances, but that was not the case then. He was a young man with pubescent stubble and a natural appearance due to the cold and rainy weather. The rain had washed away the blood and a possible unbecoming appearance. He was very handsome, with silky and curly brown hair. The young man looked more like a wax figure than a disgusting cadaver.

Fellow soldiers care little about these scenes while I cannot help being interested and taking notes. It is impossible to remain indifferent to the many bodies scattered throughout the battlefields. Many have been there for days, others fell yesterday or the day before. Still others fell a few moments ago. They are exposed to the elements, some are whole, others in pieces. Some of these sights cannot be imagined. They are on the battlefield, in the trenches, behind tree trunks, and in foxholes. Some bodies are completely or partially buried by the exploding shells. When I see all this I cannot help but think of the ungrateful nature of man. The dead are destined to be forgotten. History has no room for them and society will forget their sacrifices. Who will care about the soldiers of my *raza* after the sacrifice? There they are, Simón González, José González, José García, Moisés Carrejo, and so many others. This will not happen. Whoever survives this devastation should be responsible for selecting the right time to convince our people to erect a memorial worthy of the sacrifice of brave men who fell in the greatest war in history.

We passed by some fields with sugar beets and vegetables and could not resist eating some, though we are forbidden to do this. Aincreville was in ruins. A terrific shelling slowed us down and we sought shelter behind some old walls where we found many dead. This is where we had decided to set up our command post but since the Germans are retreating, we cannot stop. We have to try to catch up with them. We resumed our advance in the dark and, to make matters worse, in cold and rainy weather.

We arrived in Villers-devant-Dun at ten. Our headquarters was in a damaged house that also housed the French command post. All of us gathered at the same place. Barrera, Gómez, and I settled down under the table, in royal comfort. No one was really sleeping, but they acted like they were so no one would order them to do something. We were overcome by the cold, humidity, and exhaustion, but could not sleep. So much was going on.

The French were in another room but they made enough noise to keep a drunk awake. I was interested in what the French were saying and listened like "aunt Cleta's pig waiting to be discovered."[1] This is how I heard the latest news from the French. I said nothing because my buddies would have kept me from resting with all their questions. French messengers were constantly coming in from the front with news that the Germans were retreating and abandoning all the towns and other places of importance. This explained the noise with which the French were welcoming the news. I would have liked to have a map to know the exact location of our offensive, but since I did not have one and did not expect to get one, I continued to tolerate the miserable weather, the sleeplessness, and the good news. Continuous messages announced that the Allies were taking new military positions and advancing.

Hipólito Jasso Receives a Shrapnel Wound

We are in the well-known Argonne forest by the also renowned Meuse River. Today has been a terrible day for the entire world. The formidable offensive has begun along the 150-mile front. How many millions of souls have been lost? I have never seen so many dead in a battlefield nor do I want to see this ever again.

Hipólito Jasso, a humble Mexican man, is worth noting among the many wounded I have seen (in the thousands). Nobody wanted Jasso in their dugouts, trenches, or the line of fire. He loved seeing the exploding grenades and flying shrapnel. With every deadly explosion, Jasso would stick half his body out of his foxhole or trench to see where the shells had landed and how many soldiers had fallen.

We marched into the open this morning to take the village of Andevanne and came under a curtain of machine gun fire coming from trees in the nearby forest. Our advance was slow because of fallen trees and the trenches we had to jump. While facing a hail of deadly bullets, we heard the terrifying explosion of a big shell that landed between Jasso and his buddy, Juan (his last name escapes me).

When the black smoke cleared, we saw Juan get up. Hipólito was on the ground trying to get to his feet. A large sharp fragment had torn through his gas mask; it also went through his raincoat, thick jacket, and shirt, all new and made of wool. His chest—the thorax area—was torn open from side to side, but, miraculously, his lungs and heart were intact, although they came close to slipping out every time Jasso spoke and took a breath. He would say, "It's nothing. It's nothing" and would brace his chest with his hands to breathe and walk. The healthy young man did not seem to be affected by the wound and the loss of blood. He did not want to leave his company and his friends Juan and Amado Aguilar. (So many others get a scratch and ask to be sent to the hospital, while others—this is no exaggeration—have shot themselves in their hands or feet to avoid participating in the offensive!) It was not easy convincing Jasso to go to a field hospital. A very crude operation was performed on him. He was sent to another hospital, but he quickly slipped away to search for his buddies. When the captain realized he could not convince Jasso to return to the hospital, he let him remain, on the condition that he stop fighting and visit a hospital now and then.

The crude operation left Jasso in poor condition. This may spell his end because he will be breathing gases in the battlefield. May the nation and its people appreciate and remember the courage of this private from the 360th Infantry!

Sunday, November 3

The sun had barely risen when we set out for La Ferme de Sainte-Marie. We marched over unburied bodies and stopped often for fear of walking into an ambush. I told my buddies on one of these stops what I had heard at the French command post. I also urged them to maintain close relations after the war. They agreed and said they support my idea of establishing an organization of soldiers who survive the Great War.

We reached an old field house at Sainte-Marie that had once served as a German hospital. The house had four big rooms, including three in the basement. The large collection of barbed wire suggested that it served as an important German military post. We found a large pot with horse meat soup being prepared for the sick and wounded Germans. Several horses had died in the courtyard and we could tell that the Germans had selected the good cuts. The bones were beginning to show—a sure sign they had really been going after the meat. Some of the wounded had died in the rooms, either from wounds or at the hands of doctors who did not want them to become our prisoners. Some of the dead had just recently died, while others had passed some time ago. Many of them were outside and by the house, along with old and new graves and even some still uncovered ones. The house is surrounded by a beautiful garden with foxholes in every corner for sharpshooters or sentries to guard the strategically important place. Some of the foxholes had piles of casings, suggesting that whoever occupied them had been busy. The last of these sharpshooters remained in his hole. He fired his gun until he ran out of bullets and our soldiers overran his position. He had been well protected in a foxhole that looked like a grave. It had a thick sheet of metal as covering. When he fired his last round, the German jumped out of his foxhole, removed the bolt that served as a hammer for his special type of rifle, threw it far away, and stuck his rifle in the ground. The very brave soldier was walking toward the hospital when he was overtaken by one of our men. He fell, never to cause us harm again. We found the bolt in the grass. I really wish I could have sent it to America as a keepsake because we should honor courage. I did not take it because even my own is getting heavier.

Gómez took his position as a sentry under a tree at the front, the north side of the house. Barrera and I checked out the area and some houses made of tarpaper with the idea of setting up our sleeping quarters. Other soldiers had taken over the shacks by the time we arrived. We had just stepped out of the building when we saw a black cloud of smoke that seemed to be coming out of the ground. We had not heard anything but felt the shock in the air as well as the shrapnel that rained on us. We thought it had been a land mine. Gómez appeared before we had calmed down. We had been worrying about him. The shell had exploded almost exactly where we had seen Gómez set up as a sentry. He told us he had been called away and replaced by Cruttinger, from Iowa. Cruttinger was wounded and eventually died.

As soon as the danger had passed, we saw soldiers carrying Cruttinger to the house. We ran up to him at the same time that we saw some of the officers running out of the house seeking a safer place. They were going toward the nearby forest.

The doctor examined Cruttinger and gave the order for him to be taken to the closest infirmary. When they left with the wounded soldier, we asked the doctor if there was any hope for him. The doctor doubted he would make it. Several bullets had torn his intestines into pieces. The doctor was right. Shortly afterward, the soldiers returned to inform us that he had died en route. The soldier was from Iowa, serial number 2657741, assigned to General Headquarters. Our hope is that our kind and noble companion rest in eternal peace. He always shared tender memories of his beautiful fiancée and caring mother.

We are the only ones left standing to fight until who knows when.[1] Since no water was available, we decided to go down to a beautiful valley by the side of a mountain and to a small creek where we discovered a good number of German bodies. One of our buddies told us he had seen the explosion that killed them. We came up to their sleeping quarters and concluded that they were attached to a signal or intelligence unit because they had two small telephones, several rolls of copper wire, and tools. We were tempted to look into their backpacks since they were new and well packed. They were carrying everything they needed for battle, including packages they had recently received from home. It did not take long for someone to tear open the packages with rolls, candy, and other sweets, including lumps of sugar and fruit. We did not immediately start eating and were satisfied with just examining everything closely. I took a fresh and small aromatic soap, some writing paper, and envelopes. I saw someone throw away some postcards and letters that belonged to one of the soldiers. I found them very interesting and kept some for future use. The Germans also had photos of the brutality on the battlefields. These are the first pictures I have taken from the Germans. One of them had photos of himself as a civilian, before and after he married. He also had captured his image wearing the uniform he had on when our shrapnel tore him to pieces. The dead numbered five, and, by all counts, they appear to have just finished high school. Their uniforms were new, they were young and handsome. Their packages from home told us they came from privileged families, in other words, they had been born with silk diapers and silver spoons. Their bodies and uniforms look so different from the typical German soldier we have been seeing since September.

That is as far as we had gotten when some of our artillery friends arrived. They are old foxes toughened by what they have seen at the front. They wanted to know who was claiming the food and sweets and other things that were scattered on the ground. We told them they belonged to anyone who wanted them. We watched them devour everything with a delight that awakened a hunger we had suppressed. We quickly dispensed with the idea that the Germans might have sought to poison the Sammies and proceeded to finish off everything. The artillerymen continued the pillaging, removing the watches and money from the pockets of the Germans. We drew the line there and left them to claim the spoils.

We went down to the little valley where we found a stream and filled our canteens with water. The water may not have been very clean, but it was clear and fresh. We were glad to find that our mess hall was in the area and food was being prepared. The stream runs north through the middle of two tall hills that are covered by beautiful trees. One of our monstrous cannon was emplaced in one of those ravines. While we were getting our water it fired a test shot with a horrific thunderous sound. We felt a strong jolt at forty yards and were left momentarily deaf. Someone said, "The dog must be something if it even bites its masters." I added, "What misfortune it must bring on the target that it hits."

When I returned from Sainte-Marie, my lieutenant directed me to look for my buddies. Where could they be? We had not seen each other since the last day of October when I brought them from Romagne. I took my time, like that famous messenger who delivered a message to García during the Cuban war.[2] I thought they were close to the front, and that is the direction I took. Bois de Montigny was completely destroyed and covered with dead bodies. With great difficulty, I reached an area where I believed they were,

close to the machine gun fire. The cold German bullets were falling like hail.
I thought I had heard their mumbled conversations. The palisades and the
craters kept me from walking, I could only crawl. I was very quiet because I
was alone and without anything to carry. When I sensed the danger, I went
in the opposite direction. I walked and walked and cannot remember when I
changed directions, but I ended up in the same place as before. I once again
heard the muffled foreign speech and realized I was in imminent danger. This
is when I headed south and made sure I did not lose my way again. Once I
had moved a good distance away from the Germans, I set about to explore the
most horrible battlefield of the war. The Germans had abandoned so much
war matériel. I was struck by the large number of small rail tracks and railcars
for transporting the large shells to the cannon emplacements, the high caliber
mortars, and the many machine gun nests. I saw many trees with three and
even four platforms for the machine guns. These are the famous machine gun
nests that will be the object of conversations in the future. I stopped exploring. I would have gladly continued even with the danger, but it was getting
late and I had not found my friends. I finally made contact with our troops
at Bois de Tailly near Barricourt. Everyone was lying low, seeking as much
cover as possible under the fallen trees and the few trees that were still standing. The men belonged to other battalions, and although I knew many of
them, none could tell me the whereabouts of my buddies. I went looking for
the major since I knew that foot soldiers are typically uninformed. I quickly
found him. Luckily, we knew each other. He received me so well I decided to
speak candidly. He directed me to his scouts who then helped me get a better sense of the location of my friends. The scouts had not seen them since
yesterday but they gave me some good information and gave me hope that I
would find them. At this point, I met up with a friend who practically read
my mind when he asked, "Are you looking for your friends, the scouts? I saw
them close to the kitchens around suppertime. They may be in that area." I
made a charge for the mess halls. A beeline was not possible, but the danger
was not so bad around here. Finding the eating area was easy. Who cannot
possibly locate the mess halls? A good number of soldiers were still returning
from washing their utensils. I ate at the first mess hall using plates a soldier
loaned me. I reached the second mess hall as the sun was going down and
found Massenburg, as he was going for "seconds," the sly one that he is. Once
I found this bird, I had an easy time locating the nest. As soon as they finished
eating, we set out on our march. I was told to carry the heavy telescope and
serve as a guide. Sergeant Kelleher stopped me after walking a few minutes
and asked me, "Which way are you going?" I answered, "I'm going the same
way I came, on the route I know." They all said, "That is where the Germans

are." I then told them what had happened to me, and they believed me. They took out their maps and corroborated what I told them. We went in the opposite direction, to a closer destination. We reached Sainte-Marie later that evening only to find out that our lieutenant had fallen ill and had been taken to a hospital. We were sad to hear the news because he is a fellow traveler in this ordeal, but we also thank God for freeing us from an officer who has done wrong by us, or at least by me. I know others think as I do.

Dark Night, Cold Night, Horrible Night in Villers-devant-Dun

The time is around six in the evening and it has been dark for a while. All my buddies are very tired from our difficult march over a battlefield littered with dead bodies where both sides are still fighting with horrible determination.

We arrived in Villers as darkness set in under a constant rain. We had planned to sleep in the village as ordered in the afternoon. I learned of the counterorder after supper—we were to continue moving forward until we caught up with our line of fire, which is forcing the Germans to retreat in near disarray. At this time we are all leaning against our backpacks awaiting orders. I was letting some of my friends in on the order I had seen when a soldier stood up to accuse me of lying and to insult me sarcastically. This made my blood boil and I responded a thousand times louder and angrier. He did not dare respond. My friends were surprised to see me so angry. I felt embarrassed as I calmed down, but it was too late. The rain continued to come down as the bright flashes of the exploding shells tore through the intense darkness of that cold night. The sudden bursts provided enough light to make out the black walls and stones of the demolished buildings on both sides of the street. At that point we heard, as if coming from the center of hell itself, the overbearing voice of authority saying, "ready, forward!" We moved at a slow pace, pausing often. Once we were on the outskirts of Villers and out in the countryside, the darkness seemed to intensify. We could not see anything clearly, but we could detect the shelling with our feet. The awful smell of decaying blood and the numerous humps on the edge of the road or at the entrance of the dugouts told us of the many casualties that had occurred. When I realized how many bodies may have been in the area, I thought: "Forgive my trespasses as I forgive those of my enemies." We continued through that dark, cold, and horrible night all the while stepping on the many dead bodies, the remains of "our fellow man."

The underground area was the only available place for sleeping, but some dead Germans also occupied the place. We moved them to one side and prepared our beds. Some of our buddies were already snoring away. In situations like these we do not have to show too much respect for the dead since they are not too far removed from us, the living. Many of us will also be cadavers this evening or tomorrow. The danger that surrounds us may explain why the dead do not have a foul smell or an ugly appearance.

I had just gone to bed when I started thinking about the many events I had witnessed the past few days, especially the one from yesterday that I should include in my diary. I immediately started to write in the candlelight.

Yesterday, we saw the body of Simón González as we entered Villers-devant-Dun, a village in total ruin. He fell on November 1. I learned about his death from a friend of his who was marching to his right during that terrible attack on the village. The Germans resisted ferociously from their positions in the old houses. The demolished houses served the Germans well as our soldiers advanced in waves and without protection. They advanced like the waves of the sea over the fields of wheat and beets. The heavens were their only protection. In their final effort to hold their positions, the Germans have used machine guns and the "curtains of fire" against the fearless "tin soldiers," so named by the German leaders when we arrived in these lands of the old world. "The turkeys were really gobbling," I was told by the soldier who was relating the story to me. By "turkeys" he meant machine guns. In spite of it all, the waves of men dressed in olive uniforms continued to overrun everything in their relentless advance. Some fell and the others would step over their bodies to hold the ground taken with blood and fire. Our soldiers fired a bullet at every step and hit the ground at five paces, or they would kneel to load their rifles with five new rounds. Many of them would only get on one knee and then charge! This is how our squadrons moved forward, little by little, exposing their chests to steel and shrapnel.

Simón González, the humble farmworker and now overweight soldier (he had gained weight living the methodical life of a soldier), would not obey the order to kneel when loading his rifle. He never did, neither in the first front nor this one. He went after the Germans the same way he hunted quail and rabbits with his Winchester in the Texas brush country. When they came into his sights, he would shout, "Look at them, there they go," and he would shoot, steady and from a standing position!

Simón was a good-natured person who always sported a smile while resting between the battles. Everyone who fought alongside him can attest to this. Whenever Simón spotted me, he would call out, "Sáenz, here goes González!"

I usually responded with an encouraging word or with the truth, as in, "For-ward, this will soon be over." On other occasions, I would say, "Don't back away from those Germans!" He would respond, "That will never happen. Look, I'm here because of the Germans from 'Moronde' [Martindale]!" Anglo friends knew him. They would overlook his behavior and treat him fairly. The rest of the soldiers who did not understand Spanish would just listen. Simón always laughed when he saw a German fall or when he saw them run, because in this front, we have always fought them at close range. He would only curse when they killed one of his friends. Simón was like an enraged lion when he cursed the Germans. He would quiet down for a long while and then walk without saying a word.

Our offensive continued in spite of the asphyxiating gases and powerful shells raining down on Villers. The steel-tipped rifle and machine gun bullets seemed to respect Simón's stout body. He never suffered a scratch. But the moment arrived. A mortar shell landed practically at his feet. A black pall of smoke, flashes of light, whizzing sounds of shrapnel, and half a man disap-peared. Everything happened at once. An enormous shell tore off a hip and shrapnel shredded a leg and ripped his body all the way to the right side of the heart. This is how the life of that humble laborer ended. He was unknown as a civilian and will probably be forgotten after such a glorious death. How many persons from Martindale who unjustly sent him to war must now envy his heroic death!

Simón González, serial number 2244262, a private with Company G of the 360th Infantry Regiment, fell on November 1 on the outskirts of Villers-devant-Dun.

Sergeant José García of Mercedes, serial number 2228951, with Company E, also fell on the same day, close to González. This brave noncommissioned officer headed his company. While bending down to load his rifle, a steel bul-let entered the front of his helmet and exited at the base of his head. A drop of blood appeared, the hero's body stood bent over like a dove, lifeless forever.

Monday, November 4

We did nothing in the Intelligence Office the entire day. The lieutenant left yesterday and we remained without anyone to assume the command. We have nothing to do but be bored and while away the hours. We get tired of talking about all we have seen, probably because we do this at the same time we are facing danger on the same battlefields.

We keep hearing from different places on the front that the enemy is practically defeated. We should carry on and keep striking while the iron is hot. We have had an easy time meeting all the objectives given to us and until now have been suffering fewer losses than the enemy. The 360th Regiment, as well as the entire 90th Division, only stops its forward movement to maintain contact with the troops behind us.

Tuesday, November 5

The enemy's aerial activity was intense last night. They dropped a large number of bombs everywhere, especially close to the kitchens where our big cannon are located.

I spent the day watching numerous shells fall in different and random places. This means the Germans no longer have an appetite for killing and are busy running away from our "undisciplined soldiers," the very ones they thought would scatter at the first sound of the big cannon. They have been the ones who have been soundly routed. Obviously, their superiors fooled them into believing they were invincible and that the Americans were the worst. Surely, they must be the worst if they made the Germans run the most.

Wednesday, November 6

I was so glad to see Pablo Pérez. He was gassed at the Saint-Mihiel front the same day we left for this place. He has already been cleared to continue fighting. His arrival touched off a very natural reaction. Barrera, who loves Pérez like a brother, was so happy to see him he could not contain his tears as he ran up and hugged him. When Pérez asked, "Why are you crying? I am here, alive and well." Barrera responded, "They had told us you had been killed." Oh, the fellowship we nurture while engrossed in the misery of war! The unforgettable Sergeant Irwin, who fell at Saint-Mihiel, used to say, "We will become brothers if the war continues any longer."

Pérez tells of his difficult experiences in the French hospital. We recount ours in the last offensive when so many French hats, or chapeaus, littered the battlefields. Anyone who replaces us on the battlefields we have taken by force and with blood can obviously see that we came face to face with death.

We are still receiving news that peace will arrive soon. I hope this is true.

My sister Clotilde wrote and reminded me that if we survive the present troubles, loved ones will extend to us their dearest affection, and that if we fall, they will remember our passing with deep sorrow.

We continued sleeping among the dead in La Ferme de Sainte-Marie. Our officers have ordered us to the front to once and for all end our lives or finish with the war.

Thursday, November 7

The morning was somewhat cold. After breakfast we were told that Austria and Italy had stopped fighting. This was a welcomed topic of conversation. The rumors that the Germans want peace are still circulating. They should enjoy things now before it is too late. We will have to hold Germany accountable for the friends we are losing. It would be better to make peace before we start thinking about getting even. We do not harbor resentment or ill will toward our German, Austrian, Polish, and Hungarian prisoners, but we do not guarantee anything if we continue losing brothers and friends. We do not want to play out the obvious in the saying "blood demands blood."

Sergeant Schwarz went in search of a new command post. I stayed behind to write letters to my family.

We received the good news in the evening that Germany and the Allies will hold peace talks in seventy-two hours. We passed the time talking into the night amid dead bodies. We were happy to see that the newly arrived wounded are being cleared for fighting on the front line. Peace is upon us, nobody can deny it. On the other hand, we cannot be sure that we will have the opportunity to enjoy it. At the rate we are going, many lives can be lost in seventy-two hours.

Friday, November 8

All was quiet in the early hours of the day. I went to breakfast and was ordered to move to the new post. We have to march back a good distance on the same route we took to get here. The sappers left very early, eager to do their work. We will once again pass by Villers-devant-Dun. Once we arrived at the village, we had a lunch consisting of beans and hard bread, the memorable "hardtack," and then continued on our march. We reached the devastated village of Andevanne as it was getting dark; we found shelter in a large two-story house that was falling apart. We spread out some hay for a nest in a corner and rested so well. The march had been difficult and our break was satisfying.

The different furniture pieces suggest that the house belonged to schoolteachers. It contains a large collection of books that are in bad shape because the rain comes down through the large skylight-like opening the shelling caused. Our nest is in a corner of the top floor. The house has no roof or wall facing the garden. Some of the soldiers dry their clothes by the fire so they can sleep more comfortably. Poor fellows, I have seen them do this often. I am moved and saddened to see the difficult, demanding, and unappreciated lives of soldiers who come to this place to forge a nation.

Saturday, November 9

We did not sleep well last night on account of the heavy rain in the morning. We had to set up tents inside our shelter to avoid the rain, but we managed to get a bit of rest because we turned in early.

We stayed inside today and I read from the many books that were scattered all over the place. I also read some French newspapers that spoke of sweet but doubtful possibilities.

We were told we are to leave tomorrow at ten in the morning. This convinced us to turn in earlier than usual. Since we are well rested, we can expect a difficult day tomorrow. We are going to the line of fire once again. The troops are nervous because the enemy will now be able to concentrate their gun sights on the fewer of us who remain. We are comforted by the thought that many of them are "already cold and decomposing." Neither they nor the retreating Germans will fire at us. It is six in the evening and we are already in bed. I am writing in my diary by a paraffin candle, my eternal companion in this calamity. "I have two items that I will never give up," I tell my friends sarcastically, "my candles and my 'cornwilly' rations, even if I have to rid myself of my rifle and hand grenades."

Since I am not sleepy or tired and have nothing to do this dark evening, I cannot help but recall some of my most important experiences in this great slaughter. For instance, I have been armed to the teeth ever since the fighting started. I carry between one and two hundred rounds of ammunition, twelve hand grenades, a beautiful rifle, and a brand-new bayonet. However, I have not fired a single shot, even though I have had plenty of opportunities. My buddies in the Intelligence Office can make this same claim. We have been ordered not to fire a single round or else face severe punishment and even execution. On the other hand, once the scouts submit their daily reports from "no man's land," I take my turn with the old and dilapidated Underwood typewriter to pass along intelligence to the artillery. This is how I play my part in the great slaughter without firing a shot. Some kill the steer, while others hold her down. I am an indispensable tool and contribute to the killing at a mass scale. We have seen enemy carts arrive at their front to deliver what appears to be hay and other animal feed and have passed along this information to the artillery. When our artillery fired on them, a number of soldiers jumped and started running. Many of them died. This is how we have crushed the enemy, when they have tried to supply their soldiers with food and ammunition. We have also seen flashes at night and have forwarded information on the size of the shells and the location of the cannon that have fired them. Our artillery has followed by destroying enemy cannon and the soldiers manning them. I maintain constant communications—the French would say that I serve as a liaison—with airplanes, messengers, and carrier pigeons. I also translate the French wireless messages from Paris or Washington. Although I have received little or no credit for all this work, it is important to me because I stay informed of everything under the sun like no other private in the army. I am up to date on our regiment's war plans, and the experiences of my Mexican friends (they appear in "My Personal Diary") and, probably best of all I have the time to write this memoir for my family.

Sunday, November 10

After last night's heavy rain, a strong gust of wind blew the clouds away and left us with bad weather, cold enough to form a thick cover of frost that covered the entire area and burned our feet. Our orders changed, probably because of the cold weather. We left at 3:30 instead of 1:30 and returned to Villers-devant-Dun. From there we turned toward Doulcon and reached the historic Meuse River during the first hours of the morning. The Germans knew the importance of that crossing and shelled it continuously. They had blown up the bridge as they retreated, but our engineers repaired it so the infantry and small pieces of artillery could cross. Everything was destroyed, the bridge, the forest, and the town of Dun. The French and American officers had decided the bridge could not be crossed during the attack and ordered the soldiers to ford the river. Our soldiers entered the crystalline, cold water and swam in pursuit of the Germans. Imagine the sight of thousands of men jumping into the cold water at all hours of the day and night to achieve the victory that will bring an enduring peace.

A beautiful hill watches over the city of Dun-sur-Meuse, on the right side of the river. We can tell that Dun had been a lovely city of some importance, but the war has left it in an almost hopeless state. We crossed the bridge and passed Dun on our way to Milly-devant-Dun. The smell of burned gunpowder was still fresh in Milly. Numerous dead Germans were all over its streets, where they had offered resistance a few hours ago.

Before reaching Lion-devant-Dun, we came across a dead horse in the middle of the road. It was a strange sight that often occurs during terrible moments. A German soldier had made a last-ditch effort to save his life as he retreated with the "tin soldiers" at his heels. Life is so sweet it deserves all a genius can do to prolong it! The soldier disemboweled the horse with his knife, took out its intestines, and tried to hide from us. Our soldiers saw him climb into the horse, but did not understand what he was doing and opened fire with their automatic rifles. The German died as he was trying to save himself. He was not carrying a rifle or any other kind of weapon. He only wanted to save his life. The Americans did not know this. They just thought he was preparing to defend himself. War is war!—this is how soldiers from both sides justify these acts. Onward!

We also found numerous dead Germans in Lion-devant-Dun. The battle lasted all night until our troops stormed the place. We passed by a very beautiful hillside of semicircular shape and regular height. The town of Saint-Germain is at the foot of the hill, which also bears its name. The beautiful Catholic Church can be seen from afar.

We arrived close to noon and took cover in the Foret de Woevre. The name of this forest should evoke profound respect for all the patriotic Americans who shed so much blood for the cause of peace. An intense battle was being fought at an exit from the forest and the entrance to Mouzay. We could hear the shells from both sides as we waited for orders to march. We could also see the explosions in the small villages of the Meuse Valley.

During a scouting expedition in the middle of the rain, I visited the forest and several bunkers the Germans used as shelter from the rain and cold. I observed many places where heavy caliber cannon had been emplaced. They were probably the same ones that shelled us all night long. Both sides had fought a bitter battle for two days. We fought until this morning to dislodge them, at a cost of many lives.

We moved forward at two. The Germans had been shelling us heavily by the time we reached Château de Charmois, a beautiful castle that had been occupied by German officers. I cannot understand why their guns did not strike our troops. We were marching in a close four-man formation over the different roads leading to Mouzay, and the roads did not offer any protection. They could see that our serpentine movements were heading toward a definite point. We stopped briefly at the castle's garden. The heavy shelling resumed as we were entering Mouzay at four in the afternoon. Our soldiers had barely removed the Germans from the town's small buildings. The blood and the dead bodies were still fresh, and the considerable amount of gas in the air was making us sick.

The approximately four hundred French men and women who were native to Mouzay had decided they no longer wanted to live under German tyranny and decided to put their lives on the line. The Germans informed them of our attack and gave them time to leave. They refused and instead decided to expose themselves to our shelling and then the Germans', with the hope of freeing themselves forever. The locals had been under German rule since the taking of Mouzay at the start of the war. We liberated those poor people who had endured humiliation, shame, and the Teutonic yoke for four years. They were suffering misery, hunger, and hardship at the same time that they were expressing great faith, selflessness, and French patriotism. Their tears say much about their difficulties under the tyranny and arrogance of the conqueror. Take a good look at this my fellow countrymen!

We are not able to describe their suffering or the dangers they faced. They said that when the German soldiers heard we were about to attack, they grew sad and called out, "Alles kaputt, Alles kaputt." They added that when our shelling began, all they could do was to commend themselves to God and seek shelter in the basement of their homes. They said the rest was a nightmare. We can imagine the prayers they offered for our victory. Our people in the United States have never seen anything like this and we pray to God they never find themselves under these circumstances. They cannot appreciate the determination of these selfless citizens.

The shelling of Mouzay from both sides left many dead. It became more intense when we entered the village. The sky had cleared and the sun made an effort to shed its light on those Dantean scenes. Gas shells played an important part in the attack.

Some of the mess halls were set up in a house across from the plaza's public fountain. Our kitchens had fallen far behind and lost their way. I had a hard time getting something to eat because the officers knew we did not belong to their units and told us to find our own kitchen. Nothing is impossible for the soldier. We even play tricks on death itself, but we cannot be blamed if they do not always work. I managed to eat well. Just when I had finished eating, a bomb exploded near the plaza. The Germans sent it to serve as our after-dinner topic of conversation. The pall of black smoke had scarcely come out of the roof of a nearby house when I noticed the odor of gas. I immediately felt something in my stomach and started to vomit. My eyes watered a great deal and I felt an unbearable burning sensation. Luckily, I was close to the water fountain where I rinsed my eyes with plenty of water and drank until I had cleaned myself well. I lost the meal but later felt great relief. The incident left me with an intense headache.

Gassed and all, I went to inspect the disaster as I had seen many soldiers at the house that had been hit. The bomb killed a French woman and one of our soldiers. The woman had been sharing her sad story of four years under German despotism and her happiness in regaining her freedom. Poor woman, she did not enjoy her new life for very long.

I could not stand the headache and decided to lie down. This brought me such relief I felt like resuming my walk through the town with the idea of discovering something new. I went to the city hall where our command post was now located. Our brigade general was there and had given orders to everyone who could carry a rifle to move to the battle line and be ready for action at sunup. Many men were missing during roll call. Some had died, while others were wounded or lost, and still others had no rifles, but no one could disregard the orders. "Everyone should get ready. If you do not have a rifle, get one from the dead." Forward! Orders are orders! One of the officers tried to point out that the soldiers had not eaten or slept for several days. This did not work either. Once again, we were told the attack would resume the following day at six. Someone also announced that the soldiers with mortars and small cannon had left their rifles behind when they crossed the river. They were also ordered to secure rifles from the field and to form a battle line. Provisioning oneself on the battlefield is fairly easy because so much equipment is available and no one objects. At that point, we started to strengthen the line, which already included our machine gun and automatic rifle battalions. We were told to take the forest that leads into Charmois. This was not a forest, but a field with shrubs, plants, and grasses. The Germans had dug some foxholes to protect themselves from our machine guns and rifles while we were resting on our backpacks. Our battle line is weak, but we are comforted to know the artillery of the 90th Division has just arrived. I greeted many of my friends who have never been in battle and are here for their baptism by fire. The soldiers seem mentally prepared. All their equipment looked new; this inspired confidence since they were arriving at the most opportune time. Obviously, both sides will be able to claim an abundance of helmets tomorrow morning. In order to complete the line of attack, the division had to make use of "straw" troops. This is what we call the men who have only done office work. We need fighters and our reinforcements are still far away. To get an idea of our losses we only have to say that a unit of four thousand infantrymen now numbers 396.

I wanted to take in everything on that solemn afternoon and evening. My confidence grew when I saw all those cannon directing their mouths of steel toward the enemy. Hundreds of the famous 75-millimeter cannon were hidden in the vineyards, and the men who were manning them were lying prone next to them. They spoke to each other in low tones. Everything was ready. Huge ammunition caches were everywhere and prepared to supply the many cannon, as well as the rifles and machine guns. They were waiting for the late evening hours when the horrific shelling was to initiate the offensive. Our preparations lift our spirits, but thinking about the consequences makes us sad. Once it grew dark, I sought shelter with the other scouts in a house on the outskirts of town. We prepared a crude bed on top of a bale of hay used to feed the cattle in the stable. No one cared to ask about the news of the day any more. We were just waiting in anticipation of the Zero hour during the crack of dawn on the eleventh of November. The waiting was going to be a time of profound and sad reflection.

Armistice Day

Monday, November 11

I was sleeping on the bale of hay in my loft when a messenger came looking for me around two or three, or maybe four in the morning. As soon as my name was called out, I felt a chill like I think a prisoner would feel, but I responded. I was not the only one to wake up. Several other soldiers—possibly all—stood up without thinking. The messenger told me to report to the command post and not to take my gear because they needed me immediately. I got there quickly but was not feeling well since I had left suddenly from my warm sleeping area to the very cold outdoors with frost on the ground. I had hardly wrapped myself up in warm clothing and was shivering from the cold. Before entering the post, I was shaking uncontrollably and tried to calm down to avoid giving the impression that I was gripped with fear. Regarding fear, I can assure you I did not even think about it. I was as ready as the best to face everything. I quickly completed my assignment. The assignment and other information I secured allowed me to learn of the new orders to suspend the offensive scheduled for this morning at six. The orders called for continuing the artillery fire with the same intensity until eleven in the morning, when hostilities would be suspended for thirty-five days. The Germans were granted the truce so that they would enter into negotiations for the conditions for peace. Those of us who heard the orders began to breathe easier, while the rest of the soldiers continued to agonize in desperation.

The day seemed like all others because the artillery duel appeared to be continuing with even greater intensity. The horrid smell of gas was so strong that breathing became difficult. Messengers delivered the good news all over the front. This really calmed us down, although it did not do away with the danger we were facing.

We followed the same routine. The soldiers were in a pensive mood and they would occasionally ask in a hesitating manner, "What do you think, could it be true?" I could only answer, "We will see." We continued with our responsibilities. Seconds before the memorable *eleventh* hour, the enemy fired a powerful heavy-caliber projectile, which fell on soldiers who were talking and laughing, probably entertaining sweet hopes. The explosion took all six of them without leaving a trace. They belonged to a machine gun company. May they rest in peace!

The German bugle announced that it was eleven. They were very close. The Germans were sure the hostilities had ended and we did not know. They were jumping out of their small trenches and shouting loudly with excitement. Genuine joy! They were throwing down their rifles and heading toward their homeland "with the swift pace of running geese." Some were singing; all of them were making a racket. The noise gradually died down, the muttering of men of war receded until nothing was heard but the low hum of soldiers talking with each other as they leaned on their backpacks or lay down on the ground. We realized how close we were to dying when we saw so many Germans jumping out in front of us. We would not be talking of the offensive if it had been carried out.

We concluded the day holding the line and the ground that we had taken by force of arms. That afternoon we observed the burial of the soldier who was killed alongside the French woman. It was sad. We hope this funeral will be the last. Two men took him on a stretcher to the outskirts of town. We were quiet as the body passed by. We had no reason to make a fuss, there are many more. We praise men like him by saying they wear the laurels of victory. The body was tossed into an ordinary grave, wrapped in a blanket and tagged. They placed a small white wooden cross by his grave. Otherwise, the site could not be located. This could easily happen. This is the gravesite of the many! Unlucky friend, you were not able to see the triumph you helped us secure! The rest of us have witnessed this victory. Others have not seen it, but will still benefit from the sacrifice of the fallen heroes in France!

Tuesday, November 12

Last night was the first time we had peace and could rest. We slept like paupers in a sultan's bed.[1] We heard roosters crowing during the early hours of the morning. How strange, but we drew great pleasure from the singing of the bird, the king of the farm.

I explored the area around Mouzay this morning and saw the destruction from the last battle. The Germans or our big cannon had blown away many of the bridges. I also saw some planes that still displayed Germany's black cross, a symbol long flaunted with pride in the old world and respected by all the nations. The soldiers are still burying a large number of bodies. The northern entrance of the town has many graves of German soldiers who died four years ago when they crushed these towns. Their fellow soldiers had maintained the graves. The fierce helmet of the German soldier rests on each grave. Small plates bear their name and unit, as well as some words of praise. Many artillery pieces of every caliber that could no longer be used were everywhere. It appears that they tried to repair the cannon but had to abandon them because of our unexpected visit. The evidence is in the spilled blood and the abandoned equipment. The trail of the dead beasts of burden is also moving.

We had already finished our meal when we received orders to move to the rear to rest and then proceed to Germany. Some of our divisions have already crossed the Belgian border.

We left Mouzay at two in the afternoon and traveled south on a road shaded on both sides by tall luxuriant trees. The Meuse River is on our right, beyond a lovely canal that also runs parallel to the road. We crossed the Meuse on the Sassey Bridge, which had been temporarily rebuilt for our use, and then entered a town called Mont, located on the foot of a hill that was covered by a forest. We found lodging in a house that belonged to a Professor Cordonier, as evidenced by the beautiful, extensive, and well-stocked collection of books I discovered. The Germans have treated the books badly. White goose down litters every room. This means the Germans tore up all the mattresses, comforters, and pillows they found.

Since we were somewhat tired, we did not bother to prepare a comfortable bed.

Wednesday, November 13

We woke up to a thick cover of frost on the ground and a strong wind that had us shivering terribly. We went for breakfast way before it was time and had to suffer a long and horrible wait. I returned to our sleeping area and read the titles of the books scattered inside and outside the house. I was especially taken by a beautiful and luxurious set with the complete works of the renowned astronomer Camilo Flammarion. I also looked over a great collection of publications on pedagogy. I read until midday and enjoyed my well-spent time. The materials were choice morsels of knowledge for my starving mind. I long for a permanent peace. Germany is exhausted and cannot do to us by herself what she was unable to do in concert with other countries, especially since we have a foot on her neck. I also hope the owners of this literary treasure return and rebuild their thoroughly damaged home so that it may nurture pleasant memories and use its love to replace the sad miseries of war. I hope they are pleased with what we have been able to salvage from the clutches of the hawk.

After the noon hour, I visited the ruined historic section that used to be a beautiful, popular, and historic chapel. The Roman-style temple was constructed in the seventh century. Its appearance is somewhat rustic, a clear reminder of the architecture of those times. A thunderbolt destroyed the bell tower in 1912. The Germans shelled the dome because they thought the French would use it as an observation post. The church bells were gone when we arrived. The Germans may have taken them to make shells out of them or the French could have removed them before abandoning the town. The pews and altar images are also gone.

I went up a hill south of Mont and observed the aftermath of the war that has ended with a *truce*.

I hope to God these are the last horrid scenes I will ever see. The trenches are full of dead Germans who fought as the world's best soldiers but failed this time, even if the Kaiser will not admit it. Two of them are by their powerful machine guns, as if alive and holding their positions. The cartridge belts that made the gun breathe its fire of death on us are in place and half full. Anyone could take control of the sleeping monster and continue firing it. We can tell that death surprised them while discharging their DUTY of taking human lives. The machine guns fired many bullets against our charging troops. The evidence is in the piles of empty cartridge belts. The forest—the same one that is across from La Ferme de Sainte-Marie—hid many machine gun nests. Our great cannon put many of them out of commission. I now understand everything that until now was only visible from our side.

I came to the area in the afternoon knowing that such horrible scenes will remain etched in my memory for years and possibly my entire life.

Thursday, November 14

I received letters from home and some of my dear friends. I immediately responded and wrote so much I hardly had time to eat. I wrote in English, Spanish, and French and enjoyed searching for words that could express my joy and the sweet hope of soon returning to the land of my birth. Regarding our return, we are very optimistic although the dark clouds of doubt often block out the peace and happiness from the blue skies.

Newspapers bring us good news about the possibility of a permanent peace and with it a happy ending to our great crusade for democracy, humanity, and justice.

My last official act today was to sign the payroll list. Complying with this duty is hardly worth it since I make so little. I have never had the money to occasionally buy my loved ones a souvenir, although I have been carrying the helmet of a brave German that I would like to send home as a keepsake. I thought seriously about this, especially when I saw death up close and thought I might not be able to live through this. It occurred to me that my helmet might one day be up for grabs. This is when I took the German's helmet. He had held up the advance of our equally brave soldiers who charged his position. The two machine guns positioned on a ridge of a hill that served as their natural defense had stalled our advance. Our artillery was not able to finish with them and we had to seek the help of the French artillerymen who flanked the enemy. When the French opened fire, I saw the helmet jump and roll down. I lost no time dedicating it to my children with this inscription: "This German helmet is for my children, to be placed as a war trophy in my study. With everything we are seeing, it is possible that my own helmet will someday decorate a German home."

My dear brother Eugenio:

It is with great pleasure that I write you this letter. And why should I not? God willing, this war will be coming to an end. This is what the newspapers are reporting and everything they say seems to favor us. We make the news. How does that strike you? I hope that it is God's will that everything continues going our way, as it has until now.

I hope you are doing better and spending time in your little home. Read and reprimand but do less of the latter because it will not do you well. Stay inside during the rain and cold weather. If you surround yourself with books, they will be your good companions during the winter. Store your firewood and visit the city when the days are good. I promise to write often.

Your brother who loves you,

LUZ

To my loved ones:

I have written a great deal today and may not have anything else to say. I may have also said too much, but I say what I say because I only wish that all of you are well. I will be happy and hopeful to see you as long as I know you have resigned yourselves to the circumstances. Be like the Roman women of antiquity who stood proudly by the sacrifices of their children and husbands in the wars.

It looks like everyone who faithfully discharged our duty will be coming home soon.

I send you my regards,

LUZ

Friday, November 15

We had inspection after breakfast and many of the soldiers did not respond to roll call. The majority of them are crowned in glory and sleeping forever where so many heroes have turned to sacred dust over the ages in France. We grow sad when their names and deeds cross our minds, but they have saved the homeland and she will crown them with laurels of glory.

Our country is glad to return to its former state. I hope we do not forget the difficulties we shared, and that it is able to render justice to those who shunned personal gain and only sought to answer the call of our threatened homeland and the outcry of my *raza* for fair consideration in the southern states.

We found kettles for boiling clothes in a big house. The French once used them, then the Germans, and now our glorious army. I heated water in one for a good bath and in another to wash my clothes. The other soldiers followed my example.

That afternoon, our band played some tunes that tore our hearts to pieces. They brought memories of "home and country," as the poet would say. We could not help but think of our friend Pepe González whose remains rest in Toul.

I was not able to send my German helmet and other souvenirs until today.

Saturday, November 16

It was even colder this morning than on previous days. The ground is frozen and cracks under our feet. Our feet are so cold they hurt. We tell ourselves that "none of this is worth anything anymore."

I helped my buddy Gómez wash his clothes. I am paying back my overdue debts. He has been a good friend.

I received letters from my brothers Eugenio and José. I really enjoyed them. It was very cold early in the morning and I had no good reason to leave my warm room since we now have a wood-burning heater. We found the cut wood in a nearby shed. I continue to read by candlelight much of my material, which is in French. I am not tired and prefer to read until very late at night. All I read now is in French. I have no trouble understanding the language.

Sunday, November 17

Today we learned that our first battalion is heading for Germany and that it will travel through heroic Belgium. We do not know the direction we will take. I wish I could visit this sacred land where the Great War began. We may not do this and this will be our loss. The castle of "Mamá Carlota" is in Belgium and very close to us. She is the demented empress who still lives and could serve as the best example for despots who wish to usurp independent nations that do not cower before them.[2]

We fell in formation at 8:30 in the morning in an old field north of here and participated in a religious service. The chaplain noted a solid truth in his stirring sermon when he stated, "Soldiers, always remember that you have never been closer to God than during these last days before November 11." We will have to ponder and understand the meaning of these words in the future. If the harsh blows we have received do not move us to change and build a better life, it will be our fault.

We should not deceive ourselves either. Men are capable of anything, and some of them will continue to act in a prideful manner in spite of all they went through during the war. We do not have to worry or complain about the just and the brave. They will be like stars in the clear, peaceful skies, shining as they did through the fog of war. The mediocre ones will receive our disdain, while the brave will always deserve our sympathy and respect.

I took in the sights after the noon hour and visited many deserted and demolished buildings that called on me to witness the rage of man. The Germans took everything they could find. The French, on the other hand, had retreated suddenly and with ruinous results since all the essential articles for domestic life were strewn everywhere. We did not witness their wholesale withdrawal, when they carried everything they could, in caravans, on foot, or however else they could, but we had heard a great deal about this at the Belgian front. We were also told of the German atrocities. We did not believe everything we heard about unrestrained soldiers, but neither did we doubt. The Germans thought they would crush everyone and that no one would survive to make claims. These were no more than bitter dreams!

The ruins have transported me back to distant lands. They remind me of the time of the Vandals and the Huns, and the Moors and the Goths. But God lives and we have removed the Germans from the places they razed during their rapacious occupation.

I have come across many albums with postcards that help me appreciate the days of sweet peace when everyone was happy and calm. Sometimes my hairs stand on end when I think of the scattered bodies of men, women, and children who died because of the blind ambition of a few despots. The air is still saturated with the smell of blood and the stench of decomposing human flesh, in the sea and in the desert, in the fertile valleys and in the mountains that reach into the skies.

I have kept a few pictures from the many I have found because I want to remember the panoramic scenes from before the war.

Today we were told that our division has been officially named the Texas and Oklahoma Division because the majority of our soldiers were recruited in these states. A good number of Indians come from the state of Oklahoma. I will be using the term *Indians* only to go along with one of destiny's whims, but we know that they, like we Mexicans, are the true Americans in our nation.

Monday, November 18

I had indigestion the entire cold night but enjoyed the town of Mont while awake. Beautiful clear silhouettes appear on the horizon toward the valley and on the opposite side, over the black forest. The sky is clear and the moon shines over the thick cover of white frost.

I heard that one of the stands at the YMCA was opening its doors for a few minutes this afternoon. I bought some sweets, which was the only thing I felt like doing.

Tuesday, November 19

We had a good day although it seemed like it would snow. Officers told us to request the clothes we might need. I asked for a shirt and towels, got a haircut, and had a long conversation with some friends about our plans for the future. We talked about sticking together after the war to build the monument for the fallen soldiers.

I had another day of rest. I wrote, read a lot, and thought of home. The moonlit evening was beautiful although it was a bit cold. The calmness contrasts with the intense memory of the incessant thunder of cannon fire, the movement and snorting sound of the thousands of trucks, and the roar of efficient planes that rained death and fear with their bombs. What a difference! Just a few nights ago, everything seemed to rival hell. Now the sweet and coveted peace reigns. We hear that the trucks are preparing for peacetime by delivering food to our soldiers who are occupying German territory in accordance with the treaty of November 11.

Wednesday, November 20

We were issued new uniforms and our dismal appearance was changed. We no longer looked like soldiers weighed down by the misery of the trenches, the devastation of the forests, and the foul-smelling, torn bodies on the bat-tlefields. We were no longer sleeping in foxholes or whatever other place, nor were we dirty, muddy, hungry, and exhausted. We were far removed from the continuous possibility of dying or denying others their own lives with our instruments of war. The heavy backpacks and the bothersome and disgusting white, clear, conchiferous, black-striped lice of the trenches also remain in our past.

I have already said that the new uniforms have raised our morale. I will now have to participate in the military reviews. We are no longer like the mother tiger fording rivers and meeting all the challenges along the way to recover her cubs and kill the fleeing Germans.

We sewed the red emblem with the *T* and *O* on the left shoulder of our new uniforms. This is an added reminder that we will soon return to our beloved America.[3]

After a while, everything turns to the usual anxious waiting. The routine continues and we grow tired from the monotony. The streets are full of sol-diers who wander aimlessly and without purpose. My illness may be influenc-ing my perception of things. Obviously, we cannot really appreciate anything when we are sick.

Thursday, November 21

My buddies and I decided not to get up for reveille because the morning was so cold. We have no one to call us for formation since our lieutenant abandoned us at the last front, supposedly because he was ill or had been gassed. His substitute has not been appointed yet. We fear that a sergeant who does not like the soldiers from the Intelligence Office will report us and might even discipline us.

Across from the YMCA the band played some beautiful pieces in the afternoon. The staff gave us some Christmas cards to send to friends and families in America. We are writing far in advance to make sure our mail ar-rives in due time.

Friday, November 22

I exchanged my old jacket for a new one and sewed on the *T* and *O* in-signia, as well as the green Intelligence ribbon. I went out for my clothes and nothing else and returned to my place to read and to write home. I have a lot of time for writing, and if I sometimes do not write, it is because I get bored. The lack of exercise may be the reason why so many of us are suffering from indigestion. The disgusting diarrhea is affecting everyone, and it discourages me from writing. On the other hand, we should not disregard this part of our lives. We would not say anything about the diarrhea or the lice if it was not true. I believe that even the genteel sons of millionaires would agree with me.

Some soldiers found out where I got the firewood for our heater and hauled it all away. Our secrets do not last long because we are birds of the same feather and flock together. The raid on our firewood led me to search for other sources. I found pieces of firewood in another area inside the house, but they were too big. We removed the wood from the top of the stack hoping to find smaller cuts underneath. It took us some time but we found two large boxes made of new wood.

We looked like we had come across the famous treasure of Captain Kidd, the infamous pirate of long ago. Our curiosity definitely grew. We could not help imagining that the boxes contained dead bodies or maybe even explosives that could blow us up. We were certain the French were not going to leave behind anything of great value for their enemies. We found many towels, handkerchiefs, and napkins in the first box. The second box contained a lot of sleeping garments for men and women, as well as many white sheets. I stocked up on towels and sheets for my rough bed. I think the materials were placed in the boxes at the tragic moment when the Kaiser's marauding soldiers were closing in, when the Germans were using their new artillery on defenseless cities, the women, the elderly, and children. This occurred when the inhabitants, fearing for their lives, took to the roads and fields like frightened flocks of birds. God's will was served when we forced the remaining savage, murdering hordes to flee. These once-victorious soldiers have run and left behind the powerful cannon they used to terrorize all these towns. History repeats itself.

The people had no time to take anything with them and left much or just about everything to the Germans, who stormed in like pirates. We would be happy if we later found out the owners were alive and pleased with the little we have been able to snatch away from the wolf that almost finished off the flock. May God help them stand on free ground and allow them to see their flag of liberty, equality, and fraternity once again wave over their homes. We have restored all this, but do not ask for anything in return. We only want them to remember that the *powerless* demand *justice* on this day and forever!

Memorable March from Pont-Sassy, France

Saturday, November 23

The letter *C* is embroidered in all the clothing we found in the boxes. This is the same initial I found in all the books. All this must belong to F. Cordonier, a teacher from Mont.

We were paid after breakfast and were as happy as if we had been made governors of a deserted island. I imagined this because the only settlements before us are the desolate, sad villages that served as the final battlefields we took by force from the Germans on the Meuse. We can only spend our money at the canteens the YMCA operates. The staff has been following us like seagulls or sharks that want to devour us. They give out some of what America sends its children and sells the rest. War stirs the waters and makes for good fishing.

My buddies and I bought French cookies and canned peaches and acted like kids in a candy store. We bought the sweets more out of curiosity than hunger. We must be fair toward our government and acknowledge that it supplies its military very well. This was done in spite of all the crooked leaders' waste and thievery, by the bums who enrich themselves with complete disregard for the "cannon fodder." Moreover, the meticulous plans to supply an army fell apart under the whirlwind of war. We must conclude that our military really took care of us. Just compare our daily rations with those of any other army in battle. How many of us would have survived with only a bit of wine, some raw potatoes, and a piece of "army bread"?

We had just returned from the YMCA when we were ordered to move out.

Our forced march was very difficult because of our heavy load. The village of Mont looked lovely as we departed. We had a beautiful sunny afternoon and entered Mouzay as it was getting dark. A thousand memories of the tragic battle of November 10 and 11 rushed in.

Since we did not find shelter, some of us continued walking. This is how we reached Stenay, the last village we took from a stubborn enemy. This speaks well for the 90th Division. We took the village by brute force and against a terrible curtain of machine gun fire.

Stenay was already packed with soldiers on their way to Germany. This is where we met up with the thousands of French soldiers with their eternal and boisterous talk about so many topics. We found shelter in a building that may have served as a machine shop or factory for the French and then for the Germans. I was exhausted and so were all my buddies. We set up our beds right away and then had the best meal in the field, canned tomatoes with sugar, "cornwillie," and "hardtack." No king with his roasted wild boar and golden pheasant has ever been more satisfied. We were certainly the objects of envy. Soldiers to the manor born who are lazy or pretentious reject the hardtack and canned meats, whether horse, bull, or whatever. They throw the rations away soon after they receive them. I would eat something else at home, but not while at war and in a foreign land. I normally carry double rations. Dimwits are always ready to pay for them when we prepare to eat. Money has no value on these occasions.

Sunday, November 24

We really missed our Mont stove because the mornings have never been so cold. The ground was white with frost. We had just finished breakfast when the sergeant major ordered everyone to bathe immediately. We found a small cauldron in an old dilapidated house. The hovel could not be heated with all the lumber in the world, much less with the few chips and dry branches we were able to find. Many soldiers were in line for their turn to bathe. Everyone wanted to be first so they could end the torture of freezing feet. The bathing proceeded very slowly. Finally, a counterorder was given to finish with the bathing, return to the village, and continue the march. We applauded the decision and the soldiers ended the general cursing that had been directed against the person who came up with the great idea of ordering baths in that cold weather and under such bad conditions. The war is over and arrogant minds that had frozen with fear are once again victimizing us. They reappear, thirsting for glory and authority.

We left at ten and passed by two pretty little towns, Baâlon and Juvigny. During the march, we observed several landing fields for German planes. Some planes were in ruins. We also saw a good number of German graves. They are very well arranged, which makes us think they died during the early part of the war. The ones who died later were not even buried, leaving a great deal of work for our sappers.

Shortly after midday, we heard the clear roar of an enemy plane flying close to us. We were marching on a level and open field and our troops looked like a dark snake along the meandering road. We saw the German black cross under its wings and wondered at the strange sight, but calmed down when we learned the plane would be guiding us through the unfamiliar country. We were told that one of our officers was flying the plane, which had been taken from the enemy. At any rate, our nerves were on edge, they have not yet returned to their normal condition. At Juvigny I had the opportunity to see the biggest ammunition dump ever. The stockpile consisted of artillery shells of every caliber. How many millions of wasted dollars! How many millions of precious lives saved!

It was practically dark when we arrived at Marville. A dense fog in the early afternoon had already turned into rain. Marville has no sign of shell damage. The place has very respectable-looking buildings and we selected a large, old two-story house as our dormitory. We did not stay in the rooms but in the attic, where the locals keep hay for their cattle. We looked for the mess hall after setting up our beds, ate, and quickly returned to our manger to rest and prepare for the following day.

Monday, November 25

The day began with rain. The few towns we have seen lately present us with different panoramic views that are engraved in our minds. When we return home and are asked about the towns we saw, we will automatically think of the narrow, winding streets, the familiar two-wheeled carts that seemed to move without a set purpose, the different types and shapes of houses hugging the sides of the streets, the slowly rising chimney smoke that mixes with the fog and sometimes turns into continuous rain, and rainwater running everywhere, from the rooftops and over the stone-paved streets. To complete the picture, our soldiers appear as silhouettes in raincoats as they jump over the muddy, waterlogged potholes like a bunch of drenched mice. At this juncture, we can definitely say, "C'est la France par les soldats américaines de 1918."

Our usual walks through the streets are mostly meant to break the monotony in our lives. We are most noticeably excited when we eat. Chow time is important in our lives. We would never miss the opportunity to inconvenience our K.P.s for anything in the world. We can also behave outrageously. When we have the money, we buy substitutes for our breakfast or our lunch of mush, hash, "cornwillie," and "hardtack." We return to our kitchens when we run out of money. Our cooks are the men of the hour these days. We praise them when they treat us well but say harsh things when we are made to wait in line for a long time. Poor souls! They will never receive their just dues for all their troubles. They were always exposed to the cold weather and rain, as well as the downpour of shrapnel when they were feeding empty stomachs at the front.

Officers ordered us to stop marching and to remain in Marville, probably to allow our vanguard to reach Germany first. The stands at the YMCA are still very popular. We frequent them to spend what little we have left. Some of the soldiers believe we are buying many things the government should be supplying us with, but since we have no choice, we buy everything we can. We hear that in America many people think we are having a great time. We cannot explain this. Life in this place leaves a lot to be desired, even after the war. As far as the YMCA is concerned, we have little to say. We have always seen it as a business, despite its religious and missionary purpose. When we hear that a new YMCA is opening its doors, "we immediately dig into our pockets." If they are empty, the YMCA is of little interest, unless we hear they are giving away small pieces of chocolate, French cookies, postcards, or cigarettes. If this is the case, we run to see what we can get, although we know this is the bait.

The government continues to give us Christmas cards to write home.

The rain came down harder after the noon hour so I stayed in my hiding place, read the newspapers, and talked with some friends who kept me company. It was already very dark when I went out for dinner. I sensed it was getting late. I cannot say I missed it since I managed to get enough "slops" and had a good conversation with my friends, the K.P.s.

> My Dear wife:
> As much as we try to hurry and finish with everything we have to do, it will not be possible to be with you at Christmas, but we should be happy and relieved that we are still standing and can hope to see each other again. We have to believe that our children's prayers were not in vain.
> It will be Christmas when this reaches you. I wish all of you happiness!
> These are my wishes,
>
> LUZ

Tuesday, November 26

After eating breakfast, I ran into Fortino Treviño, my longtime friend from Alice. I had not seen him since before Armistice Day, and so our meeting was a happy one. We talked of all our escapades in the war and ended up sharing memories of our relations in America. Treviño was giving me a haircut when his captain arrived. He introduced me to the officer in a good-natured, down-home way. The captain treats his men well. Good for him! He spoke highly of Treviño's courage on the battlefield.

I am older than Fortino and have known him since he was a youngster in school, when we would get into fights with the "gringos." Those were the happy days of fistfights and scrapes! He was born in the Rancho de los Sáenz, in Starr County, but grew up in Alice. His parents are well respected in our community. His brothers are energetic like Fortino, but he was always more boisterous and restless, more adventuresome. I remember that he was among the very few who never allowed Anglo students to humiliate him. He followed our footsteps and suffered the worst of the blows directed at us. In the end, they showed us consideration and respect. This is what someone who fights for justice should always expect.

Few were as willing as Fortino to meet their responsibility to register for military service on the fifth of June. He always wanted to serve next to the soldiers who were to cross the Atlantic, but not with the others who were leaving for Mexico. He registered, received his classification, and was among the first to be recruited. This is how this humble soldier of our *raza* met his responsibility. He was a true representative of the good name, worth, and honor of our brave and self-respecting Mexican people.

Fortino's parents—like mine and the majority who love their children—would never have asked for a social calamity like the one that tore their children from the bosom of their homes, but they finally gave in to our wishes and burning desire to fulfill the loftiest responsibility of a loyal citizen.

Treviño never thought he would lose his life in the war. This was his faith and his form of resignation. We always saw an indestructible spirit in him. He made good use of his time while assigned to the brigade in San Antonio and during our quarantine—when we could not even go out for a haircut. He acquired a set of haircutting tools and worked on his soldier-brothers by the latrines, on a bench or wooden box. Fortino would send his earnings to his father to set up the best barbershop in Alice. He wanted to return to a good job, and if he was to die, Fortino wanted to leave all he could to his father. He sent good amounts every month. I sent several of his remittances by mail and cable. Fortino practiced his trade at Camp Travis, while traveling across the country by Pullman car, on the *Olympic*, during our last training activities in France, and in the trenches when grenades were exploding over us and he was lobbing his own and calling on us to move: Forward!

Some soldiers may have matched Treviño's bravery, but I do not believe that many, if any, outdid his sense of loyal responsibility. He faced many dangers and found himself in very critical situations, like all the rest of us who smelled the explosives at the Saint-Mihiel and Verdun fronts. The Germans tore up his backpack at Verdun, but he simply replaced it with another and, Forward!

I am grateful to Treviño for giving me the small book that became the "diary" for all my entries. A fellow barber gave him the book while on our trip across the sea. Fortino immediately came to me and in his plain and sincere manner told me, "Sáenz, you need this more than me." The book was destined for the subjects of her majesty George V of England and included valuable information.

> General Headquarters of the 180th Infantry Brigade of the
> United States Expeditionary Force[1]
> November 24, 1918
>
> MEMORANDUM
> To the officers and soldiers of the Texas Brigade.
> In his farewell letter, the division commander extended the highest praise to your abilities as soldiers. I previously reported that the commanding general of the First Expeditionary Force of the United States had informed the commander in chief that "the 90th Division was as good a division . . . that no other division surpassed it. The division is as good and worthy of our trust as any other in the military." We could not expect a greater tribute. We should recall its record so that you may better appreciate such high praise:
> On September 12 the men of the 90th Division were baptized under fire when they broke through the trenches and barbed wire, the so-called Quart-en-Reserve, far west of the memorable Bois-le-Prete. In defending the southern portion of the forest, the French reported they lost twenty-three thousand soldiers, of which eight thousand died. On September 13, we (the 360th infantry) took the entire Bois-le-Prete without any problems and significant losses— and extended our operations up to the Moselle River.
> On September 26, you advanced your lines of fire very close to Prény and Pagny-sur-Moselle, and took part in the general offensive that the entire front made from the Moselle to the English Channel. You were relieved on the evening of October 9 and 10 to march to the front of the Argonne.
> Between September 12 and 29, the 360th Infantry captured

prisoners from German Infantry Regiments 94, 106, and 155. The 359th Infantry captured soldiers from German Infantry Regiments 69, 94, and 155 and Artillery Regiment 15.

By October 23 you were at the Meuse-Argonne front and were given the opportunity to attack Freya Stellung on September 1 and 2. You advanced from Dun-sur-Meuse to the Tileries ranch, in a seven-kilometer sector. The Freya Stellung was the last German line of defense, and it served as the pivot for their whole system from the north of France to Belgium where it reached the Meuse River.

You completely destroyed the enemy in Andevanne and in Villers-devant-Dun. Your bold assault in a four-kilometer front has never been unmatched in the entire war because it was superbly executed with fierce action. This put the entire German army in danger. We later heard the cry for an armistice and the total collapse of the war.

The 360th took forty riflemen; 110 foot soldiers of the reserve infantry and of the 352nd Infantry. The 359th captured forty riflemen, 109 infantrymen, and 110 soldiers of the enemy's 120th Infantry, the 123rd Infantry, and the 426th Infantry.

The 359th and 160th Infantry (although neither one received credit) captured soldiers from 170th; the 353rd Infantry took some from the 10th, 14th, and 80th Artillery, and from 163rd, 223rd, 235th, 426th, and the 35th. They also took prisoners from other auxiliary groups like miners, machine gunners, engineers, signalmen, doctors, etc.

Between October 4 and November 11, the division captured twenty-one officers and 954 other men. They captured three 210-millimeter cannon, eight 160-millimeter cannon, nine 105-millimeter cannon, and twelve 77-millimeter cannon. The prisoners came from the 11th Infantry Regiment, the 7th Artillery Regiment, a Signal Company, and other auxiliary groups.

We will always remember Bois-de-Rappes, Bois-de-Bantheville, La Grande Correre, Andevanne, Côte 243, Côte 321, and Villers-devant-Dun. Your machine gun companies will never forget that they discharged 1,150,000 shells between November 1 and 2.

This brigade should be credited with the highest honor of never losing one soldier to desertions. You always faced the enemy, and during the night before the Armistice, you were facing them ready to strike on the dawn of the memorable eleventh. You have shared equally with the best and have deserved everything. You are soldiers and I am proud of you.

Ulysses Grant McAlexander
Brigadier General

Wednesday, November 27

The day began with rain, but the band raised our spirits. It is impossible to truly understand the power of music, especially when we are already disposed to be moved. The music has made us think that if there was ever a time to feel as we do, it happened when we found ourselves "so close to God," when we went through so much grief and suffering, and now that we are entertaining the sweet hope of returning to the love of our families.

We again bought food in preparation for our departure. We are now aware that the lack of food and exhaustive marches can make things difficult for us. The more we are prepared, the better.

The rain kept me from exploring the towns along the way.

I received a letter from Mr. Knox. He sent me a clipping of one of my letters that appeared in *La Prensa*. Mr. Knox mostly sends me his congratulations and praise for the conduct of my *raza* in these parts. He urges me to continue writing and informing our community about what we are doing. I am grateful to this good and generous educator who understands us and wants us to receive justice.

Memories of the
European War, Our Last Campaign,
Five Days and Nights

With my straightforward but honest manner, my "diary" now reports on what I believe to have been our last mission. I say that it was the final one because I trust we have been victorious, although we have only enjoyed a thirty-five-day truce granted to an exhausted enemy that has practically begged for it.

We had been resting for a few days close to the front when we were told it was absolutely necessary to make a final push to defeat our enemy. The effort was not in vain since it pleased our superiors, who are in charge of our battle plans.

On October 26, the sergeant from the R.I.O. and I received the orders to take charge of a place we expected to occupy during our regiment's offensive on the dawn of November 1. The first brigade from our division was already at the front and had reached its objective. We were now going to relieve them.

We took over the railroad station the Germans had used to supply food and munitions to their troops. Their artillery, located about four kilometers away, fired at us the five days we were there. The small village of Romagne was some one hundred meters to the southwest. Several field kitchens as well as a number of large cannon were to the south. We faced constant shelling and reported many casualties.

Small groups from our brigade began to move past us during the early evening hours of the thirtieth. The enemy soon discovered our troop movement and fired heavy artillery shells. They continued the all-night bombardment with large numbers of shells of suffocating gases. It was a night of great danger.

Our troop movement and the enemy's artillery fire continued into the evening of the thirty-first. The sergeant and I left at four in the afternoon for our command post. Two kilometers later, we reached our destination. The shells were landing constantly on the road. Many dead animals were strewn along the way. Large amounts of equipment were also scattered everywhere, the kind that soldiers discard during forced marches, when they have to attend to the enemy's resistance.

The second battalion had camped out in a small valley along the route we were taking. The soldiers were digging foxholes to protect themselves against the machine gun fire. Some tragedies had already occurred. A grenade had torn two soldiers to pieces right before we arrived. We arrived without a hitch, but I had to return to the station our brigade now occupied. I returned for my buddies who had remained behind and we reached our new location without any problems, but we continued to come across depressing battlefield scenes. Our colonel and a French lieutenant who is attached to our regiment were moving with us, within a short distance of our group. The ever-alert Germans spotted the officers with their powerful telescopes and opened fire. We moved in short intervals after each shell explosion to avoid becoming targets. Our officers escaped injury, although some soldiers were wounded in their foxholes.

As the dark mantle of the evening slowly covered us, we could now and then hear the deadly shrill of German shells followed by the terrible explosions and loss of human lives. After the explosions had shaken the ground and echoed in the valleys, a profound silence set in and regular time stretched into agonizing hours. The muffled sound of soldiers digging foxholes and moving in search of precious rest interrupted the silence. A natural instinct to survive and nothing else drove us to dig in. We absolutely knew what would happen if a shell landed on us. The heavy fortifications of cement and steel have been useless against such force. How could the quickly improvised cover of dirt and branches save us? The sole protection the spacious underground structures offered our officers was a thin galvanized sheet, also covered with loose dirt.

My buddies from San Diego and Backville, Texas, and I took more time and care than usual to build our dugout. We dug it so our heads would rest under the roots of some trees. The trees were not big but they were strong, and they offered us added protection. We had no trouble finding wood for the dugout cover. The artillery had decimated the forests and produced the necessary material. We also gathered empty munitions boxes, filled them with dirt, and placed them on the dugout's flanks to serve as barricades.

As fate would have it, our dugout was not far from the command post and between the officers' kitchen area and the munitions depot, all important places that attracted the attention of the enemy's artillery. Their aircraft spotted us and alerted the big guns by the evening of that terrible day. The most horrific bombardment hit us in the early evening. We had never seen anything like it and do not ever wish to see it again. Our cannon, made up of all manner of guns, were positioned at the lower slope of each of the hills and up to six miles from the enemy's front, but all of them, with the exception of one or two batteries that fired at intervals, watched in silence. Our artillery had been told to fire later, at eleven. Our infantry and machine gun battalions were also waiting.

We slept; we actually pretended to sleep. That was not the time to sleep! Many of the soldiers rested against their backpacks instead of preparing new makeshift beds. They waited for the supreme hour when our cannon would begin firing, believing this would silence the German guns.

We went to bed prepared for the sacrifice, yet recognizing that it would be useless to give in to our anxieties. By dismissing the danger around us, we were defying death itself. We did have our moments of deep contrition, solemn occasions when we acknowledged our insignificance next to the noble cause we serve. Nothing within a circumference of five kilometers was safe. It was the same everywhere, in the woods, foothills, valleys, and roads. None of us can forget—even if we wanted—the loud, frightful sound of the mortar rounds the Germans were using to finish us. We could hear the shells coming out of the mouths of cannon as if they were vomiting them. We followed their sound as they rose to some unknown height, paused momentarily, and then descended in search of their prey. The shells crashed on Mother Earth with their electrical discharges and dreadful explosions. They poured their deadly cargo and fragments over us.

Three powerful explosives fell near our dugout. The first small caliber shell landed three meters from our heads. It shook the earth and tossed dirt over us. Another huge shell caused such a great explosion it disoriented us. Gómez, our loyal comrade, was on guard duty and the only one standing in the vicinity. He thought we had been killed when he heard the explosion and saw where it had occurred. Gómez ran to us only to find a crater and large clods of dirt where we were supposed to be. He was more shocked when we failed to answer his calls, "Sáenz! Barrera! Are you alive?" We finally responded, "Yes, what's going on?" We did not know what had happened and only feared a new possible danger. What I mean to say is we had not even heard the explosion. The third grenade had landed while we were sleeping. Barrera, however, had decided to get up at that instant and stand at the entrance of the dugout.

Barrera was standing, we were lying down. That grenade would have ended our lives if Divine Providence had not intervened. The branches on the tree had offered enough resistance to detonate the shell. The fragments rained over us but, fortunately, did not hit us. The sticks on our cover were torn into splinters while a big one tore through one of the boxes with dirt. Other splinters fell outside and within the foxhole, and many of them plowed into the earth and tree trunks. The branches fell on us and only a small steel fragment hit Barrera on the back of his neck, as if to remind us that death was never far. His injury alarmed us, but we later discovered it was not serious. We cleaned the small amount of blood in his wound with my handkerchief. Everyone who has survived the war will recount incidents like ours because all of us faced the same dangers along the entire front.

After witnessing the enemy's attack, our artillerymen could not wait for the designated time to start firing. They took action an hour earlier than planned. We had it from a reliable source that they fired 73,000 volleys of various calibers. This occurred in the small sector of around three kilometers in width that we occupied.

Our first rolling barrage started at dawn, on the first of November. Our tanks, light infantry, machine gun squadrons, and regular infantry attacked the enemy's front with indescribable fury. Their trenches and barbed wire were of little use. Machine gun fire supported the German infantry as they tried to resist our offensive. The fighting was some of the bloodiest of the war and the human loss was incalculable. We lost many brave men. The enemy's losses, on the other hand, can be estimated conservatively at three times more than ours. Our artillery hit the tenacious Germans so well that entire companies of different types surrendered. Many of the prisoners celebrated the good fortune of surrendering to us and were more than willing to pick up the injured from the battlefield; the majority of the injured were their own.

The bloody fighting and our victory was the decisive blow that finished the Teutonic pride and dispelled forever the Germans' false dream of global conquest.

We were in possession of the contested territory by November 2. The enemy beat a retreat and offered us little resistance. The Germans mostly occupied themselves with what they called their "strategic" retreat. This is what they first told their infantrymen. Our doughboys were inspiring; they heroically swept over the enemy and disregarded the many German ambushes. They entered the impenetrable woods to displace the machine gun nests in the trees and threw themselves into river currents to catch up with the enemy columns that were on the run. In many cases, the Germans did not even have time to bury their dead.

At four in the afternoon of the tenth, we reached a beautiful town the Germans had just evacuated. More than six hundred people regained their liberty. They seemed to have awakened from a deep stupor that had lasted more than four years. We cannot really understand what they were feeling. The Germans gave them enough time to leave the town, but they risked their lives to be free again.

We had just entered the town when a large gas shell hit a home, killing one of our soldiers and a French woman who had just won her freedom. We received orders at that moment to prepare for a major attack on the next day at dawn. Our battalions and artillery took their respective places. The orders were given and everyone prepared for the order to attack.

The day that we were eagerly expecting—the eleventh of November—finally arrived. Early in the day, one of my buddies, a messenger, was told to deliver the order in spite of heavy enemy fire. He carried out his orders faithfully. When he reached the second battalion at our front line of fire, the troops were already prepared for the assault. Everyone stopped for an anxious moment when they received the order that suspended the offensive. Our troops were surprised and eager for an explanation. The order also stated that the artillery from both sides would continue firing until eleven in the morning.

Soon after this, we learned that hostilities would cease for thirty-five days beginning at eleven. The hour arrived and we still doubted, but it happened—just like that, they suspended the hostilities, that horrible shedding of human blood by the millions of men who fought for more than four years.

The truce produced beautiful scenes, but not without the kind of sad incidents we expect in war. The multitudes from both sides of the line of fire burst with shouts of joy. Their last shell landed on some unfortunate soldiers and took six lives.

This was our last operation. Since then, we have entertained the sweet hope for the desired peace. Since everyone is observing the armistice, we are confident that soon, very soon, we will return to out dear homes on the other side of the blue Atlantic.

We Mexican Americans faced the danger never doubting the character and integrity we have inherited from our ancestors. I do not know whether to feel pride or a sense of satisfaction, or both, now that we have received this great opportunity to affirm our legacy. We should be amply pleased that many of our compatriots have held the name of our *raza* high. They have known how to give themselves fully to their duties as good citizens. Even we, the common foot soldiers, are glad to have been able to make a meaningful contribution to this most sacred cause. Now that our most noble mission has been met, our happiness has no bounds because victory promises us a better future.

From Marville, France

Mr. Knox, my friend:

I cannot let this joyful occasion pass without writing you. I have nothing new or possibly significant to report for anyone except for the remaining soldiers who hope and wait for a better tomorrow.

The complete destruction of the most powerful, dangerous, and threatening autocracy to face weaker countries is obviously a magnificent and unappreciated act, especially if we take into account the price in lost lives we paid in the process.

At this moment of great expectations, we are so happy our burning faith demonstrates that Providence will rule in favor of our cause and crown our sacrifice with the desired triumph.

We also expect that someone will assume the responsibility of writing a full account of the martyred contributions of the millions of souls who sacrificed to guarantee peace and fraternity for years to come. During the few years we have left, we will be able to see the scarring over of humanity's wound. That is why we can expect that the permanent unification of the races on earth will spring from this immense shared suffering.

Luz

Thanksgiving and Then to Germany

Thursday, November 28

Today is the day for giving thanks. We had a service in a Catholic church without an altar, images, or benches. We had a protestant service followed by a friendly oration by a French priest. Most of our regimental officers as well as many of their French counterparts attended.

I received many letters and answered some of them.

The building housing the YMCA had been a German tavern with many paintings on its walls. They show how the French women behaved with the Teutonic soldiers after their occupation. One of the paintings shows German officers forcing the French barmaids to dance with them. They look like they complied reluctantly while the German soldiers respond with roaring laughter. The painting shows that the Germans have conquered everything with their big guns, except for the heart of the French women. In another image, a German officer with boots and military stripes demands a kiss while the maid resists with apparent loathing. The murals lack classic aesthetic beauty but they reveal obvious truths that we recognize as natural experiences in everyday life.

We signed the pay list and received small delicious breads at the YMCA that we have put away for our next march, which will come soon enough.

Friday, November 29

We heard rumors of entering Germany. We started to pack our typewriters and some other materials we used.

We received official notification that our pilgrimage will start tomorrow, but that we will not be conducting a forced march with loaded weapons, although we will shoulder arms.

Gómez and I volunteered to serve supper. This gave us the opportunity to fill our food containers today since we will not be able to do it tomorrow. The march will probably be exhausting. They all seem like this after a few days of rest.

Saturday, November 30

We began the day by preparing for the march. History will record the memorable march we began early in the morning. We soon passed by Le Petit Vicey, Rep. sur Reveo. The town has been in ruins since the start of the war. The Germans used to sweep over everything. They left many artillery pieces at Longuyon. It was interesting to see how Germans painted or camou-flaged the cannon to avoid the detection of our observers and airplanes. The piled-up cannon could easily exceed one thousand. They represent all calibers and makes. The large numbers of monsters with lazy yawning mouths make hairs stand on end. The Germans will no longer use them. They might become curiosity pieces in their museums. The cannon stirred so many different thoughts in me that I was unable to write. I have decided that whoever reads this should imagine the rest . . .

We marched past Arrancy and Ramemcourt, Fme. Le Fleaure. I had a grueling night after dragging what I felt was a dislocated leg. It was my most painful march ever. The ground was very wet and sticky and, with the weight of my load, I suffered a sprain that worsened as the temperature got colder. I continued marching because we were accustomed to continuing until the end. I had to raise myself up with my hands every time we moved. At any rate, I had enough strength to reach our objective. We made our beds on platforms the sappers and engineers built for us.

I sought medical care after supper. The doctor gave me the usual response, "I cannot attend to you because your name is not on the list I received this morning. Give it to the sergeant who takes up the names in the mornings." I answered to myself, "You expect me to wait until tomorrow, thank you very much!" I kept quiet because we are not allowed to speak to an officer this way, especially now that the war has ended and everyone wants to reclaim authority instead of his responsibilities.

I hobbled and grumbled until I reached a big German equipment warehouse. I found thousands of new helmets and took a small one that would not weigh me down. I then went to my sleeping area.

Sunday, December 1

The sergeant approached me very early while calling on the sick and anyone else who was unable to join the march. I thanked him and felt the holy rage of the poor soldier. Our officer may have been too tired to show up yesterday. We were not supposed to be tired as we carried the load they would never understand.

I treated myself as best I could last night and it seems to have worked because I am ready to continue.

We passed by the little town of Pierrepont and then Tunelet. Our march took us by beautiful hilly areas and over decent roads that were not paved but had good gravel. I saw an empty Ford truck overturn as it moved toward us. The driver was careless as he drove down a sharp and dangerous curve on the road. Some trucks were following him while others were fully loaded and coming in our direction. Luckily, no one died. Several buddies helped him set the truck upright and he continued on his way. The trucks are continuously coming and going. They are hauling our provisions to the areas where we will be sleeping. They now have an easier job of supplying our needs. We are no longer facing danger and the trucks can now travel ahead of us. We hear the vehicles moving day and night. Poor drivers, we are told they suffer a great deal, that they do not sleep or rest much. I tell them they should not covet our difficult life and that they should resign themselves to theirs and continue.

We passed by more munitions sites. One of them drew our attention. It had large boxes of tank-piercing shells. These were the first guns we had taken during our previous fighting at this place. The Germans had found the right weapon to fight the once-invincible steel turtle.

As we approached Thil, we saw airplane-landing platforms that were in good condition, as well as an ancient aqueduct that was still in use. The aqueduct supplies Thil with water. I regret not gathering any historical information on this ancient structure. Thil was the first French town the Germans took in this region. I would have liked to learn something about French resistance and the spirit with which they attacked the Germans, who thought they were on their way to conquering the world. We can still see the obvious marks of war in the plaza.

Our band tried to lift our spirits, but could not brighten faces, not even among the musicians. We slept in a very cold house and I shivered terribly. An unbearable sense of frustration came over me and made my night very difficult.

Monday, December 2

We left Thil early. It was the last French town before entering the Grand Duchy of Luxembourg. We reached Esch first. Since the town had not suffered losses of any kind, it was the first one we saw whose residents were pursuing life like before the war and without having to deal with the destruction associated with the conflict. We saw several factories functioning like in peacetime, and the townspeople seemed content, although we sensed indifference toward us. The inhabitants were focused on their tasks. Actually, they were giving us their backs. Neatly dressed police officers patrolled the streets. The bad reception they gave us was not surprising since we knew that they were great sympathizers of the German Kaiser who used the Grand Duchy as his base of operations. The excuse we heard was that their country is so small they could never have stopped the Kaiser's advance. This is true and worthy of consideration, just like it is also true that no one ever heard the faintest protest from them. It makes more sense to believe they always wished for a victory by the Teutonic Kaiser.

We went through another town named Dujaden and rested by a fountain on the town's only street. Several of us went looking for water. The troops were already beginning to move when we returned. This brought me a reprimand from Lieutenant George.

The rain continues as we march through muddy roads. We reached Dudelange, a beautiful town that never knew the misery of war. Several of us made our beds in a building that had served as a theater or movie house. We decided to tour the town in spite of our fatigue. We found a number of places where liquor was sold. My buddies decided to enjoy themselves in one of them by dancing with the French-Dutch women. I visited a very interesting part of the town and found a beautiful school building that was well lighted and full of soldiers who were to ready to go to sleep. This is the most impressive building. It comes closest to looking like our schools. The town is located on a scenic hill that allowed us to enjoy the panoramic view of the town. The school and the church with its tall twin towers stand out among the town's buildings. The beautiful dark color of its forest and its nearby sown fields present a lovely backdrop to its white homes. A modern castle also stands out. A three-story house with a drugstore on its first level was on the corner of a street named Hutten. I bought stamps and other souvenirs before going to sleep. My sleeping quarters were very noisy and had the bad smell of cigarette smoke. It was impossible to sleep.

Tuesday, December 3

Today, I found out that we were heading for Koblenz, a lovely city by the Rhine. We passed by Hellange, another town of little importance, but picturesque. These towns show that the region enjoys the full measure of peace. We see the carts on the streets, flocks of chickens and ducks, and small herds of sheep—all reflecting the rustic life of the peasants as they head to work to prop up the plutocrats. The last town we reached was Frisange. This is where we were to spend the night. We had found a place to rest when I received orders to report to the Intelligence Office.

I had to leave my friends Gómez and Barrera to join up with my office mates. They had already taken over a dairy shed. The cattle spend the entire winter here and we have joined them for the night. We made our beds where they feed. The serenity, the small number of people, the difference in appearance, everything is a striking contrast to the place where we slept last night. Frisange is rustic and sad.

Wednesday, December 4

We headed for Aspelt and then continued on our way until we reached Remich, a beautiful town on the Moselle. It is surrounded by vineyards, the principal source of livelihood for the towns on the river. German territory extended to the right side of the river until November 11. A beautiful and sturdy bridge joins the Grand Duchy of Luxembourg with Germany. The river is very wide here and its blue waters flow swiftly.

We have heard so many stories about how our soldiers have been received in the German towns that we do not know what to say. Some tell of a German woman who fired a machine gun at a column of our soldiers as they were entering a small town. We cannot put much stock on all of this since everyone knows that Germany surrendered unconditionally. This shows that they could not handle our offensive. We have already seen how they gave up their arms on the battlefield. How can anyone be so naive as to think they have not lost? Rumors are that we will receive ammunition this afternoon so that we do not enter these towns with folded arms. German war barons obviously continue to show their stubborn pride. There is nothing better than brute force—ammunition and machine guns—against such pride.

The YMCA is joining us as we move forward and has already put up its stalls. The soldiers have formed a long waiting line to buy something even if it is only gum. I continue walking the narrow flint stone streets, visiting several establishments, and witnessing a great deal of business activity. The locals speak more German than French, but we are told the native language is Luxembourgish. I never thought that such a language existed. I think it is a mixture of German and French. I understood the language better at the place where we slept last night. They used the two languages or a mixture of both. Of course, French is mostly used along the front in France.

People use a circular brass coin with a hole in the middle for their everyday transactions. I have collected some as mementos. The French coin is also in circulation.

Although I cannot be sure, I have heard that Pablo Pérez was sent to the hospital. I hope that it is not serious. We noticed that he lost most of his voice after being gassed.

The night has been dark and rainy. I would have liked to continue with my walk but I am tired and the weather is bad. Several of us bedded down on the second floor of a building that serves as a lumber mill. It is located on a street by the left side of the river, on the northern outskirts of town. Others slept on the first floor, next to the machinery. I tried to read and write before going to bed but I was too sleepy and all my impressions from that day faded away.

Thursday, December 5

As soon as I woke up, I sat down on the bed and looked toward Germany. What an odd feeling! It seemed a mirage or something out of a dream! I could see a small town and people moving slowly as though in mourning. Even the fog adds to the sadness as it rises from the river and engulfs the area! A diminutive train whistles its arrival at a small station and quickly departs as if nothing in the way of commercial or social activity was left on the other side, in the defeated nation. Germany, Germany, what had you dreamed?

I got up to eat breakfast and found out we would not march. I do not know what to do with my spare time, nor have I found a newspaper with news from around the globe.

The end of the year approaches, and with its passing many of our families will stop worrying. Our loved ones will soon hear the news that we are well and will look forward to seeing us.

Fidel Gleim had a good idea for fighting the day's monotony. He ordered several dishes at a restaurant and invited some of us to join him. Valente de la Rosa, Amado Cásares, and I were his guests. The idea was to enjoy each other's company. My friends smoked, drank, and ate. I ate and joined them in recalling memories of our distant homes. The food was the best that is available in these parts after the war. We said our good-byes and went our separate ways, very grateful to our buddy Gleim and happy to have been among friends. We talked about many things, but one favorite topic came up several times—once in America, we have the responsibility to continue nurturing the friendships that duty and hard times have taught us. All of us agree that this is necessary, to form some kind of organization with veterans at its center, an organization to continue addressing our social problems in Texas.

We were together until the afternoon and barely had time to grab our rifles and join formation. After the presentation of the colors, the band played for a while in front of our commander. A few of our buddies managed to slip away and visit the city of Luxembourg. I missed out on a lot by not catching up with my daring friends. They enjoyed themselves with the same abandon they showed on the battlefields.

We received orders during supper that we would cross the Moselle and enter Germany. We are eager for the new day so that we can form our columns as an army of occupation. When night fell, I washed my hair, towels, and handkerchiefs in the Moselle. I wanted to have something to talk about later, and would have bathed but no one wanted to join me. I lost my opportunity to dive into the blue and cold waters of the Moselle.

I bought some stamps on the plaza. One of them carries the images of princesses Antonia, Sophy, Charlotte, Elisabeth, and Hilda, all of them alongside the current Grand Duchess of Luxembourg, Mary Adelaide.

My favorite places at Remich were the road by the station and Moselle Avenue, which runs by the river.

Friday, December 6

The preparations for the march had begun by dawn. We were eager to enter the territory we had taken from the enemy at great cost. After breakfast, we made formation with all of our equipment as we prepared for the march in the rain. The troops began to gather close to the bridge we were about to cross. The band reached the bridge first. The colonel and the rest of the officers crossed according to their rank, and the battalions followed. The sight was amazing, worthy of appearing prominently in our nation's history. It had to be seen to be appreciated. Our very suffering seems to have prepared us for such especially rewarding moments. Participating in the grand crusade of our victorious army fills us with pride; it gives special meaning to this historic and glorious sight and allows us to enjoy the sacrifice we made for the homeland. Our flag fluttered in the open air and its colors were as radiant as ever. Even our sergeant, who acted as our standard bearer, understood the important role he was playing at that solemn moment. He looked bigger than life. We had never seen our master sergeant so happy and ready for the occasion. He gave full expression to his military "pose."

I felt as if possessed by a dream when I saw our troops crossing the bridge. I was that absorbed in my thoughts. Like Lot's wife, I decided to look back one last time to bid Remich farewell, and everything seemed more beautiful to me. Remich and Luxembourg would remain in our memories forever.

Soon after arriving at the first town, we noticed the wretched state of things among the people. They seemed to be deep in thought and suffering deep sorrow. We can never really appreciate the bitterness of a defeated people when they see an occupying army. The German people had expected their army to return victorious after hearing so much of their triumphs far and wide, after spreading fear everywhere with their new machines of war, after handing incredible defeats to the nations of the world. This did not happen. Their soldiers did not return down these roads the same way they left for the front—singing, proud, and happy. They were exhausted, dirty, broken, sad, and defeated! What an ending for men who always thought they were the first in war! Oh the deceptions of the world!

We passed by several towns and finally reached Beurig, Saarburg, Bex, and Trier, all situated by the Saar. Trier is a beautiful city, not unlike the other one on the opposite side of the river. A very old castle is located nearby. They say it was built in the sixteenth century and that Siegfried the Great lived there.

I worked in the kitchen so that I could get us a good lunch for the march. The soldier's most important concern after the fighting is to make sure he has some food. Challenges are interesting in the middle of despair; even the listless are encouraged to take action.

I bought some postcards to better remember the towns. We are moving so fast and under such taxing circumstances that we may end up only remembering the sadness and exhaustion. The region is so picturesque. Nature seems to have favored these communities. Its valleys and hills are well cultivated. They make the place look beautiful and full of life, and this is without taking into account the numerous streams on the mountainsides. The favorable changes in our lives may explain why we appreciate this. Otherwise, we would not notice anything. The ruins of the ancient castle of medieval times where Siegfried the Great once lived appear at some distance from here, on a beautiful promontory above a bend on the River Saar. We are presented with so much to contemplate and learn about the history of man! The area brings to mind the legends, tales, stories, novels, and ballads of past generations. Charlemagne the Great, accompanied by his "twelve peers" from France, roamed these lands in pursuit of the Moors.[1] Many of my buddies often ask me, "What are you thinking?" I answer, "Everything and nothing." I worry that they may think I have lost my mind because soldiers are rarely given to reflection. We have really read very little about these places and are just finding out that they existed. This is the time when some of us regret not paying more attention to world geography and history.

We left Beurig on the other side of the Saar and are now in Saarburg. I have enjoyed the place. It is situated on a beautiful hill with a view of the countryside and the two towns. As usual, our sleeping quarters are in a horse stable very near the command post. We have often wondered why our government only rents horse stables or cattle barns for us. Many soldiers could use their own money to rent a bed in every town along the way, but we have been told not to do this. Why? German families invite us and offer us their very best, including bedding and food. Our government does not want us to bother the German people in any way. We do not want our own soldiers to take advantage like the Germans did when they were victorious. The officer in charge of housing takes down the name of the homeowner and address because we expect to pay the rent at a later point. Since the German people will be the ones who will eventually pay, we do not want to be a burden on them. This is why we sleep in cattle sheds. We have nowhere else to go unless we want to be exposed to the elements. We will have to pay rent to France as well. We paid France for the water, the firewood, for the ground that we marched on, and we paid the highest price on the battlefields that we retook for them. The Germans went after the best lands they occupied. They even committed outrages on families. The soldiers that have been discharged and are returning to their homes are aware of this; their families know it too, the whole world knows. This is why they receive us so well. We want everyone to know that the American soldier is not interested in pretense, profit, or abuse. With all that we have done, we have vowed to restore some of the losses and settle scores for the outrages committed on humanity, and we will do this without resorting to the old law of "a tooth for a tooth." Our behavior is an example of how to treat the vanquished. This does not mean that some of our soldiers have not left their makeshift beds for feathered ones, but they have been subject to the harshest treatment the military hands out. German families expected abuse from irresponsible soldiers, but they are amazed at us. It is not unusual to find us talking with families almost every evening until the late hours in the towns we are occupying. It is even more remarkable that we socialize with the very soldiers who were fighting us to the death a week ago.

The lady of the house where we have just set up has offered her beds, but we have not accepted. We did consent to the humble dinner she prepared for us. We paid her, although she did not want to accept payment. We gave her what we thought was just, and she was amazed at what she considered an excessive amount. I should add that the woman thought she was obligated to feed us, but was delighted to serve us once she understood us. She thought she was to abide by the standard German practice, "to put up as many soldiers as possible and care for them as well as possible."

We have come across many soldiers in these homes; we had fought them until November 11. They are still wearing uniforms and military insignias. Some of them are friendly and talk to us. They point out their military affiliation and where they fought until the armistice. We exchange views on the things we saw. A young pilot spoke to us at length about his experiences, and we were able to confirm much of what he said when he shared dates and places we recognized. He was an officer and wears the dark iron cross with pride, although he says it is no longer worth anything. Some soldiers, however, are still seriously defiant and cannot bring themselves to accept defeat. Their faces show bitterness and they often exit quietly when we enter their homes, leaving us with their mothers, wives, sisters, girlfriends, and friends. This should make some of our citizens from the United States take pause, especially those people who boasted a burning patriotism but may have been faking all along. They used to say they were ready to die for the country if war came to our land, but not if it occurred elsewhere. They also criticized the president for sending troops to foreign lands. Those of us who came feel and see things differently, and we applaud the wise judgment of our president. We do not mean to say that we should defend the decision to go to war as a just one. It was not for the foot soldier to decide if it was our war or not. How would our opinions have been received? We believe it was a thousand times better to come and finish with the war where it was already being fought. We crossed thousands of miles by sea and left our families grieving over our departure, but we did not expose them to the cowardly, satanic, and unbridled abuse, the despotic humiliations of the boot-wearing tyrannical and merciless invader. The millions who saw action could testify to how ill prepared we were to wage a war within our borders. To restate matters, we have never favored wars, nor do we agree with the reasons for entering the war, but once we were committed and drawn into the fight, and after seeing what we saw, it was best that we fought the war in Europe.

German soldiers who committed cruelties in Russia, France, Belgium, Poland, and the Balkan states could not expect anything less than what they meted out. They were unrestrained and led by unscrupulous men, including the officers of the Kaiser. Many families have told us, "We are so glad that American soldiers are occupying this region." Are they afraid of the Belgian, French, English, or Polish? They sure are. They know better than anyone else what they did to these justifiably bitter nations.

Saturday, December 7

We passed by several towns and saw uniformed German soldiers in the fields and on the streets. The towns are by the Saar River, a tributary of the Moselle. We are heading toward Trier, which is by the Moselle.

Our soldiers had taken every place in town by the time we arrived. Few stables were available because this is a city and not a town. The towns of Konz and Karthaus once existed side by side, now they are known as Konz-Karthaus. It has paved streets and a good electrical system, the best-kept city we have seen.

Massenburg and I had to walk all over town in search of a room and were received well everywhere we went. We came across two stern-looking German soldiers in one of the homes where we found lodging. The Germans were bothered that their family members paid attention to us. They stomped out in their heavy boots, snorting as they went. We wanted to know what they were saying. The women tried to tell us they were not talking to us. We could tell that their words were not kind, and we were not off by much since they were "birds of a feather."

The kindly, fearful women calmed us down because we were clearly suspicious of those scoundrels. We continued our conversation and then a young, well-educated soldier appeared. He knew some English and we managed to understand each other even with the bad German we speak. He spoke to us about the fighting. The young soldier had fought in the last front until the last day. Now and then, he would repeat "alles vertag," which means, "the war is over," "l'guerre est fini," or "se acabo la guerra." A woman was attracted to my dark hair and asked to touch it. When I told her to be my guest and added that she not rub it against the grain, she asked "Why?" I stated that "she could cause sparks." When everyone understood that I was joking, they had a good-natured laugh.

Massenburg decided that it would be best to look for another place close to the command post. We agreed and went our merry way. We were still carrying our equipment as we headed to the center of town, away from the outskirts where the Germans had tried our patience. We decided to settle in a modern two-story house. The owner wanted to secure some beds for us. We refused and camped out in his living room. The master of the house speaks English well, and we would have liked to talk more, but we were tired.

We can take in the images on the wall from the vantage point of the beds. Some are very elegant. Two especially stand out. They are of William II, the German Kaiser, and his family. The furniture is expensive and beautiful. The family includes the father, mother, and their only son. The father gladly signed his name and address for us: F. Straup, Karthaus Trier, Deutschland.

Sunday, December 8

We gave Karthaus one last look before we left. A big building that I did not recognize is in the middle of town, and many vineyards are to the west. The river extends like a silver ribbon that seems to reach the foot of the mountains to the east. I am not sure that I have my bearings because I woke up disoriented and the cloudy sky did not help. At this distance, all the mountains look like they are full of vineyards.

The beauty of the Saar River, a tributary of the Moselle, is unmatched. Its waters are crystalline and blue like the Moselle's, and good bridges have been constructed over it. The view of the towns was more beautiful this morning due to the heavy fog that was rising from the river and enveloping them with an almost transparent veil. These are the views that have fascinated the poets, novelists, and fairy tale writers that we read with great pleasure in our schools back home. We now have a better understanding of the cultural origins of North America.

We could still see the beautiful setting when told to march toward the historic city of Trier. It was built during the beginning of the Christian era and has many ruins from the time of the Roman invasions. We saw castle walls covered with ivy and moss. They say that Julius Caesar lived here. The other ruins included public baths and a Roman amphitheater. Another well-preserved building is the Porta Nigra castle. The structure is solid with thick stone.

The barracks for German soldiers are on the way out of town. We saw several soldiers but could not tell if they have been discharged or remain on active duty.

Michel, the young volunteer from New York, tired during the march and thought nothing of dropping out of formation. A sergeant who was prepared for such things immediately ordered him to continue. The poor soul could no longer carry his pack and made it known to the sergeant. The sergeant rained down profanities on the soldier. Michel answered in kind and then the sergeant gave him a backhanded blow over his mouth. The cowardly act bothered us, but, like in the sheep's tale, we did not say anything. This was not the first time the sergeant did this. Several sergeants have it out for him, but he seems to be careful with them. He may not be very brave, but he is smart and knows how to be in the right with some people.

A short while later, a lieutenant came down on me as if he were the son of Mars. He thought I had taken an extra raincoat and assigned me to kitchen detail. I did not mind the assignment since we had already started volunteering for this kind of work.

We crossed the Moselle before arriving at Schweich, our new place of rest for the night. We crossed a long, beautiful bridge made of cement. The view of the town is more or less like the others I have described by the Moselle. Everything is beautiful and picturesque. As soon as I located a sleeping area and put it in order, I left to receive my punishment. The cooks overlooked that I had been disciplined and treated me like a volunteer. I have already spoken of my friendship with the sergeant at the kitchen. He may have acted differently if he knew the circumstances surrounding my assignment. I enjoyed the afternoon, ate well, and prepared a lunch that not even the officers will enjoy during tomorrow's march. I retired early.

The river's different vistas and the historic views of the city of Trier, its mountains, rich fields, forests, and other attractions make everything worthwhile and the difficulties with the high-ranking officers tolerable. The general feeling is that "the war is over." We will soon forget yesterday's hardships.

Monday, December 9

This has been one of my most difficult marches. I do not know if we have marched too far or if we simply need rest, but we have definitely walked over rough terrain and climbed up some sharp slopes. The scenery has varied a great deal. We have seen forests with beautiful trees suitable for lumber, tall mountains, clear streams, and fertile valleys. We will sleep in Rivenich tonight. It continues to rain, it never seems to end in these parts. After setting up my bedding, I left for a walk in the town. The first building I came across looked like a store. My buddies had bought everything there was to eat. I bought a postcard with a view of the house. It has a sign that reads "Carl Levy." The photograph includes the mother and two daughters. We knew them because they had us over for dinner. They had invited my buddy Gersbach, and he asked me to accompany him. We liked all the dishes they prepared for us. They were made with potatoes. I bid the family farewell so I could visit a nearby school. It was late and the children were gone. When I asked for the teacher, his wife wanted to send for him, but I insisted otherwise since I was not visiting on official business. I then visited a church, a very humble church, but very inviting for prayer. This is the first church I have visited since the fighting. It never closed and received believers throughout the war. How many mothers and wives must have raised their prayers for the safety and return of their loved ones, just like ours loved ones were doing for us! Blundering humanity! How can God possibly hear us under these circumstances!

Rivenich is a small rustic town, far from the larger ones and the railroad lines. It is located on a treeless plain, but surrounded by fields of potatoes and sugar beets. The residents are poor peasants, completely given to their work, and they are very hospitable. Their sincerity is undeniable and their difficulties in life leave little room for harboring malice. I can tell that they do not know what happened at the front or of the plans for peace their officials and rulers are negotiating. These places have supplied much of the cannon fodder that is now buried in France and Russia. The young men are obviously absent. Few of them returned from the war. Some parents tell us that all their sons remained on the battlefields. Did they join the military out of a sense of patriotism or were they *forced*?

Tuesday, December 10

We continued our usual march over plains, fields, and forests until we arrived at Nuremberg. Nearby, a large mountain rises in the middle of an immense valley, like a man-made pyramid. Its summit is adorned with luxuriant trees and since there is no other mountain nearby, it looks spectacular.

Some lower-ranking officers insist that I do kitchen detail or guard duty like the rest of the privates. Every time my turn comes up, a work order or something else from the Intelligence Office has rescued me. This bothers some of my buddies and even makes them angry and jealous even though I have told them not to envy my poor fate. I worked in the kitchen today and this seems to have pleased them. I stayed longer because I landed in my element. The work is not difficult or tiring, and I can leave early. I am always glad to leave but not before I prepare a "lunch." Rations are limited during the march and we only eat twice a day.

I am familiar with the work routine and know where I can find the good food. I wait until everyone has eaten supper so that I can claim a "beefsteak" and cook it to taste. Swiss cheese, California plums, and New York butter make up my lunch for the trip. If the people who dislike me and are glad to see me punished with kitchen work knew this, they would really be bothered.

I stayed late in the kitchen making my preparations. By the time I went to town all the stores had closed and I was unable to buy postcards.

Wednesday, December 11

Everything was fine this morning, and immediately after breakfast we began the difficult march that is already giving us nausea. We have covered twenty miles and are thoroughly exhausted. Many of the soldiers were so tired they quit. The trucks picked them up, but by now they are probably doing kitchen work or guard duty. The landscape looks even more beautiful than before. We are following a winding trail that takes us up and around tall mountains and brings us almost face to face with the troops who have been following us. Our columns of marching men with rifles in a shoulder arms position and drawn bayonets look like a snake moving around the mountains. With this undulating movement, soldiers who had already passed us would reappear and overtake us, but on the side of another hill, above or below us. We talk with the soldiers who are not too tired to share a word or two. This somehow lifts our spirits even as we march under the unrelenting rain. Despite the exhaustion, something inspires us and stirs our souls. It never fails; someone who is unable to hold back these feelings bursts out singing a popular song like "The Long, Long Trail." There never was a more appropriate moment. No sooner had the singing started—who knows when or by whom—than we began to hear the sweet voice of the troops rebound over the mountains:

> There's a long, long trail a-winding
> Into the land of my dreams,
> Where the nightingales are singing
> And a white moon beams.
> There's a long, long night of waiting
> Until my dreams all come true;
> Till the day when I'll be going down
> That long, long trail with you.[2]

After marching on the side of a tall mountain and by a crystal-clear stream, we stopped at midday to eat our lunch in front of a beautiful church and a castle on the summit of another mountain. I would have liked to have the binoculars we used at the front in order to get a better view of the Burg Arras castle.

A few hours later, we arrived at a town named Alf. Although some of us thought we would sleep there, we continued on the left side of the river until we reached Bremen. The railroad tracks run on both sides of the river.

We were tired from our long march when we arrived at three in the afternoon. We entered through the main street that runs along the river and had barely placed our equipment at our assigned homes when the officers called us out for formation. The bugle echoed in the surrounding mountains and we answered the call like the crusaders of the past. We fell into formation in front of a pole where the German flag and possibly the banners of the crusaders had once flown. The band played the "Marseillaise" and our national anthem as we fell into a majestic silence and supreme concentration. The flag rose so proud and beautiful with its symbolic colors against the blue sky. Below it was the ground we had just taken from Kaiser's Germany. The Germans were sad as they witnessed the spectacular display. The older ones had to hold back the bitter tears that destiny had granted them.

Our house is on a street that faces the river, and it is such a delight to see everything that passes by without having to go out. Today was a time of rest.

It is ten in the morning and no one has left the house. Resting is so good! Several of us are boarded in this place. It is cold outside, but it is not raining.

They gave us chocolate tablets at midday. We were happy to hear that the marching orders for the afternoon had been canceled.

I prepared for any possible inspection by cleaning my rifle, shaving, and washing my feet with hot water.

During the afternoon, I visited a very beautiful church situated at the highest point in town. These temples, like all the others we have seen, say so much about the generous and faithful souls who have lived here and probably also about the ones who continue to live here. They mostly remind us of people from the more distant past. No matter how lost our world may be, every town has a place like this to meditate and consider the good path the martyr of Golgotha shows us.

I climbed higher to get a better view. From there, I observed the town as if it was at my feet. The river that passes in front of it bends within a short distance and seems to flow into the interior of the mountain. A building that serves as a cloister for female novices is situated at the river bend. The roads that run on both sides of the river look like white ribbons between the dark background of the mountains and the crystal blue of the calm river waters. A gray winter sky hangs over the tall mountains.

Friday, December 13

The bugle announced reveille early in the morning. The sound cut through the morning breeze, filling us with an enthusiasm that surprised us. I was going to get up at the first call but the sergeants that sleep with us got me angry and I stayed in bed. The band played a beautiful military march whose melody wafted in through the window. After breakfast, I once again climbed to a high point to reflect on our new and beautiful landscape. The memory of places like these may be all we take to our children. I could write so much about what I see and even more if I knew its history and evolution.

Our orders to move west were not unexpected since we were supposed to have followed that direction all along. We had wandered toward the northeast. Our stay in this area has been somewhat depressing because we have not received news about how the rest of the world is doing. We are stuck here.

Saturday, December 14

We returned to Alf in the morning and climbed westward around the tall mountains with our heavy gear. The hike was tiring but the beautiful panoramic views made it all worthwhile. Some of us learned of these surroundings during our youth in books written by German men of letters. We never thought we would ever see them, especially under such difficult circumstances. German artists have painted this landscape to immortalize the beauty of their country. Many of these scenes also appear in textbooks. It is so much better to see them firsthand. This is the original natural landscape. We step on the same ground as the prehistoric giants, as the crusaders on their way to rescue the holy land, as the Franks and the Moors. The vandal hordes of Huns, Goths, and Teutons pitched their tents around here while on their victorious march to the south.

We have arrived practically dragging under the weight of our backpacks. The body is tired, but not the spirit. Our imagination is filled with visions of men from the distant past who influenced other men to settle these lands and colonize the virgin jungles of America. We see the procession of Goths, Visigoths, Ostrogoths, Huns, Teutons, and Vandals. And now, for the first time, the old world witnesses America's invasion. What will history call us, perhaps "The Vandal hordes from the West sent by Mr. Wilson?" or "The Mercenary armies that defended the Morgans and the Rockefellers?" We have every right to be called, "The Great Crusade of the West for the *rights of the suffering humanity.*" Time will tell. Which nations clamored for us to enter the war and even asked that we send fresh troops to hold back the German offensives? Which nations placed all their hopes on our troops?

We should not have to worry about history's verdict, but then how shall we explain the sacrifice of millions of men who demanded justice and shed their blood on the battlefields?

These thoughts join with the memories of my home and family as we go up and down the tall mountains and march along the Moselle River.

We began to feel the cold as we left the rough terrain behind us. We passed by a lovely town with summer homes for people of wealth. Even the trees are planted and pruned to suit the whims of men. They have diverted a stream from the mountain and formed a lake with waterfalls to properly honor Cupid.

We have completed our march for the day at a very poor town with horse stables. We were so tired and hungry our supper tasted like the best we have ever eaten. We slept in a small house near the post office where I bought a postcard with an image of the town. The owner is Johan Wolver, and the town is Strotzbüsch. I took a brisk walk and saw ill-kept alleys, houses, and garden enclosures. A small knoll is visible from here. It is called Siebenbachtal because seven streams are said to originate there. This suggests an abundance of water, but it lacks sunlight. I could not visit the place but believed what they said of its beauty.

Sunday, December 15

We were told during breakfast that we would not depart until 9:15 because it was Sunday. We marched twelve kilometers without much effort until we reached Mehren, a small but beautiful, well-kept town. Its white homes present a marked contrast to the green fruit trees in the area. The streets are spacious and clear and the roads are like white ribbons extending in different directions. Its church is not as large as the ones in other equally populated towns, but it is very clean.

Our host family treated us well. This time we did not sleep in a horse stable because none was available. They fed each one of us for a mark, and we insisted they accept payment. We read magazines, shaved, and waited for the military review in the afternoon.

Five of us stayed at the house. Since one of my buddies is of German origin and another speaks the language well we had no difficulty being understood. I am beginning to expand my German vocabulary. My friend who speaks German fell hard for the young lady of the house. He did not act in the usual and irresponsible manner of most soldiers in love. The family includes a young man who served in the German army for four years, but spent all his time at the Belgian and Russian fronts. He tells us of the horrific slaughter of Russians who charged their machine guns en masse. He was especially struck by the Russian women; he felt they were the most beautiful in the world.

Monday, December 16

We rested and ate breakfast after waiting for a long time in the cold weather. The soldiers were so anxious that they resorted to profanity. I visited the church and came by some writing paper and newspapers at the YMCA. I returned to the house after reading an issue of the *Saturday Evening Post*. I did not feel like roaming anymore and wrote until suppertime.

I felt very cold even though formation had not lasted long. Our cooks may always be by a fire, but their work is outside and very difficult, and it is not appreciated. The winters in these parts are colder than ours.

Tuesday, December 17

The morning was very cold and rainy. We only pulled ourselves out of our beds because of our sense of responsibility. We stayed inside until midday and read, wrote, chatted, and smoked because we had nothing else to do. We simply wanted to pass the time.

Some of us went to the YMCA after supper mostly to relax. We bought cakes and cigarettes and headed back to our rooms to wallow in our sadness. I read out of an official primary school textbook, the *Meine Erstes Lesebuch*. Germans use it in their schools. I read until I was too tired to continue. The trumpet called us for supper and we ran expecting something new, but soon returned to sleep for the night.

Wednesday, December 18

We continue to rest while the cold weather bears down on us. I lack reading materials for the long hours of the day and night and look forward to hearing from my family, especially since the last letter spoke of their bouts with influenza. They tell me the epidemic is causing the same kind of suffering we have seen here. I cannot understand why this worries me more now than when we were fighting. Sergeant Kelleher came to tell us that we are leaving tomorrow. As members of the same detachment and company we have forged a good friendship. Our civilian lives were similar and this encourages us to work on our relationship as we endure these trying times.

The rain is getting worse with every passing moment. It caught me by surprise at the YMCA and I got drenched despite the fact that I ran. I went for something to eat, and we passed the time eating, talking, and singing. We sang until we ran out of songs from back home. Despite everything, we enjoy these moments in the military.

Thursday, December 19

The morning brought rain and higher temperatures. Sometimes the rain turns into hail or snow.

My friends are enjoying their conversation with our Polish friend Blochaske. The snow began to fall heavily before noon, and the ground, homes, trees, and roads took on incredible and beautiful shapes.

They gave out aviator-style caps for the cold in the afternoon. Nighttime brought a bitter cold, probably more serious than last night. The trees make squeaking sounds, reminding us of the times when we would gather and hear stories of fairies, goblins, and ghosts. Those days were the best, the sweet times of youthful innocence, when things of the world had not yet distracted our hearts. On this very night we are in the land that gave us many of the legends that are now part of our memory. We have no trouble recalling the past as we sit in front of this fireplace that raises our spirit and once again stimulates us to see what only a child can see.

Friday, December 20

The dawn brought a beautiful day after snow fell most of the night. The wind is still and the trees are bending under the weight of so much snow. We have also given a stooped appearance on these blessed roads. The view of the town is typical of the brightly colored Christmas scenes in the postcards we enjoy every year in the United States. This is also where many of those postcards originate. The town is entirely under white snow and the Catholic Church with its symbolic cross stands above the other buildings. The cross is now a glowing piece of ice. Children of all ages take to the streets in their coats to enjoy snowball fights. A large number of birds are perched on the windows where the women place something for them to eat. They do this in the spirit of Christmas. Everything calls on us to contemplate God.

A friend brought the anticipated news that we were sentenced to kitchen duty for failing to fall into formation the past few mornings. This did not scare us, but we were determined to figure out how to avoid the punishment and get back at everyone who bears us ill will. We do not look kindly on anyone who accuses us of something for which we are not to blame. They should be promoted to a rank that they deserve, but not at our expense.

I decided to walk around the town to enjoy what nature offers in Germany. The hills to the north are covered with snow and the forest looks beautiful. I was about to go to a nearby town when I saw some of our squads in training. This sounded an alarm in me. I did not want to explain what I was doing and had no other choice but to hightail it over the snow, in the opposite direction, to the other side of town. I came across a good number of men, women, and children who were repairing the roads. They seemed to be doing the work without pay because they were all so happy. This is the kind of spirit these communities nurture and that we are losing in the United States. Vanity, egotism, and pretense seem to predominate over there.

Several carts were coming into town filled with sugar beets, which were stored in large enclosures. The conviviality among the people is admirable.

Saturday, December 21

We retraced our steps twelve kilometers today until we reached Strotz-büsch. Everything we had seen before seemed so different now that we were marching in the snow. The hills, forests, fields, towns, they all had a different appearance. We ate at Strotzbüsch and continued until we reached a small town whose name I cannot recall. We will be sleeping in the home of a woman with a family that includes a young man who is about sixteen years old, two hard-working maidens, and a beautiful girl who is around seven.

Some soldiers are thrashing some wheat with a US-made McCormick. The family is very poor but industrious and energetic. The snow is no longer falling in this region, or it has melted, because we have only seen mud on the roads and streets. Our exhaustion and bad weather drove us to bed early. We are so used to the rough life in the horse stables that readapting to life in America is going to be difficult. We have become accustomed to this life because we believe that part of our responsibility is to bear it. I consider it a sad experience because that is how we look when we arrive at our new quarters every afternoon, when the sun is going down. We look like lost chickens in a new roost. The small groups of soldiers of twelve or fewer arrive drenched and with a rifle in their arms and backpacks on their shoulders. They enter the chicken coops or horse stables looking overhead for a ladder to climb into a sleeping area. The soldiers who find a spot busy themselves preparing their beds, while the others take all their belongings and follow the officer to new chicken coops in the other parts of town until everyone is in their respective pen. As soon as the bugle sounds we make our last cackling sound like back at the "rancho." Everything then becomes quiet until the next day.

Sunday, December 22

We began our march at eight in the morning to Hontheim, on the same road that brought us from Bremen. From there, we headed to the right. The flat terrain changed soon after we left and the mountains to the north of the Moselle began to appear. We passed by many villages and mountains. We traveled fifty minutes and rested fifteen until we arrived at a point where we could go down to the river. While on our march, we were struck by the beautiful view of the Moselle and the many towns on its banks. We came to Kinheim, but instead of going through the town we continued on the side of the mountain until we reached Kröv.

Barrera and Gómez had already picked a school by the river in which to sleep. After supper, I went to town and bought a reading primer for 88 "pfennigs." I stopped by the church and several businesses. I was tired but the town still seemed beautiful. The noise in the home where I was to sleep was unbearable because of the large number of soldiers. I have noticed that all the public schools still have crosses in them. Catholicism predominates. I expected something different.

Monday, December 23

I woke up early to receive the orders of the day and then had breakfast. Formation was called within a short while and we were ordered to march two-and-one-half kilometers to a place near Kinheim. We crossed a river in small groups on a ferry manned by a German and landed at Lösnich, a lovely town where we are to spend the winter.

While we waited for the rest of the troops to cross, the locals offered us apples after seeing one of our soldiers trying to buy some from a youngster who was passing by.

Once we had dispersed throughout the town, I found myself in a lone house near our kitchen. I was accompanied by Sergeant Otto, the person who supplies us clothing. The old and broken house is very cold. It has a good fireplace but we have no wood to burn. The town that will serve as our winter home is beautiful, this is a relief. We will be able to sleep with warm, dry feet. We could no longer bear the long marches in the mud. The marches had lasted twenty-two days and we rested little. We only really rested when we took off our shoes and socks for the evening. I was fortunate to always have more socks than I needed. I often wore up to four pairs of thick socks because of the cold, humidity, and load that I carried. This is how I avoided the blisters that bothered the other soldiers. Many of them also contracted pneumonia.

Christmas Eve in Lösnich, Germany, 1918

As expected, I was very cold last night, but survived.

José Leal, a buddy I had not seen in some time, arrived while I was eating breakfast. I invited him to my cold house since he did not have a place to stay. He had a good supply of rations, which means he has figured out a way to survive the hard times. This is another soldier who now knows how to deal with the difficulties of a challenging life. His job is to deliver supplies to the soldiers. He told me of his difficulties when he was "short" and expecting a discharge from the military, all along carrying himself in the courteous manner typical of our people. By the time the war ended he had become an expert at supplying himself first. He now had big pieces of good bread, plenty of butter, and many other things that are like pure gold among the soldiers.

After securing a place to sleep that was better than the night before, we looked for some of our buddies in the other towns. We visited three towns but did not find them and had to return to prepare for formation.

I had forgotten that this was Christmas Eve so I ironed my uniform in the late afternoon and decided to attend mass the next day. I have also been invited to a celebration organized by Gersbach, a friend of German origin who has helped me so much as an interpreter. He shares with me whatever he finds interesting. A German family invited Gersbach to a Christmas party and he has asked me to join him. I definitely do not want to pass up the opportunity to learn how the German people observe Good Tydings.

Wednesday, December 25, Christmas Day, 1918, in Germany

I did not have to wait long for Gersbach. He arrived on time and we promptly headed for the German home where we were received with courtesy and kindness. The hosts' reception already makes us feel the true spirit of the Christmas. They had worked hard preparing the room where the gathering was to take place. They still had to paint the walls when we arrived. The two young German soldiers who did the work were very clever. They dipped rags in the paint and then glided them uniformly from the top of the wall to the bottom. The effect was beautiful and cost little. I soon learned why the soldiers were so gracious with the family. They had lost their sons in the horrible war and had nothing left but the friendship of their sons' friends. This was an example of fellowship that we, the *Mexican Americans*, could emulate in America.

I saw the soldiers work with great pleasure and self-satisfaction. The parents could not help but feel a deep appreciation for their sons' loyal friends. I felt that they wanted to cry, and they probably did not because we were there. They cried to themselves.

Two or three families arrived early. They talked a great deal and played some games that we did not join because we did not understand them, but this did not keep us from sharing in their joy. I had invited my friend José Leal and explained to him why we should be interested in the celebration. I appreciated his company as we shared memories of our own similar festivities in Texas. I could understand the festivities because my buddy Gersbach was close and explained everything to me.

A young, very attractive German woman in mourning clothes arrived. I may have been indiscreet or overtaken by the moment, but I wanted to know everything and engaged Gersbach in a conversation on the matter. The lady of the house realized what was happening and when the young woman in black walked out with her friends, she took the opportunity to explain that she had lost her fiancé during the last hours of fighting. This caused her such profound sadness that she resolved to always dress in mourning and to never marry. This is a highly unusual decision because she is young. We would rather that she does not keep the promise and seek her own happiness.

We were tired and sleepy when they placed the tablecloths. Two children, a boy of eight and a girl of ten, arrived and sat down. They were told that Baby Jesus would bring presents and they right away broke out in fervent prayer from within their youthful souls. They had prayed for half an hour when a young woman dressed as an angel entered with a large container full of fruits, pastries, and a few toys. They distributed the fruits and pastries among the children. When this was over, the children went to sleep in their rooms and we continued with our conversation. This is when the celebration turned to the bottles of the famed white and red wines of the Moselle. My buddies drank a good number of glasses. I did not share much in this delight. I only tasted a glass of each of the juices of the famous vines of the region. I regret that I was unable to note the difference in the color or the taste. Everything was grape to me. I was more obliging with the fruits and pastries. They did not have to ask me twice.

The guests gave presents to the children. We had not expected this and promised to bring some gifts the next day. We were very happy as we said good-bye to the families who had shared their Christian traditions and brought us memories of home.

The streets were covered with snow by the time we left the celebration. Who knows how long it had been snowing. It made Christmas complete. We did not feel comfortable trampling in our rugged boots through the snow that God's hand had given us. Lost in deep thought, each one of us went to sleep and enjoyed a snow-white dream in the middle of a dark void that keeps us from feeling true joy.

I attended high mass and silently longed for home and family. The church is beautiful, but I did not understand the sermon because it was in German.

I bought some souvenirs to send to my children and to comply with local customs.

Thursday, December 26

We had a grand military parade today. Both regiments participated, the 360th and the 359th of the 180th Brigade. The review took place to the west and on a beautiful plain along the river, in front of the town of Kinheim. The two regimental bands played in the historic review, our first military exercise in Germany, or in what will once again become France. Brigadier General McAlexander reviewed the parade. Other officers accompanied him.

Sergeant Kelleher came to tell me that we had to prepare for formation with the Corps of Combat engineers. It was a beautiful formation. The day lent itself for the occasion. It was very cloudy and fair. This is why we were not bothered by the long customary wait for the officers. The military setting brings to mind many other such events this place has witnessed. If the mountains could speak they would tell us much about their past. It has seen great congregations of men in preparation for the deliverance of the Holy Land, the defense against the Moorish invasion, the invasion of Russia by Napoleon the Great, the war of Napoleon III, and the last four years of fighting. We can only wonder how the roads running alongside the Moselle looked, the railroads as well, all crowded with young men in their brilliant armor expressing the most self-serving of all desires, to show off their modern armaments. These same mountains have seen the ghastly result of all this, just like they have witnessed the sad, dirty, wounded, ill, and defeated troops during the past century, marching without weapons, without officers, without their uniforms or the laurels they expected . . . and the history of man continues.

Friday, December 27

We are all taking classes; we were ordered to fall into formation and train with the combat engineers. We were ready for the task when good fortune smiled on us. The combat engineers were sent to gather firewood and we were left without an officer. We returned to our rest areas to relax another day. We cannot be blamed if a unit is not available to incorporate us. The officers in charge of the R.I.O. should be on top of these things. We had been without an officer since before the end of the war. This continues until now. We do not fit in any unit since we belong to the General Headquarters Company, which is scattered in different towns. Our officer has not returned from the hospital and we would prefer that he does not. This is not to wish him bad luck. On the contrary, we want the best for him, but we do not want him as an officer.

We decided to clean our rifles since a march is not scheduled for the afternoon. I changed my place of residence during the night and settled in room 27 in a house by the river. The gentleman of the house is an artisan and has a workshop where he and his children work. He does not seem to be setting a good example for them because he likes to drink a great deal of wine and spends more than he earns.

His children insist I learn German. They tell me I am able to converse in their language. With a book in hand, I speak to them at length for pleasure and to improve my ability.

The night brought snow and cold temperatures.

Saturday, December 28

The morning was beautiful. I woke up early and had to wait by the river because I do not have a company to join in formation and I cannot take to the streets until everyone has completed their morning drills. I have stayed inside like a prisoner and fear that an officer will discover me. I am at a loss about what I would tell the officers, some of whom are unfair and do not accept explanations. In the military, the person in charge is in the business of ordering others. All I can say is that I am not at fault and that their behavior is criminal. I will continue with what I am doing until they catch me.

I learned of an upcoming inspection of the soldiers' quarters during breakfast and returned to my room to make sure that everything was in order. I prepared my backpack and everything else like when we were in combat, but waited in vain all day because no one came. At midday, officers ordered me to report to General Headquarters.

The Schwab family treats us well, especially the kind old lady who worries so much when her husband comes home loud and drunk. She tells me—probably because she does not want to upset me—that this has been taking place for a long time. I never know when he leaves or returns, but I do know that he is always in a tavern.

Sunday, December 29

I slept well and woke up late. I noticed on the assignment chart that my turn was up. I will not mind my Monday responsibility since I am tired with the life I am leading.

Mr. Schwab was so happy to hear I was asking about the Catholic mass that he offered to accompany me. I saw my good friend Fidel Gleim at church. Everyone came out in his or her Sunday best. Mr. Schwab introduced me to some of his high-class compatriots, but I was unable to communicate with them. The Germans seem to be strong in their Christian faith. I hope this is not only due to tradition.

My fellow Mexicans and I are willing to accept whatever fate brings us. We are scattered in different towns along the Moselle. I will try to see them. The Germans have an unusual way of announcing a new law or regulation to the people. An official walks the streets with a bell in one hand and the document in the other and jingles the bell at every corner. The people gather and he reads the document in a loud voice. He does this throughout the town, much like it has been done for generations.

Despite some challenges, I have improved my knowledge of German with the help of my fourteen-year-old teacher, Peter Schwab.

I spent the afternoon in the town's outskirts and witnessed the arrival of the train with passenger cars and freight wagons. Everything is very different from back home, including the people, the railroad stations, and their technology. I carried on a conversation with an old German from Köln who works in a factory that manufactures pen knives. Many families stroll along the river and although they seem happy, their faces show the wear of living without many things.

Monday, December 30

I reported early for kitchen duty and worked alongside Domingo Pacheco from San Antonio. Our first job was to bring water from the fountain. The kitchen is responsible for preparing food for two officers. This means our breakfast was very good. The dog of the wealthy gets the best crumbs. Pacheco and I shared stories of our lives, which made the time pass by quickly. He lives near the San Jose Mission. The mere mention of the mission brought back memories from my youth. He knows my favorite places and I know much of his history. His life deserves a book all its own. I must note that Pacheco trained many of our rookies in the use of the bayonet at Camp Travis.

Most of my day was dedicated to quill work, not the plucking kind, but keeping a written account of the items in the kitchen and the like. This was not so bad. The kitchen was later moved to room number 49. I received a letter from my friend Robert Hoey who lives in Middletown, New York. This is how the letter reads in English:

> Dear Luz
>
> I received your letter of November 21 today. You asked me to write you a long letter, so I will. In it you asked me to send you a green ribbon, so I did. One side is shiny, the other is dull. The dull side is for insignias. You said you had me a notebook, from what you said, it must be very nice, a little token to remember you by. I am glad to hear you are helping your comrades to learn to speak Spanish and English. I was glad to hear you had a father, wife, and children. I have myself two brothers and one sister. It is quite some time you went through Middletown from my story "A Soldier of the 90th Division from U.S. to Germany.[3]
>
> Luz's friend,
>
> ROBERT HOEY
27 Albert St., Middletown, N.Y.

My dear sister Celia:

Now that the year is coming to an end, I want you to know where I am and how I got here. Pull out your geography book or a map of the world: We left Camp Travis, San Antonio, on June 6; that same day we passed by New Braunfels, San Marcos, Austin, and Texarkana; the following day we went by Pine Bluff, Arkansas, crossed the Mississippi, St. Louis, Mo., Cleveland, Erie, Ohio, Buffalo, Utica, Middletown, New York, N.Y., and Hoboken, N.J. We passed by the Statue of Liberty in the New York Harbor and Long Island, and on June 14 left for France. We traveled seven days and nights across the Atlantic at twenty-two knots an hour and without ever seeing a submarine. Two submarine destroyers accompanied us as we departed and six of them received us as we neared England. A submarine destroyer is a small fast-moving warship with several cannon. They are the only ones who can finish with the feared submarines. White Island, England, came into sight on the twenty-first. We slept as we entered Southampton and disembarked in the morning. We spent the whole day under a covering on the wharf. In the afternoon, we boarded England's *King Edward* and crossed the English Channel. Many of us became seasick. We came ashore and spent a day in Le Havre. The next day, we left for France in a small train for transporting cattle and passed by the suburbs of Paris. We did not see the city because it was dark and we slept. We reached Troyes and then Latrecey, where we spent a few days. On the first of July, we moved to Rouvres-sur-Aube. From there, we traveled to Toul, Saint-Mihiel, and Pont-à-Mousson on the Moselle. We fought there for the first time and then headed for the front at Verdun. We continued fighting in Mouzay and Stenay, France. The armistice came. We rested a few days in Mont; later we passed through Luxembourg and in Germany we passed by many towns, including Trier and Zeltingen (on the Moselle River) as we made our way to Koblenz. We expect to be here until peace is completely assured.

Greetings to all,

Your brother,

LUZ

I stayed in my room most of this peaceful day. I wrote, read, and picked up woolen clothing that I had been issued. The waters of the Moselle, which we have admired for their crystalline beauty, were turbulent this morning due to the heavy rain in the mountains and other high areas. Although the Moselle almost reaches the house where I sleep, the people are not concerned with floods. They know the river and they caress it as if it were a lion in a cage. I really do not trust it. The Moselle is the biggest river I have seen around here.

I attended the rosary in the evening. The rain had kept me from going anywhere, but after the rosary I took to the streets. I noticed that people were in good spirits, as they usually are at the end of the year. The soldiers carried on with the same general feeling behind closed doors. Since no one was playing music, we were able to hear rousing conversations, ecstatic laughter, and the sound of glasses as the soldiers toasted with white and red wine, or with champagne.

While roaming the dark and rainy streets, I recalled a dream from last night and realized that I am witnessing what came to me in my sleep. I again have something to share with people who do not believe in dreams. Superstition or coincidence may account for what I dreamed, but I have enjoyed this evening walk in the middle of a torrential rain and the deep darkness of night. I observe the shadows of my buddies hopping across the wet streets. I wonder if they were bored like me and went out into the rain without caring about getting wet.

The First Day of 1919

The morning was still and the life of the town unfolded like a dream. The people give themselves to their daily tasks. The soldiers move slowly. They prefer not to cross the street and show their wear from yesterday's sleepless night. The river follows its course, carrying everything in its way. The mountains serve as the river's natural barrier.

I have written home and sent good wishes for the New Year. The kindness of my hosts has moved me to give them some small gifts. I met up with Gleim at mass and he invited me to join him at his house. I consider Gleim one of us because of his kindness toward our *raza* in civilian life. This means he cannot be blamed for the racial prejudice and discrimination that is directed at us, the humble, poor, and lower-status people we are. Although he is never the object of racial insults, he does not hesitate to speak out when someone speaks badly of his mother's race. Gleim believes in the basic worth of men, but we can only convince people of this through force of arms. This is the best way to overthrow tyrants, usurpers, and despots, and who cares if they call us thieves, bandits, and murderers like Robin Hood and William Tell!

Gleim is treated well here and wherever he goes. He knows how to live among "the people" and knows how to command respect. I had a good time with Gleim, just like in America, France, and Luxembourg.

Upon returning to my quarters, I found out that a sergeant had been looking for me. He later sent me a message that the Intelligence Office was reorganizing and that I should expect a new order. This is what I dreamed last night.

Thursday, January 2

The morning was very cold and rainy, and I stayed inside all day. I find these days very useful, although I do not know if what I do will bring me good results. I was told to pick up a new blanket and shoes that had been issued to me. My load will get heavier, but it does not matter. These things are bound to come in handy.

A young German woman sewed the insignias on my uniforms.

Three buddies are leaving for America. We are happy for them. We also wonder about their future and look forward to our own departure.

I received a package from home and, as expected, I was happy. If I were to ever wish that a family member face the difficult challenges before me now, I would mean well. This is where we can really appreciate home, family, and nation.

> My dear soul mate:
> I received the package that you sent me in November. In spite of it all, we have had very good luck. The cold temperatures that I feared never came. It does not even feel like we are in the middle of winter. We have had several snows, but it warms up after it melts. The rivers rise with the snowmelt. We have not felt the cold. It may be that we have good coats or that we have acclimatized. Do you think the cold weather is going to bother me with my seven pairs of socks? I wear as many as four pairs of the heavy type. I think that if I don't lose them while on the move, I will have them for a long time after the war.
> Tell my father-in-law Gregorio that I may go to Africa from here because things are not yet settled. It may be worth going over there and bringing back an elephant trunk to turn into a totem. At this point, this Indian has learned to shoot.
> My love to everyone.
> LUZ

Friday, January 3

Today was as good as yesterday. My sister Clotilde sent me another package. I really appreciate the gift and her demonstration of affection. Anyone who sees us as idle and government-kept men could say we lack nothing, but this would be far from the truth as long as we continue to be away from our loved ones.

A group of friends and I spent a good while talking about what we had received in the mail.

I received orders to head out for Zeltingen and immediately began to prepare for the trip, all along cherishing the hope my faith gives me.

In Zeltingen, Alemania, by the Moselle

Saturday, January 4

started packing early in the day. After lunch, I went to the station where orders are posted and was able to determine the whereabouts of my buddies. I went up the river alone until I reached Erden and then Rachtig. This is where Machine Gun Battalion 345 is located. I could not help but notice all the clean, burnished instruments of war that seem to be waiting for the orders to once again make the forests and the valleys tremble under their threatening rain of death. The mules that pull them also rest. The soldiers that lord over everything are moving slowly, as if half asleep.

I visited the small but strikingly beautiful church at Rachtig.

I still wonder why I have not seen a single protestant church, neither in France nor in Germany. I thought that protestants dominated the area, but this is not so.

I rode a truck from Rachtig to Zeltingen and reported to Lieutenant Klebold. Sergeants Kelleher and Schwarz and my old buddies Gersbach and Massenburg were in the office. I also saw Gómez and Barrera and spoke to them at length.

I had to write and censor some letters and prepare the report for the R.I.O.

I slept in Massenburg's room that night.

Sunday, January 5

We had a beautiful sunny day.

General Headquarters ordered that anyone attending religious services was exempt from reporting for formation and informed the cooks to place food aside for us. The mass was solemn.

The Moselle continues to rise. Its waters have already entered some cellars at the river's banks. My work is easy. I wrote home a great deal and visited Gómez and Barrera. We had a good time with *malilla* and other card games that our ancestors played in America.

We were assigned to sleep on the top floor of the house where we have our office. We really welcomed this. Gersbach and I promptly went to sleep. Our work is getting interesting.

Monday, January 6

We did not hear the bugle and woke up late. We fear some disciplinary action for not responding to reveille. Lieutenant George is heading out, but we do not know if he is going to America or a university in Europe. Lieutenant Klebold seems to be a good person who wants to do right. He does not know the work and this gives us a say about what gets done. We are ready to do all his work but he has to treat us like office mates. It can now be said that we carry out the work of an officer with the pay of a foot soldier. This is our duty, Onward! We have left our position hoping that someone else fills it. Even though others have asked for this assignment, we remain in place and are kept in rank.

We joined the Kapp family after submitting our report. The family includes the father, the mother, and two girls, one seven and another nine. As my interpreter, Gersbach has helped me understand the German customs. We have learned the customs by critically observing others. We must take into account the provincial forms of life in this country's different regions.

We are most pleased to see that the parents raise their children in a tolerant manner and take care to educate them. They seem to have reached a point when they do not have to tell their children they need to attend elementary school, the secondary grades, and college. The children make their plans at an early age and make an effort that is second nature to them. Obeying mentors is another one of their important virtues.

Our gathering ended when the family served us waffles and wine, offerings we appreciated.

Tuesday, January 7

I received an issue of the *El Latino-Americano* with news about our town. It is worth noting that the Spanish influenza is creating much hardship and taking the lives of many friends who decided not to come to the war for fear of dying. The day has turned sad with such bad news.

I was issued a strange-looking uniform.

The day ended quietly as we continued to project our silhouettes against the buildings by the streets.

Wednesday, January 8

A large number of officers left for America. Some of them are going to complete their university studies while others are going to fill positions in the high places they used to have or that may now be available to them. They will have benefited from the sacrifice of the many who do not complain. Our roses and laurels will come soon enough, along with the war's balance sheet.

The sergeant and I dutifully attended church services.

I received a letter from George Hoey, from Middletown, N.Y., and from Juanita García, from Moore, Texas.

The German press has made a great deal of the death of a well-known count.

We need to prepare our equipment for tomorrow's military exercise.

I ended the day by reading French and conversing in German.

Mexican Americans Attend School

Thursday, January 9

We reported for formation with a light backpack and crossed the Moselle on a ferry. Our troops marched in impressive order through the valleys and fields of Wengerohr and arrived at our command post near the railroad station. We rested under a lush grove of trees while our couriers did their job. Airplanes, tanks, and cannon, as well as a formidable imaginary enemy, moved about the area. We stayed under cover until we were told to catch up with the troops and to position ourselves in front of them so that we could observe the enemy's movement and ensure the safety of our troops. The colonel displayed his old military style and he did it in good humor. The military games are interesting and make our appearance, outlook, and condition look good. Everything went well since it was all a question of mathematical calculations.

We set up our command post on a hill that overlooked a vast valley. We almost fell ill as we sweated on our march over wet, cold terrain. Also, our lunch was limited. When it came time to return, we practically ran back with a hearty appetite. It was raining the entire time. The military exercise saddened us because we could not help replaying the past battles in our minds.

Friday, January 10

We did not hold reveille and had a good lunch. Our lieutenant had to assume charge of Company M, and we took up our duties on our own. I prepared some announcements for General Headquarters and visited the home of an older Portuguese woman with a son named Juan. We have an amusing way of communicating. She uses Portuguese and I speak Spanish. It goes without saying that anyone who knows several languages can converse with the world. Her husband is German and is in Portugal taking care of his belongings. She and her son have been here since the war started. Valente de la Rosa is their good friend and they trust him. She likes to hear her piano and de la Rosa plays it with a heavy hand, but he manages to perform some old tunes from back home. We sing popular songs at her home.

Saturday, January 11

We had good weather. I spent time reading and studying in the office. The lieutenant came in to censor some letters. He has given me permission to censor the correspondence and to sign his name when he cannot come in. I am very glad for my limited Latin, my poor Texas Spanish, the English I learned in public school, and the French I picked up in southern France during the six weeks we prepared for the war. I have discovered that my languages originated alongside the ones spoken in the Balkans, or rather that my languages emerged from among them.

Our division has sixty thousand men and claims twenty-two languages. I prefer to write letters for soldiers in the languages I know instead of trying to censor the ones I do not know.

When my friends ask me, "How many languages do you know? I answer, "None, but I understand many."

The very name of our department speaks well for us, the "Intelligence Office of the 360th Infantry Regiment." Who cares if we do not have the other form of intelligence.

I sent postcards to my family.

My friend Gersbach drank a lot of the white waters of the Moselle. He got drunk, became cheerful, and was very happy.

Our band played some beautiful pieces in front of Major Allen's house. The lady who owns the house where we have our offices fears Major Allen because he is strict about keeping the town clean.

Sergeant Kelleher, Gersbach, and I took to the moonlit streets of Zeltingen on a secret service detail. We did not accomplish all we set out to do, but we had a good outing and have much to relate.

The night sneaked up on me while visiting Gómez and Barrera.

Sunday, January 12

I wrote a few letters for Sergeant Kelleher.

They gave us candies in the kitchen.

I visited the ruins of a once-lavish castle. The remains are east of us, on the hillside by the right bank of the river. Beautiful vines cover everything despite the fact that the place has a steep ridge. When I think of the thousands of tragic stories and who knows what else may have occurred next to such ancient walls, our insignificance as humans saddens me. I feel this when I think about how time erases everything. Where are their aristocratic owners? How far did their science and goodness take their pride and arrogance? The impression we leave in this world is as slight as the trace the disgusting worms make on the dirt.

We cannot be certain about how the Germans feel regarding their coming elections. They seem to prefer that someone dictate the laws to them. They will participate in the elections because they are expected to do so and not as an act of conscience. They should be further along with their suffrage.

We had a good time in the home of the Portuguese woman. She is almost seventy years old and very friendly. The woman lives by strict rules and a demanding work schedule, but we have converted her wrecked home into a social center with much beer, song, and piano playing.

Monday January 13

I have to prepare several maps for the patrols that will be participating in the military exercise next Thursday.

Lieutenant Klebold brought us the good news that the officers will leave for Koblenz on Thursday and that our division will depart on March 1. How wonderful to see that our wishes are coming true!

Lieutenant Klebold is very different from his predecessor. We know the good qualities of the person he replaced, but we give greater importance to Klebold's genuine friendship. We could care less about all the military despotism that sets the officers apart from the foot soldiers. We have simply embraced the idea of defending the homeland from present danger.

When I shared the news with the soldiers, they showed great joy in their conversations, on their faces, in everything they did. Can there be more delight than our return after such a trying exile from our country?

Tuesday, January 14

The colonel and the captain were present during morning drills. We received orders for additional drills at 1:30 because so many soldiers had been absent. Although we assembled at the assigned time, we were told to fall out and rest because we had no one to lead us.

We continued to prepare for the military maneuvers scheduled for the sixteenth. The news about our departure for America continues to arrive.

Wednesday, January 15

The morning began with a heavy rain. I received a letter from my brother Ramón.

I received some credit for my work and was told to offer a night class for soldiers who may be interested in studying. Several of us who had mentored children during our civilian life gathered at the local school. Since many of my fellow Mexicans need English instruction, I have asked for this assignment. I made this request knowing I had been denied the opportunity to study at a French or English university because I was a private.

This is how it happened. Once the fighting ended, an attempt was made to observe the law that guaranteed instruction for the soldiers. This opportunity was made to everyone who wanted to study. I filled out the following application:

General Headquarters, 360th Infantry, 90th Division
American Expeditionary Forces in Germany
January 11, 1919

Private J. Luz Sáenz
Attached to the Signal Corps, G-5
General Headquarters
Application to attend a university
1. Completed studies. I graduated from high school in 1908; completed instruction in accounting and stenography in a business school. I speak, read, and write English and Spanish. I have an understanding of French.
2. Profession. Teacher in the public schools of Texas for eight years. Clerk, secretary, and translator of French wireless communications in the Intelligence Office since August 1918.
3. I prefer to attend a French university.
4. Humanities and Science
5. I wish to leave with my division when it departs.

I was denied on the grounds that the program was limited to officers. This is for the record.[1]

I accepted the responsibility of teaching my own because no one is interested in them. This reminded me of a newspaper notice that appeared before the war, that soldiers who did not know how to read or write would not be sent to the trenches. Clearly, bullets do not respect proclamations.

I believe our close relationships will serve us well. I will do all I can to nurture a love for learning, the lack of which is our worse enemy in civilian life. I have much to say to my comrades in arms about this. I will tell them of my proposal that the government help our veterans. My plan is to establish a community with one hundred Mexican American soldiers so that they can continue their fellowship as loyal citizens to our nation. We will ask for material assistance to educate ourselves and become more useful to our community and the rest of the nation. Education is the most important way to advance our political and social development in Texas.

We have been issued gas masks and helmets for the military maneuvers. I had a long, serious conversation with the teacher of the German school. We communicated in French about issues that are important in our profession, including our long teaching experience.

My work is becoming more interesting.

Thursday, January 16

The bugle woke us up early. The moon was still bright when we finished our breakfast. This allowed us to enjoy a new natural setting. We crossed the river on a ferry and reached the trucks that were to take us to the battlefield. The name of the battle site is not important now. It is just a place where we will spend a day doing military maneuvers. We reached Wittlich by six and set up our observation post in a vacant house outside of town. Some fellow soldiers in intelligence, as well as a few couriers and I, are responsible for the observation post. From this place we can see long distances, over the fields and the nearby forests. We learned many things. The day grew cold and rainy, making the last part of our training difficult. A good number of officers came and went in cars while many airplanes flew over the town as if they were bombing it. Many persons would have died by now. We did a good job. I am sure we would have done as well in a real battlefield.

We were cold, hungry, and wet as ducks when we returned to Zeltingen.

We ate a good dinner. I did not have to attend my German class because I have been trading my English classes for German ones with the local schoolteacher.

Friday, January 17

I had a slight fever last night.

We are pleased with our work because we understand it better every day and everyone has been willing to take on his assigned tasks.

The rain lasted a long while last night and it hailed today.

My German class is very interesting. I have already said that we use French to communicate. This is how we study several languages at the same time. The interesting thing is that neither the German nor I remember when we started using French. I heard that my older brother is very sick and with little hope of surviving. God knows what He does. We do not have to go to war to die.

Saturday, January 18

The morning was very cold. I found myself alone in my office after breakfast. My friends went swimming while I prepared a bath for myself. I read, wrote, and thought the whole time. I also answered correspondence from Mr. Pedro Huizar from San Antonio and wrote letters for Gómez and Lieutenant Klebold. I am like a secretary for my friends.

A wealthy German loaned me his beautiful French and German books.

I did not hold class today because it is Saturday and I must prepare myself for tomorrow.

Sunday, January 19

Sergeant Kelleher and I went to mass. Mostly women attend the services while the men stay home to take care of the children who are still asleep. The men go to church later.

Today is the memorable day when Germans vote in their first popular election. We are witnesses to a historic day. Everyone waits eagerly to find out the results. People vote by region and they talk and pretend to know whom the elected officials will be and what they will have to do in their new lives as citizens.

> My dear sister:
>
> I received your letter yesterday, along with the ones from José and Ramón. I'm glad that all of you are out of danger. I had thought you might be sick since you had not written in a long time. God has been good to us and given you good health. My other letters that you will have received before this one show how worried I have been.
>
> I am pleased with Mr. Knox because of all he has done for you. I don't know how I can repay him.
>
> You were very sad and anxious on September 25. I also had my difficulties on the battlefield at that very hour. Life takes its natural course.
>
> Love for my little ones.
>
> LUZ

Monday, January 20

We filled out forms that asked for our civilian skills and occupations.

I wrote while in the office. Gersbach and I bathed. We do this now and then after our meals even though we are not told to do so, but we want to be ready for a physical inspection that will come when we least expect it. We are supposed to bathe weekly, but prefer to pay German women to heat our water and to then clean ourselves in a warm room rather than to suffer the cold in the open air. We should note that this is winter and the temperature is much lower than back home.

After my bath, I discovered that we are to train in full gear tomorrow. This is going to be difficult. We have not carried all our belongings in a long time. (It is eight o'clock and I am still preparing the clothes we are to take. We will probably rise before dawn.)

Tuesday, January 21

We do not give our responsibilities the same importance any more, either because of the cold or the make-believe maneuvers. They obviously want to teach us discipline, but they cannot expect this to work when everyone is doing as they please. In any event, we met our obligation. We had several incidents on our return. Somewhere near a lone village where we set up our Intelligence Office, some soldiers decided to buy "colonche" to bear the cold.[2] They drank the fermented drink until they forgot about the work and the rain. The rest of us remained at our posts. At one point, the colonel came close, but thought that everything was fine when he heard the lively conversation. He was not mistaken, everyone was getting along and happy. I taught my buddies when I returned. The class went well despite the march and our fatigue.

I wrote some letters when I returned to my office. This is my greatest pleasure because I am recalling things I do not want to forget. Now, more than ever, we look forward to returning home and sharing our experiences with our children. I ask them to save all of my letters. If they do, I will have a complete account of everything and I will be able to remember what I saw, what I did, and how I felt when I participated in the great crusade.

Wednesday, January 22

Today I received a postcard from the good priest Moura in France. It reads:

Rouvres-sur-Aube, Haute Marne, France
Professor J. Luz Sáenz,
General Headquarters, 360th Infantry Regiment, 90th Division
American Expeditionary Forces in France

My dear friend:
I am very happy to have received your kind letter and I extend
to you my profound thanks. I am especially happy to know that
you are alive and in good health. I look forward to seeing you again.
Soon after you left, I ordered the books you needed from a bookstore
in Langres, but I still have not received anything. Say hello to my
friends. I remain a friend who sends you my kindest regards.

B. Moura, Priest

They gave us a piece a chocolate during supper.

Three fellow Mexicans in my night class stand out with their interest in
learning. Men like these could help our community overcome the difficult
social conditions that result from lack of schooling and opportunities. They
are intelligent and can understand the racial problem we have in Texas. Our
challenge is to acknowledge and support our cause with more enthusiasm.
When we return home, we will have plenty of time to study and speak on
the causes and consequences of the war. We will also have to decide how to
make the best use of the difficult experiences we had in the fields of death. I
regret that my students do not even have an elementary education, and this
keeps me from teaching them about more serious and useful matters, but I
am pleased with them. I just hope we do not forget the need to struggle for
our betterment when we return to our happy homes. This is why the war did
not end for us on November 11 like it did for the other Allies and our enemy,
the Quadruple Alliance.[3]

I received a very interesting letter from Mr. Prisciliano S. Sáenz, a close
friend and partner in the fight for the rights of our *raza*. I responded immediately by expressing my appreciation and my wish to hear and see him in
person.

Thursday, January 23

It snowed most of the day, but the moisture on the ground and the warm
surroundings kept the snow from covering the ground or the streets. The tops
of the mountains have snow and the trees are white and bent over.

I wrote to the good priest from Rouvres. I found it difficult to write in

French because I use it mostly to translate and speak. He will probably have a hard time understanding me.

We submitted our report earlier than usual and had plenty of time for sightseeing.

Newspapers from the United States are reporting that the returning soldiers are having a hard time finding jobs. I can see that this is going to be a more serious problem for Mexican Americans. Some states have given land to the veterans while others have given them money. I have written to the Interior Department asking for help in the form of a loan. We commit ourselves to form a community of no less than one hundred Mexican Americans on some government land, preferably in Texas. I maintain that these men who fought in support of the nation's loftiest principles will continue to live by those principles and to teach them to their children. I ask for about eighty acres of land with a good home and implements, and possibly money for the first years. The understanding is that all of this will be paid back to the government. I also ask for schooling for our children, ourselves, etc. Everyone who knows the plan endorses it and urges me to work hard at it. Everything seems to be going well with the government, but many people back home want money and the government is not consenting to this.

Friday, January 24

The morning was very cold. We did not feel like going for breakfast but hurried to the office to write letters and to read by the warm fire we had started. We spent the whole day without anything to do until we ate dinner and prepared our report. Preparing the report was not difficult since we did not have much to say. We had much to report about yesterday and will use this information in today's report.

I did not hold class tonight because I was busy helping the Germans prepare the list of people who voted last Sunday.

A woman who claims to be Belgian came to our kitchen selling postcards. I bought some to send home. We should be suspicious of this woman who may be a spy. As despair envelops this country, more people are given to deceit.

Movies are showing tonight.

Saturday, January 25

We had another cold day. Gersbach was under the weather and missed reveille. I spent most of the day at the office. A truck arrived after midday full of athletic equipment to be distributed in the regiment. This means more work.

As soon as the report was completed, we went to the theater where members of Artillery Battalion 149 stationed in Stenay hosted a beautiful celebration. It was well done and reminded us of our distant home.

To My Children

We are in the middle of a German winter. A boring and cold afternoon and a grayish sky bring on a sadness that seems to take in everything around us. The Moselle continues its uninterrupted march until it merges with the Rhine. They travel together to disappear into the bosom of the North Sea. My location gives me a constant view of the river's grayish waters that are like the sky. The river passes by our front door and across the street. The water's edge is no more than thirty meters from my window.

I usually see fishermen, but they are not in their usual places today, probably because this is Sunday. Some of them fish with nets cast from small boats that they navigate with or against the current. Others fish with another kind of net attached to the end of long poles. They use these in the pools of water or ponds that the major floods of melted ice and snow create at a distance from the banks of the river.

A thick fog covers the area between the mountains on the other side of the river and me. The mountains are not very far; you can see the trees at the summit. I have seen them with binoculars on other occasions. They are beautiful when the days are sunny and clear, but not today.

Many people come and go to the school that is located to the north of us. This is election time and everyone is voting for the people who will lead the nation in a democratic direction. Men and women, old and young are voting for the first time in their lives, as is done in nations that are free. This is a great change because autocratic rule and special privileges have come to an end. It is also very important to our nation's cause. In word as well as in deed, we have helped make democracy where despotism reigned. What can the Kaiser say about the soldiers in gray?

My attention is also drawn to the large number of German children who spray water on the pavement to skate or slide on their sleds. Others climb hills to glide down on their sleds with their little brothers and sisters.

Four of us work in the Intelligence Office. We had been quiet, each one of us lost in our thoughts. I was writing my impressions of a sad and cold afternoon. My buddies suddenly broke the silence, singing popular songs from home. They even convinced me to put my writing aside and join them so I could enjoy myself.

At that point, we heard the call for dinner and ran to get in line. Everything was completely dark when we returned but it did not last long. The snow came down hard and covered everything. The white snow lightened the darkness and the world appeared in its new beautiful mantle.

Zeltingen a. d. Moselle, Germany

Sunday, January 26

The days continue to be cold. I attended mass and returned to my usual inactivity, which is tiring me. I pass my time reading by the light of the fire. The soldiers who do not read spend their time talking until they get tired. I cannot understand why we are not satisfied with things as they are. It would be worse to march at this hour with a load on our backs.

The German community was as calm in the second election as they were in the first.

My buddies yawn, halfheartedly read a book, tire, and head out to the streets without a purpose in mind. We have nothing to do. Thank God for our good luck. We do not have to study or raise our prayers to the heavens. Nothing! Man is by nature lazy.

I do well entertaining myself in my room as I watch the river flow some thirty meters away and across the street. My view is beautiful. The opposite bank is covered with timber. I always see people crossing from one side to the other as they pursue their daily activities.

My friend Treviño brought me a newspaper from Alice with the report that a growing number of people are dying from influenza. We will not get to see many of our friends when we return.

Monday, January 27

The morning was colder and the whole day was freezing. Our work is easy. My students occasionally apply themselves seriously to their studies. This means we lack something very important. It may be that we do not appreciate opportunities and lack the will. In the end, everyone sees the world differently.

More newspapers and letters confirm that the influenza has ravaged entire communities. We now fear for our loves ones. They once worried about our well-being.

The day was beautiful despite the cold. The young German men and women enjoy skating on a pool of water that froze over on this side of the river. Some of them show off their ice skating skills. Most of them skate well. This is a favorite pastime at this time of the year. The young people do not seem to have other forms of entertainment.

Some youngsters enjoy sledding, while others throw snowballs at each other. The adults are busy clearing the entrances to their homes. Skating is new to the soldiers from Texas. It almost never snows in Texas, especially in the south.

After bearing the cold, we went to the YMCA for some candies and then returned to our rooms to read.

The lieutenant came to tell us that we will not take part in tomorrow's activities. This is going to make some soldiers jealous, but we cannot help it.

Tuesday, January 28

It snowed most of the night and the morning was very cold. I did not leave the office. I received four letters with good news, answered them immediately, and wrote others. Sergeant Kelleher had to report to General Headquarters to play on the football team. It is not going to be easy finding someone else.

We had no trouble preparing the report. Two ladies from the YMCA visited our office. They gave each soldier candies and khaki handkerchiefs.

My class was canceled because local Germans had a meeting at the school.

Wednesday, January 29

The cold continues. I stayed in my office for a long while because my buddies are at various work assignments. Sergeant Kelleher's absence makes the hours seem longer. He is a good friend and we have much to share. I read and wrote in French, a language I am glad to have learned. My knowledge of French has served me well, and I expect to benefit even more from it.

The day was beautiful despite the cold. [*The second sentence in this paragraph is incomplete and another one may be missing. The contextual meaning in the two sentences that follow, however, suggests that Sáenz is referring to a public program sponsored by Regiment 357.*] The soldiers from Regiment 357 sponsored it. They plan to perform again tomorrow so that our second battalion can attend.

Thursday, January 30

Lieutenant Klebold fell ill and another lieutenant took his place. He reviewed our work and ordered me to make copies of the instructions that should appear in the intelligence report. The clerk from Company K came to borrow our typewriter, but we did not lend it to him because our lieutenant was gone. The new lieutenant did not know what to say. We do not want a lot of people in our office, and this is not because we wish to conserve our old, dilapidated typewriter.

Kelleher returned from playing football and reported that he had not liked it. Poor fellow, he is too old for such a rough sport. He must not feel in his element and misses the comfort of working in the R.I.O., along with the other privileges we enjoy here.

Friday, January 31

I saw Treviño and other friends last night. I find it interesting that the hardship of war and the distance from home brings men together and encourages them to unite around a common cause. This offers me a good opportunity to conduct a sociological analysis.

I met with the German teacher last night and agreed to visit his school today. Gersbach and I arrived at ten in the morning. The teacher and his family live in the same building. He took us to his living room and then to the kitchen where he and his son were working. We went up to the fourth- and fifth-grade classroom after recess. About fifty boys and girls were in attendance; all of them were adept at solving mathematical problems. Their method of reciting and maintaining silence is wonderful. The teacher's method of correcting is somewhat antiquated. They still use the rap on the head and the pulling of ears. They learn multiplications with very large numbers and read a great deal of material. This is how they taught us at the turn of the century in the rural schools of Texas.

We had to leave as it was getting late; we promised to visit other classrooms another day. I have concluded that their form of instruction comes from the educational system in the military. It will have to be replaced now that the war is over.

I sent some packages home.

My Spanish, English, and German classes were very interesting.

My coworkers have a good time drinking their smooth wines and carrying on after work.

A fellow soldier who wanted to replace me at work failed in his attempt. He managed to get himself transferred to another company where he will have to work hard. I will never forget this incident.

Saturday, February 1

We had a very cold and overcast day. I have to study and work more than usual. My buddies feel lazy and so do I.

I went to the school again at eleven in the morning. This time I visited with the children and had a good time. The teacher is a young military officer who married recently. He cannot put his military ways aside and makes the students respond like machines. The method is useful in teaching reading, with its difficult sounds and forms of expression. Constructing short sentences and then writing them on the blackboard is a good exercise.

After the classroom activities, I had a good conversation with the teacher and his assistant. The teacher was an officer until November 11. The meeting was very interesting. He told us about his long military service and showed us his many injuries from the Russian front. He did not fight in France.

Our report was extensive and highly informative. I did not receive a letter today and spent my time reading French and German. The rest of my day was peaceful.

Sunday, February 2

The morning was very cold, but we still attended mass. After breakfast, I went to Graach to see Treviño but could not find him. I saw many young men skating in a frozen pond on the other side of the Moselle.

The soldiers of the Second Battalion had a strict inspection on the care of their area and equipment.

I had a hard fall this morning as I was returning from church. I was on the street that passes by the church and my house. The ice had made the cobblestones slippery, and our shoes are very unreliable because of the nails and the steel tap on the heel. Although I was walking carefully, a sudden, strong gust of wind made me lose my balance. My legs gave out and I fell forward on the hard street. I had trouble getting up because of the large amount of ice.

The return to America is certain, we just do not know when. We are more sure now.

Chaplain Reese gave a great sermon.

An officer wanted to stay in the house with us, but we bothered him and he left with all his equipment in search of another place. An officer would have been a black widow spider among us. We are better this way. We work a thousand times better without an owl in the tree where we sleep.

Monday, February 3

The dawn was very cold and the streets were covered with ice. The nearby mountains still have a thick, heavy cover of ice. The Moselle flows as before, its bluish waters look like a gray ribbon in a white countryside. We are in the middle of winter and we do not hear, see, or feel anything that is not of this season.

Every now and then we hear the hoarse bellow of the cannon as they shoot at targets and test the abilities of the handlers. Many trucks have been moving on the other side of the river.

We had a theatrical performance last night that was not as entertaining as expected.

> My dear father:
> As always, I am glad to write you and to wish that all of you are well and happy.
> It has been some time since I received a letter from you. I've written and responded to everyone. I have been so stunned by the blows I have received in life that I would not be surprised if your untimely visits would continue as before.[4]
> Tell me about my brother Eugenio. Marce said that he was going to see you but she has not written again. I worry. I have read in the newspapers about deaths occurring daily. They predict three times the deaths we recorded in the war. May it be God's will. Here we are, in the killing fields where we were sent. We are well, unlike everyone we left behind.
> I suppose that you have been keeping up with the news about the peace treaties. The soldiers don't have much to say about it. We have quieted down the German cannon and are ready to continue moving forward if necessary.
> Make sure my brothers attend school.
>
>   Luz

> Adán and Sam:
> Before me is the Moselle with its crystalline waters and its fishermen at work. I don't have to make a great effort or leave my room and face the cold wind of winter to see how they go about their

routine. I have a good coal heater in my room. This is the only way to beat the cold. I don't see how those poor fishermen can stand it. The feel the cold but they tolerate it.

My work is in my room, just like the work of the fishermen is over there, on the river. I have to prepare a report every night, as well as take lessons in Spanish, French, German, and English. I do this so that I can learn and teach.

While at the YMCA recently, the staff gave out pieces of chocolate to the soldiers, but I decided to write both of you a letter rather than wait in line. It's eight in the evening.

I'm going to tell you about some children who live in the house where I am staying. They are little Germans, three girls and one boy. The oldest one is about Lupe's age and the youngest is like Paulita. They go to school because they are required to attend, like in the United States. They start school at six years of age and are very smart I have visited their school and have seen them work. I have enjoyed the school a great deal.

The school has many children and they all want me to visit their classrooms. The children in the house where I am staying visit me after school when they see that I am not busy. I have shown them a picture of both of you. They say you are good soldiers because you are standing next to an old soldier. Their father was also in the military for six months, and he is happy the war has ended. We are too.

I still cannot return to see you because we have to make sure the Germans don't start another war and kill more people. The Germans killed millions of other children's fathers during the war. That is why Uncle Sam was angry with the Germans and wanted to punish them.

You also came close to being without a father. I survived because God wishes that I return to see you and share my adventures. That is how good God is. Remember the two grown soldiers I once brought home named González? Well, on November 2 they killed Simón, the youngest, and the bravest soldier that ever fought against the Germans. Another buddy who slept alongside me had a splinter stuck in his neck like a needle. He had been sleeping next to me when a grenade exploded on our "dugout" and destroyed the parapet, or cover, that we had built. He wasn't seriously hurt, but got very scared. Another grenade took a sergeant's legs while he slept near our foxhole. I lost consciousness for a while underneath the dirt and garbage, but didn't even get a scratch.

I'll tell you more at a later time.

Luz

Tuesday, February 4

It was not very cold today. I wanted to get a haircut after breakfast but barely had time to bathe and make copies of past reports the officers requested.

I held Spanish and English classes in the afternoon for my fellow soldiers in a room at the YMCA. This arrangement is really good. I cannot explain why so many soldiers attended, but I had a good feeling about today's classes.

I will always remember the incidents that happen when we prepare our reports for intelligence. Our sergeant believes it is necessary to drink wine from the Moselle grape in order to write an "inspired" report. This is why he brings one or two bottles and adds much "spirit" to our work.

Wednesday, February

We woke up to a heavy snow, but it was not cold.

I received a letter from my godparent Manuel Pizaña, who asked for the whereabouts of his loved ones.

They did not pay us today like they had promised last night. The money will last us longer.

Our buddies Marks and Gersbach will have to leave for one week to Wehlen and Graach to carry out a special assignment. Two soldiers, one from the First Battalion and the other from the Second, will study with us for a week.

I had a good time with my comrades during the Spanish and English classes.

We were paid after supper.

The new lieutenant spent the whole day in the office. He is young and slow with the office work, although he also shows that he is somewhat educated. He makes a big show about being from New York. I will try to figure out how he can be useful.

I found out during my German class that the young man with whom I exchange classes will leave on Monday to resume his university studies. I will have to suspend my study of German because of this.

It is nine in the evening and I just returned from my German class. Snow has blanketed the entire area.

My coworkers are very happy. This makes me glad.

Thursday, February 6

Last night's snowfall was heavier than on previous occasions. Everything was white in the morning. The soldiers and civilians had playful snowball battles. It was all good-natured fun to pass the time.

I did not come out of my room until it was time to attend class.

The soldiers who are replacing our friends have arrived. I do not know their names, but they seem like good people.

I went to my German class for the last time. I will try to learn all I can. The day ended peacefully and under snow. The warmth of my room drew me to my bed.

Friday, February 7

The days are passing fast. The cold continues and my friends are still excited. My coworkers received numerous letters from home.

The cold has frozen the moisture on the pavement and covered everything with ice. I had a great time with my students in class. We received good news from our friends at Wehlen and Graach.

Our ideals are fading. Jealousy and envy are now evident among the Allies, like in the times of Richard the Lionheart. The criticism against the French people intensifies and the egoism among the Allies has become ugly.

We prepared an interesting report.

Saturday, February 8

This has been the coldest morning I have felt in Europe. The wet earth has turned into ice that is several feet deep. The wind seems to cut through you.

I have orders that exempt me from formations and marches. The order states:

> General Headquarters, 360th Infantry
> American Expeditionary Forces
> January 20, 1919
> Special Order No. 19
> 3. The following will be assuming special assignments as assistants in the official public schools. They are exempt from any assignment or detail that might keep them from carrying out their obligations.
> Clen. C. Thompson, Col. 1
> Wm. F. Blocher, Co. 1
> J. Luz Sáenz, Hq. Co.
> By order of Colonel Pierce
> Arthur Bowen
> Captain of the 360th Infantry

It is nine in the morning and I still feel the cold as I sit by the fire. I cannot help but feel sorry for my buddies who are passing in review along the street in front of me.

Lieutenant Boisseau reads lazily on a chair near the fire while I write and read. Sergeant Kelleher and I enjoy seeing our lieutenant sleep. The assignment and place suits him well for sleeping.

My dear brother Eugenio:

I want so much to know about you. Marce told me you left for Alice. José just told me that Marce went to see you and that worries me.

Brother, the only thing that is new in these parts is that the cold really favors us. A heavy snow fell on us about a week ago and it still has not melted. The weather continues to be very cold and the ground is quite hard and slippery. Even the river is about to freeze over. We had never seen this. Who in Texas would have thought that rivers freeze? The best protection for the Texans is the mountain range and the canyon. We would have been finished without them. I no longer suffer from the cold temperatures because I work in a well-built house. I pile on as many clothes as possible just to make sure. I still have not mastered this, but I will learn and become an expert.

I am really worried about newspaper reports of the dreadful influenza. What a life, huh? Those of us who came to face death have scared her away from the battlefields and she has turned on America. How many people who chose not to come with us must have fallen under her scythe and realized they cannot escape it. This is like the fellow who was running away from death while all along carrying her in a sack over his shoulder.

I suppose you have thought much about this because of your serious illness. But, who is afraid? We know that life is not a sure thing for anyone. Also, no one dies without a reason. Everything is a lie, only hunger is real.

I could write a lot. I found out that my students will have an inspection and will not be able to attend my class. The classroom at the YMCA is perfect for writing letters. I should tell you that I am the teacher for the Mexicans in Germany. Once the massacre ended, they gave me this other responsibility. They consider me a luminary, but they only pay me a Mexican wage. Others manage to get the high positions, honors, and cash. Someday I will tell you everything I have seen. This Indian can endure everything calmly and firmly, just treat him humanely. As far as honor, courage, and glory are concerned, I will be most gratified when they say that I brought honor to my position and not vice versa.

We will have to remain here a few days until peace can be assured. Some have said we show weakness when we become anxious about leaving for America, especially since we were nothing like this during the trying moments when we were attacking the enemy. Our situation is different, that is how we see things. We do not think it right to stay indefinitely or to be some kind of global peacekeepers.

As you can see, I have not said anything about why I am here while some of you have been ill and I am more needed there than here. Why do I do this? I want to be true to my duty as a good citizen and a worthy example to my children.

I never expected to receive my due when in battle, but now that the war has ended, we must receive justice.

I close with my love for all and may you be happy.

LUZ

I returned from my canceled class and found the lieutenant still asleep. A young German woman who came into the room to check her passport woke him up.

My students left for Bernkastel after inspection to watch a football game. The day ended with low temperatures. I translated some French.

I had a long conversation with the owners of the house, and when I was retiring for the night they gave me a warm cup of milk, which brings on a sleep that is fit for a king.

The private who sleeps in my room is a good person with a serious disposition.

The game was very entertaining and well attended. The division's squadron won.

The local priest uses his sermons to advise the young women to stay away from American soldiers. We know that some organizations of young men cut the braids of German women who are seen with the soldiers. There may be some reason for this form of patriotic jealousy, but if the situation is seen from the other side, the American soldiers lose more than the German women. Military regulations forbid our soldiers from socializing in the streets with the German women. On the other hand, they are allowed to enjoy all kinds of relations in their homes. One of the penalties the soldiers face is an extended stay in Germany—from six months to one year—beyond the point when the soldier's military unit (the division) has left for America. This is the worse punishment for soldiers who cannot wait to leave for home.

Every soldier who marries here will leave some American woman hanging, and one should expect "domestic wars" in the homes they establish in America. The lack of men here is expected to adversely affect women, and marrying them would open the doors for the same problems at home. We should expect some difficulties as a consequence of the war. We still have to face big, important battles.

The major abuses German soldiers committed when they were victorious are well known. Germans have begun to face the consequences of their actions. How must the Belgians, French, and Russians feel about them?

Sunday, February 9

It is as cold as ever and the Moselle has frozen over. We have witnessed something that we have never seen or will ever see again. Large chunks of ice have been floating in the rough waters for three days and nights, and they make an odd crashing noise. The river is almost twice as big in size and volume of water as the Rio Grande of Texas. We no longer hear the noise in the early hours of the day. The Moselle was solid ice.

Our officers had a big reunion and I attended mass.

The afternoon is cold like never before.

My buddies drink their worries away by the fire with the white water of the Moselle. They even brought champagne today, and sang, laughed, and talked a great deal. I also wanted to taste that famous wine, but it seems like all the others, except that it is more expensive. The reader must know that we are not the only ones drinking in Germany. Thousands of men are doing the same at this moment. It might not be wise to write this and put my name to it, but I do it as a sense of duty. Soldiers mimic each other with vices and other irresponsible behavior. This does not happen with the part of our lives that requires reflection, sacrifice, and constancy.

Monday, February 10

The terrible cold continues, but we seem to be adjusting. The big pieces of ice continue to pass by with their dull and oddly thunderous sound. Many of them are thick and jutting out of the water.

A sergeant who complained about us failed to convince his superiors.

They are very strict with anyone who does not appear in formation. Those stones cannot reach me anymore.

A musician was so drunk he fell in the latrine. He made a great spectacle because our colonel was passing by at the time and saw him. Imagine the scene, a man swimming in the human waste in front of his superior.

My cup was stolen at supper when I left the table to get something I needed.

The lieutenants were not in the office. Kelleher and I had a good time relaxing.

My students did not attend the class because of an inspection. Medina spoke to me about his life and the images of German and Mexican women he is drawing.

We heard rumors that a soldier killed someone at Trier. If true, this is the first such recorded case in our great army, which is made up of all kinds of men, races, and social classes. I believe the dead soldier was with the Supply Company.

I saw the order that offers schooling to anyone with the necessary preparation in London, England, and I filled out the form for a second time, simply to say that I did it. Favoritism is at play; it is nothing more than a farce common to the military. Its unfairness, nevertheless, encourages me to fight for what is just without expecting anything from the government. My wish and hope to study law and medicine are awakened again. Be it as it may, I applied again.

The following is my application to attend a college or university, which failed to receive the consideration it deserved.

General Headquarters, 360th Infantry, 90th Division
Force of Occupation in Germany
February 11, 1919
From: J. Luz Sáenz, Infantryman
To: A. C. of S. G-5, G. H. Q.
Subject: Application to attend a university.

1. Studies: Graduated from high school in 1908; completed instruction in accounting and stenography in a business school. I speak, read, and write English and Spanish. I have some understanding of the French language.

2. Profession. Teacher in the public schools of Texas during the last eight years before the war. Secretary of the Department of the 360th Infantry Regiment since last August.

3. I prefer to attend a French university.

4. Science and Humanities

5. I wish to return to my division in case it departs before I finish.

Tuesday, February 11

A very cold wind is blowing.

Someone stole a pistol from Kelleher's room. He found it in the possession of a German who was jealous and vowed to kill a woman and some soldiers.

I am studying algebra because of my love of mathematics.

We spoke about the opportunity to study while doing our report. I am hopeful and at times even believe in the possibility, but mostly doubt it.

The matter of the person who stole the gun was clarified. He was a German who wanted to commit suicide. We found him hiding in a room by the kitchen, where we eat. Walter, a young German not older than thirteen and who is the owner of the building, was hiding and feeding him. Everything was settled satisfactorily, even for the woman and soldiers who were involved. The German was left with his jealousy because the woman liked the soldiers better than she liked him.

Wednesday, February 12

More ice passes by on the Moselle every day, and it seems less navigable.

An invalid German is making baskets with reeds from the willow by the river. He does good work and makes from four to five big baskets a day. A skill or trade is necessary in this life.

Our buddies, including the ones we have sent to other battalions and the ones who are receiving instruction from us, are eager in their work as Public Information Workers.

Barrera did his detective work and told me how to find my cup. I took it away from the fellow. We did not have to fight because the cup has my name.

I see a need to teach our own. They need me and I am also glad that some of them manage to learn everything I teach them. It would be wonderful if they continued with their learning in America. I am studying more algebra.

I received a letter from Mr. Knox and I answered my good friend.

Zeltingen, Germany
February 12, 1919

My beloved:
We have just set up at Zeltingen, by the Moselle, Germany. My unit is the same, Hq. Co., 360th Infantry Div. I am doing very well.

Luz

Thursday, February 13

It was less cold today. The sun came out, although the day was not very clear because of a thick fog over the river.

I sent some newspapers home.

The young man who stole Kelleher's pistol was tried today. He was sentenced to three months of work in the public roads program. A wealthy wine merchant from Graach was fined and sent to work for three months on the roads. He offered to pay 12,000 marks, but this was not allowed. A government truck killed a woman in Bernkastel-Graach.

We prepared our report without a problem. I retired to my room because of a headache, but before falling asleep, I contemplated my life and thought of some good plans for the future, all the while knowing they will probably turn into smoke, ashes, and sadness. Nevertheless, that is my life.

Friday, February 14

The weather was better this morning. The floating chunks of ice that had been blocking the river and forming a solid mass are moving. The local residents say that despite the river's strong current, the waters have previously frozen over, allowing the passage of small artillery pieces and soldiers.

An important football game will be played in Wittlich. We decided not to go because we are not interested in sports while we are chained down by the strict rules of the military. We are free men and resent any form of oppression.

I bathed and went to class. At three in the afternoon, Kelleher and I crossed the river again to see the Germans skate on the lake.

We prepared our report and were left with time to think and worry over our situation. I thought about what awaits me at home once I am relieved of duty.

Saturday, February 15

The day began with rain and very cold temperatures. The ground was slippery because the ice has not melted.

We lost the football game against Division 89.

Funny incidents happen in our chow line, the formation that no one wants to miss. We witness fights, jokes, conversations of all kinds, and no few harsh words, and even profanity.

Mayor Allen issued strict orders to keep everything clean.

I received a letter from Robert Hoey.

Lieutenant Boisseau has been kind to me.

Someone died in an accident with a truck during the game at Wittlich.

Sunday, February 16

The morning was warmer and we attended the seven o'clock mass. After preparing our weekly report, we informed our friends from Graach and Wehlen that they should return tomorrow. We missed supper because we arrived late.

I wrote family members and friends the entire afternoon.

The festivities of the 143rd Infantry were great; we enjoyed good music.

The day passed peacefully, the mass was very well attended.

> Alice, Texas, February 15, 1919
> Priv. J. Luz Sáenz

My dear brother:

My wish is that you are always well.

Brother, there is a lot happening here, but nothing is new. We have many dances, but as you know, I am not a dancer nor do I plan to be one. We had the pleasure of crossing bats with San Diego for a second time last Sunday. We won in their home turf with a score of 32 to 9. It wasn't much of a game, as you can see. We will most probably have to play Falfurrias next Sunday. I'll let you know how we do.

This shouldn't have been the letter where I would have to tell you of the passing of our beloved brother, but you ask me to tell you everything.[5]

We were asleep at home when Gilberto arrived to tell us that our father was calling to tell us that my brother was very sick. Crispín and I went and from then on no one slept, but my brother got better during the day, or least that is what we thought. Father came home, I left for work, and Crispín stayed with him. Crispín says he saw him doing so well he didn't think anything about returning home. My sister Clara says she saw him bend over as if he was going to get up to put his shoes on and then he laid back on his pillow and that is how he remained, serene forever.

In the last letter Crispín writes from San Antonio, he tells me that he is well. Mother has been sick for some time and cannot get well.

I hope that you return soon. We will be happy to see you.
Your brother,

Jose

Sergeant Kelleher writes to his family telling them to make use of the opportunity to ask for their loved ones to be released from military service, that it is necessary that they do this. He suggests I do the same, but I am not thinking that way. I will wait.

Monday, February 17

It was raining in the morning and I had a slight headache. I can say I was lucky my illness was not severe and that it did not put me in bed.

During the class at the YMCA, I felt a strong pain in my heart that worried me a great deal, but like my headache, it did not last long. The doctors have told me that the pains in my head and heart have the same cause.

This day ended without fanfare; it was pleasant.

Tuesday, February 18

This day began hotter than usual. Lieutenant Boisseau and I had a heated discussion over Mexico and its people. He knows nothing about Mexico and little about the United States. Sergeant Kelleher and I quickly showed him up.

My fellow Mexicans are more diligent and this pleases me.

I went to the theater in the evening, but I did not think much of the performance.

The river continues to rise as a result of the rain that is falling everywhere.

I continue to study algebra, German, and French.

Wednesday, February 19

The morning was beautiful. I feel anxious because I have not received a letter from home.

Sergeant Kelleher and I had a long conversation about the history of Mexico.

My superiors gave me beautiful books to hand out to my friends in class. I selected a lovely book on universal geography and another one on mathematics.

A *New York Herald* correspondent commits some serious errors when he writes about Mexico and France. He tells us that Carlota, the mentally unstable empress, still lives in Belgium and describes Juárez as a murderer simply because he ordered the execution of a royal despot and usurper who went to Mexico hoping to enslave our people. This is a lesson the Kaiser and José of Austria should not forget.[6] I regret that I was unable to visit the castle of "Mamá Carlota."

The Moselle is rising and threatening.

Thursday, February 20

The day began peacefully. I received letters from home and Roberto and responded immediately. I sent Roberto a book. I also received the following letter from Mr. Knox.

> San Antonio
> January 20, 1919
>
> My friend, Mr. Sáenz:
> I have received several letters from you and have responded promptly. The last one was dated December 13. I'm glad to hear you are well and enjoying "Germany's scenery" under "very pleasant conditions."
> I have visited your sister, wife, and children now and then. Your brother who was sick asked for me one day. He left to live with his father. He has been very sick.
> San Antonio continues to be in a very cheerful mood with the many soldiers who are here. Some have been discharged while many injured soldiers have returned with their "chevrones" on their uniforms that indicate they were wounded and that they served overseas.[7] Every one of them is very happy to have returned to the United States.
> I suppose that you will have much to tell us when you return. We are more than glad for the part you have played.
> Yours Sincerely, Your Servant
>
> W. J. Knox

We did not go to the theater because we were waiting for orders from Lieutenant Klebold for the maneuvers that are scheduled for tomorrow.

Friday, February 21

The morning brought rain as we prepared for a military operation. We rode in a Ford and crossed the Moselle on a ferry. It was cold, especially after we left the river and climbed the mountains. Many piles of ice are still by the sides of the road. I did not take my overcoat but I did have my raincoat. Luckily we did not have to go to the open fields and risk contracting pneumonia or a cold.

We placed our command post in a home owned by "Carl." Sergeant Kelleher once again drank the Moselle "water" and practically rolled over drunk. We prepared a good report and returned in good spirits to our camp. The YMCA had a celebration in the evening that was not very enjoyable. I did not sleep well.

Saturday, February 22, Washington's Birthday

This is a great day for the American nation. It brings back memories of happy days. I have a slight headache, a trace of yesterday's chills. It has rained much today and I sat down to write letters to Roberto and José.

My headache continued until I could not stand it anymore and I went up to my room to rest. I stayed in from eight in the morning until four in the afternoon, at which time I prepared the report. I felt better later.

The soldiers play, drink, and wander through the streets.

> Zeltingen, Germany
> February 22, 1919
>
> My dear wife:
> I just received a letter from José telling me that all of you are doing well in Alice and that Marce returned to San Antonio on January 29, but he does not tell me anything about you, and it has been some time since I have received word. I'm all right for now. I had a migraine headache this morning but it went away by this afternoon. I just felt disoriented. We marched about twelve miles yesterday. It was cold and rainy and we were marching fast, need I say more? All of you know I am a sensitive person and today I had a migraine headache. I was dying at eight in the morning but look at me now—I am like the muleteer's donkey, ready for the journey. I had not had problems with my head for months and I was beginning to think I was free of the headaches.

I do not have much to say. Tell me, how have all of you been? Do you receive your payments on time? What arrangements have you made with the owner of the house? What have you done with the youngsters? Mr. Knox wrote last month and told me some things about all of you.

I'll stop writing so I can prepare my report.

I close with my love for all of you.

LUZ

Sunday, February 23

I felt better today and went to mass. The Moselle River continues to rise. Captain Bowen refused to sign off on some passes for us. We wanted to go to Koblenz. Lieutenant Klebold has returned and will soon find out all we have done for him. I censor all his correspondence. We oversee the athletic department and intelligence and assume other responsibilities in this office.

Kelleher and I went to Lösnich. We left on foot at 2:30 and visited a small but very wealthy church in Rachtig. Our old friends at Lösnich received us very well. Kelleher spent a good amount of time drinking with Speece at the YMCA. The "Fräuleins," the German tavern workers, served them liquor. I talked to Rivera (Puerto Rican), Pacheco, Jesse Pérez, Neri Pérez, and Pablo Pérez. We did not want to walk back so we risked the trip by train. We have orders not to ride on the trains, but we disobeyed and they did not even charge us. We shared memories about our lives in America during the short ride.

While at Lösnich, I visited Jesse and he told me much about San Antonio. I visited the Schwab family, but Peter and Stephen were not in.

After returning to our office and writing our report, Ms. Kapps gave me sweet cow milk and offered my buddy some "Schnapps." We retired after enjoying such a humble delight.

Monday, February 24

The dawn was beautiful. The mornings seem like spring with the warm and joyful feeling they provide. I woke up feeling better with only a rough voice and a buzz in my head.

My buddies were working seriously in my class. Some of them are moving along rapidly. I am glad, although I think they can do better.

Today we thought we had lost our buddy and good friend Lieutenant Klebold. We received an order that he would have to go elsewhere and that a captain named Thomas would take his place. All of us, including Lieutenant

Klebold, felt bad about this. He has been a good person. We do everything for him so that he can flatter, please, and keep the colonel content, and keep us from the difficult marches and other activities. We do all the work and he gathers the profits. Everyone says he will be promoted to captain. We will make him general if he continues to be generous and good-natured with us.

Tuesday, February 25

I completed a year of military service today. What an experience!

I woke up feeling a bit under the weather, but never gave up. We turned in our hats and "jerkins" (a type of shirt without sleeves made of leather and canvas). I met with my class, which continues to do very well, and bought pastries at the YMCA. The chaplain started a class on history and another on civics. We found out that they were not going to cancel reveille. A sergeant directed a very sarcastic remark at us. Wretched thing! He shows how small he is! The planned entertainment was canceled and we had to retire to our nests early.

Wednesday, February 26

I still sounded hoarse today. We did not have reveille and had a good early breakfast. I had little to do, so I studied algebra, German, geography, and French. Nothing unusual occurred in my class.

Kelleher and Gersbach were drunk in the evening when we were preparing the report and they had to go to my room to rest. Their antics gave us plenty to laugh about. Lieutenant Klebold found a sergeant and me working on the report. He asked for Kelleher and we told him he had retired because he was not feeling well. Kelleher slept with us on blankets placed on the floor. I do not know what sorrows he wishes to drown with his heavy drinking or if he does it for pleasure.

Friday, January 28

The mornings continue to be beautiful and peaceful. We had inspection and I later studied my lessons and prepared materials for my class. I plan to write Mr. Knox and my sister. I received another letter from my brother José. I read and studied at the YMCA and had beautiful thoughts about the future of Mexican Americans in Texas.

I continue to feel sick. I think about seeing the doctor and I change my mind. I will wait some more.

I read a fine editorial on the future of the world's nations in the *Saturday Evening Post*.

Headquarters
American Expeditionary Forces
France, February 28, 1919
Order of the Day:
No. 38-1

My Fellow Soldiers:

Now that your service with the American Expeditionary Forces is about to end, I cannot let you go without a personal word. At the call to arms, the patriotic young manhood of America responded enthusiastically and became the formidable army whose decisive victories testify to its effectiveness and bravery. With the support of a nation firmly united to defend the cause of liberty, our army has executed the will of the people with resolute purpose. Our democracy has been tested, and the forces of autocracy have been defeated. To the glory of the citizen-soldiers, our troops have faithfully fulfilled their trust, and in a succession of brilliant offensives have overcome the menace to our civilization.

As an individual, your part in the world war has been important in our entire achievements. Whether keeping lonely vigil in the trenches, or gallantly storming the enemy's stronghold, whether enduring monotonous drudgery at the rear, or sustaining the fighting line at the front, every one of you has bravely and effectively played his part. With your willing sacrifice of individual circumstances, with your strength and indomitable will made effective by thorough organization and cordial cooperation, you inspired the exhausted Allies with new life and turned the tide of possible defeat into overwhelming victory.

You have served your country loyally with a consecrated devotion to duty and a will to conquer. By your exemplary conduct a standard has been established and maintained never before attained by any army. With mind and body as clean and strong as the decisive blows you delivered against our foe, you will soon return to the pursuit of peace. As you leave the victorious battlefields, I wish that you take to your homes your high ideals and continue to live as you have served—in honor of the principles for which you have fought and of the fallen comrades you leave behind.

With the greatest pride in our success, I congratulate you and extend to you my sincere appreciation for your heroic service to the army and to the entire nation.

Faithfully,

JOHN J. PERSHING,
Commander in Chief
Official: ROBERT C. DAVIS,
Adjutant General
Copy furnished to the soldier J. Luz Sáenz
ANDREW J. CARR.
Captain, 360th Infantry

Saturday, March 1

This is a beautiful day. We had a change in the weather for an hour. The colonel and other officers took in the sights at Trier. The Germans are celebrating lent. We, the Mexican Americans, agreed to have a Mexican-style gathering with as many of our own as we can bring together. We are working hard to do this. On my initiative, we have agreed on a program and a fee to participate in the celebration, with the understanding that our guests will not have to pay anything. This will take place tomorrow evening.

Sunday, March 2

I attended mass and, upon my return, sent two buddies to Graach and Wehlen to invite our Mexican friends and brothers. I sent Medina to Lösnich to invite Jesse and all the others he could find. Everything was ready early in the day. The festivities will take place at the home of the Portuguese woman. I plan to make a list of the names and addresses of all the participants and write a report for publication in America.

Monday, March 3

Last night brought us great pleasure. More than fifty Mexicans came together as planned, and we reminisced and thought of the land of our birth and our loved ones. Several companies from our regiment were represented. We had wine, chocolate, bread, card games, music, and song. Everything was well ordered, to our credit. The Germans also enjoyed the festive event. We entertained and discussed beautiful plans for the good future we desire. I seek the well-being of our people and am glad to see such noble and intelligent

people among us. God bless them for the good of our people. I wrote this
letter for *La Prensa*.[8]

A Celebration by the Texas-Mexican Soldiers in Germany
A Communiqué to *La Prensa* by One of the Soldiers
Zeltingen a-d Moselle, Germany, March 3, 1919.—

Ever since we arrived in Europe, I have tried to maintain contact
with fellow Texan-Mexicans who serve in the 90th Texas Division. I
was able to meet most of them during our training in France. Since
then we have spoken to each other in confidence about the effort
we would have to make to remain true to the martial spirit of our
people. They all assured me they would be loyal in carrying out their
assigned responsibilities. Their heroic sacrifice speaks louder and
clearer than the promises they made.

The Texan-Mexicans participated and continue to do this in all
the branches of the service. Our young people enlisted in all of them.
I have always sought to record the views and actions of our soldiers
while they were falling or being taken out of action. I believe these
observations will now help relieve the pain among the families whose
sons are not returning because they remain in the European fields of
honor.

Last night, the Mexican-Texans who survived the terrible catas-
trophe had a lively social gathering in the form of an open public
program. I attach a complete list of my comrades in arms who attended. They were all members of the 360th Infantry Regiment. We
each made the event our own, while our short improvised program
unfolded in a joyful setting. At the same time, thousands of plans
took shape as we spoke of our return. I made a brief presentation to
my compatriots during the festivities that I also attach to this report.

This is our first gathering. I will continue to use *La Prensa* to
inform our community—for which we have fought in Europe. We
must not forget that we are in a hostile country and that a short distance separates us from the enemy that we forced to retreat to his last
barricade. J. Luz Sáenz.—Hq. Co., 360th Inf., 90 Div., A. E. F.

My presentation follows:

To the Mexican-Texans of The 360th Infantry Regiment
Fellow Soldiers:
I am not exaggerating when I say that this great occasion has

given me a joy like no other since we arrived in the old world. This feeling is greater than the day we first saw the mainland of the Eastern Hemisphere, even though our arrival was already announcing the end of an uncertain voyage, a very dangerous passage, a daring shortcut the terrible German submarines would have wanted to prevent, but failed to do.

This is not to say we did not enjoy good days. Consider those amazing days of victory in September, on the Saint-Mihiel salient where our division received its baptism of blood. Reflect on the subsequent days of our great advance and complete victory in the glorious sector of Verdun, in the Argonne woods, and along the Moselle River where each one of our soldiers basked in glory. Joy overwhelmed our hearts the day the enemy asked for a truce and the jubilation rose within our souls the morning of November 11 when we heard that the armistice had been signed.

All of you know we were ready to attack again on the morning when we received the order to cease all operations. With that said, the joy in my soul is even greater. None of that equals what we can sense now. The tempest has not only ended, it will not return. The rainbow of hope is clear and beautiful as we are about to return to our homeland to see our loved ones who are eagerly waiting with outstretched arms to pour out their sweet and sincere love.

This may explain why our feelings as the descendants of a noble race in the battle-hardened 360th Infantry Regiment run deep today. Our hearts should also be filled with the righteous satisfaction of consciously meeting our responsibility, of completing our assignment during the great global struggle. Our brothers who remained on the other side of the Atlantic expected much from us, and I am sure we have not let them down. They are eager to hear what we have done while defending our flag and our good name. Nothing fills us with more pride than the heroic conduct of our brothers during the supreme hour when the war tested the will of the races from around the world.

Mexicans have once again demonstrated their stoicism and their disregard for their own lives as they fulfilled their duty to country and maintained high the good name of our people.

I could not overlook these important issues that give us the pleasure we deserve to have tonight. Let us now talk about the reason for this gathering and what is before us. In the first place, we should thank the fine lady who made our meeting possible. She is Elisa

Norder, a woman of German Portuguese extraction who is largely responsible for the happiness we are enjoying. Thanks to her boundless kindness and extensive knowledge of the Latin races of America we are able to gather tonight and receive her affection as well as the esteem she has generously extended to us and our *raza*.

This is also a day of celebration in Germany that no one race can claim. It is a festive occasion without political, civilian, or military intent. The Germans as well as our people in America observe it. The *Carnaval* has a long tradition among us, and although we cannot enjoy it fully at home, we can at least recall the sweet memories from a distance and take pleasure in them. The Germans have been preparing for the traditional celebration of Shrovetide.

Since the major reason for tonight's celebration is to recall our past, including longings and distant loves, we must remember our aging mothers and our beloved and kind wives, the cause of our sleepless nights and objects of our precious dreams. Such sweet memories will no doubt turn into a deep sigh that the breeze of this valley will take to the other side of the ocean as intimate thoughts and settle like a mist over the sad bedrooms of our homes. Let us raise our glasses with this rich Moselle wine to the good health of the people who love us and wait for us in a free America. I have spoken.

List Of The Mexican-Texans Who Are Members Of The 360th Infantry Regiment Of The 90th Division

1st and 2nd Battalions—Genaro Castañeda, Mercedes; Jorge Cavazos, Harlingen, Ramón González, San Benito; Pedro Vidal, San Antonio; Juan Benítez, Corpus Christi; Juan Salinas, Edinburg; Juan Rodríguez, Uvalde; Fortino Treviño, Alice; Victor González, Port O'Connor; Agustín Sáenz, San Antonio; Ricardo Vallejo, Harlingen; Clemente Espinosa, Asherton; Apolinar Gámez, San Antonio; Luis de León, Del Rio; Santiago Ortiz, San Antonio; Filomeno González, Martindale.

3rd Battalion, Company I—Pedro Rocha, Laredo; Prisciliano Medina, Canutillo; Pablo Buitrón, Laredo.

Company K—Agapito Salinas, Alice; Ernesto Martínez, Point Isabel; Amado Anguiano, Victoria; Francisco Hernández, Spofford.

Company L—Teodoro Aguilar, Seguín; Samuel Ramírez, Houston; José Gómez, San Marcos.

Company M—Feliciano Carter, Eagle Pass; Manuel Cantú, Woodsboro; Andrés Rosales, Eagle Pass; Casimiro Vázquez, El Paso; Fidel

Velázquez, Oakville; Domingo Garza, Cuero; Hipólito Jasso, Jesús Moreno, Petters; Jacinto Garcia, Floresville; Juan Monjarés, Fort Davis.

Supply Company—Trinidad Rodríguez, Rio Grande City; José Leal, Seguín; Gregorio Tamayo, San Benito; Eligio Martínez, Point Isabel; Florentino Aguilar, Point Isabel.

Machine Gun Company—Jesús Pérez, San Antonio; Fidel A. Gleim, Shafter.

Mortar Company—Felipe Neri, San Antonio.

Regiment Assistants—Eduardo B. Barrera, San Diego; Eulogio Gómez, Bracketville.

Military Band—Vicente de la Rosa, Austin; Amado Cásares, Seguín.

Sappers—Domingo Pacheco, San Antonio; Juan Martínez, San Antonio.

R. I. O.—J. Luz Sáenz, San Antonio.

Tuesday, March 4

I woke up with a stomach ache, but it went away as the day progressed. I appreciate the lady of the house for the remedy she gave me. My buddies also treated me well. We are more understanding and considerate as we get to know each other better.

I felt better and went for a walk in the early afternoon and joined a celebration after I completed my report. It is two in the morning and I am still in a good mood after the show we saw. The five American performers sang and played beautifully. The organizers served chocolate and hosted a dance after the performance. My friends and I enjoyed a short conversation.

Wednesday, March 5 (Ash Wednesday)

The mornings feel like spring. Since it was Ash Wednesday, I thought about my many friends who came to rest as part of this continent's dust. I went to mass.

It has rained a great deal and the Intelligence Office has been unable to take a photograph. We want a memento of the entire office staff. I will also try to take a photograph with my class.

The 358th Infantry put together a pitiful program.

Pacheco did a terrible thing in beating up a poor buddy who was behaving badly.

We turned in the typewriter and will now have to do our work by hand.

Thursday, March 6

We had another beautiful day. During breakfast, I saw some friends who are very happy with the course of events. It is time to make some observations on our historic contribution to the war. A German lady came in to process her passport. She had a short conversation with a sergeant who acted as her interpreter and asked him about my racial background. The sergeant told her in a sarcastic and flirting way that I was an Indian. His form of expression revealed the racial hatred his people show us in Texas. This fellow forgets that the Indian overlooks everything except the people who treat him well and the ones who insult him.

Friday, March 7

We had a new situation today. A young German woman came from Berlin claiming to be visiting her relatives in the area. One of our officers suspected her of spying and subjected her to a trying and thorough interrogation. We have used some of the information secured from her. This added variety to our work and made it more interesting.

I received letters from Moore and Devine and traded in my overcoat for a new one. I had worn a long one since I was in America. When we arrived here, everyone had to exchange them except me. I liked mine very much because it kept me warm. Someone took it during the night of the festivities and left me a very short and dirty one, which I have now exchanged. I was also issued a new chapeau, or hat, and a new raincoat and the letters *T* and *O*.

We talked at length about our losses in the Great War and noticed a difference between US newspaper reports and what we have seen and are seeing. They almost always exaggerate things. The French, German, and English are the same, and I suppose everyone else is too. It would have been best to place all those people who are writing and know nothing of the meaning of the war on the front.

Saturday, March 8

I wrote letters after breakfast. Yesterday, I sent out four copies of the account I wrote about the gathering of March 2.

Today was a beautiful day, and I have no idea what is ahead of us. The noncommissioned officers had an inspection yesterday, and the officers will have one today.

The young German woman from Berlin visited us and left us with much useful information.

We took a photograph of our staff in the R.I.O. today.

Sunday, March 9

What a beautiful morning! Everything is beginning to take on a new appearance after the rainy and cold days of the past. I attended mass, and after breakfast we prepared the weekly report, which was very long and interesting.

> Zeltingen, Germany
> March 9, 1919
>
> Adán and Samuel:
> I hope this finds you well. I am writing both of you, but ask your mother to answer my letters. I expect to be with you by the time school starts.
>
> Marce:
> I have not received a letter from you since October. Say hello to Crispín.
> I'm sending you this proof of a photograph that I took yesterday. It's not good but it gives all of you a sense of your brother's appearance in Germany.
> Your brother,
>
> Luz

My students and I have long conversations after class about what we witnessed at the battlefields and the conduct of our fellow Mexicans. They told me how and where Pedro Rocha, Hipólito Jasso, and others were wounded. We took a photograph of everyone who attended class and got together at night in Norder's home. We sang, drank, and talked while playing cards.

Monday, March 10

The morning was extraordinarily beautiful, but everything seems to be changing. The *Chicago Tribune* published a protest by A.E.F. soldiers in France that appeared in *The Herald* of New York on February 19. It carried an opinion on President Wilson.

The issue of *El Latino-Americano* I received includes part of a letter I sent last November. It also announces the death of my good friend Guadalupe Flores. My hope is that he rests in peace.

The protest made by Roy E. Nelson, the unstable person in the Medical Corps, is one of the most popular issues of the day. He was a conscientious objector and predicted the end of the war on several occasions. He decided to no longer wear a uniform a few days ago. They put him in jail and he took off all the buttons from his uniform. We wait for the end to this case with great anticipation. The crazy man deserves justice.

I enjoy the epigrams that appear in *El Latino-Americano*.

Sergeant Kelleher wrote a beautiful article on the death of Sergeant Irwin at Saint-Mihiel.

Tuesday, March 11

This is a beautiful day. I took a bath and then made entries in my diary. Last night I had a terrible dream and then a sweet, pleasant one. Our frailties even haunt us in our dreams. I continue studying algebra.

A program at the YMCA noted that Mexican soldiers from Graach would sing this night. I immediately invited the rest of the group and we agreed to go see, hear, and encourage them.

I received a letter from home. We had a nice evening walk in Graach.

> Alice, Texas
> March 11, 1919
>
> Soldier J. Luz Sáenz
> My unforgettable and beloved brother:
> I write with the same pleasure as always and wish you are well, just as we are here. Thank God almighty.
> Brother, as always nothing is happening in these parts. Regarding the "European War," I don't have to tell you anything since you have been one of the actors in it. Isn't this so?
> Many soldiers who crossed the "so-called puddle" have been returning. They come back happy and satisfied for having served. Manuel Flores is among them. He says he did not participate in any battles, so he doesn't have much to say. In any case, he brings us some news. How much more will we hear from the soldiers who really fought with the enemy?
> Pedro Flores has also returned. He too says he did not do more than reach the water's edge. Sixto Flores did not come back. As you know, he died with the sinking of the *Tuscania*. Florencio Heras and Guadalupe Garza, from Alice, also fell there. They sleep in peace and glad for having assisted in such a grand cause. We are especially sad that some men left for Mexico to avoid military service. They are beginning to come back to pay their sentence.

I'll back up to tell you that a grand celebration is about to take place to honor of the returning servicemen. We had another commemoration after the sinking of the *Tuscania* in honor of the fallen heroes of the nation.

Many people have died from the Spanish influenza. We suffered from it, but thanks to God we are now well. Mother is the only one who is still feeling bad. Crispín was also sick, but he is doing well now. You probably know that my brother Crispín is now in San Antonio with our sister Marcelina. Did you know this?

Clotilde and Juanita have been writing me from Moore and they tell me that they too have been hearing from you.

Brother, this typewriter is in bad condition. That is why I am making so many mistakes. It may also be my fault. Today, I ordered a new one, an Oliver. I will pay it in installments. This means that when you return you can use it to your heart's desire

All right now, why don't you ever tell us anything about the young women from over there? Are they good looking, beautiful, or ugly? We'd like to know, although we understand we may never visit unless we have another war soon.

Our thoughts are with you. With the love of always, from your brother who wishes you happiness.

G. José Saenz

Wednesday, March 12

We went to Graach last night and had a good time with friends. We walked under a lovely moon and warm breeze. Our boys sang, but not as well as in other times. A sergeant and a corporal participated in a boxing tournament and the corporal won. I also found a Greco-Roman wrestling match interesting.

We returned after ten, it was a beautiful walk.

I began to draw a postcard with the different insignias of our division. I answered some letters and studied. We hear that Lieutenant Klebold and Colonel Price will be promoted, but nothing is said about the members of the Intelligence Office. We might be promoted during the next war. We must hope.

Thursday, March 13

Flam is a young man who has worked as a page for the colonel and has learned to make the best of it. Householder is another good person who does not draw attention to himself and seems satisfied with things as they are. Flam slept at the guard post for getting drunk. Others met the same fate for breaking house windows. The chicken coop is beginning to show some excitement.

I am very tired and need to rest in order to study and continue with my class.

We have learned much from the German people, above all, that that they are blindly given to a racial hatred against people from around the world.

They do not seem to belong to the twentieth century because of their backward state. I cannot understand how they dare to criticize the whole world. I could write a great deal on this subject, but at this moment I am mentally exhausted and will leave it for later.

Zeltingen, Germany
March 13, 1919
Mr. Gregorio Garza Martínez

My dear friend:

I am not surprised about what you don't know. You tell me in your short note that "we are told that all of you are having a good time with new ideas and that everything you see is worth recording, etc., etc." If things are worth recording, it's because we have had to pay for them. Don't fool yourself my friend. A great distance separates appearances from reality. I will tell you everything. You think that I benefit from my very misery. That is already granting me due credit. You know I have never given up over small things? I repeat, don't fool yourself. We haven't said everything because we can't. The law is the law. The vile law, the one imposed by man.

I don't doubt that you consider me a hero, but your goodwill can really blind you. I appreciate your generosity. I have seen much injustice in the way we recognize real heroes, that I don't believe much in them, that is, in many we have idolized. I won't say heroes do not exist, I never would. I have seen many who have earned this honor, including many from our *raza*.

I now turn to your life. Don't be impatient my good young man, we have to suffer some to deserve. I don't doubt that you have had your share of misfortunes. Do you really believe I am in a bed of roses? Well I'm not. Don't be influenced so easily and with so little.

I hope we will soon see each other over there and if you wish, we could study the wide world a bit more. Expect my arrival, I will return like Plaza "laden with laurels to face the hard times."

Say hello to Mingo, to Mrs. Luz and her husband, to the young ladies González and García. I haven't forgotten anybody, I have thought of everyone when writing for *La Prensa*.

Wait for me. Your friend who cares for you will soon be with you.

LUZ

March 13, 1919

Father:

I'm enclosing a poor photograph of me in the field with my fellow workers. We had been eight, but as I told you on September 15, one of the soldiers died. Another one of French origin behaved badly and he is no longer with us.

We represent many races in the office, but all of us are Americans. This is really a bad mix. We do not get along, but hardship has produced some good moments that we will always remember. We have had many interesting experiences that I hope to share with you in detail.

Your son who cares for you,

LUZ

Friday, March 14

The day began cold, but the sun came out and everything took on a different look.

A boat that travels up and down the Moselle arrived yesterday afternoon to load up with wine from warehouses in the area. The men who load the large barrels are a sight to see. They are like beasts of burden carrying the barrels in small carts to the boat, the "Prince Heirrich."

I wrote to Mr. Velázquez and sent my photograph home. Gómez and Barrera worked in a horse exhibition at Bernkastel-Kues sponsored by our American division. They say it was beautiful. I did not feel like going and stayed in my room to write and read. Many of our compatriots who did not participate in combat were at the exhibition.

Saturday, March 15

The mornings have changed, they are now cold and warm up when the sun rises and adds life to everything. The beautiful change of seasons affects us in ways that cannot be understood. We have beautiful moonlit nights that make us long for our distant homeland and our families. I read works that describe Rome in splendid fashion and long to know it personally. I wish I could visit Rome even under these difficult circumstances. Others have visited the place under better conditions, but we have only seen it through different eyes and then formed our own opinion. My poor financial situation and my strong interest in visiting Paris keep me from visiting Rome and to fulfill the happy wish of a poor man. Night fell as I dreamed of so many things.

Sunday, March 16

I went to mass before my friends woke up. This allowed me to enjoy the views they denied themselves. Only the townspeople who attend church are on the streets at that hour. They see more and live more. The peace that envelops the little town is wonderful.

Last night, I went to the theater for a while and to a public performance by the 359th Infantry Regiment. Everything was good, especially the movie and its touch of comedy and truth. The movie treated the theme of money and its vices and of a protagonist who refused to sell herself. This was odd. Some of our own *raza* from the 359th singing group stayed with us. We enjoyed talking with them.

Monday, March 17

We gathered in a room and sang, drank, played cards, and enjoyed talking about the past and our sweet hope of soon returning to our loved ones.

When I returned to my lodging, the door was shut. The lady did not know that someone was missing. I slipped in through the office window and slept until the next day. What an experience.

This was St. Patrick's day, a time to remember the patriarch of the Irish. Bumberry and Kelleher celebrated the holiday the whole festive day. I could not accompany them because they were going on a drinking spree. Some of my buddies went with them. I visited my good friend Gómez who had been sick, but is now well.

Lieutenant Ayers, who has taken over the R.I.O. until Klebold returns, has been somewhat overbearing. I cannot continue with him and have already told him to let me do my work if it meets his expectations, otherwise, I would be willing to resign. Remember that as a teacher to my fellow Mexican soldiers I do not have to serve in intelligence. I do it because of my sense of fellowship. A fly in the ointment; it never fails.

Tuesday, March 18

The morning was beautiful. I can hear the sergeants and officers from my window giving orders to the soldiers. It has been so long since I have participated in this kind of training that I fear the day when we receive orders to do it again.

A great deal of baseball equipment arrived yesterday. This has been a great pastime since we were always fans in civilian life.

We received the good news that we will depart for America in May.

I finished drawing several postcards and passed them out among my friends. I made some for the lieutenant who requested them.

It grew cold by nightfall while snow fell on the mountains.

Wednesday, March 19

The cold weather continues. Things warmed up by midday, but then it got colder.

Today we were given a shot and at this point—eight in the evening—I do not feel well.

We watched a program by a group of "Indians" from Oklahoma last night. The performance included a well-educated "Indian" princess who graduated from a university in New York.[9] They presented typical scenes of the disappearing race and accurate depictions that tell us of their efforts to survive as the aboriginal *raza* of America. They also spoke of their struggles to survive in urban centers. Many of the Indians who are fighting for the nation are not treated like citizens, but they will demand it when they return. And what about those who died?

I drew several postcards for Colonel Price. They represent my modest ability.

I received and answered several letters, but none were from home.

Thursday, March 20

I woke up with a very sore arm, the same one that was inoculated. I did not feel like going to breakfast and stayed in bed the whole day. When Gómez visited me, I got up but then returned to bed. Snow fell most of the day, but it melted quickly.

I did not prepare a report nor did I attend class.

Friday, March 21

Thank God, I woke up feeling much better. I continue drawing postcards. An Anglo had the idea of making postcards with the images of an Indian and a Texas cowboy; he sells them for fifteen cents.

During breakfast, one of my buddies reminded me that I had promised to draw something to commemorate the Indian from Guelatao, the most important representative of our *raza* since the Spanish conquest.[10] I promised to do it. We gathered again early in the day and had a good time but not before we talked about Juárez. Some buddies drank wine, others sang. I spoke to them about Juárez, the model historical figure of our people.

We did not write a report until ten in the evening. I visited Gómez at his house.

I signed off on the payroll. Before saying good-bye, we agreed to get together the next day with the same idea in mind and to talk more about the life and work of Juárez.

Saturday, March 22

It was snowing at dawn. We were ordered to clean up because our regiment had to pass inspection by the commander of the division and possibly by General Pershing himself.

The inspection was solemn. Several officers from other parts and some French officers were present. Everything was acceptable to the visitors.

We gathered again as planned and celebrated. The festivities were lively and cheerful because of the friends who joined us.

Sunday, March 23

I went to mass and then returned to the office to read. I visited the YMCA and my friends in the afternoon. On one of these visits, I found out that a German woman had died of typhoid fever.

We were given several letters after dinner. One of them brings the sad news that my brother Eugenio has died and that my other brother Crispín is still sick. The death of my brother has affected me deeply. Little by little, we are losing loved ones who were with us in our youth and helped us during difficult moments. May your soul rest in peace, my brother! I will never see you again!

Monday, March 24

I got up with a slight headache and a chill. We heard a rumor of another more difficult and demanding inspection that will require our presence. I try to write, but I cannot do it. I will in the afternoon or whenever possible.

We had the review despite the cold, snow, bad weather, and rain. The poor soldiers were dying of cold on top of the hill while waiting for the officers. They had to present themselves very early. We were assembled and ready for the inspection by six in the morning. The soldiers put up with the load they were carrying and the cold, but as is the custom, the officers arrived in town around ten and after a few toasts and good conversations by the fire, told the troops, "This is fine, let's go." That was it. It was truly a farce.

Tuesday, March 25

Much snow, hail, and rain is falling, but it is more obvious on the mountains. Gersbach and I were awoken very early. It looks like the sun will come out today. The sun did not appear as we expected, and it rained several times. Lieutenant Ayers came looking for a Spanish teacher. I refused, saying I had a lot to do. I was told that I could be allowed to leave my intelligence work, but I again declined. I cannot be of service to someone who is not the same way with me.

My students appear to be advancing in their learning. This pleases me more than teaching officers who need much less instruction.

A rich, single German owns most of the vineyards in the region. His name is Jacinto Merren, he speaks little English, and is a loyal supporter of the Kaiser. He gets excited easily. I like to challenge Jacinto to make him angry. Otherwise, he seems like a good person.

Wednesday, March 26

I dreamed of my brother Eugenio last night. He was happy and pleased to tell me how mischievous Samuel is. I attended church services.

I had a long conversation with Jacinto when I returned from class. We heard of an American priest, and Kelleher and I joined Jacinto for confession.

The surrounding woods are part of the Eifel hills and the region is called Hunsrück.

I went to visit Agapito Salinas but I could not find him, although I am sure he lives in town.

The Moselle rises again.

Thursday, March 27

"Winter howls, the rain and the white snow falls, but despite all, the season of the beautiful flowers will come."[11] The morning was very cold while I went to mass, studied algebra, wrote home, and had another conversation with Jacinto. Our work continues as usual. It rained in the afternoon. My buddies are departing and Lieutenant Klebold went to Koblenz on leave. Sergeant Kelleher and I had a good time playing catch with a ball.

Friday, March 28

The morning was cloudy. Gersbach and I reported for reveille. I finished translating my German lesson and received letters from Mr. Velázquez and my family in San Antonio. Mr. Velázquez makes me think much about my sad, dark future.

The weather continued to be inconsistent. The lieutenant from Koblenz arrived. I returned to Salinas's house after class and met up with Martínez. I had a good time with them.

I read some magazines in my room and studied German. Sergeant Schwarz plans to travel to London and Paris. Soldiers who take these leaves do it with government money and authorization. We will always appreciate this government gesture.

Saturday, March 29

We woke up to heavy snow. The snowflakes are beautiful, probably because we have never witnessed such a sight. The ground is so warm it does not allow the snow to remain long. The trees on the mountain, however, are covered with it.

The Moselle is still rising. I have seen an infinite number of birds that have come from the mountains where it is obviously colder. A goldfinch that rests by my window trills early in the morning. This reminds me of the mockingbird that sings so sublime during moonlit nights or the spring mornings in South Texas. Bird of our people, daughter to the virgin forests, you will live while our people live.

Schwarz left and this complicates the work of preparing passports for the Germans. Since we do not want to create any problems, we will not receive many applicants.

Sunday, March 30

I attended church with the hope of later visiting the town of Graach, but I did not go because it was very cold. It snowed all day. I decided it was better to visit Gómez and Barrera. I spent most of the day talking to them and playing cards.

We spent a quiet day, but with the energy to do much more. It was a good time to sleep and that is what most of us did.

Monday, March 31

The morning was cold. I went to the school and later passed the time by the Moselle hoping the fresh air would alleviate my headache. It did. The sun appeared slightly and everything turned for the better. I was very happy to receive five letters from loved ones and acquaintances. The letters are the greatest source of joy. Our friends tell us to write while they fail to do so. They may be saying the same thing about us.

> Zeltingen, Germany, March 31, 1919
> To my dear father and brothers:
> I received a letter from José eight days ago informing me of the passing of my brother Eugenio. I anticipated this. We seem to receive unfavorable news through premonitions. He hoped for a recovery in his last letters, but a friend of mine from San Antonio was less optimistic. May this be God's will.
> I am now concerned about Crispín, who I am told is ill.
> The loss of my brother has been a terrible blow, and I can imagine how hard it must have been for all of you. The same fate that took him has placed me far away from you. We must have Christian patience.
> I had hoped to write you more, but I have had headaches in the mornings that do not leave me until the afternoon. I am in pain right now and find it hard to concentrate.
> We are told that we will leave this place in June. It is almost over, right? It was really hard when things were hopeless.
> From someone who will always love you.
>
> Luz

Tuesday, April 1

It was a beautiful morning. I got a haircut. Lieutenant Bartlet, currently in charge of the R.I.O., gave me a Koblenz coin, the type that was minted for wartime use. It reads, "Good until a year after the end of the war." The iron coin will remind me of the lieutenant and Germany. It was quiet and lovely the rest of the day. The civics class was very interesting. I took a bath. I am learning German in a class taught by Jacinto while I am teaching him English.

> Zeltingen, Germany
> April 1, 1919
>
> Sister:
> I hear you are well but that all of you lament that others are sick. That's life. What can we do? I don't see any reason why you should try to secure my discharge. It would immediately do more harm than good. The reason for getting out of the service would be to help you, but I would be out of work and joining the unemployed the moment of my release. A discharge works for veterans who have a job waiting for them. I noticed that a notary public sealed your letter. Why did you do that? I once suggested to my brother Eugenio to register a letter so it would arrive quickly, but this was only necessary then. You don't even have to use stamps now. Did the notary charge you? Was he that shameless?
> All of you should be patient, especially now that I am no longer in danger. Don't believe the liars. No one wants to be out of the military and by your side more than me.
> Your brother,
>
>

Luz
27 Albert Street
Middletown, N.Y.

>
> March 13, 1919[12]
>
> Dear Luz:
> I received your letter of November 21 today. You asked me to write you a long one, so I will. In it you asked me to send you a green ribbon, so I did. One side is shiny, the other is dull. The dull side is for insignias. You said you had me a notebook, from what you said, it must be very nice little token to remember you by.
> I am glad to hear you are helping your comrades to learn to speak Spanish and English. I was glad to hear you had a father, wife, and

children. I have myself two brothers and one sister. It is quite some time you went through Middletown from my story "A Soldier of the 90th Division from U.S. to Germany.[13] That was on June 12, 1918, and your departure from the United States was on July 14. Nine months of fighting must be horrible. I understand why you would want to be at home in Texas. From what I have heard and seen, I think Texas must be our best state.

Here goes something in French: "Celle est petite francais—Monsieur Saenz est soldat. Il demeure a Texas." (This is a bit of French: Mr. Sáenz is a soldier. He lives in Texas.) "Luz est sur Allemand. Est Luz sur Etas Unis, non, il est sur Allemand, Oui, Oui!" (Luz is in Germany. Is Luz in the United States at this time? No, he's in Germany.) What do you think? "Vive la France!" (Long live France!) I'm having problems with my French. I'm debating the League of Nations in English. What do you think about it? I'm confused since everything that man does has its good and bad points. Let me know when you return home so I can get a train ticket to New York on the O&W. I saw New York's 27th Division when it returned home on the huge transatlantic German steamer, the *Leviathan*. Now, that's a ship! Four tugboats were needed to bring it to port. You will disembark in Hoboken like all the other troops and maybe I can see you. I don't think you will return home through here, but perhaps. Well, this is all and I remain yours,

Robert E. Hoey

P.S. I received a letter from your son. I've been writing to him since you left the United States. He asked me to read one of his letters and send it to you.

Luz' Friend

ROBERT E. HOEY
27 Albert St., Middletown, N.Y.

Wednesday, April 2

I did not respond to reveille. The band played, and I set about writing letters after breakfast. I write in German, French, English and Spanish. I have discovered that this is a good way to pass the long hours of idleness after completing a major obligation. This will surely bring me great benefit.

They set up the pole for our flag today. A police sergeant supervised the Germans who helped out. Hoisting our flag in the afternoon was a grand sight. The band played more beautifully than ever.

I spent a good amount of time writing home.

Thursday, April 3

They showed a movie last night that was shameful. The heroes are two Yankees who put down an entire revolution in a South American country with their Colt pistols. The saddest thing is that many ignorant people believe it and even encourage this thinking.

I wrote to the War Risk Insurance Department in Washington, D.C. after receiving my pay. Only four of my buddies came to class, the others went to collect their pay and to drink, which is disappointing because they are not patient.

I spent the night with Gómez and Barrera.

Friday, April 4

It was raining and a little cold this morning. We were told during breakfast that everyone who missed reveille would have to attend a training session and that we had to fall into formation at 8:30. We went along. Captain Bowen insisted that we explain why we were not reporting in the mornings and we did not respond. Tamborcello offered a feeble excuse that the captain rejected. He then told us we would not participate in physical training and that we would be denied passes for a month. This may be the work of Sergeant Menchon, who does not like us. We have always thought he does not hold back and do not doubt that this is his handiwork. He got angry yesterday because we refused to provide him some baseball equipment on Lieutenant Kebold's orders. We think this is the cause of his anger. We are not losing much. He has never given us a pass.

I sent souvenirs to some friends.

Saturday, April 5

I did not go to the theater or visit Gómez and Barrera last night but reported for reveille this morning. I studied Tennyson, algebra, and French and wrote another letter to the Secretary of the Interior. I requested support for a settlement of one hundred Mexican Americans in fallow Texas fields by the Nueces River. This is how we wish to make use of the aid the government offers its veterans. I ended this lovely day in conversation with a German friend. We bathed so we do not have to do it at our port of departure. We are so happy to leave for home. The childlike excitement that comes from going home will stay with us for a long time.

The sergeant and I played ball until we dropped.

Sunday, April 6

Salinas, Hernández, Gómez, and I enjoyed playing *malilla* last night. I attended mass. Gómez and I walked to the mountains that surround Zeltingen. Our binoculars helped us see for a great distance in all directions. I am intrigued by the bad impression that German civilians have of us. It begins with some mean-spirited soldiers who debase themselves when they speak badly of our *raza* to court social favor. I have had serious and even heated conversations on the subject with some Germans and have figured out how to handle their weak arguments. I do not concede anything like others tend to do nor do I exaggerate my views. I force them to see the error of their ways and bring up the war. They wash their hands of it, like Pontius Pilate. I do not let them get away with anything because they act so arrogantly over so little. I am one of the few Mexicans who can stand up to them. Many of them have discovered how prickly I can be. When I now pass by a group of them in conversation, they stop talking and stare. On some occasions when I have wanted to debate them, they have declined. That is fine by me.

Monday, April 7

After reveille I drew a postcard for my buddy Gersbach. He found a string and a hook and set about to enjoy his favorite pastime. Gersbach caught a small fish, which he threw back into the water. He tells me a lot about his calm and peaceful civilian life.

We did not hold classes because of a military review at Wengerohr.

Tuesday, April 8

We had a beautiful morning. I finished some postcards and attended my class.

The lady of the house and a man from the YMCA got into an argument and she denied him lodging. Protestant services were held at the YMCA. The day was boring and slow, and turned calm and cold by the afternoon. I received *El Latino-Americano* and enjoyed reading about the town of Alice.

The pleasant, moonless evening was not as cold as expected.

The Texans and Oklahomans
An Occasion for Drawing on a Postcard

A member of the staff of the YMCA had given me his last sheets of paper so I could write letters for my buddies and students.

At that point, six men I did not know entered through a door on the other side of the room and caught my attention. When I noticed that they were asking for paper, I invited them over to use what I had at my table. They did not seem to understand what I was saying, and the more I spoke to them in Spanish, the more confused they appeared. For some reason, I felt they were making fun of me when they laughed, especially since they were not responding or treating me seriously. I then spoke to them roughly and "with the language of the soldier." They still refused to pay much attention, but I was glad to have told them off. I continued writing without thinking much about them, and my blood pressure began to come down little by little.

I had practically forgotten the incident when one of the men approached me and courteously asked me in English, "Have you any writing paper left, please?" I insisted on answering in Spanish, "Did I not just ask you a while ago? Why did you ignore me?" He replied in a serious tone, "We don't speak Spanish."

"What are you then?"

"Indians."

"You can't be more Indian than I am. What kind of Indians are you?"

"Oklahomans."

"Well, I'm of the Texas kind, but we're the same, right? What is sad and even embarrassing is that we should have to resort to the language of the last conqueror in order to communicate. It pleases me to see that you still preserve some of the indigenous language."

I gave them paper and envelopes and we had a long conversation. I learned that they too hope for a better future for their people and rightfully expect to be treated better.

394

Many of the men are very rich and educated. They were required to fight for the stars and stripes without being recognized as citizens of the United States. They belong to the Second Division in our brigade. I had already heard that they acted like tigers in combat. They tell me—and the Indian people are not self-serving in saying it—that many of their buddies have fallen in battle, and that they discharged their duty the same as other men, white or black.

The conversation impressed me so much, and I am glad that we have been faithful to our duty. To record this thought, I picked up a pencil and compass and traced a circle, which I painted blue. The blue field represents an unconditionally defeated Germany waiting for the terms of peace. On this field, I have linked a *T* and an *O* to represent the great army of occupation and the courageous Indians from Oklahoma and the Indians from Texas (Mexican American). We feel a deep sense of pride to be in these lands that were taken from the blind despots who ignored *the voice of justice*. I have placed our coat of arms over the field so no one forgets that we came to defend *mankind and democracy*. The *T* and *O* denote the 90th Division, which is also known as the Texas and Oklahoma Division. I have made liberal use of our national colors, as if I was hearing the words from *Over There*, "the red, white, and blue," the colors we came to defend with our blood.

We have given our all in the fight against Germany, just like we will devote ourselves to addressing all the hardships brought on by the *German* war.

I am proud to see each one of my Mexican brothers show off the uniform of our victorious army. I see them as giants in their humble appearance. They are bigger and more genuine than all the warriors of the distant past who clashed in bloody conflict on these same battlefields.

The years will pass, they will become centuries, but over time people in these mountains and valleys will likely remember the silhouetted images of the Mexican Americans and the Indians from Oklahoma as the spirit of the indigenous people of America demanding justice in their first crusade in the Old World.

I used all of today's drawings to make a postcard.

Wednesday, April 9

This was a quiet day. My friends Barrera and Gómez are going to Paris. The reports from the soldiers who have been visiting the city of light are interesting. While some soldiers say it is very beautiful, most of them disagree and say that our cities in America are better by far. No one believes they have seen anything worthwhile. The truth of the matter is that they are not prepared to appreciate a great city. They discover what they expect to find.

The soldiers who say that Paris is the most corrupt city they have ever seen may have been seeking vice and finding it. The soldiers who know nothing of the history, language, and customs of the ruling and educated classes must have felt they were in a desert. Some of them are so uninformed they cannot accept that their ignorance is the sole reason for their mistaken conclusions.

We received the best news of all today. Our division will be leaving for America on May 23. Colonel Conrad telegraphed the message from Koblenz. My class is going well. I sent souvenirs to my little friend Roberto, and to my loved ones as well.

Thursday, April 10

The days seem long. Everything is depressing and we are eagerly waiting for the wonderful day of our departure. Nothing else concerns us more. Even material for my diary seems to be running out. Nothing interests me, everything seems insignificant and unimportant. I follow the same routine every day, and this makes life monotonous.

A lot of planes have been flying over the area. I have not had much time to study and have had more chores than usual. I received a letter from my brother José that he wrote with his new "Oliver." Good. I did not go anywhere and continue to accept my lot indoors.

Friday, April 11

The morning brought a rainstorm, and we did not have reveille. I went to class and grew concerned that my friends are so bored they have lost much hope and give themselves to hopeless pleasures. They do not seem to understand the seriousness of their condition as illiterates, even as they are about to return home, and they are incapable of understanding that they have lost an opportunity to learn. They are returning to civilian life and leaving behind the hardships the sweep of destiny brought upon us. We are not worried by what the future has in store for us. We will soon see our brothers in the clutches of the "German" from Texas. This time, they will not have a rifle to defend themselves as they did in Europe. I tell them to continue studying. They promise to do it, but I fear that they will not and that our sacrifice, if they understand it at all, will be of little use.

Lieutenant Klebold is now a captain. Good for him, he knows how to make use of opportunities. His service record shows how much the humble soldiers have done for him. We do not think he will forget and wish him the best. He is going to Paris tomorrow to show off his stripes, to rest, and enjoy the life of leisure for a few days.

Marks had to go to the hospital today. Poor fellow, we fear for his health!

Zeltingen, Germany
April 11, 1919

Marce:
I hope all of you are doing well.

I know that by the time you receive this letter, others will already have reached you. I realize now that the reason you had not written was because you were ill. That's what I thought.

I can see that you need me, but a discharge will not make things better for me because I would be there without work or money. I don't know how you asked for my military discharge. Everyone has a right to request it for a family member. The trick is to get the government to agree simply because you ask for it. You obviously need a good reason. I fear some crafty devil convinced you that my discharge could be secured quickly. Don't be fooled by the many deceitful people who are around. I also noticed that you sent the letter "special delivery." I don't know why you went to that expense. The postage does not matter at all. It got here just like the others.

Do not make the usual $20 payment on the house. Remember that the understanding was for $10. That will probably help. I will settle with the old man when I get there. I wrote Washington today to arrange the final payment.

I look forward to seeing you soon.

Luz

To My Little Ones

The time is 3:20 p.m. and it's been cloudy and drizzly almost the entire morning. This is April and we are in full spring. The "railroad station street" is across from our office. The Moselbahn railroad runs between the street and the side of the Moselle River. The window to our office faces south. No houses appear across the river, only the Eifel Mountains that are covered with tall trees. A road runs on the other side of the river, alongside many vineyards and gardens that the local Germans tend. The cold front ended a few days ago and everything is beginning to look beautiful.

New leaves are beginning to appear on the trees, and many have already flowered. The German people really love exquisite flowers, and they maintain manicured gardens. The warm weather has encouraged them to take out the many plants they had kept in their basements and greenhouses. A large number of birds are showing up. I cannot tell where they come from, perhaps from the south or the nearby woods where they spent the cold days of winter. I do not recognize most of them, but they are beautiful. Their feathers are different from the birds' feathers in America. People from here do not know of mockingbirds, cardinals, or orioles. A finch that sleeps near our window always announces the good and pleasant days with song. The owner of the house tells us the bird has been sleeping in the same tree for years. The little bird had already sung a lot by the time the bugle called us to do our soldierly duty.

Children from a nearby school march by our street every Wednesday, Thursday, and Friday during Lent. The school is an official one, but the teachers and students are Catholics. I have visited the school and know the four male and female teachers. They usually pass by at quarter of twelve.

Their locomotives, boxcars, and passenger cars are very different from ours. They are not as fast and big, and they are even ugly when compared to the ones we see in America. Some small, nice-looking steamboats occasionally travel upstream, almost always with several small barges in tow. The boats drop off the barges at the towns along the way. They are loaded with large wine caskets. The barges are then set free to move downstream to towns where the wine is consumed.

I always thought that our humble, working Mexican people were the most backward in the world. Others have described us this way for so long we have even come to believe it ourselves. As you can see, this expedition has served us well, even if it was only to see and compare with our own eyes, and repeat what our aunts have said, "seeing is believing." We have seen backward people in the northern part of the United States, in England, France, Belgium, Luxembourg and, now, Germany. I now know that the heavy and eternally squeaking, two-wheeled cart pulled by horribly treated oxen is not the absolute low point of civilization. In Germany as well as in France, people use the few cows that are left, whether milk-producing or not, to pull their carts and plows. We have often seen dogs and horse-cattle combinations pull their carts, and it is not unusual to see men, women, and children do this work. The strange thing is that they do not use pack mules. It seems that these humble people would rather use cows to produce milk, calves, meat, and leather, and as beasts of burden, all rolled into one. I thought all this had resulted from the war and its hardships but we have also seen how their artists have long immortalized these same scenes.

One of the typical tasks performed around here is carrying cow dung up the mountains to the vineyards. This is how they fertilize the soil-washed ground below the vine, which is the life of these people. Every day, long caravans of men, women, and children carry baskets on their backs filled with the rich bovine treasure that has been collected during the winter and carefully kept in covered holes. Imagine this sight!

I am intrigued by the possibility that this place may have originated racial prejudice, the fuse that will no doubt set the globe on fire during the next world war. They tell their children of their racial superiority over all the other races on earth much like they would teach the ABCs.

May God remind us what the war made patently clear—"weapons are the great equalizers." We will have peace as long as we do not forget this lesson. Otherwise, we will have to pick up the rifle again.

With love, your father,

Luz

Prodding That Produces
Favorable Results

Time unfolded joyfully after we silenced the destructive cannonade of war. The American forces are the Army of Occupation stationed along the Moselle, from France to Koblenz. I have spent several months teaching Mexican American soldiers to read and write. I worked in the evenings at first, at the official school for German children. I now teach during the day in one of the YMCA buildings.

Some of my buddies have made significant improvements. Others just show up to avoid the demanding military duty. My great hope and desire is to impart new and well-grounded ideas from our past into these minds. Above all, I intend to fight for the social advancement of my people. I have taught basic writing skills, the English language, and the essentials of math, citizenship, Americanization, and civics. The idea is to prepare them to be better citizens during peacetime.

We have made plans to continue learning when we return and to maintain our unity with a fellowship that will be passed on to future generations. We have even come to believe in the possibility of forming a community composed entirely of people who will have worn the uniform on this side of the ocean. We have already contacted the US government with this idea. All this stems from the need to advance socially, to build good homes, and to set the example of good citizenship for our children—to form a people worthy of our name and the sacrifice we made for the nation.

Everything had been moving along nicely until we heard the encouraging rumors of our departure for America. Military inspections and reviews are starting to consume our time. I notice the discouragement. Some buddies show up with unfinished class assignments. Others prefer to contemplate our departure rather than learning to read and write.

I understand the feeling completely; I feel it, sense it, and deplore it. I am in a better position than many of them to see the challenges we will be facing as civilians. What can we expect from men who have experienced little intellectual and professional improvement? They will no doubt continue working on farms and railroads. Many or all of the privileges associated with the uniform and the fresh memory of their sacrifice for the common good will come to an end.

We need to prod these hardened minds with effective force because of their age as well as their rough lives, difficult work situations, and the hardships they will be facing. We must fire up their passion to maintain the flame of hope we lit here.

When I arrived in class today, I found that the students had lost interest. They were into their animated conversations and discussions and did not seem to be giving much thought to the class. I did not say anything but studied them to figure a way out of the situation. Time passed until one of the students asked, "What is the matter, teacher, why are you so deep in thought?"

"Nothing is the matter. I have much on my mind, but it is not worth stating. Who cares about the thoughts of the poor?"

"Why? What can you tell us about returning to our beloved home?"

"As it happens, I was thinking about our return and the challenges that each person will have to face on his own. Wise men do not know the future, much less us. But upon seeing the lack of enthusiasm among you, it might be best to talk tomorrow. Do you know that classes will be terminated soon?"

"Really, why? When?

"As far as this being true, it is a fact. It seems more important that we know how to handle a rifle and charge enemy positions than to read and write. The general view is that money for education is an overinvestment. We have been ordered to give an account of the progress each man has made. You are going to see that many men will have to once again pick up the rifle and abandon the books. I do not know what you are thinking, but it might be better to return to the simple life of a soldier. What do you think?"

"No. They should and must teach us to read and write. We would prefer to study than to march. We must learn."

"You are right, but you also cannot forget that we are soldiers. Yesterday, we were formidable, strong, and brave while defeating our enemies and making them respect the interests of the Morgans, the Mellons, and the Rockefellers. However, if we claimed our rights, any ignorant and mean sergeant would quickly shut us up. The best thing of all is that our departure for America is a done deal and it gets closer and closer with each passing day. We want to return, but we also want to learn something new and useful to take back with us. The former will come true; the latter, who knows?"

I can see the unmistakable signs of our departure, the military deployments and the frequent reviews and barrack inspections. It will not be long before we are told that a two-stack steamship is waiting for us on the Atlantic coast. That wonderful day will bring us such joy! So many soldiers will be waving good-bye to the beautiful "Boches" from these parts! I can already see the small trains that will carry us, "straining" under the weight of fat soldiers, many of them claiming children and German or French wives. Who would have believed or thought this when we were crossing the "sinister ocean" a few months ago? We will not have any fear when boarding the steamship. Our voyage will be a pleasure. The steamship's whistle will no longer warn of submarines and our only thought will be our arrival. Each passing day will mean that we are closer to our loved ones. Oh, these men who have suffered much are so fortunate! We will soon see the enormous receptions in American ports in honor of the humble yet tough soldiers. What a contrast to our cold farewell from New York Harbor or our arrival in England and France! And even more joy awaits us when Pullman cars reach our destinations. None of the many receptions we will get will be as joyous as the ones in our home-towns, where our loved ones wait with open arms. Our fathers will be there, also our beloved women who own our hearts, our sons, brothers and friends, and last but not least, the little girls with black eyes, our little turtledoves that we never forgot while in the trenches or in the midst of fiery explosions.

Even as these pleasurable and happy images come to mind, we cannot really measure such joy. Pleasant and sublime moments await us. We will experience moments of complete abandon when it will not be unusual for men and women to be crying. Holy tears of joy will roll down the cheeks of sphinxlike soldiers.

Even the future father-in-law who could not stand our sight will offer his congratulations. That will be the most propitious moment we realize our golden dreams. With well-earned frankness, we will be able to firmly embrace our tender dove, the woman we love. She does not ask for this expression of affection, but it is her greatest desire. Let us not waste the opportunity for firm embraces and acts of forgiveness.

But this will not be all. The joy will come later, when we are alone and face to face with our sweet bride to be who will ask so many things with her penetrating eyes and profound silence. But those moments are best left for expressing our yearnings of love. It will be like a dream when we are once again in the presence of this beautiful woman who filled so many of our private moments. As objects of their delight, we will look bigger than we really are, even in our coarse uniforms of war. But that dear perceptive woman will make a quick and thorough assessment and tell us as she comes out of her trance,

—"I like everything, my love, except for one thing. (And she will sigh with deep sadness)."

—"What could this be, my love? Can you tell me?"

—"I am afraid to offend you."

—"The only way you can offend me now is if you insist on not telling me."

That beautiful woman with the tender eyes will take in our entire being, from head to toe. We will feel more important than ever under that feminine scrutiny.

—"Be frank with me, my angel."

Making a supreme effort and almost trembling, she will very softly but clearly,

—"Almost everything pleases me, but what really saddens me is that . . . after all is said and done, you have returned from Europe, the continent of enlightenment and science, as much a *brute* as when you left.

Saturday, April 12

We had a beautiful morning. Everyone seems happier. I had to look for the sergeant who takes the names of soldiers needing to go to the hospital. I did not find him in his room and decided to bear my discomfort another day. I have already noted that we fear the hospital more than illness. We were not happy with the hospital service. The war is over and the officers show the arrogance of their rank even though they have never looked kindly on the poor cannon fodder. I have been ill for a few days, have not slept well, and had a fever during the night.

The last we heard about Marks is that he had food poisoning, perhaps from the canned fruit he eats, and that they had little hope for his recovery. I hope this is not the case. Bad luck has taken some of our dear friends.

Sunday, April 13

I went to church. The day was rainy but the attendance was very good. The service was one of the most beautiful I have seen in these parts. I had such pleasant thoughts about home! The morning continues to be peaceful, and it is not cold. The fields and mountains are turning very beautiful. I have to find the photographer who took our picture a few days ago.

Salinas, Hernández, Anguiano, and I had a good time this afternoon.

Monday, April 14

A beautiful sun came up this morning. Yesterday, before going to bed, I wrote a letter to old man Graebner, my family's German landlord in San Antonio. I can see that the fox gets cleverer as he grows older. He has taken advantage of my family, but we will get squared away when I return. The old man is one of the parasites who stayed behind to suck blood. He must have been sorry that I did not die and he could not confuse my family with government regulations. The German visited me at Camp Travis before I left to find out if I was really going to war. He came to tell me not to desert.

Sergeant Schwarz returned from London and had many things to tell us.

All I have to do is to look out my window to enjoy the beauty of nature; the sky is blue and birds warble in the green fields. I have not heard a thing about my friend Marks and continue to have problems with an unbearable, haughty, and wretched officer who always keeps crossing my path.

It rained a lot as nighttime fell.

Tuesday, April 15

We had another lovely sunrise, and the Moselle is flowing with more water from rain that fell elsewhere. The sergeant and I had a discussion about my *raza*. He seems to have a very poor opinion of us, but I have told him that if he wants to test his strength, he can try his cowardly hatred on me.

I received *El Latino-Americano* today and learned that some of my buddies from Alice are nearby. They are Lupe García, Manuel Flores, and Jesús Lopez. Barrera has received his discharge. The Moselle River continues to bring new waters. The electrical plant is not working and we continue in the dark.

Zeltingen, Germany
April 16, 1919

My loved ones:

My old friends, the books, have completed their military career with me. I am sending them home and hope to follow them soon since our emergency mission is now over.

If they arrive before me, they carry my regards. I am sending my books separately so that I will not carry a lot when we leave.

From someone who loves you very much,

Luz

Wednesday, April 16

I got up early to enjoy the breeze and to take in the German sights. Everything is lovely at this time. An infinite number of magnificent flowers are starting to appear in the countryside and the gardens. All Germans seem to love flowers. This is evident in their beautiful gardens and the amount of work they put into them. The natural environment is perfectly suited for this. Everything favors the growing of flowers. This reminds me of our poor people who grow flowers under any circumstance.

I sent all my books and much of my correspondence home. Writing letters is my favorite pastime and the best way to remember everything I see. I cannot save the letters from America. I am sorry that I have to destroy most of them. I continue to make plans to hope for a rewarding future.

A German family that is related to our hosts received a letter from Trier informing us that Marks was well despite a long illness that left him weak and thin.

We had an inspection. I had a good time at Salinas's home after class.

Thursday, April 17

We went to the movies last night, and today Kelleher and I attended mass. I also visited Salinas. I have made it a point to visit him because his house is close and I have to pass by it every day on my way to class. I had a conversation with my friend Blocker. He promised to help me with a plane geometry project that I did not prepare as well as I would have liked. I am reading universal geography.

The last letters from home were not very encouraging, and I am concerned because I have not received any more. It is very difficult to receive bad news while thousands of miles away from home. I do not wish this on anybody, not even my enemies.

Friday, April 18

Our windowsill guest, the finch, announced a lovely spring day. The morning was hot and sunny and the flowers perfumed the breeze. Oh, the fragrance that wafts through our place of sleep is so sweet!

I sent all the coins I have collected in a letter to my loved ones. Sergeant Kelleher engages the lady of the house in long conversations. They are funny as they try to understand each other. The lady sometimes thinks we want to say something important and gets anxious. She does not understand that we only want to practice our German.

Zeltingen, Germany
April 19, 1919

My loved ones:
I am well and I hope this letter finds you well too.

Today is Saturday and I hope to receive a letter from you, if not today, perhaps tomorrow. I write because I have the time for it now. I sent you my books yesterday including some keepsakes for my little ones. We are told that only government-issued material will be allowed on the boat. Some of the items I am sending you are not very important, but save them.

Everything is pointing to a June departure. Great!

I can imagine that your tribulations must have been many and serious but you will be sharing them with me soon. I suppose Crispín is with you. Tell him he needs to take care of himself and calm down.

Keep writing every week, whether you receive a letter from me or not. I want to hear from you.

Greetings to all,

LUZ

Saturday, April 19

It has been a lovely and happy day. Not so for a German who was stupid enough to challenge the law on septic-pit cleaning. He was fined 1,000 marks this morning. The poor fellow was seething, but this will send the message to others who want to avoid the fine and teach them to obey the laws of the invader, conqueror, and defender of the rights of the downtrodden! He was especially bothered by his three-month jail sentence. The Germans felt for him but they will also learn their lesson. The offender is a highly respected person in the community.

Most of my day was spent reading in the garden by the street and the river. I was also given the photos of my class. The students looked good. I wrote a response to Mrs. George T. Guernsey, the head of the Daughters of the American Revolution, and other superpatriots of the day and will send the letter to America for publication. I also mimeographed materials today.

My friends had a good time at the expense of a pedantic officer named Barker who took charge of our post today. His antics cost him dearly.

I received letters from home, they were such a pleasure.

Sunday, April 20

I was eager to attend Easter services, they were more than beautiful. We need to give much more thought to the holiday's importance and record it forever in our minds.

I had a good time with Salinas, Anguiano, and Hernández. We talked about the film from last night. We were especially bothered by the horrible scenes with those big men and their women. Each to his own.

I took a stroll along the Moselle and reflected on the German people and their past. They are in their silk outfits today. The clothes are older than Easter itself, but they are true to form when their pride lifts them from the miserable wartime conditions. Sometimes we empathize with the poorest Germans, but they do not endear themselves. They believe they are superhumans in spite of being forced to accept defeat.

A good number of trees are blooming.

The Portuguese woman had a long conversation with Merren, the bachelor.

I am having my own exchange with the pigheaded Johnson.

Monday, April 21

The morning was cold; we did not have physical exercises. My buddies are going to Wengerohr on maneuvers and I am staying behind to study geometry and world geography. Much of our artillery passed by on the way to Wittlich, where it will remain until peace is finalized. The maneuvers will be interesting.

I received the following letter:

Eagle Pass, Texas
March 10, 1919
Mr. J. Luz Sáenz
Zeltingen a-d Mosel, Germany

My dear friend:
I have your letter of February 16, 1919.

Thank you so much for your kindness, my good friend. I am very sorry that you did not know my new address and that your correspondence was sent to El Paso and returned to you, so I hear.

I arrived from Kingsville at the end of May, 1918. I am now at your service in this city.

I have read some of your letters from Europe in *La Prensa*. I have always spoken well of your good conduct. You were not a "draftee" but a "volunteer," and this ennobles you even more. I am sure that when the time comes to assign credit, this will surely speak well of you.

I was happy to receive your letter, not only because I am always glad to hear from you, but because you have once again shown how sincere and steadfast you are with me. These qualities—sincerity and steadfastness—are rare today, perhaps more than any other time. You are clear in this, that is to say, you do not have a scintilla of inconsistency or insincerity, which brings you added praise from prudent and honest people.

Many young Spanish-speaking men from the United States went to war against Teutonic tyranny in support of freedom. I have said it once and will say it again (without making this an exercise in adulation, which is foreign to my being), that among those patriotic and self-sacrificing young men, you hold a special place for your honesty as well as for your patriotism and learning. You are one of the most honorable members of our community in Texas and a fine model for our youth.

My friend, I do not only say these things because of the high regard I have for you, but because it is the truth and I want to extend to you the praise you deserve.

Turning to another matter, I want to address the obstructionist work in this country against our illustrious President Wilson by persons who wish to see him fail in his admirable efforts to establish the League of Nations. I do not believe they will be successful and that the president and all men of sound reasoning who support his realistic goals will succeed. Their success will truly be a cause for celebration because we will have taken a major step toward peace and order, and culture and democracy. I am not mistaken in stating that a large segment of the American people is on the side of our popular president during these critical times. We should hope this for the good of all mankind.

Now you know where to send your good letters. It will be my pleasure to respond.

When I hear that you are receiving my letters as expected, I will send you some printed materials as gifts.

I regret that I cannot write more as I am moving my shop to a new location today and tomorrow. It gets so complicated when you have so many things to do.

I send you warm greetings from my entire family.

Again, my warm regards to you and my best wishes for your health and general well-being, pledging once again my sincere friendship.

Your trusted friend and loyal servant who holds you in high esteem,

Eulalio Velázquez

Tuesday, April 22

Last night, we heard the singing of the "Cu" bird. We could still hear it this morning. This brought to mind many local stories about this strange bird. Daybreak was beautiful. The regiment's instructors led some short physical exercises at 9:30. They were very intense although we did not benefit much due to the current circumstances. My class continues to show some progress.

We watched a good film last night about the 90th Division, which is going to mislead the public as these kinds of films usually do. The movie showed our military maneuvers. We could avoid future wars if they had filmed real battlefield scenes. As good as the actors are in presenting the action, they can never come close to what happened. Someone is going to make money at our expense. The scenes look good, including the simulated combat and the decoration of our heroes, but we are also seeing that people who never fought and who "schemed" after the war are receiving more medals. They have filmed many scenes of military reviews and battlefield sites in Germany.

Wednesday, April 23

It was a little cold early this morning and I do not feel well. The gases seem to be having their deadly effects. I went to class, and wrote for *La Prensa* and *El Latino-Americano* with the typewriter in Sergeant Kruger's office. The soldiers are busy preparing for final maneuvers. The loud noise reminds me of those terrible days when we were close to the front, ready to kill or be killed and ready to make the supreme sacrifice for humankind.

It was lovely at the end of the day. I cleaned my cartridge belt and am studying the German flora.

The Last Minute Flag Wavers
(For the *Latino-Americano*, from Alice, Texas)

General Quarters, 360th Infantry, 90th Division
Army of Occupation
Zeltingen, Germany
April 23, 1919
Mr. Amado Gutiérrez
Alice, Texas

Dear Sir:

I am sending you the following for your consideration, to see if it merits publication:

The insolent bluster of the flag wavers can already be heard even as the horrific cannonade that did great injury has ended and the makeshift hospitals are treating victims of the great conflict. They have tried to put on a show and praise themselves to the sky. They are so active we find their handiwork everywhere.[1]

We can start with the ones who lament loudly and falsely—as if it was their greatest misfortune—that they were not among the men who gave their lives for the nation. Many of them claim that they would have made the sacrifice if the draft had required it. A good number of them volunteered, but we do not know of one—if one ever existed—who sought to take the place of the many unfortunate men who would have lived if justice had been served. Their ashes remain here, buried in oblivion forever.

Next are the people blinded by a patriotism they wish they had. They will always stand out because of their raised voices, but they will never win over the gratitude and approval of informed people.

We should concern ourselves with the latter group. They are so close minded they cannot see that their nonsense only brings them contempt and disrepute. They deserve this from the poor but truly patriotic and brave men they injure with their shameful word play that is nothing less than well-intentioned insults.

The states of Massachusetts and Texas must be fed up with the interesting polemic between that illustrious "Bostonian" and the arrogant "San Antonian." Word of this has even reached Zeltingen, Germany. What provoked this controversy and what caused them to speak in such base terms? They leveled a cowardly insult against two races of humble nobility that played an important role at the supreme

moment when they defended the violated rights of humankind and
upheld democracy and the integrity of the nation. They demonstrate
their mediocrity with foolish judgments directed at the citizens of the
United States of America who represent these races! This will never
pass for real patriotism! Our best response to the call of the nation was
to go to the slaughter in silence, as was expected. We also continue
wearing the uniform and are still waiting for the final resolution on
the battlefield. There are no distinctions between "Bostonians," San
Antonians," etc. Does this not shame the "noted polemicists"?

The adversaries from San Antonio and Boston cannot say that
members of my *raza* deserted in the fields of honor. I refer to them
because I am of pure MEXICAN extraction, even though this might
not square well with my compatriot from Boston. If they had pointed to one single desertion, just one, the enemies of my people would
have rewarded them with thunderous applause. When they could
not find the desertions to justify their deep hatred, they resorted to
petty ideas that always earn their proponents what they deserve—the
worse disdain they could imagine.

We now find Dennis Chavez (notice the metamorphosis in the
name and racial origin) before us (not surprisingly). He is the "distinguished reformer" from New Mexico who proposes—in an outburst
of patriotism—to radically change the ethnography of a people. The
nation of his children demands other forms of sacrifice, not hypocrisy or petty expressions.[2]

Besides Dennis Chavez (and his well-known ideas), our attention
is drawn to a matron who directs the respected organization Daughters of the American Revolution. In a recent speech in Washington,
DC, she called for the prohibition of the use of languages other than
English in the schools. This lady also stated that using any foreign
language constitutes the worse kind of treason (and this is supposed
to be sound reasoning). Deadly myopia! Fortunately, millions of our
nation's sons—and perhaps one of her own—can dispute this and will
soon return to proclaim loudly the value of knowing other languages
in military and civilian life. We made full use of this knowledge in
defense of the nation, for which we have sacrificed everything.[3]

We do not question the passion with which the Madam President defends the English language. Like Chavez, we know the tender
feelings that come from hearing and speaking the mother tongue.
This is why her views would deny citizens the right to improve their
ability to speak their mother tongue and to learn any other language

that fills their heart's desire. We also believe that accusing someone of treason for speaking another language is contemptuous, especially in the case of our children. They face this problem in the public schools. I made my most important contributions during the war as a translator of French and German correspondence for the 360th Infantry.

My own life allows me to demonstrate—and I do this—that it is not treasonous to claim our rights as citizens of the United States of America without knowing a word of English. Many of my brothers as well as those of other races who perished in the war did not know a word of English. Were they heroes or traitors when they fell under the hail of our enemy's bullets, when they were defending the stars and stripes to make Democracy possible?

J. Luz Sáenz

Thursday, April 24

Sergeant Krugger arrived yesterday from Rouvres, where we once trained for battle. He brought me the souvenirs I had left with the good Father Moura, including my bag with the mementos and the last letter that was to be sent to my wife and children in case I had fallen in battle.

The final grand review of our division will take place today. The troops began their preparations very early. The military trumpet called out three times, as it used to do during battle. We did not take part but stayed in the office doing our work.

I am waiting for Barrera and Gómez to return from their trip to the most beautiful city in the world. I look forward to their stories. I was sick last night and did not sleep well.

General John J. Pershing, the commander in chief of American forces, will oversee our grand review. The infantry fell in formation in a beautiful valley during the early morning hours. The cold was unbearable. Our brothers in misery were on their feet, wearing their full gear. This is how they stayed in line, standing and waiting for the great general. The announcement that the commander had arrived circulated around ten. The officers did not seem to be in any hurry to review the troops. When the order was given to play the grand marching music, the wind instruments malfunctioned and the review was done without music. Some soldiers suffered frozen feet and ears, but they stood steady as lead.

Like in other reviews, we were told "very good" and that was the end of it. The soldiers, numb with cold, scattered in all directions. The grand parade of fully supplied, well-dressed, and clean infantrymen was a sight to behold. The shiny artillery was immaculate and the railroad kitchens and supply cars were in good order. We were not without the noise of the trucks, officers' vehicles, airplanes, and heavy tanks. This may be the final spectacle we will see. We did not want to participate in the review because it is mostly a vain attempt to show off uniforms and insignias. Some people will accuse us of envy for saying this. They are free to think what they want. All we have done is observe the movement of troops and feel sorry for our friends. We may be wrong, but our nation cannot possibly benefit from these farcical maneuvers. We should be offering our lives for justice; our record shows that we have done this (we think differently twelve years after the war and the maneuvers are once again a part of military life).

Our soldiers were very tired and hungry when they returned from Zeltingen. This was real.

Friday, April 25

Colonel Price declared a holiday and we had no reveille, work, physical exercises, or classes today. We had a good time at the YMCA and then went to the Moselle to watch a game between companies K and L. The day was so cold we could not wait for the end of the game. Tamayo, Leal, Anguiano, and I reminisced about our homes.

Saturday, April 26

We saw western movies last night. We saw Agustín Sáenz, my cousin, and Fortino Treviño from Company G at the movies and Filomeno González at Salinas's home. I wrote a letter for Fortino and received one from my friend José G. González of *La Prensa*. I sent home a beautiful picture of Zeltingen that my buddy Gómez gave me. Kelleher drank quite a bit last night and now says he is going to stop drinking. The day ended with rain and more low temperatures.

San Antonio, Texas
April 18, 1919
Pvt. José Luz Sáenz
Hq. Co. 360th Infantry
90th Division
American Expeditionary Forces in Germany

My good and dear friend:
I was so glad to receive your letter of March 21 with the two

postcards. They are certainly interesting and priceless. A few days ago I saw one of your sisters; she told me they are receiving many letters from you.

Tell me if you have received the newspapers I sent, including the one in which you wrote about your celebration over there.

Today is Good Friday and I am curious about what you do at this time. I believe that *Carnaval* starts tomorrow, and as you can well imagine, we will have plenty of noise for a few days.

My wish is that you stay in good health and I hope to see you soon in San Antonio. I remain your good friend and trusted servant who wishes you well,

JOSÉ G. GONZÁLEZ

Sunday, April 27

I attended mass and received a letter from home after breakfast. It was well drafted, typewritten, and certified. I was sure my friend Mr. José G. González had prepared it. I sent photographs of the soldiers enrolled in my class and another one that Filomeno gave me with some of his friends dressed as women. They all look drunk and very happy. Long live free Germany!

The afternoon got colder despite the occasional appearance of the sun. It snowed a little and Gómez, Barrera, and I played *malilla* in the evening.

Zeltingen, Germany
April 27, 1919

To my family:
I received a typewritten letter today and I could tell who had written it. I am very happy to hear that all of you are well.

I am sending my little ones a box with some mementos by separate mail. My mailing date appears on the outside of the box. I have sent other items that I hope you have received although I know they will arrive after the letters. Later, I will tell you about many of the things I am sending.

Be checking the English and Spanish-language newspapers to find out when our 90th Division returns.

Petra, please purchase a book for me if you can. It is our regimental album, the best memento I could possibly have. I ordered two when they were published but I have no idea why I was not charged or why they were not sent. You can find them at the following address:

H. I. Hymans
San Antonio Printing Company
San Antonio, Texas

Marce:
You told me in one of your letters that, while on his deathbed, my brother said that he wanted to give us one of his little girls. I would be very happy to have either one of the girls, but I doubt that my sister Clara sees it that way. It might be best not to pressure her in any way, especially at this time. I would love to have Lupita because he had already suggested her for us. But either one would be fine.

Tell Clara that Lupita could stay with us while in school and that I would send her home every year until she finishes her studies. Take care of Crispín.

With affection, as always,

Luz

Monday, April 28

The weather changed from bright sunshine to snow, and then to a cold wind. Feliciano Carter gave me the wooden soldier I carry in my backpack in remembrance of the war. Gómez gave me another gift. I cannot offer anything in return but my friendship and some favors.

Tuesday, April 29

This was an important religious and social holiday for the locals. Each community has a religious holiday every year and today this town has its turn. The people observe it religiously. Many groups from the neighboring towns arrived singing with great joy. We had an inspection. The weather changed again today, to snow, cold weather, and sunshine.

I did not hold class on account of the inspection. I responded to a letter from my brother.

Article of War No. 105 and 2,175 Bottles of Champagne

On December 26, 1918, 674 soldiers of the Third Army, including corporals and sergeants, 174 second lieutenants, ninety-two lieutenants, fifteen captains, and three majors, received orders to attend a military school in Châtillon-sur-Seine. One of the students was our good friend and companion Corporal Jesse Pérez. On December 28, they arrived in Toul, France, and came across a shipment of 2,175 bottles of champagne meant for Monsieur Charles Barlaband. The warrior spirit did not fail them as they took the shipment of bottles by storm. The joy that came from that unexpected event is impossible to describe, but it rivals their surprise on April 29, 1919, when General Headquarters handed them Article of War No. 105. They were forced to make restitution for the value of the liquor, some damages, and other losses. Each soldier or officer was fined according to rank. Corporal Jesse Carter was fined 14.98 francs. Jesse still sighs to this day when he recalls the escapade. He states, "I don't feel aggrieved, what I feel is pain." The others would agree and will want to forget the incident. They believe they paid a just price.

Wednesday, April 30

The morning broke with much snow on the mountains and everything was very beautiful.

I made each one of my students a postcard.

We received passes to go to the great city of Paris. Sergeant Kelleher and I will go together. We have shared wretched moments and now look forward to an enjoyable trip. Besides, we think the same and share a general view of the world. We started our preparations. Salinas, Barrera, and Treviño have loaned me some money. Lieutenant Ayers offered to help. I cannot explain why I never took the time to visit him and accept his offer.

Thursday, May 1

THE AMERICANS VISIT THE GREAT CITY OF LIGHT—PARIS

We were ready for the trip early in the morning. We had prepared all our passports and the many other documents the military required. Some say that France does not offer enough sightseeing to justify all the trouble we are going through. The problem may be ours and not that France offers little to see and enjoy. In any case, we will carry the documents in case we need them.

We ate a good breakfast and prepared our lunch. Although we do not know what we are getting into, we figured out the train's departure time and set our watches to the clock in the office. The train—if that is what we are to call the poor excuse of a machine that is to take us—arrived ten minutes early. We had to run after it. Luckily, it runs slow or we would have required a good running start to catch up. It reminded me of the slow-moving trains from Kansas.

We enjoyed the scenery once we settled into our small seats. Most everybody stood because of a lack of seating. The tracks run along the river's left bank. In Bernkastel-Kues we saw the circus the 90th set up for the troops. I hear that the circus is complete, especially in terms of horses and other beasts of burden they paraded about. We had a three-hour layover in Trier, went for a walk, and made our first stop at a Knights of Columbus stand to get all the information we needed on the place. Afterward, we visited the historic Porta Nigra castle, which dates back to the time when these towns were part of the great Roman Empire. We visited the basilica, an amazing and magnificent building that serves as a Pauline church. Lastly, we saw the old Roman public baths and the ruins of the sumptuous castle of Augustus Caesar, the Roman Emperor. We ate at a Red Cross station for a nominal amount.

We left for Paris at 1:45 and passed by Schweich, Karthaus, and Remich (Luxembourg) on the other side of the Moselle. This last place brought back memories. We finally arrived at the fort city of Metz and spent four hours waiting for another train. We have been on the trip for a day but have only traveled two hours. The soldiers are frustrated to no end because they have been ordered to stay in the train station. The place is very beautiful but it is a prison to us. Heavy gates keep us from reaching the lovely city. I have no idea why we are kept inside. We apparently took the city to hand it over to the French, but we cannot visit it now that they have taken possession of it. The only official explanation is that officers fear the "Boches" left many mines behind since this was their most important fortification after Verdun. So be it. What a fate for the poor Sammies if we had attacked this wall of China!

This is the little job the French had given us. Who knows what we would have suffered or what would have happened if we had not taken it. What I do know is that the Germans hightailed it out of there as soon as they heard our cannon. They called the truce the next day, on November 11. The Germans do not admit fear. They prefer to say they took "precautions."

Our long stay here gives us no choice but to strike up conversations with the other waiting passengers. Trains are constantly coming and going with civilians while the victorious soldiers ride in wagons meant for horses. Who knows when we will be able to say "the best for our troops." During the fighting we would say, "We cannot expect the best while at war." Now that we are at peace, or in a truce, we will say, "Let the lion get his fill first, the rest of the wild animals can eat later." We were not able to enter into good conversations with the people from here. If I am not mistaken they are all Germans and resent the Sammies that spoiled their dreams. I met a poor "poilu," or French soldier, who could have told me everything, truth and all. The poor fellow really wanted to talk but had to board a train right away. Our rest time was taken up by moving between the upper and bottom platforms of the station because the trains were arriving at both levels. We left for Novéant-Toul at nine. I do not recall when we arrived but it was very late. We were worn out but happy because we were on our way to the city of light. Such human misery! We will have to tell everyone in America about this so that when we have another war they do not miss the opportunity to travel at the government's expense.

We were barely able to locate some worn cots at a place run by the Knights of Columbus. They were in such bad shape we decided to sleep on some tables. We were fine-looking tourists traveling the beautiful and free France and enjoying the privileges reserved for victorious soldiers.

Friday, May 2

We did not sleep much, "ours was not a bed of roses." We were told that a train was leaving for Paris at 6:30 a.m. and asked the ticket agent if we could buy tickets with our own money. He agreed to sell us the tickets but warned us that military orders prevented us from using them. We were so angry we decided to proceed with our plans. We made the mistake of believing a French soldier who offered to buy our tickets. He bought them, but this did not help. When we tried to board a passenger train, the officers stopped us and severely reprimanded the agent. What do we care! The train for the soldiers and animals was arriving at 9:30. We had breakfast and toured Toul. Our MPs, or military police, were everywhere. They gave us hostile looks, but

ARTICLE OF WAR NO. 105

would not tell us anything. We were tired and visited a cemetery for a short peaceful rest.

Our luck as American tourists was so bad we even feared that the dead would rise and scare us. The cemetery was very interesting and since no one could tell us anything, we explored to our heart's content. We asked an MP as we walked briskly out of the cemetery if Sammies were allowed to walk the city streets while waiting for the train. He said we could and even recommended some interesting places to visit. That is the first friendly policeman I have met. We went into a fort since it seemed the most appealing site for the soldiers that we are. We found so many old cannon with hellish mouths to kill the barbarians of this world! This is the St. Michael fort. Another less important fort was situated at the nearby Barene hill. We visited the cathedral, a beautiful and historically important building. We also visited the door known as the Joan of Arc. The general vista of Toul is very beautiful from the hills. We had to climb down because it was starting to rain and it was time for the cattle train to arrive. I bought some postcards at one of the stores. The rain turned cold and everything took on a grayish look as the water poured from the buildings.

We arrived in time to catch the train and pile up alongside French soldiers. We had never seen a more pathetic sight when we got off at Bar-le-Duc! The name of the place, Bar-le-Duc, will always have a familiar ring to our ears! The barracks were dirty and deserted. We had a difficult time finding something to eat and what we did find was very bad and expensive. More soldiers began arriving from all over. Most of them were French. I was able to carry on good conversations with them. This is how I learned about everything we want to see in Paris. I found it strange that most of them are not from Paris. They are backwoodsmen who only travel through Paris and know nothing of the city. That was one of our most wretched nights, just a notch above dying. The French soldiers look so bad! What must they say of us? They do not act like saints simply because they are soldiers.

Saturday, May 3

We left for Paris at 6:30. It was a lovely day. Everything started to look up when we took note of the good speed of the train and the circumstances of our trip. We would have loved to visit many of the important places along the way. The entire route is lined with white crosses in fields of red poppies. They mark the graves of the French heroes who gave their lives for the homeland. Nothing else appears before us, the entire area looks like a big cemetery. This gives an idea of the great loss of men that France suffered. All the crosses bear an emblem with the colors of the French flag. This is Holy Cross day and the whole area has been made to look attractive, but it still looks sad when we think about what all this represents. These men died resisting the German offensive. On the sides of the railroad tracks, by the foot of some hill, and in trenches or ditches of all sorts, so many crosses remind us that brave men fought until they died and that they made the Germans pay for every inch of territory they took. The fighting was horrific for the ill prepared. German soldiers were well equipped, especially with their truck-mounted artillery units that protected the infantry. They would always catch up with the retreating French troops, who inevitably died. The Germans rode roughshod over them on their way to Paris. I cannot place a flower on each grave, but I have one in my thoughts for all these French martyrs. Glory to them! Red poppies, like in Flanders Field.

We continued in deep thought until someone announced that we were close to Paris. The train had actually already reached the eastern entrance leading to the gardens of the great city. The engine's whistle finally stopped and we realized we were at the East station. A large number of French and American soldiers were waiting when we arrived. Not one familiar soul appeared in the immense sea of people, nor did they give us a friendly welcome. We arrived in Paris at 1:15 and ate at the French Red Cross. We were joined by another soldier who knew nothing about Paris and had come to discover the city on his own. I bought a map so we could get our bearings. After our meal, we took Chabrol Street until reaching Lafayette and the nearby Grand Opera. We rented a hotel room and met up with a very young Frenchman who knew some English. We talked at length and discovered that he was a Parisian. My friends asked that he accompany us. He readily accepted, probably because that is what he wanted to do all along. We ate at a luxurious nightclub, but we were self-conscious because of our ragged appearance, and especially of our lowly rank. The meal was also very expensive. We had an especially difficult time handling the slow rhythm of life among the class of people frequenting these places. They spent at least two hours drinking a cup of dark coffee. The place was meant for talking, not eating. We then went to the French Theater, one of the most famous in Paris. We once again took note of our boldness as we entered the theater in a soldier's uniform. It did not matter, we had fought for these institutions and we believe in our right to step on the soft carpeting with our well-worn boots. The Germans would not have shown any respect and would have damaged the carpeting with their boots and spurs. A delightful work was presented on stage. I could not describe the luxury that paraded before us that special evening, which included so many important people from all over the world and all kinds of nobility. The theatrical presentation was either "The Seasons of the Year" or "The Life of a Man," and the beautiful paintings depicted the Follies of Jean de la Bruyère. The stage setting with the sublime music seemed so strange to us. We did not stay to the end but we did not arrive on time either. We were not interested in a full, critical analysis of the play, but wanted to see as much as possible in a short period of time. We left and made room for people with binoculars and monocles in a standing-room audience. Regarding the Parisian ladies, I could not see past their ostentatious luxury and overdone colors and powders. The meager supper and the theater tickets were too expensive at 28 francs for each of us.

The rain was coming down hard when we left the theater and we were forced to call it a night.

Sunday, May 4

MORE LIGHT THAN THE RAYS OF THE SUN

This is Sunday and we had a miserly, expensive, and bad breakfast in a French restaurant. From this point on, we went about the city without a guide since our French companion had disappeared. We immediately decided to visit the Notre-Dame Cathedral. While at the cathedral, we were given some mementos and bought others for our children and wives. The Seine flows on both sides because the cathedral is located on an island. A small garden and the Palace of Justice are to the far west. A good number of bridges cross the Seine. We followed its left bank and visited an institute, the Orleans train station, the Chamber of Deputies, Saint Sulpicius, and a bridge that led us to Concorde Square. We saw many beautiful statues at both ends of the bridge. Concorde Square is very lovely, with an obelisk in its center that Napoleon I is said to have brought from Egypt. We visited the Tuileries Garden and saw the famous statue of Gambetta. We went by the Nouvéant Circus, stood before the Royal Palace, then at the Champs-Élysées, the Crystal Palace, the Royal Palaces, the American Episcopal Church, and the Arch of Triumph. Many captured German cannon of all calibers were at the Arch of Triumph and Concorde Square, as well as in other squares and at the beautiful Place de l'Étoile. We also saw the statue of Victor Hugo on Victor Hugo Avenue, Trocadero Square, and the Palace of Gardens. Trocadero Avenue is now known as the President Wilson since July 4, 1918. Our sightseeing took us to the Eiffel Tower and the great Ferris wheel. At the Pantheon, I asked two Mexicans about the whereabouts of General Porfirio Díaz's tomb and remains and was told that they had already been returned to Mexico. Our next destination was the tomb of Napoleon I and a private museum. We came to the museum by accident. Its owner was kind enough to let us see his wonderful collection of art. It is situated across the street from the National Hotel for the Disabled.

We were very tired and found lodging at the American Red Cross. After supper, we went for a walk that did not turn out well because everything got dark quickly. We saw something at a large public area that we did not like. Some Parisian beauties were taking a stroll with two black men who seemed rich and educated. After wandering around aimlessly, we retired for the night.

I forgot to note that we went to the popular business district where we bought souvenirs and saw the biggest displays of silks and textiles in Paris. Some businesses remain open on Sundays. We especially liked their wide boulevards with few cars in the streets, especially in areas reserved for pedestrian traffic. A place like this would have been noisy in America. We also failed to see utility wires, which detract so much from the beauty of American towns. We missed our unsightly streets with so many cigarette and vehicle advertisements.

Paris, city of light! Fate has granted me the opportunity to come and see you as you really are. Lovely city of indescribable charm, of pleasures never imagined by men from other lands, men lacking in the "light" of intellectual achievement and practical development. The city has inherited much from advanced civilizations that have disappeared from the face of the earth. Vice and virtue walk your streets and flow through the center of your heart. The light of Lucifer is mistaken for the light of the Archangel Michael, the hissing of tempting serpents intermixes with the music of the divine, Satan's palaces appear close to the Louvre and Notre-Dame, and the enticing songs of sirens seek to eclipse the sweet assuring cooing of doves and the resonant rhythm of Christian prayers.

My partner in adventure and I were walking in the middle of that unknown place after a night that had been so completely new to us. We dismissed our interpreter because we wanted to experience and enjoy everything directly and immediately.

I do not know if we have found what we were seeking or if it was time to find it. We gave ourselves to the study of aged walls of the many palaces with world appeal, all the while listening to the sweet and harmonious sounds that make up this great city on a pleasant day in May. Military tunes, music, the trilling and warbling of innocent birds, the gurgling of happy fountains, the rustling leaves of luxuriant trees, the happy laughter of people doing their daily chores, and the songs and laughter of women who are full of life and ready for pleasure. Out of nowhere, an American soldier approached us in the street and told us, "Yes, my friends, this is the place you were searching. Make sure you go inside, otherwise you will miss the best that Paris has to offer." The soldier's austere appearance reflected a deep sadness rather than joy. He was not your Bohemian-type person, but neither was he the virile soldier at inspection. He was in a daze. We did not know him. He quickly disappeared into the crowd of animated pedestrians.

We went up the few steps to the door of the palace-looking building without knowing what we wanted. Instinct or mere curiosity moved us forward. We did not have to knock. A well-dressed young man invited us in with the typical Parisian politeness that either reflected a way of life, natural ability, or the results of good breeding. We asked where we were and the meaning of the place. In a very refined language and with the accompanying gestures to spare, he proceeded to explain something that we could not understand until he noted the admission price. My buddy asked me to explain what the young man was saying, and I replied, "I don't understand anything. The only thing I know is that the admission is 30 francs or 6 dollars. It might be best to see if such a steep price is worth it or not. We could come back." The young salesman had started his spiel again when my buddy announced with some enthusiasm, "Let's go in. Let's see what they have to offer so we don't have to hear it from someone else."

The door to a luxurious room opened up as soon as we paid. Streams of brilliant light and waves of sweet aromas filled our senses. Our ears were filled with the sweet cadence of delightfully harmonious sounds that came from an unknown place. The entire room was covered with rich carpeting and sumptuous veils and silks. A ravishing woman rested on a soft divan of blue-green velvet. This evoked the memory of Eve, the woman who has been exalted and celebrated over the ages because of her God-given beauty. We took in the human spectacle with eyes aflame. We could sense that she was breathing alluring sensations into our being.

"You can take off the covers to get a better look," said the guide. With our rough hands, we removed the few fine silks, the transparent veils, and sheer fabric that barely covered the entirety of her form. She was a faithful representation of Eden's gardener during the first days of creation. Her rosy cheeks would occasionally form a sweet smile that was a distant memory of a modest life that had been recently lost.

We entered another room that was even more impressive. Another beauty was reclining on a soft divan. Her attractive features took on a different appearance, in color, size, shape, and position.

Entranced, dazed, and practically disoriented, we followed the guide from room to room. We were not in a condition to count them. We later figured out that we had toured seventy-eight rooms. We took in the parlor scenes with eyes of wild passion, as bold men of the world at the peak of our strength.

We were out of place with our unwelcoming, tough, and rough appearance. It contrasted with the beauty that graced the rooms of light and wealth. We were uniformed and right out of the war's front and with the obvious signs of fierce battle experiences. We had also been walking on the expensive carpeting of Cleopatra's elegant confines with our heavy shoes with steel heels, rows of large-headed nails, and leather soles.

Our coarse uniformed appearance was not all. We also displayed a fierce base instinct seeking the magnetic lure of regenerative forces that perpetuates the human race on earth. This paints a reliable picture of the American soldier in the city of light.

We were not in a condition to truly admire and appreciate those curly, silky locks, the small eyebrows, and the eyelashes over eyes that beckoned. These looks did not necessarily belong to the sensually debased, enslaved, or wild woman, but to the woman who is educated in our schools and colleges, the product of our modern civilization, but nevertheless a prisoner in her own chains. It was impossible to deny that her incomparable mouth could send out the unmistakable sense of infernal fire that can give life, delight, inspiration, or death to man.

An eclipse seemed to be blocking the sun when we walked out into the street. This is when we came to understand why the soldier looked stunned when he said, "This is where you will find the best and most beautiful in Paris."

Monday, May 5

We prepared for our return early in the morning. We had passes to continue going out, but had run out of "coins," and we felt it best to leave and let Uncle Sam continue taking care of us until he turned us loose. We arrived early at the train station and bought our tickets. There are many things to buy. We regret having wasted five and a half francs on a ticket at Toul. As the saying goes, "No matter how early you get up, you can't make the sun rise any sooner."

We once again spent a few hours at the military camp in Bar-le-Duc. The visit was boring and agonizing. To make matters worse, it was very hot that day, with nowhere to hide from the sun or to find fresh drinking water. We saw all types of French soldiers with various kinds of uniforms from different colonies or French possessions. Most of them are black and may be from Africa or islands close to Africa or from Asia. This is one reason—as forced as it may be—why the Parisian women feel they should associate with black men.

We left very late for Toul on a train that was not assigned to us. We acted as if we did not know anything and boarded. The conductor checked our tickets and told us we were on the wrong train but that we could go on to Toul where we could catch our own train the next day. This was a thousand times better than waiting at the camp, riding the same train all night, sleeping in a poor bed, and eating badly prepared food. Everything is different in the city. If we do not eat, it is because we are out of money. The city has all the amenities that are lacking in a military camp for privates like us. The camps also usually look bad.

The train had few soldiers because it was not designated for us. We got good rooms and beds in Toul and ate at a Knights of Columbus restaurant where we had long conversations with soldiers traveling to and from Paris. They included green recruits as well as seasoned foxes, worldly men. We had made our plans for the next day by the time we bedded down for the night.

Tuesday, May 6

The train we should have taken arrived at dawn. We did not regret switching trains, especially since the one we took was clearly better. The soldiers who had just arrived would not leave until the afternoon. We boarded the first train that arrived and relied on our "best judgment" to answer questions from the conductor. When he asked if we had been on the train that had just arrived, we answered that we had not and showed him the tickets from the previous day as proof. He shook his head and informed us that the train we wanted was only going to Nancy and that we would not be gaining much by taking it. We insisted and he let us on. We did not want to ride on a cattle train. Best of all, we would be visiting Nancy, something that would be impossible to do if we took the other train. We stepped off the train at the historic and beautiful city of Nancy.

We took Constitution Street to the cathedral, Nancy's solemn home for Christian prayers. The city has many old, heavy metal and bronze doors. The locals have preserved them as works of arts from a distant era. Artisans from a long time ago forged them with hand and hammer over iron anvils. The lamps over the doors were once lighted with wicks of cloth or candles, later with oil, and now with electricity and gas. Who knows what else will light them in the future. Another public place of note is Place Stanislas with its Governor's Palace and the Cathedral behind it. The semicircle at La Carrière is just as beautiful.

Soon after our walk, we boarded another train that took us through some of the most important places we could ever imagine: Jezainville, Pont Mousson, Norroy, Novéant, and Epagny. We passed by fields that we painted red with the blood of our companions in military life. The Saint-Mihiel sector will live forever in our memories. Our minds replayed many unforgettable experiences. Everything was like a dream, except that our memories were real.

We arrived at Metz, but all we did was transfer to another train and continue on our way. A German who was about fourteen years of age and spoke English boarded the train. He came to the school in Metz every day. When we asked where he had learned English, he said the Metz school requires English and French. He does not know what changes the war will bring, but French will probably serve as the official language and students will be expected to also study English and German.

The 89th Division occupies the towns on the route to Trier. We saw many of its soldiers quartered along the way and arrived in time to retire for the evening. Since the trains will not be leaving for Zeltingen until the morning, we located a place for the night and went sightseeing around the city. It looks beautiful with all its lights. Everything was new to us. We are a day ahead of the train that had been assigned to us. This has given us the time to visit and learn about the towns that we passed through. This is the first and last time the military will have given us a pass to see Europe. We may never have this opportunity again. We have enjoyed the trip as much as a low-ranking but intelligent soldier is able to do and are grateful to Uncle Sam for this.

Wednesday, May 7

We greeted the morning in good spirits and felt well rested after a good night's sleep. We know Trier well since we have visited it several times. Despite this, we decided to visit it again, perhaps for the last time. It is unbelievable, but we are ready to get back to our barrack.

We did not have to wait long for our train. We boarded quickly and seemed to have reached Zeltingen in a shorter amount of time. While resting by the Moselle, we gave our friends an account of everything we saw, but not about what we did. Few people share their disappointments.

We checked for mail, and, sure enough, many letters and even newspapers were waiting for us. We barely read all our letters during the assigned time and then prepared our report to close the day and rest.

Thursday, May 8

We awoke to a beautiful day and busied ourselves with the preparations for our trip home. A strange and unfortunate turn of events occurred today. A fellow in a nearby town had been eagerly waiting for the day of his departure. He had bought many nice gifts to take home. While saying his good-byes around the town, he climbed a pole with a live wire that supplied electricity to the region. The soldier slipped and fell on the cable and was immediately electrocuted. It took a while for the plant to cut off the electricity and remove the body. Once the service was cut off, the body fell but the shoes, including the feet, stuck to the wire. It was a horrible death.

I sent some things home, the soldiers organized a ball game, and we marched some. We will only be here a few more days and our happiness will begin.

Friday, May 9

The morning was beautiful and we started the day in good spirits. I went to my class and told my friends that we would soon finish with our studies but that they should continue with their learning in America and that I would be checking on them. I felt inspired when I saw the changing of the guard with the musical sound of the band.

I am overjoyed that my companions have done well as soldiers, and I have even noticed that the major, "the Indian" as he is called, prefers them as guards for our grand reviews. The Indian makes a good soldier when a real one is needed here or anywhere else, but please do not make him into someone he is not.[1]

During the afternoon, I visited some friends who I am also teaching to read and found them sad and discouraged. They were gambling with dice. What a shame that they cannot find a better way to spend their time! How can we expect them to be any different when they return home! Will their military service have made them so full of themselves that they will repeat the mistakes of the character in "The Sleeper and the Waker"?[2] I can see that the majority of them will not make good use of their contributions in the war and will think they served simply because they could not avoid the draft. Mexican Americans will face a tremendous challenge as civilians. The very unfortunate circumstance of war was just beginning to bring us together and teach us some useful lessons.

Some Americans beat up several Germans, and the authorities condemned the act as despicable and cowardly. Our soldiers exploited many advantages they had over the Germans.

We had a good time playing baseball.

Saturday, May 10

The morning was beautiful. Nothing is more pleasant than the aroma of the many flowers in the gardens and on the mountain. The tall trees that someone planted in straight lines are now well-planned and productive forests, and the vegetation has grown beautifully after much rain and snow. The warmth of the sun brings life as it moves along on its tropical journey. I am contemplating all of this from a bench in the garden.

We had to go to Bernkastel-Kues for our pay. We made the trip by train. Although we could have walked, we wanted to have something to talk about and more time for sightseeing. Bernkastel-Kues are two towns that are joined by a beautiful bridge across the Moselle. The mountains that rise from the banks of the river are a source of sustenance for the towns. They also provide a beautiful panorama. Some very old castles rest on the mountaintops. Each one of them represents a chapter in history. We returned as soon as we received our pay.

We noticed a horrible hatred toward the French in these places.

I passed the time with Gómez and Barrera at their home.

Sunday, May 11

The German people are happy to see us leave, but they also fear the French might come and take charge. The followers of the Kaiser fear the enemies they made when they mistreated defenseless women and children.

Someone in church sermonized against mixing with the Americans. We see nothing wrong in trying to protect their women from irresponsible soldiers. We also appreciate their precarious situation because the American soldiers are the only ones with a lot of time on their hands and money to spend freely. The German men, on the other hand, do not have the means to please their women, and it makes sense that they should take up with Americans rather than their own countrymen. Someone captured the meaning of things when he said, "Hardship can be made to justify anything"[3] We could also say that there is nothing odd about soldiers marrying women from countries they have defeated in war. Many of our soldiers have chosen French wives and others have married Germans. How long can this continue? We cannot answer this question, but can say that marriages will improve relations between nations. We have seen this after the conquests of Alexander the Great and in many other cases. This is natural. The German people can expect a generation of their own children among the poor and needy classes. After losing so many men in war, this will be their best gain. They win by losing. This leads the

Germans to criticize their women, often with a good number of posters with caricatured images. One of them is ingenious and satirical. It shows the US government sending home a boat full of soldiers followed by another one of equal size with their wives and children. These posters have appeared in towns where American soldiers are stationed. Many soldiers are sending ahead of themselves their French and German wives. How many American girls are going to be left out! How many women will remain alone and without a husband! Some people are predicting that a scarcity of men will produce a wave of vice, crime, and moral laxity all over the world.

Many of our soldiers take leisurely walks by the Moselle, while others lie in the shade under the trees. They talk about the much-anticipated departure. Who can fault us?

Monday, May 12

We did not have reveille today. The horses that pull the machine gun and small cannon have been turned in so that they can be taken to the dock. We have received orders to turn in all the baseball equipment and to no longer lend it out. We know our voyage is no longer a dream.

> Zeltingen, Germany
> May 12, 1919
>
> My dear loved ones:
> May God take care of you! I am doing well.
> I have little to say but this may be the best news for you. We are packing all our things as we prepare to leave this land to return to our own. Absent any problems, we will leave next Sunday and see each other soon. Everything is going so well that it is hard to believe.
> With love,
>
> LUZ

We received a letter from our division commander today with a message from General John J. Pershing, commander in chief of the Expeditionary Forces in France. It states:

> 90th Division Headquarters
> American Expeditionary Forces in Germany
> April 3, 1919
> Order of the Day No. 16:

1. The division commander takes great pleasure in making public the following letter from the commander in chief of the Expeditionary Forces.

2. Each officer and each private of the 90th Division shall receive a copy of the letter

American Expeditionary Forces
Office of the Commander in Chief
France, April 26, 1919[4]

To Major General Charles H. Martin
90th Division Commander
American Expeditionary Forces

My Dear General Martin:

It gives me much pleasure to congratulate you and, through you, the officers and men of your division on the splendid appearance you made during the inspection and review of April 24 at Wengerohr. The fitting appearance of your personnel and the good condition of the draught animals and artillery are clear signs of the high morale that permeates the ranks. We did not expect anything less from a division with such a fine fighting record.

Arriving in France toward the end of June 1918, it underwent training away from the fighting until the end of August. It was then placed in the Villers-en-Hays sector and there took part in the Saint-Mihiel offensive, where it attacked the fortified positions on the Hindenburg line immediately to the west of the Moselle River. It achieved complete success in three operations, mopping up the Bois-des-Rappes, occupying the town of Vilcey-sur-Trey, the Bois-de-Pretre and the Foret-de-Vencers, and advancing for more than six and one-half kilometers. The division joined the Meuse-Argonne offensive on the night of October 21, taking the town of Bantheville and the high ground north and northwest of that town. It continued with its splendid record during the incredible attack of November 1, reaching the Freya Stellung, crossing the Meuse and taking fourteen villages in its advance. The Carriere Farm, the Bois-de-Raux, Hill 243 (the capture of which was vital to the advance of the division toward the left) and Hill 321 were the scenes of desperate fighting on the opening day of the attack. The division took Villes-de-Tailly, Bois-de-Mont, Bois-de-Sassey and the town

of Montigny-devant-Sassey on November 2 with an offensive that
was as quick as it was far-reaching. It took Halles on the fourth day.
By the tenth day, the infantry had crossed the Meuse and taken the
town of Mouzay. The division was pressing the enemy hard when
the armistice was signed.

As part of the Third Army, the division participated in the march
into Germany and the subsequent occupation of enemy territory. I
am pleased to note the excellent comportment of our soldiers under
these difficult circumstances as well as for their record in battle. They
are a source of pride for the American people. I wish to express my
own gratitude to each man for their splendid manner of serving
their country and to assure them of my heartfelt concern for their
well-being.

Sincerely yours,

JOHN J. PERSHING
By order of Major General Martin:
John J. Kingman, Chief of Staff
Officer: Owen J. Watas, Adviser
For the soldier J. Luz Sáenz

I received another letter from Secretary of the Interior Franklin Knight
Lane. He commends my plan and good intentions to contribute to the Americanization of the many sons of our nation who took part in the war but who
do not feel or have ever felt like complete Americans in body and soul and
who have not been extended this privilege or been accepted politically and
socially for who they are. I am very pleased if Washington finds my plan acceptable, and I really hope it does not remain a proposal.

Gómez gave me a picture of himself and other soldiers in K.P. uniforms.

I wrote home. The rain came down hard in the afternoon. I gave away
some things to my friends.

Tuesday, May 13

The dawn was beautiful. After breakfast, I searched for a newspaper to
get the latest news from home. A possible war with Mexico is receiving much
public attention. I read something about it but I do not believe the conflict is
imminent. Things have been postponed, I can believe that.

Spring is here in celestial splendor. Our happiness may have something
to do with how we observe things. We would not be the same if circumstances were different. What we now consider marvels of nature might not
have drawn our attention when we were trudging along during the war. At

this time, it is enough to view the fields or to be more attentive to know that life has changed completely. The green in the fields has never sparkled so beautifully, the melodious birds have never trilled so sweetly, and we can now appreciate the picturesque streets we disliked just a few days ago. If things were not as they are, this would not be Europe. I viewed this from a bench in the garden.

Wednesday, May 14

I saw Captain Joe Maxwell yesterday. I thought he was already in America but he is still around. I sent a gift to my brother José.

The usual slow pace cut into this beautiful, warm morning, but an order to inspect our equipment broke the monotony. We dressed quickly and put everything in its place. Hopefully, this will be the last inspection, at least in Germany. We were also ordered to burn all the Intelligence Department files. We gladly complied but not without feeling that a good part of our souls went with the records, including the best we had rendered in war and peace. We also destroyed the other files in our office.

Rumors of the impending war with Mexico continue. This is interesting. We came to build peace in Europe and now find that the roosters are all stirred up at our own ranch. It could not come at a worse time! Many people talk about a war between Mexico and Japan and that someone's ship has been sunk. We could care less about the ship. We were in Paris when we read that the Morgans and other millionaires are planning to ask England and France for their approval—not their support—to intervene. The opportunistic drones were not satisfied with Europe's honey. When asked for my opinion, I have stated, "I'm ready with my rifle, cartridge belt, and knapsack to take a position on the front lines, as long as I am accompanied by greedy millionaires like Morgan and Rockefeller, malicious journalists who have sown discord between other nations, all the slackers, and everyone who bears ill will against my *raza* in Texas and other states."

Zeltingen, Germany
May 14, 1919

My dear wife:
I am writing this letter with great anticipation. Everything points to our departure. This may be the last time I write from Germany. Everything is ready. We will leave on Saturday rather than Sunday,

which is so much better. No submarine will impede our way this time. This does not mean the sea is free of danger. Our voyage, like overland travel, has its risks. Who can deny that? We could even die eating *pinole.*[5]

We should thank God for everything he has done for us since we are returning with a load on our backs and not in a coffin. It is better to be flying our flag instead of being wrapped in it, even if the honor is the same.

You told me in your last letter that the countryside is beautiful and the year seems to be starting out better than previous ones. I pray to God that this year will be better for everyone. The hardship of the war may entitle us to this.

Spring has also just arrived and everything is beautiful. This season's changes are new to me and this is why they are so delightful.

Tell my little ones that I will soon be with them and that I will tell them stories of the old world and the sea.

I will close because I want the letter to go out today. This is the last day that we are allowed to write from Germany. This means I will be close to home when you receive this letter. Who knows, I may get there first. This would be best, right?

I send all of you my very best regards.

Luz

A Portrait of Zeltingen

Thursday, May 15

I have followed the news that Mexico and the United States will be at war by the time we arrive.

We are marching to Wengerohr tomorrow and then to Brest or some other seaport. I felt like bidding a last farewell to the area around Zeltingen. I took a boat to the other side of the Moselle. Three mountains surround the town. They are not very tall but of sufficient height to offer shelter from the wind and protection from a military attack. The town extends along the right side of the river and may only have three small streets. The church sits prominently on the far west by the foothills and stands out over the other buildings in town. The view of the town contrasts against the deep green color of the vineyards on the mountains. The train passes close to the river, which has no bridge over it. A barge that takes the place of a bridge allows the villagers to work their vineyards. Nearby bridges also provide passage to anyone needing to cross. I will never forget the many times I climbed the foothills after mass to pass the time and exercise until it was time to eat. I would do this on Sundays. The view from above is beautiful. I have many reasons for giving this town a special place in my memory.

The staff of the YMCA invited us to a party. After some songs, they served us chocolate and exquisitely tasting cookies, their last gift in occupied territory.

We did not prepare a report. This gave us time to ready our knapsacks for our trip home, the greatest and happiest of all the marches we will have taken.

Friday, May 16

We fell in formation soon after we finished dressing.

Jacinto, the rich German bachelor and owner of the best vineyards in

Zeltingen, invited me to his warehouses, and I asked my friends to join me. The warehouses are large subterranean cellars holding great amounts of aged wine. I invited Kelleher and another friend because I thought they would appreciate the wine tasting hosted by our wealthy, single German friend. We had just arrived when Jacinto asked a beautiful German maid to bring some glasses of wine. The glasses were expensive, finely polished crystal with beautiful transparent color, like a diamond made for wine. My friends downed the contents in one gulp and indicated with facial gestures, "I want more." I only sensed a bitter taste that left me with a burning sensation. Jacinto insisted that I drink more. I declined and asked that we visit the warehouses. We went in with glasses in hand. The warehouses must have been the size of a city block. They were full of big caskets or barrels (I am not aware of the names they give them) with aged wine of various vintages. We figured that some of it was more than twenty years old. He would take a small sample from each container and ask for my opinion. I would respond that it all tasted the same. The German and my friends laughed and kept drinking. I could not be faulted for not telling the difference since I had never been around so many fermented grapes. My friends' eyes were starting to look so red and sleepy that we decided to say good-bye to the rich bachelor from Zeltingen.

Jacinto lives in a splendid, expensively furnished three-story brick house. A lovely self-portrait from a not-too-distant past hangs in the foyer. It is a true work of art. Jacinto dresses elegantly and has the familiar look of a despot of the German empire. He is a learned man who enjoys the flowers and trees, a true student of nature. A beautiful fountain graces the center of his garden, which has numerous hyacinths, Jacinto's favorite flower.

The bugle that once called us for combat sounded at two. We quickly said our farewells to the owners of the house where we had stayed for so long and practically flew to the assembly point. It seemed like a dream. If we ever had an occasion for believing in fairy tales, this was the time and place. Our joy had no bounds and we did not seem to have any other care in the world. We were experiencing a moment in our lives we would never enjoy again.

We crossed the Moselle on a barge at 2:30 in the afternoon and waited a short while for the 2nd Battalion as it made its way from Wehlen. Like on previous occasions, we rested on our knapsacks and were able to take in a relaxed view of the town. We placed the memory of Zeltingen inside the book of our lives knowing that we might never see it again. The only thing left to do was to say good-bye to Zeltingen, its vineyards, mountains, and people.

We must have left at three, behind the thousands of soldiers who had been marching by all morning toward Wengerohr, our point of departure for America. The walk was difficult and tiring. I think my buddies created a problem for themselves when they said their farewells with "the white beverage from the Moselle." Others made the same mistake on that very hot day. The sun appeared for a while, making the march seem harder. Some soldiers had to drop out of formation while others dragged along. They also had to march without a meal. The load felt heavier because they did not feed us on time. Once in Wengerohr, we bought some sandwiches at a YMCA stand, but they were cold and dry and did not do us any good. I had a long visit with my friends from the signals platoon, including a soldier with whom I have argued about the duration of the war. I maintained that Germany would not give up as easily as some people thought. It turned out that Germany had no choice but to surrender unconditionally when her allies began to fail her. Each nation held up according to the means at their disposal.

Wengerohr is an important small town because it is a rail hub. We had several military maneuvers and inspections near the town. The field is perfect for it. The sun began setting slowly and closing a memorable chapter in our lives. Barrera, Gómez, and I decided to sleep in the same boxcar. We wanted to travel together again. This is how we left America and crossed the sea, how we lived in France, how we endured the thick of the action, how we spent our time after the armistice, and how we wanted to return to our native soil. We made our beds and visited our buddies in the other boxcars. We always found some friend in each of the Pullman wagons who was happier than when we were given five-cent coins as kids or were allowed to go fishing in the creek. Sergeant Baton will be in charge of our cattle car as we cross the France that was once at war.

On the Last Cattle Train
and Cars 40 and 8

Saturday, May 17

We slept well and were ordered to rise very early and put away our beds. We ate breakfast and waited for our train. The trains began to leave, but ours did not depart until ten. We were already worrying that we would never leave. Some friends even wondered if we were not being taken into the interior of Germany.

We finally left Wengerohr and began to take in the new vistas. We were so deep in thought that no one had spoken in a long time. Once in a great while someone yawned or asked for a light for his cigarette as the train rolled downhill sounding like a jalopy and shaking us about with its constant jerking movements. Each time we reached another hamlet, the engine's whistle was so weak it was barely audible.

We got off at Trier and did some physical exercises. This helped with the blood circulation and gave us a sense of new life and a good appetite. The Red Cross gave us cigarettes, a cup of hot coffee, and a sandwich, which we gladly accepted. We were later given a bag with shaving material and a deck of cards. Sergeant Krugger and I played rummy once we resumed our ride.

Our bugler and the director of the 360th band, Lieutenant Banberry, makes his beautiful silver cornet resonate a new order now and then. We ate and took two trains to a place about thirty-five kilometers from Verdun. This is where the war's destruction ended, the last battlefield of gruesome fighting. I will regret it if we do not make it to Verdun and "The Ladies' Path," the site where the prince of the German crown sacrificed more than half a million men to retake Verdun. A man's whim resulted in such a costly loss of lives! It is six in the afternoon and we have stopped near a cemetery containing the remains of French soldiers who fell in the area. These are sacred sites for France as well as for everyone who cares about our civilization, which almost disappeared under the weight of despotic ideas. This is where we broke the pride of the most formidable emperor in history. The signs of battle are still visible wherever one looks. Over there, we see a town in ruins, its houses torn to pieces by cannon fire. Farther up, we can see the thick barbed wire that blocked our nightly offensives against enemy positions. War material is strewn everywhere as if a battle had just ended. A truck in ruins is before us, probably overturned by cannon fire. The crater left by the explosion is still visible. What happened to the soldiers in the truck? They were probably nearing the front. We would not be off by much if we said that they are sleeping in that cemetery.

We did not pass by Verdun during the day as I had hoped. The rain started coming down early in the morning and the train stopped for a while at a distance from Verdun. We saw large stockpiles of war matériel the Germans left. I took the opportunity to quickly look around and found many German steel helmets. I took one and so did the other soldiers.

Sunday, May 18

THE BATTLE OF VERDUN

It started to rain very early last night. It got so dark that we never would have been able to take in the entire view of the historic Verdun fortress. The mountains on the approach to Verdun were completely demolished. The dense fog and rain kept us from seeing more.

We traveled all night. If we had not been soldiers on our way home, we probably would not have survived that infernal trip. The reeling, jerking, and bouncing movement of the train kept us awake until very late, when we finally fell asleep, or at least it felt like we went to sleep. Our sergeant had ordered us to close the only door to our car, leaving a small grilled window for air circulation. The cool night kept us from asphyxiating. I have already noted that the Pullman cars have unattractive names. Their plaques read "10 horses, 40 men."

I did not know our whereabouts when we woke up and someone stated, "I hope that we are not going into the heart of Germany." We were able to see the green farmlands with the early morning light. We passed by Joinville and Bessons and thought that we would reach Orleans because of the direction we were taking, but that was not the case. The beating we took from that rough train ride did not keep us from enjoying the sights. Everything was new to us since we had only seen the parts of France destroyed by war. France seems different now that we are traveling through its southern region. The people had always appeared sad and quiet, but they now looked cheerful, in short, an entirely different nation.

Monday, May 19

The train thrashed us around again last night and the motion kept us from sleeping well. We arrived at Saint-Pierre-de-Corps in the morning and ate breakfast. "Chow time" produces the liveliest moments. This is when the tensions of life are most evident. No one wants to be the least among us. The best thing to say at this time is, "We're born to die, count me in!" We have two meals a day and take full advantage of them. Uncle Sam is not saving any money by cutting out the third meal. The view from the train on the way home brings back memories from 1898, when I was a boy and we were at war with Spain. I remember seeing the soldiers traveling by train, either to the Mexican border or directly to Cuba. The children would say, "Someday we will be going too."

We passed by Angers and wished we could walk its streets. We felt the same way when we came to the lovely city of Nantes. Our train would not stop. It seemed to want to quickly rid itself of the American plague or it understood how eager we were to return home. We do want to return home, but no harm would have been done if we had been allowed some sightseeing to appreciate the France that we will be hard-pressed to describe. We have been enjoying the most wonderful sights as we travel along the beautiful Loire River.

We arrived at the port of Saint-Nazaire around five in the afternoon. One of the first things we saw was the blue sea, the Atlantic that we often thought we would never see again. Ships of all sizes were in dock. Which one will take us to America? Large train engines were being unloaded from two big steamships that had just returned from the United States of America. Enormous cranes were placing them on the rails. The plaza is beautiful. Many ladies and sailors are conversing in French on the beach while some soldiers are swimming. A good number of the women are "sharks" who follow the soldiers in search of money. Many of the soldiers are American. The march to the first camp was strenuous. We felt right at home in the American-style barracks and quickly made our beds. We ate very late and were quick to hit the sack.

Saint-Nazaire will become one of the most important ports in Europe once a permanent peace is established and the United States supplies the reconstruction of France, Belgium, and Germany.

Tuesday, May 20

We had just finished breakfast when the officers announced a physical examination. It was complete, much like before the war. Afterward, we marched to camp No. 2 and took possession of new barracks, which were better than the first.

Some of my buddies told me that a soldier who knows me would be coming to see me. He is one of the soldiers who stayed behind and did not make it to the front. I am eager to know who he is.

The soldier arrived shortly thereafter. He was no other than an old student of mine from Cotulla whom I had taught in 1910. His name is Pablo Gutiérrez, a sergeant with the Special Operations Squadron (SOS). We talked at length about our past and his experiences during the war. In short, I learned he has moved around and that he has always wanted to improve his social and economic standing, as well as his intellectual understanding. He had to venture out of that poor town of Cotulla, resigned to toil like every other man who is poor financially but rich in noble and dignified aspirations. Gutiérrez is a brave soldier and a very worthy example for our youth to follow in the future.

I saw many other friends from my regiment and sent my children the German helmet I picked up in Verdun, but I doubt it will reach them. Other soldiers are sending their souvenirs, but swindlers in the service are stealing and selling them.

I have been assigned a task for tomorrow and have heard that it is not one of the most pleasant.

Wednesday, May 21

I was able to get out of doing the job that I was assigned. In military life, ingenuity and strategy are essential in the hands of someone who knows how to use them. I used my wiles to make "some other fool carry the load."[1] Sergeant Kelleher and I had a good time making our rounds through the YMCA and the Knights of Columbus halls and a few other places in the camp. We bought souvenirs and planned on sending them home because we are told that we cannot take anything with us.

We read an announcement at the Knights of Columbus hall that an important baseball game was scheduled for the afternoon, and we went to see it. The field was well-kept and spacious. The 88th Regiment of the Health Corps and a marine regiment battled it out. It was a hard-fought contest, one of the best games we have seen on this side of the ocean. Twelve innings were required to decide the outcome. It was impossible to tell who was going to win. The marines finally scored the winning run to end the game with a score of 4 to 3.

The 359th Infantry band played during the baseball tournament, and its counterpart from the 360th entertained us in the evening. This is where I saw Pablo Pérez.

Thursday, May 22

It rained quite a bit last night. Many soldiers arrived in the evening and everything grew lively early in the morning. Platoons of soldiers are roaming in search of the rest of their buddies. We took a bath today. I was assigned to work at General Headquarters. After supper, Gómez and I went to the camp that housed the 359th Infantry and the 343rd Artillery. I saw several of my Mexican friends, some from Alice. They came to our barracks and we had a long discussion about our past, especially when we saw "the grim reaper" up close. Someone commented on the bad behavior of a certain Jack (more stupid than an ass), a scheming and malicious coward.

Friday, May 23

Today was beautiful. I went to the Knights of Columbus after my meal and read for a good while. I later spent some time with Gutiérrez at his workplace, where he disinfects soldiers' clothing using a steam pump.

We went to see a ball game but it did not take place; we returned to our barracks right away. The machine gun companies were playing a team from the SOS when we arrived at our barracks. The former won with a score of 22 to 8. Gleim and I went to a shop and bought some souvenirs. I later accompanied Sergeant Kelleher to buy his souvenirs.

Some black soldiers from America played baseball until very late. The game must have been closely fought since they played until they could no longer see the ball. You could hear them playing with the same enthusiasm that everyone else expressed.

San Nazario, France
May 24, 1919

Dear Family:
Thank God, we are at the port of embarkation. We have not been able to leave but we are headed out. Be attentive to the news so that

you know of our arrival. We are told that our first destination will
be Houston, where a banquet will be prepared for us. Screams from
the platform and clouds of smoke will complete the homecoming
scene. We'll see what kind of reception awaits us in San Antonio, the
birthplace of the 90th Division.

Luz

Saturday, May 24

We lost our patience when a counterorder delayed our departure. Very
little amuses us now because "we have set our sights on the ranch."[2]

We have no entertainment other than baseball games. The 343rd Artillery
played against a machine gun battalion today. The artillerymen won 8 to 1.

Our colonel conducted an inspection and found problems in our barracks. He disciplined us with four hours of daily physical exercises. Nothing
was wrong with us but we agree that the exercise and discipline can keep our
minds occupied and settle our nerves. As the saying goes, "the less a private
thinks or has time to think, the better." In the Intelligence Department, we
know how most of these orders are put together and relied on our astuteness
to get out of things. "You don't need horses from another corral when fighting
the bulls from Jaral."[3]

Sunday, May 25

We had a minstrel show with song and dance by blacks from the south. I
went to mass at a Knights of Columbus hall. We did physical exercises after the
services and later attended very interesting talks by Dr. Barton and Mr. Manos.
The speakers were very good. They moved the audience on several occasions.

Last night we heard the pathetic bellowing and whistling of the arriving and departing steamers. The whistles reminded us of the sounds on the
high seas that warned us of fire or threats from submarines. They now seem
like dreams, but we are ready to hear the warnings and are hearing them
again. Those were horrifying times for the men on the war-torn seas. No coast
was safe from the enemy submarines. How many men must have heard that
mournful whistle, their last alarm while on this world?

Monday, May 26

Our captain led the physical exercises this morning. All of us thought he
was half-asleep because he would order us to do something and forget to give
us a new order until we were completely exhausted.

We had to prepare our report, which kept us from participating in the maneuvers.

It is two and we are waiting for the start of a baseball game. I have spent several hours resting and reading until the heat and the humidity of the day got me tired and put me to sleep. I am at one of the Knights of Columbus halls. We had mass this morning.

Word is spreading that we will be leaving this evening, but we have not received orders. Others tell us that we will definitively leave tomorrow. This has made everyone happy. We will never experience anything like this again, waiting eagerly to return to our beloved homes after suffering terribly in the greatest of all wars.

Many soldiers were in joyful conversation, others sang, while still others played instruments. This is how another day of waiting comes to an end, caressing sweet dreams but getting older.

The *Mongolia*, American Steamship

Tuesday, May 27

W e had another rigorous inspection after breakfast, as if to keep us from entertaining bad thoughts. We readied our knapsacks and the rest of the things we will take on our return trip. The overwhelming noise, the pleasure that abounds in us, and the need to have everything ready are killing us and filling us with a sense of desperation.

The heat is unbearable. All of us sweat heavily and seek out the little shade the barracks offer, not unlike the sheep from West Texas in search of the few trees of the region. It is already ten in the morning and the ship has yet to arrive, but we are ready. We would really appreciate it if our bugle were to sound its call an hour early. We would never respond more gladly. This does not mean we would not also obey the call if we were facing death. Anyone can see the difference between discharging a military duty and the joy that comes from finally returning home with the laurels earned for meeting this same responsibility.

I had a pleasant dream last night. I was already in my father's home. He was asking that I tell him about my adventures. I was about to do this when I questioned the thought and woke up.

We fell into formation around four and marched to the dock where our anchored ship was waiting to take us home. It felt like we were moving at a snail's pace even though we were marching as fast as possible. We could see the wonderful name on the American transport, the *Mongolia*. It was smaller than the *Olympic*. The movement was slow because so many soldiers were waiting to board. Large numbers of soldiers gathered along the wharf as more continued to arrive. We will always remember this. The dark columns turned into one solid mass of men, each carrying packages on their shoulders and articles in their hands plus an untold number of souvenirs hanging from their knapsacks. Thousands of eyes that brightened with profound happiness stood out in the dark mass. Joy was not just a dream anymore. We could sense it and gave ourselves to it.

I thought our turn would never come, then the boarding started. The other soldiers probably felt the same way as they rested in somber silence. Most of them smoked to pass the time. The moment finally arrived when our company began walking across the ship's narrow bridge. This was also a slow process, only two men could board at a time. The ship's officers and some of the lazy sailors were indifferent toward the great army that had saved the imperiled nation and now returned with the wounds and dust of trench warfare, but we were happy with our victory.

When the supreme moment arrived, my heavy boots made the bridge crackle and squeak. I was reminded of Texas cattle being loaded on railroad cars. We were really no different in the crude way we boarded.

Troops continued boarding at night. These men were left over from the armed conflict and were now survivors in peacetime. The company from the 360th Infantry's General Headquarters was already situated on the second level of the *Mongolia* by six in the afternoon. The sun was setting and darkness was beginning to envelop the port of Saint-Nazaire. We will be doubled up and suspended in the familiar hammocks.

Wednesday, May 28

The boarding lasted until sometime in the evening. The ship made use of the tide and started pulling away at one in the morning. We were not able to see the landscape we were leaving behind. Everything stayed in the shadows much like the past, which will soon be forgotten, perhaps forever.

I could no longer see France when I got up at six. France, the name that had served as our rallying cry in democracy's great crusade! We could only see a tiny island to the north. I was seasick all day, as were many of the soldiers. The sea received us with furious waves and suffocating heat.

The navy's band, along with the band of the 360th, gave a nice concert.

I stayed on the upper deck after midday and contemplated the sea. I saw many of the same soldiers who had crossed the ocean with me several months ago. A good many of the ones who are not returning with us are resting in peace in the fields of heroes.

The sick soldiers have cursed a great deal. Others have gambled a lot of money with the sailors. I did not to eat supper.

Thursday, May 29

I feel better today. We woke up late and had fire drills after breakfast. The drills were difficult to execute because we had been sick yesterday.

All of us are on the bow after resting and sunbathing. The noon hour is approaching.

Some of my friends and I spent time on the ship's bow until very late as we took in the immense beauty of the sea and played *malilla*. The card game may not improve our lives, but it gives us some peace and good company.

The day ended with rain, but it was very pleasant.

Friday, May 30

Our major concern is that we will miss the opportunity for fellowship. The losses in life will come soon enough. We returned to the bow and continued to play cards and talk about our plans. We will begin our first project as soon as possible, a campaign to erect a monument to honor the memory of the fallen in France. We are confident that the sacrifices and heroic deportment of our Mexican brothers merit such a tribute by those of us who survived and everyone else who is coming after us. We discussed this project in Germany. The idea surfaced as we witnessed the very actions we wanted to immortalize. I am pleased that everyone likes the idea and that they are ready to participate in the campaign.

The ocean has been calm and beautiful today, although sailors are said to fear such serenity in the sea in the morning. I have not been able to read.

Officers and soldiers are at odds because of the poor system for feeding us. It occurred to me to go up to the pilot's observation deck. The seas are still calm and the hour for dinner is near.

Martinez, a friend who has fished and faced storms at sea since he was a boy, told us, "You'll see how rough this old sea gets at night." It turned out as he predicted. By the time it got dark, the weather had turned cold and the sky cloudy. We continued playing *malilla*, trusting in the ways of the Sammies.

Saturday, May 31

The morning was very cloudy and foggy and the steamship constantly blew its whistle to make its presence known. This is one of those famous fogs that cause disasters at sea.

After breakfast, we went up on deck where an officer was speaking. He read us the latest news that had come through the wireless, "The tombs of our soldiers were decorated yesterday. Pershing visited Romagne. Carranza is about to fall. González will be president and Pancho Villa will become the secretary of war." The wireless is a marvelous invention. It brings us the news of the world every day, in the middle of the ocean.

The YMCA handed out sweets and oranges to the soldiers in our company.

Sunday, June 1

The waves were very high and my spirits were down. I was seasick and stayed in my cabin and on my hammock all day. You can only be comfortable while in bed. I could not eat during the day. Some of the soldiers who were also sick tried to eat and lost everything, including the chance to go to the dining area. I fear this illness. This is why I decided to stay inside the whole day, rereading material about the ocean. I am glad to have experienced first-hand what I read about. We trusted in the strength of the ship and enjoyed climbing to the deck to witness the terrible storm.

Monday, June 2

I went to the deck again after breakfast and remained there all day. The day stayed clear and the sun shone beautifully. We have already traveled half the distance. The sea is stirring and the wind is so strong it whips up big waves against the sides of the ship. Some of them break over the steamship and water enters the cabin area. The water mostly douses the soldiers who sleep in the lower open-air deck. The sun warms us on the exposed side, the wind freezes us on whatever side it hits us, and the ocean soaks us.

I feel hungry for the first time in several days. I went down to my cabin and ate the food I had put away for later use. We were given apples and candies, which upset my stomach and brought back the nausea. After supper, Gómez and I sat at the tip of the ship's first deck until sunset. We have spent one more day on this earth and have one less to live.

Tuesday, June 3

The wind blew hard last night, but it settled down by midnight and it was peaceful this morning. The marines tell us we will have a storm again by four in the afternoon.

Luckily, the marines' forecast did not pan out. The afternoon came, and the sky is still. The day went so well. I saw two steamships passing us in the opposite direction, one on the left and the other on the right.

The marines of the Signal Corps are very good at what they do. One needs to see them to appreciate their quick movements when communicating with other steamships.

The Knights of Columbus gave us candies, stamps, scapularies, and checkerboards.

Wednesday, June 4

The day dawned beautifully. The blue ocean is completely calm and looks like a mirror. We grow happier with every day that passes because we know we are that much closer to the land where joy awaits us.

We see many steamships coming and going, both nearby and on the distant horizon. We gather to talk and plan our projects. I wish these men would form the working nucleus needed to lift the name of our people. We are not understood and are not given due consideration or justice because we are different from the Anglo people. Our obvious loyalty and manliness may have demonstrated once and for all how we meet our responsibilities as faithful citizens.

Barrera, Gómez, and I went to the front of the chow line and ate first. We remained on deck until sunset. We were given oranges, candies, and more stamps.

THE STEAMSHIP *MONGOLIA* OF THE UNITED STATES OF AMERICA AND THE FIRST SHOT OF THE WAR

The New York Ship Building Company built the *Mongolia* steamship at Camden, N.J. in 1903. It was one of the regular steamers of the Pacific Mail Steamship Company of San Francisco, California. The ship was involved in trade between San Francisco, Honolulu, and China.

When the Allies were in great need of ships to transport food and munitions across the Atlantic, the Atlantic Transport Line bought it and sent it around Cape Horn in December, 1915. The ship later sailed between New York and London. When the imperial German government organized its famous submarine blockade in March 1917, the *Mongolia* was armed with three six-inch cannon and with a crew of one officer and twenty-two soldiers. It was the first boat to sail after the Kaiser's proclamation of a "restricted zone" and to engage a German submarine in March 17, 1917, in the English Channel, six miles southeast of Beachy Head. The battle ended badly for the submarine. This was the first time after the declaration of war that the United States fired on the high seas.

The U.S. Armada used the ship in March 1918 to carry supplies. The Navy equipped it to transport soldiers in May 26, 1918.

On May 26, 1918, it sailed with a good number of troops to rendezvous with the rest of the convoy. The ship departed in the company of the *Siboney*, the *America*, the *Tenadores*, the *Henderen*, the *Mercury*, and the *Huron*, all escorted by the battle cruisers the *North Carolina* and the *Von Steuben*.

The *Mongolia* made its first round trip with France in 28 days over a distance of 7,006 miles. The ship has been used constantly since then, and it is now bringing the soldiers back as soon it can complete its voyages between New York and Brest. The name of the *Mongolia* will go down in history for its good work and will be remembered for delivering the first blow at Fritz and firing the first volley of the war.

(Taken from a magazine during our trip to America. The *Mongolia* carried us back home.)

June 6, 1919

I am aboard the *Mongolia* crossing the Atlantic as an American soldier, and my fellow travelers and I are on our way home as a victorious army.

Thursday, June 5

Today was a day for remembering Camp Travis. One year ago we were about to leave in search of death or victory. We are now returning with our lives and the coveted laurel. Let the nation open its arms to receive us and we will know to place the crown of victory on its august head.

We had a good time contemplating the ocean after breakfast; we talked about fishing with some friends who had been fishermen as civilians and who will return to the same pursuit as soon as they remove their fighting uniform.

The Knights of Columbus gave us a handkerchief and candies. I sewed my green ribbon on my jacket and filled my employment card. My buddies and I continued with our conversation about our future. Many of them have high hopes for their civilian lives. I urge everyone who can stay in the military to do so. I tell them that the men who stay in the military will benefit from the laurels we earned in war. I volunteered to remain in the standing army but was not accepted due to my large number of dependents and my inability to support them with the earnings of a soldier. As God is my witness, this was not an obstacle when I presented myself for the slaughter. I want it to be well understood that I did not wish to leave the military. I do not harbor regrets either. After serving my nation, I will focus on my family. I want justice for my people.

The ocean was calm during the day, but the temperature dropped in the afternoon and a cold wave forced us to move into our cabins. We saw many steamers heading toward the old world.

Friday, June 6

It has been exactly one year since we left for France. We guarded so many illusions back then and have brought back so many bitter experiences! For what? Who knows. Destiny now brings us back over the blue and briny waters of the Atlantic.

The morning brought a dense fog while the *Mongolia* blows its whistle at every turn. The sun was so faint it looked like a cold moon without the strength to drive away the thick fog.

I ended the day on the deck, while other soldiers were inside in an absolute state of euphoria after receiving the welcomed news that we would reach American soil tomorrow. It was the best reason to be happy.

We will disembark in Boston.

Gómez and I bathed with ocean water in the sailor's quarters. The ship takes in the cold, salty water for daily bathroom use.

How Boston Receives Us

Saturday, June 7

We woke up early and prepared our knapsacks. Our joy is indescribable. If death were as sweet as this, we would all want it.

Soon after breakfast we climbed to the upper deck to be the first to see land. It must have been ten when we set eyes on the first islands that guard the entrance to the city and bay of Boston.

We will never forget the beautiful reception the cradle of liberty of the United States of America prepared for us. Tears of joy came streaming down, as no doubt they would have if an invading despot had set up camp in the land where our loved ones wait for us. Here we are, after subjecting ourselves to the suffering of the most horrific war that has befallen humanity. Standing steady and tall!

There were so many small passenger boats coming out to greet us! All of them were decorated with the national colors. Many of them had orchestras or other kinds of musical bands. Everything was joyful and colorful. What a contrast to our departure from New York when we were ordered to close every single skylight and retire to our cabins until we were far from the coast! No one bid us farewell when we were departing to face death. Now everyone is greeting us. Why? The reason is that the hardship weighs heavily on us, but also because we have restored peace and safeguarded prosperity for the entire nation.

The navy inspector came in a boat to conduct the inspection the law requires. The steamships came next. All of them sounded their greetings. One of the boats brought gifts from the YMCA, and staff members lobbed them to the soldiers on the upper deck. We finally arrived at the major dock and disembarked. The Red Cross provided free telegrams for our loved ones. We also sent postcards.

We were unable to make note of so many other moving scenes. The people of Boston released thousands or millions of small and colorful balloons as we approached the dock. Even the heavens thought of us, despite the fact that many of us did not even thank God for his Divine Goodness. As soon as we reached the dock, a strong rain drenched us and changed everything.

It was impossible to overlook the colorful view of the balloons against a gray sky and to hear the continuous whistling from the factories, ships, and other machines. We accepted all these greetings with profound gratitude.

We went from our ship to a train that was to transport us to Camp Devens. The weather was unbearably hot, as if threatening to rain. We witnessed the worse of it in Boston, especially along the railroad line. Later, we passed by Concord and Junction until we reached Ayer, on the edge of a rural area. As soon as we marched on the open terrain, a heavy downpour soaked and chilled us. We marched in the middle of the rain and a storm, but this did not matter, "if we had escaped the bullets, why could we not bear a heavy rain." We are now in the America of Liberty and Justice.

We made our beds in the barracks and ate our supper in the middle of all the commotion and the busy talk one finds among soldiers about to be discharged. At twelve midnight, we signed our first discharge documents. We cannot sleep.

Sunday, June 8

It was cool in the morning. Everything was very beautiful, all because we were in the bosom of our country. We bathed, took a physical examination, ate a good breakfast, and had an even better lunch. They know how to eat in these parts. We washed our clothes after the meal and later fell into formation and received our mail. I searched everywhere for Company G. They are giving eight-hour passes to visit Boston.

The mail I received today included *El Latino-Americano*, which brought me news from home. While at Camp Devens, we visited the Robbins Pond Club and other well-known places in the small town of Ayer.

Monday, June 9

We could not secure passes to go to Boston because the person who issued them—his excellency—took one for himself and left for the famous American city. What does he care, the war has ended and if a soldier has problems with this, he should wise up. We see this as the best time to demonstrate our mettle. If we really want to visit Boston, we have no choice but to manufacture passes for ourselves. Our superior has set the example. It would be our own doing, but also our own risk.

We rented a cab from the many that were available. Seven of us went to town. My buddies Gómez and Kelleher accompanied me. This made the trip even more enjoyable. We went by the historic town of Concord. I discovered how little I knew of the town. I was comparing the old Concord I knew from books with life in the modern birthplace of the American Revolution. I stood under the tree where General Washington was promoted to commander in chief of the American forces during the war against England.

It was starting to rain when we reached Boston. We visited the "White House," the City Hall, and the Public Garden, where we saw several German cannon captured in the war. The 2nd Division had taken the cannon at the Marne. We also saw a statue of the heroes of Boston from the civil war of 1862. I cannot remember exactly what the inscription said but I recall that it did not speak well of the heroes from the South. It expresses the feelings of the time, the hatred of the North toward the South. We also visited a statue of General Washington, a public library, a Christian Science Church, a modern theater, and Fenway park, where we expected to see a baseball game but it had been canceled because of rain. We also visited the area with the major clothing stores and other businesses. Finally, we visited the historic Old South Church and moved quickly from one historical relic to another. An older man showed us everything. We could not tell if he was the minister.

It was soon time to return and we had to give up visiting places we would have enjoyed. We had dinner at a Red Cross restaurant in the public gardens. We came back in the rain and arrived "wet but happy" after an eight-hour outing.

Tuesday, June 10

Our company took a photo this morning. Some of our buddies who were visiting the city were not included.

I had a good time working in the kitchen after lunch. I have already stated that this is one of the details the soldier dreads in peacetime and that he most wants while in war. We now say, "This is the life," when we used to say, "This is the war."

We heard a rumor that we would leave tomorrow. We are so pleased and happy. Soldiers who arrived yesterday are being discharged. Good wishes to our buddies who suffered like us.

Wednesday, June 11

We began dressing as soon as we woke up and carefully prepared the bigger bags that had been issued. The soldiers are very restless. We are part of the commotion because of our departure. The soldiers who are to remain in the military will stay with the arriving troops. They will be transferred to another point where they will remain a few more days. The soldiers are not all foolishly quitting the peacetime army and foregoing the benefits available to them.

Our greatest wish is to see our loved ones, although we cannot deny that we are leaving behind a life so full of adventure and danger. We are also beginning to regret that we will no longer be a part of the peacetime army that will draw benefits from everything we did in the war.

We marched a short distance to a hospital for a throat examination.

The Pullman cars began to arrive. These were the real thing. They felt different in the United States. We left Camp Devens about three and arrived at Troy, New York, by nightfall. Later, we passed by Albany. We felt very happy, ate supper, and recalled everything that occurred a year ago, at the same hour and the same place.

Thursday, June 12

We made daybreak at Binghamton, New York. The other trains with the 360th Infantry caught up with us. We left on the second train and passed by Oswego, Elmira, Olean, and Salamanca. In Salamanca, the American Red Cross gave us ice cream and postcards, which we sent home. They gave us coffee, ice cream, two cigarettes, and matches in Meadville, Pennsylvania. Gómez and I slept in the lower bunk, Barrera in the upper one. I took the lower one so I could note the names of all the towns we will be seeing on our way home.

Friday, June 13

We ate breakfast before reaching Dayton, Ohio. Pullman cars provide all the amenities to wash and shave while traveling at high speed toward the south, the land of our birth. After passing by Dayton, we arrived in Cincinnati at 11:30 a.m., crossed the Ohio River, and entered Indiana. We stopped at Covington, Kentucky, for fifty minutes to do physical exercises. Covington is two miles from Cincinnati. We saw the famed horse track at Latonia, Kentucky, where major races feature the best horses in the country. The Red Cross gave us a lot of ice cream, sandwiches, and cigarettes in Louisville, Kentucky. Nightfall came as we left Kentucky. The last beautiful scene we saw was the state's famed "Blue Grass" region.

Saturday, June 14

On this day last year, we left New York for France on the expedition that forever marked the lives of the soldiers who embarked on the *Olympic*. We just passed through Tennessee and its beautiful capital, Nashville. We are traveling toward New Orleans. We arrived at Birmingham, Alabama, at 10:30 in the morning. The Red Cross gave us ice cream. I bought postcards and did some writing. We bought a watermelon for $1.50. At about two thirty, we crossed the Alabama River on the northern side of Montgomery. We were so happy to see our first fields of corn. In Europe, we saw fine-looking fields of wheat, potatoes, and sugar beets, but none of them compare to the king of the American diet.

In the middle of so much bonanza and beauty, we see the wretched existence of the black population, a moving blemish in this country's history. This is a vestige of the horrible institution of slavery. The whites of Europe brought the curse from Africa.

We passed by Montgomery. It grew dark at Flomaton, Alabama. We began to feel the intense heat of the south.

Sunday, June 15

We reached the historic city of New Orleans by morning and spent a few hours there, but without leaving the train. I saw many rice and sugar cane fields. The corn looked very bad. I saw the famous levees of Baton Rouge for the first time. They hold back the fury of the biggest river in the world. The city is the capital of Louisiana. The Red Cross gave us more ice cream and sandwiches. We have traveled toward the north all morning with the Mississippi to our left.

A newspaper brings us the news of the battle of Ciudad Juárez, Mexico. The rumor spread quickly that we were no longer going to San Antonio but to the border as a rear guard.[1] We have also heard rumors that we will be supplied with munitions.

I wanted to get a sense of how my fellow Mexican soldiers felt about what we were hearing and I asked one of them, "What do you say friend, shall we go fight Mexico? He answered me in the cool and calculated manner of our people, "We are committed and have no choice." How many people can truly understand the meaning of such a humble response?

The Mexican American soldier's response gives us pause. A war against Mexico would be the most important test the American citizen of Mexican origin would have to face. It would be the same kind of challenge that was presented to the German American citizen in the recent war. Our participation would not represent an act of treason. Ever since Texas was sold to the United States with everything and its inhabitants, we have been cut off politically from our brothers on the other side of the border. If treason occurred in the case of Texas, others were to blame, not us. It surely would be distressing to see soldiers of our *raza* in the invading army, just like it was during the Spanish conquest, the war of the 1860s against France, and the wars against the United States.[2] We would meet our responsibility and join the fight, although without the same enthusiasm and willingness we displayed against Germany, Austria, Turkey, Bulgaria, etc., etc. Why? It would be because of the bad treatment, injustice, and racial prejudice we face in Texas. We gave a good account of ourselves against the claim that we were not brave or were not good citizens. We are also speaking for many of our own who did not register for the draft on June 5, 1917. We challenge anyone who saw us on the firing line and in the offensives against the Germans to demonstrate otherwise.

We crossed the wide Mississippi River in two trips on a steamboat. Each crossing included eight Pullman cars. The railroad engine brought us to the steamship. Another one was waiting for us on the other side of the river. I could not tell the distance across the river, but I believe it was over a mile. I can also say that the current is very strong. The moving luminous waters reminded me of many moments in history.

Monday, June 16

We passed by the city of Beaumont last night and reached Houston at daybreak. This made the sergeant in charge of our kitchen very happy. Silver, who is Jewish, and Berner are from Houston. They did not wait to reach the railroad station. They stepped down while we were still moving. No one can blame them. I would have done that and more. We really want to see our loved ones after the long absence the war caused.

It was raining hard when we reached the station. I cannot explain it, but I had a bad feeling about the place, it was different from the way we have felt when arriving at other cities.

Samuel Gómez's family was waiting for him. He was so happy to see his parents and siblings. I will experience the same joy in due time.

The rest of my buddies appear oblivious to everything except the present moment, which smiles upon us.

We ate breakfast in the city at our own expense.

As Colonel Price, our regimental commander, promised, we marched triumphantly through the streets. We did this in a torrential rain and did not stop until we had reached the city auditorium where General McAlexander and a congressman gave stirring speeches. The program was long and tiring.

I should express my appreciation for a German who approached a buddy and me and thanked us for our part in the war. His upstanding character surprised me, I will never forget it. The racial conditions under which Mexicans find themselves in Houston are not very good. The friendly German is obviously different because he is from the north and sees things through a different lens.

We enjoyed a sumptuous, exquisite lunch after the speeches. I do not know who we should thank for all of this, but we are grateful to everyone who was involved. They should know that members of my *raza* also know how to be thankful for such sincere and friendly acts.

After our meal, we rushed to the Pullmans to leave our bags and then walked the streets of Houston. We had a shave in a barber shop owned by one of our own and talked at length with several local Mexicans. We concluded from the conversations that many Mexicans still do not understand that we need to improve our condition so that we can claim our rightful place in society. We are accused of being lazy and for insisting on maintaining our traditional way of life. We concede some ground on this and believe that we should adjust our ways for a better life in this country. We will be treated as a problem if we are a hindrance to Anglo-American progress.

A concert was held in the auditorium in the afternoon. Some ladies sang while others played the piano.

A building with a dilapidated appearance and even sorrier reputation named the Salón para Mexicanos is situated next to the auditorium, actually in front of it. To add to the insult, its name is written in bad lettering on a long and ordinary-looking plank. This image alone makes it obvious that we need to make progress. Vice-ridden behavior—not economic conditions—closes doors and denies us the full measure of justice. I am not saying this is characteristic of Mexicans in Houston, but the place leaves a bad mark next to the place where Anglo-Americans express their full appreciation to the sons of the nation who return with the greatest well-earned victory. This makes Mexicans from Houston seem irresponsible and oblivious to the bad image their behavior bring us. It also undermines the sacrifice we just made in the fields of honor. There it is for everyone to see, that disgusting house with its wide open doors and its prostitutes who are calling out to the Mexican soldiers.

Why are they doing this? They do it to draw them into the mire. How many must have gone to them.

The reader must understand that the municipal auditorium is the social center of the great city and the Salón para Mexicanos is a business that corrupts. This is a sad situation for our poor community of working people. Even though they may be more than willing to cooperate for their advancement, they lack the necessary environment for social development. We need more people who will fight for justice. For this reason I have urged my fellow Mexicans to join the cause in peacetime. We now face new problems that require our experience, skills, and energies, and we have the opportunity to teach by example, like Archimedes's fulcrum and lever.

People who do not understand, act poorly! Comrades in arms, what a sad day it will be for us if the quiet peace of our homes causes us to forget the horrible hardships and other forms of suffering. This is a high price that we will have paid for bringing our children the honorable laurels of victory and success.

We received another kind gesture before the celebration ended. A ladies' organization from Galveston extended its courtesies. We appreciate them as bright rays of sunlight falling on a darkness of profound proportions, a hostile environment the poor and uneducated working community faces in Houston and its surrounding area. The problem emerges out of the injustice and racial prejudice of the past that continue as aberrations in a civilized society without any justification in history.

I attended a public program in the evening at the famous Rice Hotel. The orator showered praise on the heroes who fell on the battlefields, as well as on the survivors who will serve the nation in peacetime. The big dance for the officers began once the ceremonial program ended. Some soldiers had partners and danced while the rest decided to wait until they saw their loved ones. It goes without saying that the dance was of little or no interest to the Mexicans. Why? It was because of the well-known animosity expressed toward our people in these parts. I do not know that any Mexican was snubbed this evening, but neither did any of us give them an excuse. I also do not know that anyone was nice enough to ask one of our own to dance. Houston! Houston, you may be beautiful, wealthy, and forward looking, but you do not inspire confidence, and may our cause live on!

While seated in a luxurious booth in the comfortable waiting room of the Rice Hotel, I mulled my past in light of what was before me. I thought anxiously of the many dark moments and my wishful thinking, of the numerous memories and encouraging hopes for the future. All of this may soon fade away like smoke. We may have to face harsh realities and bitter truths tomor-

row. Already, we are subject to so much but ready for anything. We will know
to respond with strength.

Short of money and alone, my friend Francisco Hernández joined me to
eat in a restaurant. The world has yet to hear about him and others like him.
They have retreated into their private lives like snails into their shells, and this
is why history will fail to notice their sacrifices. Even his friends and fellow
Mexicans will forget them after a generation. Hernández was among the few
heroes who faced dangers and the possibility of death by himself. During
an evening patrol in no man's land, he surprised a German patrol and killed
three of them with his bayonet. There you have him, this quiet young man
shrouded in mystery. He will soon be behind the plow, wielding the lariat and
ready to rope, or working on the railroad, all the while waiting like Cincinnatus, to defend the nation at the first sign of danger.

We returned to our train late after dinner, but not before we had bid
farewell to our poor brothers who were staying behind. Good-bye my dear
companions, I hope we do not meet again under the same circumstances that
brought us here! Good-bye!

Tuesday, June 17

I do not know when the train left, but we were very near Yoakum by
daybreak. The Red Cross handed out candies and cigarettes. Much rain has
apparently fallen in the past few days. The crops look beautiful. Corn, the
historic plant of our indigenous *raza*, shines in all its splendor and beauty.

When I set my eyes on the first cactus, the legendary symbol of our Aztec
past, I saw a beauty in the humble plant that I had never imagined. Like
other plants, it is condemned to extinction. The Europeans have declared an
all-out war against it like the one they leveled against the indigenous people
who lived here.

Mesquite trees and dark brush began to appear after we passed Cuero.
When we came to the sandy soils and the vast cotton fields that employ so
many Mexicans, I could not help recalling my experiences here. A while later,
we passed by Nordheim, Runge, Kenedy, and Karnes City. I poured out my
sweat in all these places as a youngster. This is where I made a living and
earned the means to pursue my education, where I tasted the bitterness that
has been the lot of my people, where I realized we must struggle to become
like the educated people on this earth. I suffered horribly as I witnessed the
inequality, contempt, injustice, and bad treatment directed against my people. They come from Mexico or other parts of Texas intent on making a life
for themselves and determined to earn an honest living picking the valuable

crop to clothe people around the world. In the middle of this suffering, I felt a burning desire to educate myself and to become a mentor to the children whose parents clamor for help. I also wanted to give voice to our indignation and outcry so that the whole world could know. There is no better time to do this, now that a wounded humanity is waiting for the official word to establish world peace and place our civilization beyond the reach of barbaric rule. The fresh memory of our service and loyalty makes this the opportune time; this is when we can say that we knew how to sacrifice everything to fulfill the most sacred duty among men who desire to be free.

We reached San Antonio at two in the afternoon. A sweltering heat beat down on us as the factory whistles announced that the sons of San Antonio had arrived with the laurels of victory. A large crowd that included my wife and children was waiting for us. I felt the greatest joy in the world. My most profound desire and my fondest dreams were realized as I took them in my arms and reached for my Supreme Creator in prayerful gratitude for such a wonderful blessing. The idea of the nation came to me as I kissed my loving wife on her forehead and embraced my children.

After formation, we marched from the old Aransas Pass railroad station and into South Flores. We were actually walking on roses and other flowers the grateful citizens of San Antonio had laid at our feet. The flowers were for everyone who had marched over the soil of liberated France, ground turned mud with the heroic blood of our nation's sons. What a profound sense of satisfaction to witness such a deep-felt appreciation for the consummated sacrifice!

This was the best tribute our fellow citizens could have given their victorious sons. From South Flores we proceeded to Commerce and then to South Alamo where we turned toward the historic Alamo Plaza and the Alamo mission, "the cradle of Texas liberty." They had built a large triumphal arc like the ones raised for returning Roman legions. All the accomplishments of the 90th Division were written on it. We were allowed to join our friends for a good while once we had passed under the arc.

Mr. William J. Knox, one of my longtime friends, a *profesor*, and a fellow professional, did not wait for us to fall out. As soon as we stopped, he made his way through the troops until he reached me. He gave me a welcoming embrace with the same sincerity I would have expected from my father.

Friendship from men like him encourages us in our difficult and demanding cause for the justice and fair treatment we deserve. *Profesor* Knox fully understands the challenges and injustices we have faced. He recognizes our potential as citizens and encourages us to hope for the justice we seek.

The soldiers and civilians heard eloquent, provocative speeches given from a public stand that had been built for the occasion.

From there, we marched to the Sunset station where railroad cars were waiting to take us to Camp Travis. As soon as we arrived, we took all our military-issued clothing to the old and familiar barracks, opened up our metal cots, took off our packs, and left for the city. This is how we came to spend our first night with our loved ones, after the depressing absence we took while meeting our patriotic duty.

Demobilizing the 90th Division

Wednesday, June 18

I t is impossible to describe the happiness we felt during our first night in our homes. One had to have been there. I suppose that what happened in my home was repeated everywhere else. My loved ones wanted to know everything and I wanted to hear about what they had done while I was gone. Happy and unpleasant memories, dreams, illusions, and experiences overwhelmed us and made it impossible to talk about everything. We all wanted to talk but no one really said anything. Joy was in all our hearts and everyone had a smile on his or her face.

We hardly took notice of the humble, traditional banquet my family prepared. The visit turned into a virtual "barrage" of questions and incomplete responses, but we did everything with complete joy and pleasure.

After waxing on the glory of the moment and our good fortune, the harsh reality began to set in. I will soon return to civilian life, and I need to decide what I am going to do with my children and myself. I thought about my teaching profession. Mr. Knox had told me that the classes for teachers had begun and that I should enroll because I had to take the examination. I did this. I went to the high school on Main Street where I had a good time seeing old friends and making new ones. I am once again grateful to Mr. Knox because he was kind enough to pay my ten-dollar enrollment fee, and he absolutely refused to accept my money. Mr. Knox instead spoke highly of me because I had met my patriotic duty. He added that his sacrifice was insignificant next to mine. Who else thinks this way? I should add that this is not the only favor I owe this generous and responsible man. Everything happened so fast when I was preparing to go to war that I was not able to visit all my relatives and tell them about my wishes for my family. I briefly told Mr. Knox I was on my way to fulfill my duty and I trusted that people who were to remain on the home front would understand what I was doing and offer my family a helping hand in time of need. I asked him, "Please visit my family whenever you can, I know they will need your help now and then." I advised my family, "Go to this man when you are in a bind, trust him completely." My dear friend was true to his word and I thank him for being a gentleman. Gold cannot repay this debt. Knowing that such reasonable, honorable, self-respecting, and fair men exist helped us bear the bad treatment and insults that ignorant, insolent, narrow-minded, and wicked citizens directed at us.

I returned to the camp, where I figured out what I had to do for my discharge. Gómez and I went back to the city later in the day. I bought some everyday wear and visited my old friends, Mr. Ignacio Lozano and José G. González at the offices of *La Prensa*. I promised to share with them my experiences from the Great War.

A soldier who had just returned from Europe invited me to a dance that evening. Gómez joined me. He really shook up the dance floor. I could not locate Barrera; otherwise, I would have also made him dance up a storm. We were very pleased with the reception our people prepared for us as the defenders of our racial pride and good name.

Thursday, June 19

I attended classes for teachers in the morning and went to the camp in the afternoon. My friends are turning in all their government property. We are to keep a complete uniform for ourselves. Of course, we will keep the best one. We joked around and even acted as if we were happy when we said good-bye to everything that had become a part of us. When I turned in my carbine, I could not help remembering two horrible nights—the evening of our first advance and the night when I wandered into no man's land. Many of the soldiers had the nerve or were simply bold in refusing to turn in everything. I would have wanted to keep our eating utensils and would have paid for them. I was not interested in their material value, but wanted to keep the memories that came with them.

I placed the rest of my clothes and other personal items in my blue canvas bag. I wanted to take it home as a souvenir to remind me of the equipment we carried in the unforgettable trenches of France. We can only wear the government-issued uniform for sixty days. This would give us enough time to buy civilian clothes. Our uniform consisted of the raincoat, chapeau, overcoat, gas mask, steel helmet, blue woolen bag, undergarments, and military shoes.

Friday, June 20

It rained for a good while, and this made me late for my teacher examination, but I finished and never lost hope that I would do well. Although I had not reviewed the books for almost two years, my ability to recall was unfailing. I took the examination to teach while still in the military.

Felipe García, a good friend from San Diego, works with me in the office where we process the discharge papers. I was very happy to see him, but we had little time to talk.

I filled out my questionnaire this afternoon. The information they are collecting is probably useless. Many of the forms are so badly filled out that they will be difficult to use regardless of the intentions of the military. They will present the same problems as the ones that we filled out when we left for Europe.

I headed for home, happy but worrying about tomorrow's challenges.

We have to return tomorrow, maybe for the last time. So be it.

Saturday, June 21

We ate breakfast on the government's tab for the last time. We will begin paying our own way tomorrow, if we have any money to spare. We have claimed victory, we must now pay up.

We fell into formation for our last pay, but it was not the same. No one felt the military spirit. Who knows what was racing through our minds. We were stunned. As much as we tried to make sense of the animated conversations like we used to do, it was impossible. Our companions in arms are entering General Headquarters, where they are receiving their pay. As soon as they went outside, they acted like animals throwing off their binding chains. They were leaving without saying good-bye to their brothers in misery. When our turn came—we were among the last—no one was around to bid farewell. This is how man yearns for freedom, as he is abandoning military discipline or subliminally seeking the slavery of the sweet obligations of home! He is oblivious to everything!

I would have given anything to have been able to say goodbye to every one of my Mexican brothers. It was impossible. May they go in peace and may their homes give them sustenance and serve as sources of pride and honor for our children, for whom we have made the greatest sacrifice and in whose name we have helped write the latest page in our national history.

We were given a discharge document, a bonus of $60, permission to wear our uniform for sixty days, and a government-issued pass for our trip home.

What a great deal! Many of us would have been unable to pay the cost of transportation and a set of civilian clothes.

I ate with my family. At one in the afternoon, I took the train to Alice where my father and the rest of my brothers lived. Other discharged soldiers traveled on the same train.

Although I had seen my wife and children, I could not really be happy until I visited with my dear father. The train arrived a few minutes after five. I said hello to some of my brothers and walked home. I wanted to walk the ground of my youth. My father was already heading toward me and that is how I was able to take the poor man in my arms before reaching home. He is the kindest father in the world.

I take in my surroundings but it all seems like a dream. After our joyful greeting, my father, brothers, and sisters leave to finish their day's work and I find myself alone to rest for a while. I am exhausted, sad, and deep in thought. It is six in the afternoon. We will be gathering at Salón Salazar at eight o'clock. At the suggestion of our dear friend Mr. Ascencio Treviño, some of our friends are eager to celebrate our return.

We will have to accept our friends' good wishes, although I would have preferred to stay home, my dear place of joy, which I often feared I would never see again. I want to talk to my family and to hear from them until we can no longer speak.

YEARNING

I am beginning to feel the full effect of the memories that were etched in my mind during the sixteen months of military service. I recall the reasons for pursuing such an adventure and understand that if I gained nothing, at least I feel fulfilled.

Like in a movie, I see myself arriving at New Braunfels, my presentation before government officials, a short and lively conversation with an old German, my observations at the tavern before we ate, our meal at the Plaza Hotel, the railroad station and our trip to Camp Travis, our first impressions at the camp, scenes of our training, and the military preparations for our departure. Our camp became a virtual ant colony during those days. I see many military trains arriving, every one of them with a chain of Pullman cars to carry millions of men to the Atlantic coast and the high seas. I see our car, the *Inverary*, my travel companions, our exit from the camp, and our farewell to San Antonio. On our way to the northeast, we pass by New Braunfels, San Marcos, Austin, Dallas, Greenville, Texarkana (Texas), Smoky River, Pine Bluff (Arkansas), and "the father of all rivers," the Mississippi. We arrive at the Great Lakes, Cleveland, Buffalo, Utica, Albany, Norwich, Middletown, and Hoboken, NJ. We cross the New York bay, near the Statue of Liberty, on the steamship *Catskill*. We disembark on Long Island and spend one night at Camp Mills. The next day we cross the bay, this time on the *Washington*, and dock at a huge wharf in New York City. The massive English steamship *Olympic* is waiting for us. Some ladies from the Red Cross give us a sandwich and an orange (we haven't eaten breakfast). A YMCA representative gives each soldier a postcard with a printed message. The card informs our family members about our arrival. We sleep on hammocks that night while the ship is tied to the dock. We will never forget the small servings of bad food the English gave us during our first days—horsemeat, potatoes, unsalted fish, rotten bread, and poor quality tea. This was such pitiful food for the soldiers of democracy on the precarious crusade to help save our civilization.

We leave on June 14. Two destroyers escort us the entire day. The *Olympic* travels day and night at 22 knots per hour. We see land on the twenty-first, believing that we have reached Ireland. The F52, the H6A1, the 48, and the oo join us. They belong to the US Navy. In the afternoon, we pass by Whit Island and enter Southampton Port, England. We sleep on the ship, disembark in the morning, and stay indoors. We cross the English Channel on the *King Edward* at sunset, arrive at Le Havre, France, in eight hours, and rest for a day in an English military camp. The next day, we head to the south of France. After reaching Lautrec, we march to Rouvres-sur-Aube, Haute-de-Marne. On August 18 we leave for Toul and later to the first front at Saint-Mihiel. We spend time at Villers, Fey, Jezainville, Montville, Norroy, Pont-à-Mousson, Bois le Prete, and the Moselle River. On October 10, we leave the front for Toul and then Rampondt. From there, we march through Nixeville, Blecourt, Dombasle in Argonne, Avocourt, Melancourt, Montfaucon, Dead Man Hill, Hill 304, Cierges and Nantillois. We end up on the outskirts of Romagne. On the first of November, we begin to throw out the Germans from Mantheville, Aincreville, Villers-devant-Dun, Dun, Mouzay, and Stenay. The armistice comes. We leave France for Germany, crossing Luxembourg and reaching Zeltingen on the Moselle, where we spend six months as the army of occupation. We travel to Koblenz and Paris. Our next departure takes us across Germany and France until we reach Saint-Nazaire. The *Mongolia* transports us to the United States. We reach Boston, Nashville, New Orleans, Baton Rouge, Beaumont, Houston, San Antonio, Camp Travis, and my home.

I am home, safe and sound, and reviewing all these memories as if in a dream. All of this pleases me. I have been faithful to my duty.

REFLECTIONS

Have we saved democracy, civilization, the nation, humanity? I do not know. What I do know is that the Mexican American has distinguished and asserted himself. The glorious stars and stripes we have defended with our lives in European battlefields will no doubt serve as our children's banner for years to come. These are the kind of sacrifices that forge a nation and honor a flag. It is only right that when the last glorious chapter of our National American History is written we do not forget that *Mexican Americans* have made a contribution with their blood.

Fini la Guerre!

Epilogue
The Voice of a Claim That Demands Justice

Three decades have passed since the world celebrated Armistice Day, on November 11, 1918. On that memorable day, at eleven o'clock, hostilities ended for the nations that had fought in the air, on the ground, and on the high seas. During these thirty years, many people have been able to see the terrible hardships the war visited upon civilians and the soldiers who lived the dangers and horrors of those dreadful battles.

We, the survivors of the war, observed and continue to witness man's capacity to be inconsistent. Under different circumstances we might have agreed that my observations, written as the events unfolded, could have been easily taken as "complaints that were out of order," but they stand on increasingly solid ground. I have labored patiently for the last ten years to prepare my views for public presentation and have waited for the right time during the last five years.

The time to publish has arrived, especially because of the recent events in our nation's history. This has prompted us to act. We are no longer the only *complainants without a cause*, as some would still insist on calling us. If our bitterness once caused us to doubt that we would ever receive justice for our great sacrifice to the nation, recent occurrences tell us we were not far from the truth. Insofar as the ingratitude we might receive, we could point to the guns and violence directed at the men, women, and children last year in Washington. The victims were defenseless veterans and their families who had come to the Capitol on a crusade demanding payment from the government for their services to the nation. We can agree that this might not have been the best time to make demands, even if conditions were enough to otherwise cause revolts and revolutions, but neither did their actions justify deploying armed troops who did not hesitate in using asphyxiating gases against the wives and children of the same men who in 1918 defended our flag in foreign lands.

Like a disturbing voice from the past, the memory of the war of 1918 reminds us that we have not raised a memorial equal to the martyred sacrifice the American soldiers of Mexican descent offered for us. Grateful people have erected so many monuments on the old battlefields that France has placed limits on the number and type of structure that can be built. The press tells us that even the animals—horses, dogs, and pigeons—that died like heroes for our cause have warranted statues that safeguard their memory with dignity.

We sounded the first alarm of our pending responsibility in 1928, but self-serving and base individuals divided us and blocked our way. Some people could not bring themselves to understand the difference between the intrinsic value of the idea and what could be classified as a personal motivation. The proposal stood on its merits and favored us, but we could not move forward and postponed the project. Men fall, ideas last. We do not lose hope that we will see the grand monument rise majestically in our lifetime in a Texas city, or in San Antonio. We wish to erect it in the Alamo city, on the Main Plaza, to the east of the Casa de Cortes and in front of the old San Fernando Cathedral.

We have published the book against all odds. This has been the history of the book since its beginning. The diary was born amid the sad and historically significant events of 1917, when our nation entered the global conflict. Gathering the facts required that we risk everything, including our very lives.

Fifteen years have passed and the nations of the world still do not have the peaceful and friendly relations that existed before the war. Many of my people have died and been forgotten. It pains us to see cases like the wife and children of our fellow veteran Hipólito Jasso who live in oblivion, abject poverty, and isolation in Beeville, Texas. This reminds us that we were right when we stated before the grave of Simón Gonzáles of Martindale, Texas, the hero of Aincreville, "No, my friend, the war for us will not end when we finish with the Germans, unless they finish with us first. We will have to face a more difficult fight, a battle in the heart of the Nation, against the people from Martindale who killed your father and unjustly sent you to war."

Future generations will continue to present our demands over the lack of gratitude shown to the Bonus Expeditionary Force in Washington.

What should we say about our own who kept us from completing our monument by saying, "We should not be doing this. It is the responsibility of the government that took you to war," or "We will contribute but it must not say anything Mexican. We fear this will provoke more racial prejudice and hate. The Anglos may not like it." You fainthearted souls of limited nationalist vision, blinded by the glare of personalities, lacking a principled education and trumpeting pessimism, you carry the complex of inferiority and are incapable of rising above your depraved surroundings.

We need more sacrifices, and these offerings require more broad-minded men prepared to fight for the common good of our *raza*.

To the Memory of
the Mexican American Heroes
Who Died in the Great World War
Defending the Democratic Principles
of the American Union

Heroic nymphs of the New World,
Sing our civic virtues with poetic glory,
Place laurels on proud intrepid warriors
Who fell defending our freedom.

    The immaculate, American Eden,
    Washington's homeland, turned the storm
    Into triumph and victory, our magnificent Spartan home,
    You wear grand dignity as a crown.

Over there, beyond the seas, the vile despotism,
The idea, the cowardly acts,
The German nation conspired
To entrap our heroes with egotistical snares.

    The eagles of America flew over the high seas
    And planted in Europe their military might
    Because Joseph William, that tyrannical monarch,
    Sought to claim the glory of our triumphant fight.

Over there, in foreign soil, where the heartless War
Would display its sorry and destructive way,
There too, our people offered an eternal example
Of our nation's sense of civic worth.

They left their happy and sacred homes,
Their beloved parents and women, their angelic love,
To bequeath us honor, Oh intrepid warriors!
You return with glory and bright grandeur.

Our very own who in trenches fought
Gave us testimony of bravery, our legacy of glory,
They fell fulfilled in trenches, while honoring the flag
That led them into the greatest battle the world has ever seen.

A breeze from America sings its praises,
Palm and olive trees send them our way.
The Lord who commands, prepares a place for them.
To the world they are dead . . . to us, they live!

Flag of stripes and glimmering stars,
Your profound meaning commands respect.
What heroic example you have left
For the nations of the distant old world!

They died honorably for our democracy,
Mexican Americans, still appear in history!
If pride is our inheritance, let us honor their courage,
By erecting a pedestal of glory for them.

MARGIL LOPEZ
Sarita, Texas

List of Honor

We most sincerely appreciate everyone who has made this book possible. Future generations will have to judge us according to our deeds. People who made a sacrifice to advance the subscription cost without even requiring the usual receipt once again demonstrate undeniable loyalty, and this has been the life-giving support that sustains us in the struggle until the end. Their children and their children's children will now be better able to appreciate their modest efforts in favor of a just cause. They deserve to be called collaborators because this publication would not have been possible without their help.

J. LUZ SÁENZ

ALICE, TEXAS

Fortino Treviño
A. A. Hinnant
Sra. María Luera
Alfredo Munguía
Francisco Pérez
Lawrence Broeter
Manuel Sáenz Escobar
Eduwiges Pérez
Sra. Florencia Vda. de Flores
Ascencio Treviño
Julián Gómez
Melesio Pérez
Fidel Rul

CORPUS CHRISTI, TEXAS

Constantino M. Rodríguez
(Tex-Mex News Stand)
Guillermo Cuellar
Zeferino Perales
Cipriano R. González
Federico Quiroz
Andrés de Luna
José G. González
Luis G. Wilmot
Ezequiel Meza
Vicente Lozano

FALFURRIAS, TEXAS
Maximiliano Hinojosa

Juan H. Vela
Juan V. González
Doroteo González
Sra. Lucrecia Vda. de López
M. G. Pérez
Adalberto B. Cruz
Rufino García

KINGSVILLE, TEXAS
Eduardo Salazar
Maximiliano Figueroa

POINT ISABEL, TEXAS
Gregorio Tamayo
Florentino Aguilar

PETTUS, TEXAS
Ramón D. Sáenz

PREMONT, TEXAS
Luis Gonzáles
Félix Barrera
Albino Canales
J. M. Canales

SALINENO TEXAS
Juan Hinojosa, P. M.

SAN JUAN, TEXAS
Srita. Adela Sloss
Zacarías González

SAN DIEGO, TEXAS
C. G. Palacios
Dr. José García
Juan Rivera
Pablo Pérez
Guillermo Jaime
Juan Solís
Eduardo B. Barrera
Eliseo Cadena

Lorenzo García
Daniel U. García
Daniel Tobín
Avelino E. García
Manuel García
Carlos Peña
J. O. Treviño
Filomeno Hinojosa
Fernando de Peña

VICTORIA, TEXAS
José G. Sáenz
Pablo González (Brownsville)
Sra. Teresa M. de la Garza

GRULLA, TEXAS
Prof. J. M. Longoria

HEBBRONVILLE, TEXAS
Rafael M. García
Servando H. González
Arístides Barrera
Raúl P. Montalvo
Armando Vázquez
A. W. Saldaña
Eliseo Cuéllar
Aurelio M. Cisneros
Sinecio Gutiérrez
José A. Canales
Eduardo Barrera
Fernando Ximénez

BEEVILLE, TEXAS
Alfredo Dereause
Felipe Martínez

LAREDO, TEXAS
Luis S. Perales
Prof. Juan T. González
Blas García
Laureano Salazar

SAN ANTONIO, TEXAS
Lic. Alonso S. Perales
Priciliano Sáenz
Antonio Elizondo
Samuel E. Luna
Florencio R. Flores
Lic. Manuel C. González
Prof. Edmundo E. Mireles
Prof. W. J. Knox
Humberto Rivas
Luis Rodríguez
Dr. H. N. González
José C. Ramírez
Gonzalo García Jr.
S. Vidaurre Jr.
H. Rodríguez

RIO GRANDE CITY, TEXAS
Jesse Pérez
Pedro Díaz
Enrique González
A. H. Gutiérrez
Hernán Contreras
Casimiro P. Alvarez

REALITOS, TEXAS
Julián Gonzalez
Ernesto Ramírez
R. A. Acebo
J. M. Benavides
Emeterio Guerra
Ponciano Ramírez
Enrique Ramírez

DONNA, TEXAS
M. Mendoza
B. C. Escobar
Enrique Zúñiga
Salvador M. Hinojosa

MERCEDES, TEXAS
Arturo Torres

ABRAHAM, TEXAS
Antonio Sandoval

PEÑITAS, TEXAS
Humberto Cavazos

ROBSTOWN, TEXAS
H. P. González

POTEET, TEXAS
Benjamin A. Treviño
Fidel García

McALLEN, TEXAS
Severo Barrero
Gregorio P. Sáenz
Dr. F. Godines
Luis Vela
Miss Zara Thigpen
"Diogenes"
Flavio Salazar
"Orientación"
L. Yañez
Cruz T. Kelly
Victorino García

MISSION, TEXAS
R. E. Austin
Felipe García
P. H. Longoria
J. Martínez
Alberto Díaz
Adán Contreras
Camilo González

Moore, Texas
Pedro Múzquiz
Srita. Pfra. Concepción Múzquiz
Francisco Múzquiz
A. Chapa
J. M. Dominguez

San Benito, Texas
Ramón González

Cotulla, Texas
J. E. Villarreal

Brackettville, Texas
Eulogio Gómez
Ignacio Gómez
Tomás Falcon
Emilio González

Del Rio, Texas
Amado Gutierrez
J. B. Rubio
Rodolfo H. Gutierrez
Pilar García
Concilio No. 18 de Del Rio
Fidelio Cortinas
C. H. Gutierrez
El honorable Comité Pro Defensa
Escolar de Del Rio, Texas, que
sostuvo la causa de nuestra niñez
cuando injustamenta se le segregó
en una de las escuelas oficiales de
aquella ciudad, en el año 1930.
Pres. Jesús Salvatierra
Sec. Pilar Garza
Tes. Nazario Rodríguez
Voc. Francisco Sánchez
Voc. Felipe Oldrete

North Pleasanton, Texas
Frumencio Cásares

Benavides, Texas
Ramíro González
Gilberto González
Alfredo Sáenz
Gabriel Guevara
Gregorio Guevara
Prof. Samuel G. García
Francisco Vaello Puig
Octavio Sáenz
Servando H. Gonzáles
Manuel Ramírez
Liborio Cadena
Trinidad Salazar
P. N. Hinojosa
Edelmiro Farías
Miss Eudelia Sáenz

Eagle Pass, Texas
Carlos Carter
Feliciano Carter
José Angel Martínez
Ricardo V. Cook
H. T. Harper
T. H. González
Andrés Rosales

Spofford, Texas
Francisco Hernández
José Pereas

Brownsville, Texas
F. C. Garza

Notes

Introduction

1. Most of the biographical information on Sáenz is drawn from two of his unpublished autobiographies: "Yo, Omnia Mea Mecum Porto," 1944, and "Short Autobiographical Sketch," May 1947. Copies are available in the José de la Luz Sáenz Papers, 1908–98, archived in the Mexican American Library Program, Nettie Lee Benson Latin American Collection, University of Texas at Austin (hereafter cited as Sáenz Papers).

2. Other Mexican-origin soldiers may have also put their pens to paper when they returned from the war. The San Antonio newspaper *El Imparcial* reported that a veteran named José Canal published a war diary titled *Hazañas de un Mexicano en las trincheras de Francia* (San Antonio: Companía Publicista Lagunera, 1919). Only Sáenz's war diary seems to have survived in published form, however. Despite extensive searches in the catalogs of libraries located in the United States and Mexico, I have been unable to locate a copy of Canal's book. The editors of *El Imparcial* described Canal's diary as "a true history of the achievements and heroism of José Canal, a young man from Coahuila who enlisted in the American army to fight the Germans and avenge the blood of his father who was beaten to death by a German from the region of La Laguna, México. The valor and heroism of the Mexican people is so evident in this history that a reading of it should fill Mexicans with a sense of pride." *El Imparcial*, February 20, 1919, 4. Previously noted in Emilio Zamora, "Fighting on Two Fronts: José de la Luz Sáenz and the Language of the Mexican-American Civil Rights Movement," in *Recovering the U.S. Hispanic Literary Heritage*, vol. 4, ed. José F. Aranda Jr. and Silvio Torres-Saillant (Houston: Arte Público, 2002), 231–32.

3. The history of many settlements on the South Texas-Mexico border region, including outposts like Realitos, began when the Viceroy of New Spain commissioned José de Escandón to establish a colonial presence in the area during the late 1740s. The now shared history across this transnational region allows numerous Mexican families from Texas and northern Mexico to trace their ancestry to the first colonial families in places like Reynosa Viejo, Mier, Camargo, Revilla, and Laredo. See Florence J. Scott, *Historical Heritage of the Lower Rio Grande: A Historical Record of Spanish Exploration, Subjugation, and Colonization of the Lower Rio Grande Valley and the Activities of José Escandón, Count of Sierra Gorda, Together with the Development of Towns and Ranches under Spanish, Mexican, and Texas Sovereignties, 1747–1848* (Rio Grande

City, TX: La Retama Press, 1970). I use the terms *Mexican, Mexican American,* and *Mexican-origin* or *Mexican origin* interchangeably, mostly in accordance with Sáenz's usage.

4. The following publications address the life and work of Sáenz, as well as the Mexican American civil rights cause that drew much of his attention between the 1910s and 1940s: Carole E. Christian, "Joining the American Mainstream: Texas's Mexican Americans during World War I," *Southwestern Historical Quarterly* 92, no. 4 (1989): 559–95; Zamora, "Fighting on Two Fronts"; Zamora, "La guerra en pro de la justicia y la democracia en Francia y Texas: José de la Luz Sáenz y el lenguaje del movimiento mexicano de los derechos civiles," *Revista de Historia Internacional* 4, no. 13 (Summer 2003): 9–35; José A. Ramírez, *To the Line of Fire: Mexican Texans and World War I* (College Station: Texas A&M University Press, 2009); Zamora, *Claiming Rights and Righting Wrongs in Texas: Mexican Workers and Job Politics during World War II* (College Station: Texas A&M University Press, 2009); and Jesús Rosales, "José de la Luz Sáenz: Precursor de la literatura del movimiento Chicano," *Camino Real* 1 (2009): 153–73.

5. Sáenz provided little information on his Mexican teachers. The following is a useful secondary source on one of them: "Eulalio Velázquez," Handbook of Texas Online, http://www.tshaonline.org/handbook/online/articles/VV/fve4.html, accessed July 15, 2009.

6. Consult the following studies on Mexican American history in Texas and the educational experience: Arnoldo de León, *Mexican Americans in Texas: A Brief History* (Arlington Heights, IL: Harlan Davidson, 1993); Emilio Zamora, *The World of the Mexican Worker in Texas, 1900–1920* (College Station: Texas A&M University Press, 1993); Guadalupe San Miguel, *"Let All of Them Take Heed": Mexican Americans and the Campaign for Educational Equality in Texas, 1910–1981* (Austin: University of Texas Press, 1987); Carlos Blanton, *The Strange Career of Bilingual Education in Texas, 1836–1981* (College Station: Texas A&M University Press, 2002).

7. For a substantial and substantive statement by Eulalio Velázquez on the merits of teaching Spanish and Mexican history and culture, consult his sixty-page pamphlet, *Escuelas mexicanas en Texas, artículos publicados en El Cosmopolíta* (Alice, TX: Tipografía del Cosmopolíta, 1906). The publication includes articles by Velázquez as well as by educators and journalists from Mexico and other places in Texas taking issue with the editor of another newspaper from Alice, *El Sol,* who reportedly claimed that independent Mexican schools were not preparing Mexican youth for life in the United States. Velázquez and his allies responded that public schools often refused admission to Mexicans, while the Mexican schools provided them instruction in Spanish and Mexican history in accordance to accepted pedagogical methods—including the use of native and second language instruction—and the popular wishes of Mexicans in the United States. The persons and the organizations they represented included Rodolfo Menéndez, director of the Escuela Normal (teacher's college) in Mérida, Yucatán; the School Board of El Colegio Altamirano (Hebbronville); and the editors of *El Demócrata Fronterizo* (Laredo), *Guarda del Bravo* (Laredo), *Puerto de Matamoros* (Matamoros), *Progresista* (Ciudad Victoria, Tamaulipas), *Observador* (Ciudad Mier, Tamaulipas), *Porvenir* (Brownsville), *Libertad* (San Diego), *Liberal* (Del Rio), and *El Regidor* (San Antonio). Also consult the

following study on the historic statewide meeting that addressed the issue of schooling and school exclusion and segregation as central concerns in the larger Mexican political world of Texas: José E. Limón, "El Primer Congreso Mexicanista de 1911," *Aztlán* 5 (Spring, Fall 1974).

8. The previously noted autobiographical statements by Sáenz do not include information on the Canary Islanders, but they are relatively well known in Texas history. Fifteen families from the Canary Islands arrived in San Antonio in 1731—thirteen years after the establishment of a presidio—and formed a community they called San Fernando de Béxar, which had the first organized civil government in Texas. The Aztec pilgrim story anchored him to the larger hemispheric world, but it required elaboration because only family members knew it. According to Luz, a group of indigenous survivors fled to the north soon after the Spanish forces had conquered the Aztec defenders in present-day Mexico City. After a long but undetermined period, some of them reached the area close to the northern town of Ciudad Victoria where they established a town they called Tula, in remembrance of the ancient Toltec capital, Tollán (now called Tula, in the state of Hidalgo). When Spaniards arrived in 1617, they moved again, into a canyon where family lore claimed that the mountains ended. Some of them eventually established settlements along the Rio Bravo, probably during the late 1700s or early 1800s. "From here," Sáenz added, "it was very easy to cross and roam over the grassy prairie land of the Tejas [tribe]. This will explain well enough of how I came to be born in Realitos and being at the same time an Aztec." Sáenz confirmed the pilgrimage story in 1946 while attending a teachers' seminar in the northern Mexican state of Tamaulipas. According to Sáenz, a respected historian from Ciudad Victoria named Candelario Reyes provided him the corroboration he sought. Mattie Alice Austin, "The Municipal Government of San Fernando de Béxar, 1730–1800," *Quarterly of the Texas State Historical Association* 8, no. 4 (1905): 277–352; Sáenz, "Short Autobiographical Sketch, May 1947; Sáenz, "Mi linaje Azteca," three-page typescript, Sáenz Papers.

9. Local Anglos knew the community of El Palo del Oso as Rogers. The school was named after a businessman from Corpus Christi who responded to requests for help with "great enthusiasm and generosity." Sáenz, "La Escuela Laica 'Vicente Lozano,'" *La Verdad*, February 23, 1951. Although there is no record of the curriculum Sáenz used in his one-room school, he probably used English and Spanish to offer the children basic instruction in reading, composition, and arithmetic, as well as in Mexican history. The evening classes may have emphasized the teaching of English to predominantly Spanish-speaking adult learners.

10. Phone conversation, Eva Olivia (Sáenz) Alvarado (San Antonio), with author, October 4, 2009.

11. José María's wife, Manuela (Leal) Esparza, and their sons, Enrique, María del Jesús, and Manuel, were surviving eyewitnesses to the battle. Sáenz took pride in his wife's family's roots, which established a claim of prior occupancy, much the same way he did with his own matrilineal and patrilineal connection to a colonial settler community in Texas and indigenous communities in Mexico. Information provided during telephone conversations with Sáenz's daughter Eva Olivia (Sáenz) Alvarado of San Antonio, October 4, 2009; see also Reynaldo J.

Esparza, "José María Esparza," *Handbook of Texas Online*, http://www.tshaonline.org/handbook/online/articles/EE/fes2.html, accessed July 12, 2009; Linda Peterson, "San Augustine, Texas," *Handbook of Texas Online*, http://www.tshaonline.org/handbook/online/articles/SS/hrscf_print.html, accessed July 12, 2009.

12. Information provided by Eva Olivia Alvarado during our telephone conversation, October 4, 2009.

13. The following are the first in a series of newspaper articles that appeared in Spanish-language newspapers between 1928 and 1930: "En Octubre sera colocada la primera piedra para el monumento a los heroes," *La Prensa,* July 23, 1928, 10; and "Ha dado principio la colecta para un monumento, Se trata del que se levantará a los México-Texanos," *El Crónista del Valle,* August 3, 1928, 4.

14. In one of his earliest articles that appeared in *La Prensa* in July 1915, Sáenz urged readers to help defeat a proposed amendment to the state constitution that would establish a strict English-language literacy exam that would disenfranchise Mexican voters. Less than a month later he was using his other preferred method for communicating his ideas to Mexican audiences—he was speaking in a public program commemorating Juárez and paying homage to the historical figure's grand example of patriotic service to nation and exalted source of national unity. Sáenz, "A los México-Texanos," *La Prensa,* July 16, 1915, 5; "Conmemoraron el aniversario de la muerte de Juárez los vecinos de Moore, Texas," *La Prensa,* July 24, 1915, 4, 5.

15. Consult the following for histories of LULAC: Benjamín Marquez, *LULAC: The Evolution of a Mexican American Political Organization* (Austin: University of Texas Press, 1993); Cynthia E. Orozco, "League of United Latin American Citizens," *Handbook of Texas Online,* http://www.tshaonline.org/handbook/online/articles/wel01, accessed July 9, 2012; Orozco, *No Mexicans, Women, or Dogs Allowed: The Rise of the Mexican American Civil Rights Movement* (Austin: University of Texas Press, 2009); and Zamora, *Claiming Rights and Righting Wrongs in Texas.*

16. *Independent School District et al. v. Salvatierra et al.,* 33 S.W. 2d 795 (Tex. Civ. App.—San Antonio 1930), cert. denied, 284 U.S. 580 (1931). For details about this case, see Steven H. Wilson, "Brown over 'Other White'; Mexican Americans' Legal Arguments and Litigation Strategy in School Desegregation Suits," *Law and History Review* 21, no. 1 (2003): 145–94.

17. A sample of Texas newspapers containing his articles and letters to the editor can be found in the Sáenz Papers: *Corpus Christi Caller* (Corpus Christi); *Diógenes* (McAllen); *El Continental* (El Paso); *El Paso Times* (El Paso); *El Tiempo* (Raymondville); the *Denton Record-Chronicle* (Denton); *Justicia Social* (San Antonio); *La Prensa* (San Antonio); *La Verdad* (Corpus Christi); *La Voz* (San Antonio); *Mañana* (Mission); *Revista Latino-Americana* (Mission); the *San Antonio Express* (San Antonio); *Skyline* (Alpine); the *Valley Evening Monitor* (McAllen).

18. Alonso Perales, "Arquitectos de nuestros propios destinos: Una nueva sociedad para el progreso y bienestar de nuestro pueblo en Texas," *La Prensa,* May 11, 1952, 3.

19. Perales, "Arquitectos de nuestros propios destinos: Interesante carta de un gran lider

Mexicano," *La Prensa,* September 14, 1952, 2. Sáenz died at the Veteran's Hospital in Corpus Christi on April 12, 1953. He is buried at Fort Sam Houston National Cemetery in San Antonio.

20. "Diogenes . . . he aqui un hombre! La personalidad del prof. J. Luz Sáenz se nos revela mas grandiosa," *La Verdad,* July 1952, 1.

21. "Fallecio un gran líder, el professor J. Luz Sáenz," *La Prensa,* April 14, 1953, 2.

22. According to family members, Sáenz sketched a battle scene that was to appear on the book's cover and commissioned the artist Humberto Cavazos to prepare a painting. However, the cover of the published volume—which depicts a battlefield scene of attacking tanks and airplanes, bursting shells, barbed wire, and soldiers bearing the brunt of battle from within their trenches—is the work of an unknown artist named L. Correa. The Cavazos painting is at the Austin home of Mrs. Edelmira Sáenz, the widow of Enrique, one of Sáenz's sons. A copy of that painting appears on the cover of this publication. Mr. Cavazos had a distinguished career that included his teachers José Arpa y Perea, the renowned Spanish landscape artist from San Antonio, and Diego Rivera, as well as associates like Pablo Picasso. He spent most of his professional life teaching in the Rio Grande public schools. Interview with Humberto Cavazos Jr., by author, April 4, 2013. For further information about the publisher, Artes Gráficas, and its important contributions to Latino print culture, see Nicolás Kanellos, "Recovering and Reconstructing Early Twentieth-Century Hispanic Immigrant Print Culture in the US," *Hispanic Literary History* 21, no. 2 (2007): 438–55.

23. Not content with the limited reach of the diary, Sáenz translated it, but his efforts to interest two New York publishers, Fortuny and Fleming H. Revell, were unsuccessful. Copies of the translated text have been lost. Consult the Sáenz Papers for Sáenz's extensive correspondence with the publishers as well as a couple of surviving pages of his translated work.

24. Congress had approved the World War Adjusted Compensation Act authorizing certificates to be redeemed in 1945. The hard times of the Depression, however, led veterans to seek their payment for military service at a much earlier time. Their protest ended when President Herbert Hoover ordered the army to forcibly clear their campsites. Paul Dickson and Thomas B. Allen, *The Bonus Army: An American Epic* (New York: Walker and Company, 2004).

25. Sáenz uses the term *raza* throughout the diary primarily to signify the community of Mexican-origin people in the United States, although he also applies it to the Spanish-speaking people in Latin America. Its usage as a sociological self-identifier meaning "our people" or "our community" is widespread in Latin America and continues to be popular among Mexican-origin people and other members of the Latino community in the United States.

26. The copious correspondence in the Sáenz Papers (and letters Sáenz wrote that are included in the papers of Alonso Perales), as well as the numerous articles and letters to editors that Sáenz published in various newspapers, point to high levels of time-consuming activities. Moreover, he planned and undertook many trips, and he and his family relocated frequently as he accepted new teaching and administrative positions in towns throughout South and Central

Texas. These activities all placed significant demands on his time. See Sáenz Papers and Alonso S. Perales Papers, 1898–1991, Records Relating to Hispanic Americans, University of Houston Libraries, University of Houston.

27. The postcards are the only surviving materials that family members kept for Sáenz to use upon his return from military service. His postcard notes correspond fully with the corresponding diary entries and their dates, suggesting that he sought to provide an account that was consistent with his experiences.

28. Refer to pages 170–72, 198–205, and 374–77 in the diary for copies of the following articles: "Demostraremos que somos dignos de ocupar un sitio en estos campos donde se lucha por un noble ideal," *La Prensa*, August 12, 1918, 1; "El diario de un soldado México-Texano," *La Prensa*, October 27, 1918, 2; and "Una fiesta de los soldados México-Texanos que se encuentran en Alemania, Correspondencia Dirigida a *La Prensa* por Uno de Aquellos Soldados," *La Prensa*, March 31, 1919, 5. Sáenz also published six diary entries in *La Prensa* ten years after the recorded events and five years before he published the diary. This article is a verbatim account of the entries between October 7 and 12, 1918. "Mi diario particular; Lo que hacíamos los México-Americanos en Francia," October 9, 1928, 8.

29. Refer to pages 334 and 390–91.

30. "El profesor Sáenz en San Antonio," *La Prensa*, January 22, 1933, 3.

31. I point this out in my first article on Sáenz. I also remind readers that Sáenz almost singularly anticipated the idea of "Fighting on Two Fronts" during the interwar period. Zamora, "Fighting on Two Fronts."

32. I am especially grateful to Angela Valenzuela for reviewing portions of my work and offering valuable technical suggestions on my writing and editing. I also appreciate the assistance of Katherine Mooney, a colleague who is highly proficient in the method and art of editing.

33. Zamora, "Fighting on Two Fronts," *Claiming Rights and Righting Wrongs in Texas*, and "José de la Luz Sáenz: Experiences and Autobiographical Consciousness," in *Mexican American Civil Rights Pioneers*, ed. Anthony Quiroz (Champaign: University of Illinois Press, forthcoming 2014).

Prologue

1. Sáenz included the following note at the bottom of the page: Felipe García, born in Bess, Duval County, State of Texas, on January 23, 1891. He was sent to Company 48, Twelfth Training Battalion, Brigade Division 165, on October 11, 1917. He was assigned the position of company bugler on October 1917, from which position he was relieved on November 21, 1917, to become a common soldier in the same company. García became a corporal on January 17, 1918, with Special Order Number 15, General Headquarters, Brigade 165. He was promoted to sergeant on April 29, 1918, with Special Order 100, General Headquarters, Brigade 165. On October 16 he was transferred to the Company of Machine Guns. On October 1919, he was transferred to Battery F, of the 54th Field Artillery Regiment of the 18th Division. On

February 6, 1919, he was transferred to the General Headquarters Detachment. García was promoted to sergeant major on March 21, 1919, and became aide-de-camp on June 1919. He was honorably discharged on October 8, 1919.

2. The original English-language copy of the letter can be found in Sáenz Papers.

3. Alfred was a small rural community twelve miles northeast of Alice, Texas. The Texas and New Orleans Railroad established a station there that contributed to the appearance of the town during the early 1900s. "Alfred, Texas," Handbook of Texas Online, http://www.tshaonline.org/handbook/online/articles/AA/hna21.html, accessed on July 20, 2010.

4. The term *rinches* is a derivation of the word Rangers, as in Texas Rangers. It is popular among Mexicans in Texas and carries a pejorative meaning that emerged in the early 1900s when Mexicans accused the state police force of committing atrocities in South Texas. See the following work of Américo Paredes, for a critique of the Texas Rangers that gave voice to Mexican antipathies against the *rinches*: *With His Pistol in His Hand: A Border Ballad and Its Hero* (Austin: University of Texas Press, 1958).

5. A German submarine sank the steamer on February 5, 1918. Approximately two hundred soldiers perished. This was the greatest loss suffered by the US military on a single day since the Civil War. The dramatic news received widespread newspaper coverage. José A. Ramírez, *To the Line of Fire. Mexican Texans and World War I* (College Station: Texas A&M University Press, 2009), 94.

6. Two colloquial terms in this sentence presented the kind of translating challenge evident throughout Sáenz's book. Sáenz refers to Mr. Luna's "expresito," a diminutive term that referred to a mode of express or conveyance. Sáenz could have meant a car, truck, or even a wagon that transported goods or people on a regular or intermittent basis. According to an article that Sáenz wrote in 1947, "Las Caleras," or lime kilns, was a community near New Braunfels. Sáenz, "New Braunfels," August 1947, Sáenz Papers.

7. The use of "cherished" and "dear" represent the translator's effort to communicate the wistful and melancholy meaning that Sáenz gave his reference to the building and the children with the terms "aquel edificio" and "aquellos niños." A direct translation would have rendered the less meaningful terms "that building" and "those children."

8. The San Agustín community no longer exists. It was established between 1850 and 1860 when Manuel, Enrique, and Francisco Esparza and their families settled the area north of the present-day town of Pleasanton, located about thirty-five miles south of San Antonio. Sáenz may have made San Agustín his home to be near his wife's family. Aside from the historical marker identifying the church the Esparza brothers built at San Agustín, only the vast Esparza family network and their large reunions bring attention to the site of the ranches and the community associated with Gregorio Esparza, one of the children, who, along with his mother and siblings, survived the 1836 battle at the Alamo mission. "San Augustine Church," Atascosa County, Texas Historical Commission Markers, http://atlas.thc.state.tx.us/shell-county.htm, accessed September 12, 2010; "José María Esparza," Handbook of Texas Online, http://www.tshaonline.org/handbook/online/articles/EE/fes2.html, accessed on September 12, 2010.

9. Sáenz probably meant that his age and dependents would have helped him obtain a deferment from military service.

Reporting at New Braunfels

1. The person named Wells cannot be identified.

2. Sáenz's reference to farm Spanish suggests that the old German spoke a limited Spanish that he most probably used to communicate with his farm laborers. Texano or Tejano is a popular self-referent used by Mexicans in Texas.

3. Sáenz used "las viejas," an old regional term for cigarette butts. The term literally means the old ones, signifying butts, or cigarettes that had been smoked and discarded.

4. American infantry companies had 256 soldiers led by a captain. An infantry battalion consisted of a headquarters and four rifle companies. It had 1,027 soldiers and was commanded by a major. A division brigade included two brigades of infantry and one brigade of artillery with an engineer, machine gun, signal, medical, and transportation units and a headquarters. It had 28,105 soldiers and a major general at its head. Center of Military History, *American Armies and Battlefields in Europe* (Washington, DC: Center of Military History, US Army, 1992), 529.

5. Barbarita, or Barbara, was the aunt of Sáenz's wife, María Petra. Barbara was a special person in María Petra's life. She was the sister of Antonia, María Petra's mother. When Antonia died, Barbara married María Petra's father, Gregorio, and became her stepmother. Barbara was apparently living with María Petra when Sáenz wrote this letter. "Mocha," on the other hand, was the shortened version of Marcelina, Sáenz's older sister. Marcelina was married at the time to Samuel Luna. "Sam," or Samuel, was one of Sáenz's nephews. Phone interview, María Cruz Esparza Garza, Pleasanton, Texas, September 14, 2010, interview notes in author's possession; phone interview, Eva Elizondo, September 22, 2010, interview notes in author's possession.

The Brigade Station

1. Cortéz led the expedition of 1519 that defeated the Aztec empire and initiated Spanish colonial rule in the Americas. Cortéz ordered the burning of his ships soon after landing on the coast of Mexico to discourage mutiny among his troops. See the following recent reprint of the firsthand account of the Spanish conquest: Bernal Díaz del Castillo, *Historia verdadera de la conquista de la Nueva España* (Tuxtla Gutiérrez, Chiapas: Gobierno del Estado, 1992).

2. Pablo Martínez and Ignacio Zaragoza are important figures in Texas history. Martínez was the editor of the Laredo paper *El Chinaco* who supported the 1891–93 insurrection of Catarino Garza in South Texas against the regime of President Porfirio Díaz. He was jailed and eventually assassinated for his views. Zaragoza was born in Goliad, Texas and led a cavalry unit in the successful defense of Puebla in May 5, 1862, one of the first battles against French occupation. Like Garza, Zaragoza recruited troops in South Texas. Mexicans have celebrated the battle of Puebla, mostly in the American Southwest, but especially in Texas. Elliott Young, *Ca-*

tarino Garza's Revolution on the Texas-Mexico Border (Durham: Duke University Press, 2004); Ana Luisa Martínez Catsam, "El Regidor, the Regime of Porfirio Díaz, and the Transnational Community," *Southwestern Historical Quarterly*, Vol. 112, no. 4 (April 2009): 388-408; Rebeca Anne Todd Koenig, "Fiestas Patrias," *Handbook of Texas Online,* http://www.tshaonline.org/handbook/online/articles/EE/fes2.html, accessed on July 10, 2013.

3. When Rosalío referred to the young *pomocas*, he meant Luz's younger brothers. The term *pomoca* may have been associated with the residents of the small indigenous village with the same name in the state of Michoacán. As noted previously, Marcelina, Luz's older sister, was called "Mocha." Rosalío's playful use of the term "Malinche" could have been his way of underscoring her sense of independence, as exhibited by the indigenous historical figure of Mariana, the Indian princess who served Hernán Cortéz as his interpreter while on his colonizing march into the interior of what is now Mexico.

4. Sáenz refers to a "cabeza cocida" in the Spanish text, which literally means a cooked head. He was most probably referring to the delicacy in Mexican American cuisine that involved steaming a steer's head in an earthen hole into a "carne de cabeza," or "barbacoa de cabeza." See Mario Montaño's study of the social meanings of the Mexican diet, which includes the barbecue: "The History of Mexican Folk Foodways of South Texas: Street Vendors, Offal Foods, and Barbacoa de Cabeza" (PhD diss., University of Pennsylvania, 1992).

5. "Colorín" refers to a playful, poetic refrain that Spanish-speaking adults customarily use to announce the end in the telling or reading of a children's story:

> Y Colorín, colorado,
>
> este cuento se ha acabado;
>
> El que se queda sentado
>
> Se queda pegado.

6. Sayings such as this one will appear in the notes in their original Spanish form, regardless of whether I am able to locate sources that explain them: "No hay más que ajustarnos al sol que nazca, al viento que sople, y al agua que corra."

Camp Travis

1. Eulalio Velázquez was a teacher and the editor of *El Cosmopolíta* in Laredo and Alice when Sáenz was about to graduate from the local high school. While in Alice, Velázquez mentored a group of young men that included Sáenz. Sáenz acknowledged that Velázquez was a major influence during his early years, especially when he opened his library to the young men and taught them a considerable amount of Mexican history. Agnes G. Grimm, "Eulalio Velázquez," Handbook of Texas Online, http://www.tshaonline.org/handbook/online/articles/fve04, accessed January 9, 2012.

2. Sáenz may have been referring to the popular poem "Primero es la Patria," by Juan de Dios Peza, an influential writer and political figure from Mexico during the late 1800s and early 1900s. Juan de Dios Peza, *Hogar y Patria* (Paris: G. Hermanos, 1891).

3. Sáenz provided an English translation to the Spanish in parenthesis, most probably to underscore the familiarity of the offensive language to Spanish-speaking readers.

4. The novel may have been written by the Spanish writer Armando Palacio Valdés, *José (novela de costumbres marítimas)* (Boston: D. C. Heath, 1905). The essay "Will Power" could not be located.

5. President Wilson's daughter was most probably Margaret Woodrow Wilson. She was a trained singer, a member of the National War Committee of the YMCA, and a frequent visitor to military encampments in foreign lands during the war.

6. The "fully grown" saying reads as follows: "Todos, hombres de pelo en pecho, como hubiera dicho cualesquiera de nuestros antepasados."

7. Samy, Sammy, or Sammies was a popular slang term used in England to refer to American soldiers, or soldiers of Uncle Sam.

8. The celebration commemorated the defeat of the Mexican army by Texas insurgents at the battle of San Jacinto on April 21, 1836.

9. Knox was a well-known teacher and principal who worked in several predominantly Mexican schools from San Antonio. He established a personal and professional relationship with Sáenz mostly through Knox's work in the teacher training workshops that he organized in the early 1900s. "Fallecio el Profesor William J. Knox, *La Prensa*, April 14, 1940, p. 12.

10. The popular saying, "ya tenemos puesto el pie en el estribo," means that someone has his foot in the stirrup and is ready to depart.

11. Sáenz and his friends may have been ridiculing the English spoken by their fellow Anglo soldiers as a way of countering Anglo claims that Mexicans did not speak English or were not fully proficient in the language.

12. Sáenz uses the term "putees" to refer to "puttees," the leather leggings that soldiers wore above their ankle boots. They also wore wool and canvas wrap leggings, but Sáenz was obviously referring to the leather variety because he describes them as shiny.

13. This article appeared in *El Latino-Americano* from Alice as a reprint from the *Notas de Kingsville*, a weekly published in Kingsville, approximately fifteen miles southeast of Alice. Amado Gutiérrez, the proprietor and editor of *El Latino-Americano*, also published the weekly *El Demócrata* in San Diego during the 1930s. Sáenz maintained contact with Gutiérrez after he returned, and his newspapers continued to publish materials on and by Sáenz.

14. This last sentence demonstrates Sáenz's knowledge of Mexican colloquial expressions. It reads, "No escatiman gastos en proporcionarle al soldado cuanto le haga pasar el tiempo, el corto tiempo antes de que vaya a estacar la zalea." The phrase "estacar la zalea" refers to death, more specifically to the "staking," or securing an animal's skin on the ground to skin it and dry it. In other words, Sáenz was suggesting that within a short period of time other soldiers would be putting them to death. The linguist Juan M. Lope Blanch identifies the phrase as a common Mexican expression referring to death. Juan M. Lope Blanch, "Algunas expresiones Mexicanas relativas a la muerte," *Nueva Revista de Filología Hispánica* 15 (1961): 79–80.

15. Brian Michael Todd Kryszewski, "Oakville, Texas," Handbook of Texas Online, http://

www.tshaonline.org/handbook/online/articles/hl004, accessed September 9, 2010. Spanish colonials knew the town of Oakville, located about eighty miles south of San Antonio, as Puente de Piedra, or Rock Bridge. It was a natural rock bridge over the Nueces River, two miles east of the town. This is yet another instance in which Sáenz asserts local historical knowledge from a distant past that lends greater authority to his voice as a Mexican from Texas.

16. Sáenz made use of the popular term *pinole*, or dry corn meal. *Pinole* is typically prepared as parched corn, ground and mixed with cinnamon and sugar. It can be used as a base for making a chocolate drink called "champurrado." Mexicans from Texas have also used the powder as a sweetened treat, often for children and, as Sáenz indicates, as a ready-made source of nourishment during trips, as in "pinole para viaje." Sáenz was obviously contrasting experiences to add a light touch to an otherwise uncomfortable event. Dust was so severe that he tasted it as the dry sensation of *pinole*, but this time without its familiar sweet taste and far removed from the more enjoyable travels of his past.

17. Sáenz refers to the execution of Archduke Ferdinand Maximilian Joseph of Austria in Querétaro on June 19, 1867, and the end of monarchical rule in Mexico. The French had invaded Mexico in 1862 and within a year had extended military control and established a monarchy with Maximilian at its head. The national cause against foreign intervention and the monarchy catapulted Benito Juárez, the deposed president of Mexico and leader of the opposition, into legendary fame as one of the most important unifying figures in Mexican history. Sáenz calls Maximilian a "Kaiser" to suggest that he usurped established democratic rule, much like German Kaiser Wilhelm II contributed to the start of World War I and the violation of national sovereignties. Moisés González Navarro, *Benito Juárez*, 3 vols. (Mexico City: Colegio de México, 2006–7).

18. American troops occupied the port of Veracruz on April 21, 1914. President Wilson issued the order to gain the release of American sailors who had been arrested for entering an area in the port of Tampico that was off-limits. This may have been a pretext to enforce a US arms embargo against the administration of President Victoriano Huerta. Sáenz reminds us that US citizens were known to give popular expression to their anti-Mexican feelings and ideas to their support of such US foreign policy decisions and actions in Mexico. Robert E. Quirk, *An Affair of Honor: Woodrow and the Occupation of Veracruz* (New York: W. W. Norton, 1962). For a broader and more critical view of US military actions in Mexico, see the following: Gastón García Cantú, *Las invasiones norteamericanas en México* (Havana: Casa de Las Américas, 1981).

19. Sáenz is no doubt alluding to the famous 1917 telegram from Arthur Zimmerman, the foreign secretary of the German Empire, to a fellow diplomat in Washington, DC. The intercepted note raised the possibility of an offer of an alliance with Mexico and the return of the vast territory lost during the Mexico-US war of 1846–48 if the United States gave up its neutrality and joined the Allies in the war. Although Mexican officials never openly entertained the proposal, the incident contributed to the decision by the United States to declare war on Germany. In the accompanying crisis, Doroteo Arango (also known as Pancho Villa), a major

and popular figure in the Mexican Revolution, responded to another US arms embargo with an assault on Columbus, New Mexico. His brazen anti-US actions in the border region won him both admiration and condemnation in Mexico and the United States. Linda B. Hall, *Revolution on the Border: The United States and Mexico, 1910–1920* (Albuquerque: University of New Mexico Press, 1988); Friedrich Katz, *The Life and Times of Pancho Villa* (Stanford, CA: Stanford University Press, 1998).

20. Zurdo and Picudo are nicknames. The first term refers to a left-handed person, a lefty. Picudo may refer to a skinny and long-nose appearance or an association with cotton picking and the dreaded tubular snouted cotton boll weevil that migrated from Mexico during the late nineteenth century.

21. The song could not be located, although the title's reference to a child praying at dusk suggests Sáenz's deep religious sensibilities and an endearing focus on children.

22. The song, "Goodbye Broadway, Hello France," was a popular march written in 1917 by C. Francis Reisner and Bennis Davis and staged in the New York musical "The Passing Show of 1917." Sáenz made minor changes to the letter and structure of the tune. The most noticeable ones are the occasional combining of two stanzas into one and the substitution of Texas for Broadway in the chorus. See the following for a copy of the song: http://www.first-worldwar.com/audio/goodbyebroadway.htm, accessed November 11, 2010.

23. Matalote conchos are a type of scaly fresh-water perch found in Mexico and South Texas.

24. The quote most probably originated with Marie-Jeanne Phlippon, known as Madame Roland, the wife of Jean-Marie Roland de la Platière. Madame Roland and her husband are best known as early supporters of the French Revolution who were imprisoned when they lost favor with its leadership. Madame Roland is credited with making the statement before a clay statue of liberty as she faced her execution by guillotine in 1793. Brigitte Szymanek, "French Women's Revolutionary Writings: Madame Roland or the Pleasure of the Mask," *Tulsa Studies in Women's Literature* 15, no. 1 (1996): 99–122.

25. Sáenz employs a version of the popular Mexican saying "hasta que llovió en Sayula," or, "it finally rained in Sayula," when he says, "parece que llovió en Sayula." He means to say that something one wishes for has finally occurred. Sayula is a town in the southwestern state of Jalisco, Mexico.

26. Sáenz's use of *amasarnos*, or to work us like dough, is a play on the word *masses* and suggests a form of easy manipulation and defeat the Germans were to be entertaining.

27. On a later occasion, Sáenz notes that German officers derided American doughboys by calling them tin or toy soldiers, that is, servicemen who did not measure up. This is the first time that Sáenz uses the term with understated intent.

28. This entry stands out because Sáenz once again uses an idiomatic expression that reaches back into Mexican history and folklore. His use of *borrego* in the last line of the original underscores this. It reads, "al menos se darían cuenta que no compraba borregos en Europa," meaning that "they would at least now know that I do not entertain falsehoods in Europe." According to

a dictionary of popular Mexican sayings, *borrego* means a lie or a ruse. This is captured in the following proverb: "No hagas caso de la gente alarmista que solo suelta borregos para desorientar a los demas," or "Do not be bothered by alarmists, they simply let loose sheep to disorient everyone." Jorge Mejía Prieto, *Asi se habla el mexicano: Diccionario basico de muerte* (Mexico City: Panorama Editorial, 1984), 25.

France

1. The celebration honoring the memory of John the Baptist was an early Christian event with "pagan" origins that was observed in South Texas every year on June 24. The running of the cock, or "el correr de los gallos," was a game associated with ranch culture. A Mexican horseman would ride at full speed, snatch a live rooster buried in the ground or hanging from a tree, and race back to a predetermined place while other riders would try to take the rooster away. Mary Lou LeCompte, "The Hispanic Influence on the History of the Rodeo, 1823–1922," *Journal of Sports History* 12, no. 1 (1985): 24.

2. Martel, a Frankish military and political leader and the grandfather of Charlemagne (Charles the Great), is credited with stopping the Islamic advance from Spain and Portugal into the rest of Europe in the famous battle of 732. David Nicolle, *Poitiers AD 732: Charles Martel Turns the Islamic Tide* (New York: Osprey, 2008).

3. Sáenz is referring to the monarchical regimes of General Agustín de Iturbide and Archduke Ferdinand Maximilian. Iturbide led an eight-month rule soon after Mexico's independence. He was deposed in 1823 by troops headed by General Antonio López de Santa Anna, who subsequently ushered in the Republic. Maximilian assumed the position of emperor in 1864, as noted earlier. Sáenz is referring to Maximilian as the Kaiser's relative.

4. Sáenz once again demonstrates his adept use of language to express a thought. When challenged by his friends on his decision to learn French, he suggests that he will not allow a game of chance, as in card playing, to determine his decisions in life but that he will take charge and demonstrate that "de aquí en adelante las cartas pierden," or that "from here on out the cards will lose."

5. The manual of arms was a standard guide for the use of weapons issued to American frontline soldiers during World War I. The weapons included the M1903 Springfield clip-fed, 5 shot, bolt-action service rifle that Sáenz and his buddies used.

6. The historical figures Sáenz noted made significant contributions to literature, science, and politics. Victor Hugo's literary work is vast and significant within the romantic movement of the nineteenth century, but he is especially known outside of France for his highly influential novels, *Les Misérables* and *The Hunchback of Notre Dame*. Nicolas Camille Flammarion, also a nineteenth-century man of letters, is best known in the United States for his translated book on astronomy. León Gambetta, a major statesman in the last half of the 1800s, played both radical and moderate roles in the establishment of the French republic. Napoleon Bonaparte was one of the most prominent political and military leaders of France in the early nineteenth century. He was appointed emperor of the French in 1804. Graham Robb, *Victor Hugo:*

A Biography (New York: W. W. Norton, 1997); Camille Flammarion, *Popular Astronomy: A General Description of the Heavens* (London: Chatto and Windus, 1894); John P. Tuer, *Gambetta and the Making of the Third Republic* (London: Longman, 1973); Robert B. Asprey, *The Rise and Fall of Napoleon Bonaparte* (London: Little, Brown, 2000).

7. Sáenz refers to Carnot but he probably meant Jean-Baptiste-Camille Corot, one of the best-known landscape artists in France during the 1800s. Vincent Pomarède, Gérard de Wallens, and Lisa Davidson, *Corot: The Poetry of Landscape* (London: Thames and Hudson, 1996).

8. Sáenz was probably thinking of an Aesop fable to suggest that it may be better to hold's one tongue than to risk obvious repercussions. His comment comes from the figure of the bull that was refused refuge by a goat in a cave but decided not to protest for fear of calling the attention of the threatening lion that was nearby. Aesop, "Of the Lion, the Bull, and the Goat," in *Aesop's Fables: with a Life of Aesop*, trans. John E. Keller and L. Clark Kating (Lexington: University Press of Kentucky, 1993), 180.

9. Dulcinea was a peasant woman who became Don Quixote's beloved in *Don Quixote de la Mancha*, the first modern novel written by Miguel de Cervantes Saavedra in the early 1600s.

10. D'Annunzio's novel appeared in 1889 as *Il piacere* and translated into English as *The Child of Pleasure*. The novel's close and exaggerated treatment of romantic relations may have disturbed Sáenz's moral sensibilities.

11. "como los asnos de los arrieros, que todo lo que necesitan es revolcarse."

12. The hobnailed shoes got their name from the thickheaded nails on the heels and soles that were meant to give soldiers traction on most terrain except smooth and hard surfaces.

13. According to Roman legend, squawking geese saved the day by warning of an attack by the Gauls in 387 B.C. See the following for a children's book on the subject: Terry Deary, *The Goose Guards* (London: A & C Black, 2008).

14. The Indian from San Pablo de Guelatao, Oaxaca, was Benito Juárez, the historical figure noted above.

15. President Venustiano Carranza, a revolutionary leader from the northern part of Mexico, served between 1914 and 1920. The apparent wartime printing of French currency reminded Sáenz of the inflated money Carranza issued soon after assuming control of the government. Enrique Krauze, *Venustiano Carranza: Puente entre siglos* (Mexico City: Fondo de Cultura Económica, 1987).

16. This entry appeared as an article with the same title in *La Prensa*. It included an introduction and a conclusion by the editorial staff of the paper and the letter by Sáenz to Mr. Ignacio Lozano, the editor of *La Prensa*. The diary reproduced all the material that appeared in the paper; three minor revisions included the deletion of two words and the replacement of another one. This means the published diary offered a true rendition of the letter in the newspaper and added the editorial commentary between August 12, the date of the diary entry, and sometime before 1933, the date of the publication. In either case, Sáenz's letter appears in almost identical form in the diary and the newspaper, suggesting that the publication offers

a reliable representation of his entries in 1918 and 1919. Sáenz, "Demostraremos que somos dignos de ocupar un sitio en estos campos donde se lucha por un noble ideal," *La Prensa*, August 12, 1918, 1.

17. The Latin phrase stands for "the law is harsh, but it is the law."

18. Once again, the Indian from Guelatao is Benito Juárez. Hidalgo refers to Miguel Hidalgo y Costilla, the parish priest from Dolores Hidalgo, Guanajuato, who led the first major insurrection against the colonizers from Spain's Kingdom of Castile. Zaragoza, as previously noted, refers to General Ignacio Zaragoza from Goliad, Texas, who led the Mexican forces against the invading French army during the Battle of Puebla on May 5, 1862. The Mexican forces were defending two forts, the Loreto and Guadalupe, against a French army that had won major battles at Magenta and Solferino, Italy, in 1859. In both cases, according to Sáenz, Mexican fighters demonstrated skill and bravery against impressive military foes.

19. Sáenz's use of "first line of fire" obviously refers to the commonly known front-line trench that was usually situated between fifty yards to one mile from the German trenches. The other trenches typically provided additional men and supplies to support the first line of fire. In this instance, Sáenz notes a trench of resistance and a rear guard. Elsewhere he makes note of consecutive lines of fire, underscoring the fact that the troops in reserve also saw action behind the front line. See the following for examinations of trench warfare: John Ellis, *Eye-Deep in Hell: Trench Warfare in World War I* (Baltimore: Johns Hopkins University Press, 1976); Simon Jones, *Underground Warfare, 1914–1918* (Barnsley, England: Pen and Sword Books, 2010).

20. Sáenz uses an old saying in the last sentence to denote Barrera's close brush with death and to once again demonstrate his understanding of Mexican folklore. He notes that "lo mejor de todo es que Barrera no estacará la zalea por andar cuidando brutos." As noted previously, to "estacar la zalea" literally means to treat or tan a sheep skin by stretching it over stakes. Lope Blanch, "Algunas expresiones mexicanas relativas a la muerte."

21. Sáenz may have been referring to Hans Christian Andersen's famous tale of the snail. The snail taunts the rose tree from his protected shell until both he and the rose tree complete their final cycle of life and disappear into oblivion. The patience of the snail and the innocence that it shared with the rose tree as they face one of destiny's fates may have attracted Sáenz's attention at this important point in the front. Andersen, *Fairy Tales and Stories*, trans. Henry William Dulcken (New York: Hurst, 1908), 18–19.

22. The article in the diary appeared as "El diario de un soldado México-Texano," in the October 27, 1918, issue of *La Prensa*. It offers an opportunity to comment further on the reliability of the diary. The narrative in the diary is more than twice as long (approximately 3,050 words) as the one that appears in the newspaper (about 1,340 words). Sáenz explains most of the difference by noting that he had not able to provide a full account to the newspaper but that he now intended to do this. He no doubt was referring to military censorship, a practice that he knew well and may have applied on himself. Much of the material missing from the newspaper article included sensitive information, such as the names of places and soldiers, as

well as moving descriptions of deadly hand-to-hand fighting. The internal consistency in the diary's use of chronology and names of places and persons suggests he had a very good memory, but it is more probable that he wrote the complete account at the front but only sent a portion of it to the newspaper. Sáenz no doubt revised parts of his diary after the war. In this instance, however, self-censorship may explain much of the change. The difficulty in speaking with any certainty is Sáenz's form of expression. To say that "I have expanded that letter with details that I could not write" could be interpreted to mean that he had prepared the narrative at the front but that he could not write it entirely into the article, or he could have meant that he waited until he returned home before he could write the full account.

23. The battle at Marathon occurred in 490 BC during the Persian Wars. Its name recognizes the legend of an Athenian soldier who succumbed after running a marathon of twenty-five miles to announce the defeat of the Persians. Peter Krentz, *The Battle of Marathon* (New Haven, CT: Yale University Press, 2010).

24. Momentarily inspired during Mexico's day of independence, Sáenz anticipates the famous saying that was coined by José Vasconcelos, the head of the Office of Education and the Rector of the Universidad Nacional Autónoma de México during the 1920s. The phrase, "Por la raza hablará el espíritu," captures a national sense of unity beginning during Mexico's reconstruction period after the Mexican Revolution. It appears as the motto of the national university on its administrative tower. For an examination of the significance of the Mexican holiday among Mexicans in the United States during the early 1900s, see Emilio Zamora, "Las Escuelas del Centenario in Dolores Hidalgo, Guanajuato: Internationalizing Mexican History," in *Recovering the Hispanic History of Texas*, ed. Mónica Perales and Raul Ramos (Houston: Arte Público Press, 2010), 38–66.

How Carrejo and Four Others Died

1. The quote may originate in one of Juan Antonio Mateos's works. Mateos was a well-known writer and participant in Mexico's liberal reform movement and the military campaign against French intervention in the 1860s. He wrote on Mexico's independence movement and its nationalist cause against the French. The following are his better-known historical novels: *El cerro de las campanas (Memorias de un guerrillero)* (Mexico City: Imprenta de Ignacio Cumplido, 1868); *El sol de Mayo (Memorias de la intervención)* (Mexico City: Imprenta de Ignacio Cumplido, 1868); and *Sacerdote y caudillo (Memorias de la insurrección)* (Mexico City: Imprenta de Ignacio Cumplido, 1869).

Toul, Choloy, and Rampondt

1. Sáenz is making light of the moment when he says that someone will search for horns on the soldiers because they look like sheep in their uniforms. He is alluding to a popular saying in Spanish that associates "poner cuernos" (literally, the placing of horns on a person) with infidelity, typically a woman's infidelity.

2. See note 1 in the chapter "How Carrejo and Four Others Died" for references to Mateos and one of his subjects, Pablo Martínez, an officer in the nationalist army that fought against French intervention.

3. This is the second time that Sáenz refers to the end with a reference to Andersen. See note 49 in the chapter "France" for possible sources.

4. Although the author of the quote is unknown, Sáenz is obviously suggesting that we tend to construct social realities but that satisfying hunger remains a basic human need, especially during times of war when the soldiers' major preoccupation is to stay alive.

Five Days and Nights in a Foxhole in Romagne

1. Xicoténcatl and Cuauhtémoc were heroic figures who fought against the Spanish occupation of the Aztec city of Tenochtitlan in 1521. Their execution made them martyrs in the indigenous fight against Spanish colonial rule.

Simón González and Others

1. Sáenz notes that he was eavesdropping and waiting for the rap on the head with a popular Mexican saying, "De allí, desde donde estaba durmiendo 'como la marrana de Tía Cleta, que solo esperaba el cascarrazo.'" Mark Glazer, *A Dictionary of Mexican American Proverbs* (New York: Greenwood Press, 1987), 189–90.

Hipólito Jasso Receives a Shrapnel Wound

1. Sáenz once again makes use of a colloquial expression signifying death. Here, he states that the soldiers who were still standing would continue fighting, "tirándole muy fuerte a la gamuza y arrastrando la guaracha, quien sabe hasta cuando." His use of *gamuza*, or swede, brings to mind the previously noted tanning process that can be used to prepare a drumhead with the use of the brains of an animal. The traditional sandal, or *guaracha*, also invokes animal hide as the covering for one's own skin. The allusion to the pulling of a skin over a drum alongside the reference to the dragging of leather sandals during the course of the war implies violence and death, especially for working-class Mexicans, the usual wearers of the *guarache* or *guaracha* in the United States. Lope Blanch, "Algunas expresiones Mexicanas relativa a la muerte."

2. Sáenz is alluding to Lieutenant Andrew Rowan who carried a message of cooperation in 1898 from President William McKinley to Calixto García e Iñiguez, a Cuban general who was leading an army of insurgents against Spanish colonial rule. The intrepid messenger was memorialized by Elbert Hubbard in an 1899 article that attained great popularity as an American saying—"to take a message to García"—primarily because Rowan had demonstrated initiative and an abiding sense of duty that resulted in US support for the Cuban independence movement and its eventual success. Hubbard, *A Message to Garcia* (Chicago: House of Hubbard, 1970).

Armistice Day

1. Sáenz is clearly drawing on literature again when he underscores with quotation marks that the soldiers slept as "méndigos en lecho de sultán." The word "méndigos," or paupers, has popular usage, while "sultán" suggests a literary source such as the classic *One Thousand and One Nights*, also known as *The Arabian Nights*. The collection of Middle Eastern and South Asian stories was available in English and Spanish by the late 1800s. Although the exact quote in the diary could not be located in *The Arabian Nights*, the publication does contain references to paupers sleeping in beds owned by sultans. Consult the following recent edition: Husain Haddawy, trans., *Arabian Nights* (New York: W. W. Norton, 2010).

2. Princess Marie Charlotte of Belgium, or "Carlota," had been married to Archduke Max-imilian when the latter assumed the position of emperor of Mexico after the French invasion of 1862. Mamá Carlota literally means Mother Charlotte, and it originates in a popular song written by Vicente Riva Palacio ("Adiós Mamá Carlota," 1867) that derisively bids farewell to the princess after her husband is deposed and executed by nationalist forces led by President Juárez. Carlota lived until 1927 and suffered from a mental collapse after her return to Europe. See note 17 in the chapter "Camp Travis."

3. The letters *T* and *O* appeared on an official insignia patch that the members of the 90th Division wore on one of their sleeves. They stood for Texas and Oklahoma. The soldiers, however, would often read the insignia as "Tough Ombres" to signify their prewar service on the Mexican border.

Memorable March from Pont-Sassy, France

1. This is a translation of a document that originally appeared in English and that Sáenz translated into Spanish. The original English-language document could not be located. Another Spanish version of the document appeared in a San Antonio daily as part of a report by Agustín Sáenz, a San Antonio soldier attached to the 360th Infantry Regiment of the 90th Division in France. Neither Agustín nor José de la Luz acknowledged a family relation. "Hechos realizados en el frente occidental por los soldados de San Antonio: La 90a Division pelea bizarramente contra los Hunos, ningún soldado dio muestras de cobardía y todos cumplieron a satisfacción de sus jefes," *El Imparcial de Texas*, February 13, 1919, 1, 4.

Thanksgiving and Then to Germany

1. Sáenz is referring to the twelve peers, or major warriors, of Charlemagne's court. The story was a literary invention that brings to mind King Arthur's Knights of the Round Table. Alfred John Church, *Stories of Charlemagne and the Twelve Peers of France: From the Old Romances* (London: Stelley, 1925).

2. The chorus that appears in the original song does not correspond exactly to the stanza that Sáenz includes in his diary. The soldiers may have altered the song to match the marching cadence or some special experiences. On the other hand, Sáenz may have inserted a version of the opening line of the famous Mexican song, "Canción Mixteca." The Oaxacan composer

José López Alavez wrote the song in 1912 to capture the yearning for home or the homeland. It opens with "Que lejos estoy del suelo donde he nacido" ("I am so far from the land where I was born"). Sáenz's Spanish translation is as follows: "Que lejos está la tierra de mis sueños, Cuanta marcha penosa para llegar allá, Angel mío, qué feliz seré, El día que tú y yo recorramos esa senda."

3. This letter appeared in English, most probably as a verbatim version of the original.

Mexican Americans Attend School

1. The translation "This is for the record" stands for Sáenz's word "Conste." In South Texas, the word signifies more than a desire that the experience be remembered. It also suggests, "Let it be known that I tried," or "Let it be known that they rejected me," or "I have spoken."

2. Colonche was a Mexican alcoholic drink prepared by fermenting the juice of the fruits of the prickly pear cactus. Sáenz probably used the term to suggest the use of local ingredients in the preparation of an alcoholic drink.

3. Sáenz obviously includes Japan, alongside Germany, Austria-Hungary, and Italy, in what is commonly called the Triple Entente.

4. This is one of the rare instances when Sáenz is unclear. He seems to be saying that his father's visits have been untimely or inopportune, suggesting a long-held grievance about erratic or inconsistent parental support during his trying moments in life. This kind of critique was uncharacteristic of Sáenz. Moreover, the rest of the letter does not express any form of animus toward his father. The more reasonable explanation would be that Sáenz was suggesting that his father came to him unexpectedly in his dreams or thoughts.

5. This letter appears out of place, suggesting that assembling the materials in the right order occasionally presented challenges for Sáenz. The letter appears next to his February 16 entry, implying that the letter had made its way from the United States in one day. It should have appeared immediately before his March 23 entry when he acknowledges the central message in the February 15 letter, the death of his brother.

6. Sáenz is referring to Franz Joseph the emperor of Austria-Hungary, and the older brother of Archduke Ferdinand Maximilian, the emperor of Mexico. Franz Joseph was also the uncle of Archduke Franz Ferdinand, the heir to the throne, whose assassination in 1914 led the emperor to declare war on Serbia and triggered World War I. Kaiser Wilhelm II was the German emperor and king of Prussia during the war.

7. Aside from indicating the wounded condition and overseas service of the soldiers, the V-shaped sleeve badge acknowledged they had been discharged from military duty. Mr. Knox called the chevron badge "chevrones," the Spanish plural version of the word.

8. The article appeared in the San Antonio newspaper as follows: "Una fiesta de los soldados México-Texanos que se encuentran en Alemania, correspondencia dirigida a *La Prensa* por uno de aquellos soldados," *La Prensa*, March 31, 1919, 5. The newspaper article is a verbatim copy of the corresponding account in the diary.

9. The princess may have been Atalie Unkalunt, an artist from New York City who

served with the YMCA during World War I. Unkalunt, also known as Sunshine Rider, was a well-known Native American artist and advocate for Native American rights during the early 1900s. "Native Performance in New York City at the American Indian Community Center," http://hemisphericinstitute.org/cuaderno/aich/history.html#layerpoint, accessed January 5, 2012; Atalie Unkalunt, *Biography* (New York: Self-published, 1924).

10. Sáenz's friends were referring to Benito Juárez, the indigenous figure of Zapotec origin who served as head of the Mexican Supreme Court and as president of Mexico between 1858 and 1872, including the period of the French intervention. He was born in Guelatao, in the southern Mexican state of Oaxaca.

11. Sáenz did not identify the author of the quote.

12. This letter has been reproduced as it appeared in the diary, in English.

13. An almost identical English version of the first paragraph and most of the second in this letter appeared in a previous letter from Robert E. Hoey that Sáenz entered into his diary on December 30. The obvious difference is that the earlier version appears in English while the latter includes a sending date (March 13, 1919), two additional paragraphs, and a postscript. A serious issue emerges when Hoey uses two different dates when he is responding to the same letter from Sáenz. In the first instance, Hoey says that he is answering a November 21 letter from Sáenz. In the second case, Hoey cites a February 21 letter from Sáenz. We could attribute the obvious inconsistency to a technical error if the dates did not correspond so well with the time of their placement in the diary, December 30 and April 1. The inconsistency suggests that Sáenz altered the narrative.

Prodding That Produces Favorable Results

1. Sáenz is commenting on a series of articles on race and Mexicans that appeared in the *San Antonio Light* during the first and second weeks of February 1919. Someone from San Antonio—most probably an Anglo—had apparently written to the paper that people from the north denied African Americans equal rights; someone from Boston responded by offering racially charged observations about Mexicans. The debate cut a broad cultural swath when a writer for *La Prensa* with the pseudonym of Audifaz interpreted the Bostonian's association of chile con carne with Mexicans as a racist characterization because he did not understand or appreciate the heritage of classic culinary traditions and other broader considerations like the technological and cultural achievements of pre-European times. The two writers to the *San Antonio Light* touched off a flurry of responses by Mexicans that appeared in the *San Antonio Light* and in *La Prensa*. "Por que atacar a los mexicanos? Alderrededor de una polémica en el 'Light,'" *La Prensa*, February 23, 1919, 19; J. A. Reyez, "En defensa de la cultura Mexicana," *La Prensa*, March 2, 1919, 11; (reprint) J. A. Reyez, "En defensa de la cultura mexicana," *El Imparcial de Texas*, March 13, 1919, 9; Audifaz, "Cosas del destierro chile con carne," *La Prensa*, March 16, 1919, 14.

2. Sáenz is referring to an article by Dionisio "Dennis" Chavez published by *La Voz del Pueblo* from East Las Vegas, New Mexico, and reprinted by *La Revista Mexicana* from San

Antonio. In 1940 Chavez was the first person of Mexican origin to be elected to a full six-year term in the US Senate. He worked as a clerk in the office of the secretary of state at the time that his article appeared in the San Antonio paper. Sáenz obviously agreed with the critique the editor of *La Revista Mexicana* leveled against the New Mexico paper and Chavez when the paper argued that the Spanish language impeded the learning of English and the Americanization of Mexicans. Sáenz's entry adds to an obvious national Mexican debate over ethnic identity and Mexican claims of cultural autonomy in the middle of a highly charged nationalistic period in US history. He believed that Chavez's Americanizing call sought to reshape Mexican culture and insinuate disloyalty when a Mexican identity was affirmed. Sáenz also noted hypocrisy in Chavez, either because he was calling for a demonstration of loyalty far from the battlefields of Europe or because he was discouraging the use of Spanish while obviously lacking mastery in it. Dennis Chavez, "Por los fueros del idioma," *La Revista Mexicana*, February 23, 1919.

3. Mrs. George Thatcher Guernsey delivered her speech before the annual convention of the Daughters of the American Revolution at the Memorial Continental Hall, Washington, DC. Address by Mrs. George Thatcher Guernsey, *Twenty-Second Report of the National Society of the Daughters of the American Revolution, March 1, 1918 to March 1, 1919* (Washington, DC: Government Printing Office, 1921), 16–22.

Article of War No. 105 and 2,175 Bottles of Champagne

1. Although Sáenz introduces his comments on Indians with a reference to an officer's nickname, he uses the opportunity to speak about the exemplary conduct of Mexican soldiers and to attribute this to their Indian ancestry. He uses a saying, "pero, por favor, no le pongan corbata al indio," to suggest that Indians are culturally disposed to act responsibly and that society cancels this possibility by stripping them of their cultural identity. The text can be literally translated to mean, "but, please, don't dress up the Indian with a tie." Sáenz's manner of depicting the Indian as unsuitable for a more formal and modern appearance could also be interpreted as a condescending view of a community that was best left alone in its uncivilized state. His purpose, however, is to bring positive attention to the wartime conduct of Mexicans and not to demean Indians.

2. "The Sleeper and the Waker" refers to a story in the *Arabian Nights*. Abul-Hasan, the major figure in the story, had given away most of his inheritance only to discover that his acquaintances did not reciprocate with their own generosity when he needed their help. Consequently, he became a loner. Abul-Hasan decided to forsake friendships with local people and limit his generosity to outsiders visiting his town, but only for one day since they too could eventually abandon him. Sáenz uses the Spanish version of the story, "Historia del Dormido Despierto," to suggest that his students could disregard the relationships and commitments to fellow Mexicans in the military and dedicate themselves to their own form of misguided personal ventures.

3. The saying reads as follows in the diary: "La miseria tiene cara de hereje."

4. This letter appeared in its original English form in a history of the 360th Infantry

Regiment. Sáenz's translation into Spanish was a reliable rendering of the original document that is reprinted here. Army of Occupation, American Expeditionary Forces, *A History of the Activities and Operations of the 360th United States Infantry Regiment in the World War, 1914–1918* (Zeltingen: Army of Occupation, 1919), 2.

5. *Pinole* is roasted and sweetened maize flour popular among Mexicans. It can be eaten dry or in a drink with hot or cold water. The reference to dying brings to mind the warning that anyone from South Texas would recognize, that is, if *pinole* is taken as dry meal and in large single amounts, a person risks choking to death. Sáenz, in other words, is underscoring that though death on the seas is as improbable as eating *pinole*, it is still possible.

On the Last Cattle Train and Cars 40 and 8

1. Sáenz used the saying that "otro tonto cargará a Tacho" to indicate that someone else would do the chore, or that "some other fool will carry Tacho."

2. The original reads "ya pusimos el pico para el rancho," literally meaning that we have pointed our beaks toward the ranch. His use of "rancho" harkens back to the distant past of Mexican-owned cattle ranches that were lost during the racialized conflict that began in the 1830s and continued into the latter part of the century. Mexicans continued to use the term *rancho* during the twentieth century to refer to their significantly smaller properties, including small homesteads and even urban properties.

3. The saying originated in the central region of Mexico during the 1700s when bullfighting enthusiasts claimed that the Hacienda del Jaral de Berrio, owned by Don Miguel de Berrio y Zaldívar, bred the best horses in the Mexican tauromaquia (bullfight) tradition. Sáenz meant that his superiors did not have to go far to find the right persons to do the job since he had already demonstrated his abilities. The saying is still used in South Texas. According to my dearly departed father, the popular saying claimed that "Pa' los toros del Jaral, los caballos de allá mesmo," meaning that an hacienda known for breeding good bulls could be trusted to produce their equivalent in horses. Interview, Emilio Hinojosa Zamora, by author, December 23, 2011, notes in possession of author; "Geneología NovoHispana," http://genealogianovohispana.blogspot.com/2011/04/pa-los-toros-del-jaral-los-caballos-de.html, accessed May 19, 2011.

How Boston Receives Us

1. The battle of Ciudad Juárez took place on June 15–16, 1919, when the forces of Francisco "Pancho" Villa, led by General Felipe Ángeles, took the border city away from the carrancistas, or the federal forces led by President Venustiano Carranza. The takeover of Ciudad Juárez represented a major blow to Carranza and contributed to his overthrow less than a year later. US troops fortified El Paso, presumably to prevent the violence from flowing across the border. The following sources provide a history of the border cities and the battle and a running account of the conflict: David Romo, *Ringside Seat to a Revolution: An Underground*

Cultural History of El Paso and Juárez, 1893–1923 (El Paso: Cinco Puntos Press, 2005); "Los Villistas se posesionaron de Ciudad Juárez," *La Prensa*, June 16, 1919, 1, 7.

2. Sáenz was referring to instances when Mexicans found themselves fighting against each other. The Spanish conquest, for instance, included alliances with native peoples, and the French invasion of 1862 resulted in a civil war that pitted Mexicans against Mexicans. His reference to the North Americans no doubt referred to the Mexicans who sided with the Texas insurgents of 1835–36 and the supporters of the US conquest of Mexico in the 1846–48 war.

Index